Living with Myanmar

The **ISEAS – Yusof Ishak Institute** (formerly Institute of Southeast Asian Studies) is an autonomous organisation established in 1968. It is a regional centre dedicated to the study of sociopolitical, security, and economic trends and developments in Southeast Asia and its wider geostrategic and economic environment. The Institute's research programs are grouped under Regional Economic Studies (RES), Regional Strategic and Political Studies (RSPS), and Regional Social and Cultural Studies (RSCS). The Institute is also home to the ASEAN Studies Centre (ASC), the Singapore APEC Study Centre, and the Temasek History Research Centre (THRC).

ISEAS Publishing, an established academic press, has issued more than 2,000 books and journals. It is the largest scholarly publisher of research about Southeast Asia from within the region. ISEAS Publishing works with many other academic and trade publishers and distributors to disseminate important research and analyses from and about Southeast Asia to the rest of the world.

Myanmar Update Series

Living with Myanmar

EDITED BY

JUSTINE CHAMBERS
CHARLOTTE GALLOWAY
JONATHAN LILJEBLAD

ISEAS YUSOF ISHAK INSTITUTE

First published in Singapore in 2020 by
ISEAS Publishing
30 Heng Mui Keng Terrace
Singapore 119614

E-mail: publish@iseas.edu.sg
Website: http://bookshop.iseas.edu.sg

ISEAS Library Cataloguing-in-Publication Data

Name(s): Myanmar Update (2019 : Canberra, Australia) | Chambers, Justine, editor. | Galloway, Charlotte Kendrick, editor. | Liljeblad, Jonathan, editor.
Title: Living with Myanmar / editors : Justine Chambers, Charlotte Galloway and Jonathan Liljeblad.
Description: Singapore : ISEAS - Yusof Ishak Institute, 2020. | Series: Myanmar Update Series. | Papers originally presented to Myanmar Update 2019 held at the Australian National University, Canberra, from 15 to 16 March 2019. | Includes bibliographical references.
Identifiers: ISBN 9789814881043 (softcover) | ISBN 9789814881074 (hardcover) | ISBN 9789814881050 (pdf) | ISBN 9789814881067 (epub)
Subjects: LCSH: Myanmar—Politics and government—21st century—Congresses. | Myanmar—Social conditions—Congresses. | Myanmar—Economic conditions—Congresses.
Classification: LCC DS530.4 B972 2019

Cover photo: A street scene from downtown Yangon, September 2016. Reproduced with permission of Justine Chambers.

Copyedited, typeset and indexed by Maxine McArthur

CONTENTS

LIST OF TABLES

LIST OF FIGURES

ACKNOWLEDGEMENTS

In March 2019, the Australian National University's Myanmar Research Centre hosted the bi-annual Myanmar Update. Bringing together academics, researchers, policymakers and active members of Myanmar's NGO and civil society sector, the theme of "Living with Myanmar" sparked strong debate, conversations of which are included in this volume.

The Myanmar Update is a major venue at which to present cutting-edge scholarship on political, social and economic affairs in Myanmar. Now in its third decade, it is one of only two long-standing, regularly held international conferences on the country and has consistently produced high quality publications since the 1990s. We thank the conference speakers and participants and encourage everyone reading this volume to forge ongoing connections that will further enhance our knowledge and understanding of Myanmar.

International conferences such as the Myanmar Update require tremendous collective effort and we thank those members of the MRC who supported both the conference and preparation for the volume. The MRC was launched in 2015. Since then, the Centre has served as the university's academic hub for Myanmar activities. The Centre provides a flexible and inclusive structure to maintain its activities, build relationships with our Myanmar partners, and create new opportunities for ANU staff and students. The strength of these partnerships is reflected in the growing attendance of Myanmar scholars in the conference series and this volume.

We want to thank the ANU for their ongoing financial and institutional assistance for both the conference and the volume series. We are especially grateful to the College of Asia and the Pacific and its Department of Political and Social Change for their ongoing enthusiasm and commitment. Particular thanks to Maxine McArthur, whose assistance with copy-editing, indexing and the layout helped to ensure the volume's high production standards. We also acknowledge the generosity of the Myanmar studies community whose ongoing support and scholarly reviews provided critical feedback and commentary on each of the papers.

Special thanks to the collective efforts of our amazing contributors. The strength of the analysis in each of the chapters is testament to your hard work. We appreciate all of the time and effort each of you have put into developing these chapters, and for your patience and collegiality throughout the publication process.

Finally, thanks go to the ongoing support of Ng Kok Kiong and Rahilah Yusuf at the ISEAS – Yusof Ishak Institute in Singapore. Once again, it has been a pleasure working with you on this volume and we look forward to doing so again in the future.

CONTRIBUTORS AND EDITORS

Aung Kyaw Thein is a consultant working on political, social and economic issues in Myanmar.

Aye Thiri Kyaw is an MSC candidate of International Social and Public Policy (Research) in the Department of Social Policy, London School of Economics and Political Science, UK.

Michael G. Breen is a McKenzie Postdoctoral Fellow in the School of Social and Political Sciences at the University of Melbourne, Australia.

Peggy Brett is a senior researcher at the Center for Diversity and National Harmony in Yangon, Myanmar.

Mary Carroll is an Associate Professor in the School of Information Studies at Charles Sturt University and a member of the Faculty of Arts and Education Library Research Group (LRG), Australia.

Justine Chambers is a sessional lecturer and Research Fellow in the School of Culture, History and Languages at The Australian National University, Australia.

Renaud Egreteau is Associate Professor in Comparative Politics, Department of Asian and International Studies, City University of Hong Kong.

Hitomi Fujimura is a postdoctoral fellow in the Graduate School of Global Studies at Sophia University, Japan.

Charlotte Galloway is the Director of the Myanmar Research Centre and Senior Lecturer in the School of Art and Design at The Australian National University, Australia.

Rick Gregory is a specialist in coastal and freshwater fisheries and aquaculture, with more than thirty years of experience working in South and Southeast Asia, and Africa.

Baogang He is the Alfred Deakin Professor and the Chair in International Relations at the School of Humanities and Social Sciences, Deakin University, Australia.

Andrew M. Jefferson is a Senior Researcher at DIGNITY – Danish Institute Against Torture and co-convenor of the Global Prisons Research Network.

Khin Khin Mra is a consultant working on gender, governance and development in Myanmar.

Marie Lall is Professor of Education and South Asian Studies at the UCL Institute of Education in London, UK.

Jonathan Liljeblad is a Senior Lecturer in the Law School at The Australian National University, Australia.

Deborah Livingstone is a senior social development consultant specialising in gender equality and social inclusion.

Stephanie Spaid Miedema is a dual degree PhD-MPH candidate in the Department of Sociology and Department of Behavioral and Health Sciences, Rollins School of Public Health at Emory University, USA.

Roxanne Missingham is University Librarian (Chief Scholarly Information Services) at The Australian National University.

Nyein Ei Cho is a Research Associate of the Myanmar Development Institute, Naypyitaw, Myanmar.

Nyein Thiri Swe is a Senior Research Officer at the Enlightened Myanmar Research Foundation in Yangon, Myanmar.

Ikuko Okamoto is Professor at the Faculty of Global and Regional Studies, Toyo University, Japan.

Sean Turnell is Special Economic Consultant to the State Counsellor, Myanmar, Director of Research, Myanmar Development Institute, and an Associate Professor of Economics at Macquarie University, Australia.

Peter Warr is John Crawford Professor of Agricultural Economics, Emeritus, at The Australian National University, Australia.

Yin Nyein is the Coordinator of Learning and Action Group for Local Governance in Yangon, Myanmar.

Zaw Min Oo is a Senior Research Officer at the Enlightened Myanmar Research Foundation in Yangon, Myanmar.

I

Introduction

1

INTRODUCTION: LIVING WITH MYANMAR

Justine Chambers and Charlotte Galloway

When Myanmar's first democratically elected officials took their place in the *Pyithu* (lower) and *Amyotha* (upper) houses of Parliament in February 2016 it heralded in a new era – one of hope and optimism – for the greater part of Myanmar's population. The National League for Democracy (NLD) led by Aung San Suu Kyi held an 86 per cent majority of elected seats. Clad in orange as a mark of their difference from the military's light green, a collective sigh of relief was felt across the country, as the new members of parliament took their seats. After half a century of military rule, the process of installing the new government was by all accounts a triumph for democracy. Fears that the military, who by constitutional rule are reserved 25 per cent of seats in both the lower and upper houses, would agitate and refuse to hand over power to the NLD did not eventuate. While the 2008 Constitution, written by the former military junta, barred Aung San Suu Kyi from taking the position of president, the NLD-led parliament created the new role of State Counselor for her – a role effectively seen by all as the head of state, "above the president" (BBC 2016).

Significant gains in reforming Myanmar had already been made during the term of the military-aligned Union Solidarity and Development Party

(USDP), which formed a majority government after the flawed general elections of November 2010. While there remain many questions over the state of Myanmar's "transition", it marked the starting point for the country's move away from military rule toward a halting process of democratisation (Kyaw Yin Hlaing 2012; Cheesman et al. 2014; Crouch 2017a; Jones 2014). President Thein Sein, a former military general, led these changes, praised as a "champion of democracy" (Hunter 2014). And yet, built on the 2003 commitment to a roadmap to a "discipline flourishing democracy", efforts to reverse a legacy of isolation also cemented the *Tatmadaw*'s power in the nation's "democratic" future under the guise of liberalisation (Egreteau 2016; Jones 2018; Brooten et al. 2019).

One of the key election promises of the NLD government in 2015 was the enactment of constitutional reform to limit the role of the military in national affairs. Alongside their control of security-related cabinet portfolios, important sections of the constitution entrench the *Tatmadaw*'s influence over the parliament and legislative affairs, marginalising civilian rule (Crouch 2019a). However, the NLD's commitment to this area was soon subject to critical scrutiny after the historic elections, when Suu Kyi reached out to the *Tatmadaw* leadership and they agreed to "cooperate on peace, the rule of law, reconciliation and the development of the country" (Senior General Min Aung Hlaing cited in Fuller 2015). The concurrent release of the *Tatmadaw*'s first Defence White Paper in February 2016 was also telling, outlining the ongoing importance of the military in national security and political affairs (Maung Aung Myoe 2018, 204–205). As the country's most powerful interfacing agency between the government and the nation's people, the transfer of the General Administration Department (GAD) from military to civilian control in 2019 was one indicator of important public sector reform (Arnold 2019). There were also raised hopes in January 2019, when the NLD put forward a legislative motion to form a committee to consider constitutional amendments (Crouch 2019b).[1] However, in many ways the NLD has done little to overtly challenge the military's entanglement in national affairs (Maung Aung Myoe 2018; Selth 2018).

Great things were expected of the NLD government when they were elected in 2015. It can be said on reflection that many of the expectations of the new government for an almost overnight improvement in political, economic and social wellbeing were unrealistic with the military maintaining their constitutional control over parliamentary and national affairs. Another major challenge was the simple fact that the party lacked sufficient resources and preparation for the execution of major policy reform. Enacting rapid change in a government system that lacked experience and infrastructure was always going to be a challenge. More than four years on, many of the same concerns and questions about Aung San Suu Kyi and the NLD's ability to govern and enact meaningful change are still there.

Nowhere has this been more evident than in their approach to addressing the country's complex identity politics. Not long after the 2015 elections the ongoing conflict between the *Tatmadaw* and Rohingya communities erupted into a major humanitarian crisis, causing one of the largest exoduses of refugees in Southeast Asia since the 1970s (MacLean 2018; see also OHCHR 2018). The overwhelming majority of analyses on the situation have not minced words, condemning the Myanmar government and the military's operations in northern Rakhine State. Several international and domestic investigative bodies were formed, with the Independent International Fact Finding Mission concluding that "crimes in Rakhine State, and the manner in which they were perpetrated" had "genocidal" intent.[2] Subsequent international manoeuvrings saw the Republic of The Gambia take Myanmar to the UN International Court of Justice on charges of genocide against the Rohingya. Aung San Suu Kyi represented Myanmar at the ICJ hearing in the Hague in December 2019 and firmly rejected the charges made against the military. Although she acknowledged serious crimes may have been committed by the military's security clearance operations, her position made it clear that she supported the *Tatmadaw*'s response to what she perceived as an armed "terrorist" group.[3]

Myanmar's management of the Rohingya crisis had immediate consequences. The tragic events of 2017–18 shattered an already tentative international confidence in the new government and Aung San Suu Kyi's reputation as a champion of human rights and democracy icon. Her silence on the military's brutality reinforced the complexity of Myanmar's ethnic divides, revealing an unpleasant "truth" that there was negligible humanitarian spirit within the new government in the management of a community largely seen as "Other" (Cheesman 2017; Kyaw Zeyar Win 2018; Schissler et al. 2017; Wade 2017). International funds for investment, which had risen significantly since the 2015 elections, were markedly reduced. Both the United States and the European Union imposed sanctions against senior Myanmar military commanders. Foreign tourism declined dramatically and pushed back targeted growth forecasts. Myanmar also increasingly saw itself forced back into the orbit of China, who sought to maximise their own advantage from the crisis in exchange for political support (Zhang 2020).

Not only did the justice icon fail to acknowledge the scale of the violence and subsequent suffering of Rohingya communities, but she failed to use her "moral authority" to stem the virulent anti-Muslim sentiment that proliferated in the wake of the violence (Chambers and Cheesman 2019). However, while Suu Kyi has been widely criticised by the international community, she has benefited domestically from the crisis and a widespread nationalist antipathy for the Rohingya. On the same day that she represented Myanmar in the Hague, rallies were held in support of her across major towns in Myanmar as well as amongst the diaspora community, backing her "defence of the nation" (Naw Betty Han 2019). And yet, domestic support for *Amay Su* (Mother Suu) has also been accompanied by growing unease amongst ethnic nationality communities due to what is perceived as her ongoing defence of the military's actions in other parts of the country.

In addition to the Rohingya crisis, armed conflict in Rakhine, Shan and Kachin States has intensified and the peace process is on rocky ground. When the NLD came to power, Aung San Suu Kyi declared the peace process to be *the* national priority, hoping to end the multiple ethnic insurgencies that have plagued the country since independence. After decades of experiencing violence at the hands of the *Tatmadaw*, the ushering in of the civilian government also raised hopes for a genuine peace accord and ethno-religious reconciliation. However, the loss of human life and material destruction in borderland areas continues to incur heavy social and economic costs to ethnic communities (Hedström 2016). For Ethnic Armed Organisations (EAOs) participating in the peace process, there is also a growing sense that the same political-economic dynamics that drove the resumption of conflict in Kachin State in 2011 are now occurring elsewhere (Gabusi 2018; Sadan 2016; South 2018a).[4]

In 2019, formal peace negotiations stalled when both the Karen National Union (KNU) and the Restoration Council of Shan State (RCSS), the two most influential signatory groups of the Nationwide Ceasefire Agreement (NCA), suspended their participation. While all parties to the NCA have agreed *in principle* to building a "democratic federal union", the challenge of forging an inclusive national identity on the basis of which a new federal state can be imagined is an ongoing challenge, particularly in a state beholden to cultural and categorical determinisms (see Cheesman 2017; Ferguson 2015; Robinne 2019; Walton 2013). After numerous rounds of informal negotiations, another conference was held in August 2020, but little was achieved and key EAOs remained absent (Mathieson 2020). Indeed, the peace process remains hindered by ongoing issues over inclusivity (Lwin Cho Latt et al. 2018) and the *Tatmadaw*'s focus on disarmament, demobilisation and reintegration. There are also ongoing obstacles to implementing the NCA and basic principles for a future federal union. The negotiation of interim arrangements in ceasefire areas, for example, fails to properly take into account existing administrative and justice systems of EAOs (Harrison and Kyed 2019; Lue Htar 2018; South 2018a, b). Significant challenges also remain to securing a political settlement that would establish how populations and territories should be governed, including the rights to preserve and protect minority customs, traditions, languages and literature (South and Lall 2018; South 2018a, b).

Outside the official peace process, the NLD's inability to take seriously the voices of ethnic communities has had significant consequences. In many ways Suu Kyi appears to continue to impose a singular cultural vision of the nation and its history on the country. This builds off decades of Burmanisation throughout ethnic areas under military rule and what Walton and Haywood (2014, 4) describe as an "entrenched wariness, if not outright fear and hostility" towards the Bamar majority and the central government (see also Walton 2013). Controversies over the naming of a nationally funded bridge in Mon State, where local preference was overridden by central government, and protests against erecting statues of the Burmese independence hero Aung San in ethnic towns across the country, are being seized on as examples of Bamar ascendency (see Medail 2018). This is also reflected in the NLD's engagement with ethnic parties. The Arakan National Party (ANP), for example, had a strong showing in the 2015 polls but was denied major roles in the local administration, fuelling local resentment and a resurgence in support for the Arakan Army (AA) (Smith 2020, 95, 107–110) – recently declared a "terrorist organisation" (Nyein Nyein 2020).[5] As detailed by Cecile Medail (2018, 278) in our previous volume, while self-determination lies at the heart of civil conflict in Myanmar, these ongoing controversies illustrate "the incompatability of ethnic aspirations with a particular notion of national identity promoted by the Bamar militarised elite."

Beyond the peace process and identity politics, the NLD government has come under increasing criticism for their lack of progress on other fronts (Moe Thuzar and Cheong 2019; Nyi Nyi Kyaw 2020; Pederson 2019). Key economic, social and political reforms are stalled and the justice system also faces significant structural issues, continuing what Nick Cheesman (2019) refers to as a "routine practice of impunity" embedded in "mundane juridical and administrative arrangements" (2019, 891). With conflicts over land a key issue affecting rural communities (HRW 2018; Lue Htar 2018; Mark 2016, 2017), the continued centralisation of the courts, the limited realm of judicial authority and a "culture of procedural authoritarianism" leaves little room for restitutional justice (Crouch 2019b). Under Suu Kyi's leadership, many expected the government to further liberalise colonial-era press censorship laws and policies that restrict human rights and freedom of expression. However, there are still significant risks to journalistic production and the work of civil society activists, in particular (Brooten et al. 2019; Eaint Thiri Thu 2019; Salai Thant Zin 2019). And yet, to focus on what is lacking in the country's reform process, also neglects what is also occurring and the complex dynamics of what it means to *live with* a country going through profound social and political change.

The wide-ranging, myriad and multiple challenges of "Living with Myanmar" is the subject of this volume. Taking the call from Elizabeth Rhoads and Courtney Wittekind (2018), any analyses of Myanmar's present political reform process must take into account the various levels of "interaction and agency" at all levels of society. Rather than focusing on the stasis of the current government, the chapters in this volume instead highlight dynamics of the various levels of change and contestation occurring, including the various "processes of change and the agents that propel such processes forward" (Rhoads and Wittekind 2018, 174). Each of the authors explore the multiple and productive ways that people, activists, state officials and external actors are engaging with Myanmar's historical, geographic and institutional complexities. Split into four sections, this includes an analysis of parliamentary and economic life and the ways that various groups attempt live with institutional legacies and plural identities. Many of the authors in this volume are change agents themselves, and their work helps to highlight the contradictions, ambiguities and complexities of what it is like to live with and navigate the political institutions, socialities and historical legacies that continue to shape the country's ongoing political transformation. This is not a comprehensive coverage of what is happening in the country. However, what is clear is that while there is a great sense of frustration and impatience with the various hurdles that stymy reform, there is a diversity of actors deeply committed to making change at all levels of society.

PARLIAMENTARY LIFE

With 25 per cent of seats reserved for the military, there is no denying their ongoing influence over parliamentary life. It appears that under the NLD the *Tatmadaw* has actually strengthened its parliamentary delegation and expanded its involvement in lawmaking activities and legislative oversight (Maung Aung Myoe 2018). Yet in parallel with the ongoing restrictive presence of the *Tatmadaw*, in Chapter 2 Egreteau shows that during their first four years in power, NLD parliamentarians have been busy working to improve the country and the argument of a parliamentary deficit is "misplaced". Under the top-down leadership of the State Counselor, the balance of power appears to have shifted to a core elite, with a dominant executive controlling parliamentary debate and oversight (Barany 2018). In what is widely regarded as a strict standard of party discipline, draft proposals and motions prepared by individual legislators are routinely dismissed by the house speakers and backbenchers are continuously warned against using their oversight duties. However, when interrogating the activities of NLD legislators pre-and post the 2015 elections Egreteau suggests that while the State Counselor Office and the presidency do dominate the legislative process, the parliament has consolidated its position as the prime site for policy discussion and popular representation. In particular, there has been a strong focus on NLD parliamentarians engaging with their electorates and representing their constituents' views in the legislature.

The ability of MPs to represent the interests of their constituents is further examined by Nyein Thiri Swe and Zaw Min Oo in Chapter 3. Drawing attention to the views of MPs in sub-national parliaments, they explore how parliamentarians construct and enact their representative role both in and outside of the *hluttaw*. This chapter nicely complements Egreteau's research in the national legislature, showing the emphasis placed by MPs on the importance of representing the needs and concerns of their respective constituents in the sub-national parliaments. However, the authors also reflect on how these MPs feel frustrated by the structural limitations and institutional constraints that limit their representational performance. One of the biggest challenges identified is the constitutionally mandated dual role that many MPs have to fulfil in sub-national parliaments. The role of the military also necessarily inhibits the representational performance of MPs. The difficulty in changing their control of 25 per cent of seats of parliament according to the constitution is seen to corrode the representational performance of the parliament, as a democracy should. However, one interesting dynamic which the authors point to is the increased level of engagement of citizens with the parliament and their evolving expectations. Indeed, in many ways the "social contract" – the terms with which people interact with the state – is being rewritten in Myanmar as pro-democracy parliamentarians find their feet (see also Pursch et al. 2018).

In Chapter 4, Jefferson gives us a more intimate insight into the lives of some of these new parliamentarians, and their experiences as former political prisoners. Moving beyond simplistic narratives of change and transition, he reveals the importance of attending to personal trajectories as mutually constitutive of the socio-political in Myanmar today. Rather than focusing on narratives of interruption and rupture as many do in tales of former prisoners in Myanmar, in their stories time in prison is viewed as part of a life narrative that continues to evolve. Central to his interviews is a theme of frustration with the slow pace of reform in Myanmar, but tempered by the knowledge that the time *will* pass. Indeed, what comes out of the narratives Jefferson presents is a story of an unwavering optimism and pragmatism. For many of the former-political-prisoners-cum-parliamentarians, their memories of the infamous prison system is not always negative. Rather, for some it provided a family and even an education of sorts. For others, it was part of their time "doing politics". Indeed, as he notes:

> I hesitate to characterise the interruptions and disruptions as rupture per se, that is as only an expression of brokenness... They are links as much as breaks and as such imply continuity as much as discontinuity.

These narratives also have implications for how we think about Myanmar's social and political changes and the way that we study it. Rather than seeing what has occurred in Myanmar over the last ten years through a grand transitional narrative of political revolution, these narratives instead reveal the slow and subtle "mutations" to Myanmar's political landscape and its people.

ECONOMIC LIFE

Mutations to the country's economy over the last four years have also not always been so positive. With Suu Kyi's focus on peace and national reconciliation, economic reform was pushed to the side and foreign investment declined significantly as a result of the humanitarian crisis in Rakhine State. This lack of confidence is reflected in the World Bank's "Doing Business 2019" ranking of Myanmar as 171 out of 190 countries, showing just how far the country has to come into making the country more attractive to investors (World Bank 2020).

In Chapter 5, Turnell and Nyein Ei Cho examine the NLD's progress in the economy, focusing on the challenges to macro-financial reforms. They argue that the structures put in place since 2015 have been significant, but the benefits have perhaps not been so evident to the public. In various speeches after the inauguration of President U Win Myint in 2018, the government signalled a renewed emphasis on the economy. In August 2018 the government released the long-awaited Myanmar Sustainable Development Plan (2018–2030). Based on the United Nations' Sustainable Development Goals, the objectives and principles of the plan recognise that bold measures are needed to "reinvigorate reform" (Ministry of Planning and Finance 2018). Importantly, this includes recognition of the need for policy change that supports sustainable, broad-based growth, good governance, fiscal discipline and increased equality. Indeed, as the authors show, the government has been focused on implementing a long-term vision for the country. This has included tackling corruption, opposition from vested business interests and the development of the new Myanmar Investment Promotion Plan which aims to expand public investment over the next two decades. It will take time, as the authors show, to tackle corruption and untangle the strands of personal and institutional ties that the military still holds over the economy and government policy (Ford et al. 2016; Gabusi 2018; Jones 2014, 2018). However, there are building blocks being put in place to do so.

Like efforts to implement macro-financial reform, indicators of economic development reveal some improvements while other figures are not so promising. As Warr details in Chapter 6, when tracing the indices of poverty and inequality over more than a decade, there is now a widening gap between the financial health of urban and rural populations, the former being the main beneficiaries. While this is not entirely unexpected if we look at other countries' development paths, the impact of this gap is significant in Myanmar where 70 per cent of the population still resides in rural areas. Warr argues that while spending in both rural and urban areas has increased since 2015, the inequalities between the two groups have not been adequately addressed. Improved transportation corridors and reliable power and water are still fundamental services that are unequally distributed across the country. He also makes clear the difference between poverty and inequality, and signals a warning that greater economic growth may indeed prove damaging to the Union as inequities will likely widen. In particular, the ongoing fracturing of the peace process will also only further marginalise ethnic populations from developments occurring elsewhere and fuel fires for future conflict.

Despite these warnings, it is important to acknowledge the scale of change in rural areas of Myanmar. In Chapter 7, Okamoto details the place of Myanmar's agricultural sector within its economic development and the significant shifts that have taken place since the relaxation of restrictions on freedom of movement imposed under military rule. In the early phase of the transitional government there was strong investment in industry and expansion of manufacturing. Agriculture fell significantly as a percentage of exports and there was a parallel reduction in the percentage of people employed in agriculture as a result of rural outmigration and rapid and widescale mechanisation (see also Myat Thida Win et al. 2018). For many farmers and their families the promises made by the NLD are yet to be felt, with the majority still largely relying on their own self-enhancing "coping strategies" developed under military rule (Thawnghmung 2019, xvi) and the work of social welfare groups (Griffiths 2018; McCarthy 2019). The NLD has, however, commenced reforms which have assisted in supporting the agricultural sector, including through access to rural credit. Like Warr, Okamoto acknowledges that efforts towards poverty reduction are plagued by well-known issues that other nations in the region face. What is distinctly different about Myanmar is the rate of change and rapid engagement with international agricultural methods, including mechanisation.

The impacts of government reforms in the agricultural sector is further detailed and addressed at a micro level in Chapter 8 by Yin Nyein, Rick Gregory and Aung Kyaw Thein. Through a thorough examination of reforms made to the fisheries sector, they discuss the complexities of existing controls and licensing regarding freshwater fishing and the way the country's citizens and growing civil society community have taken advantage of new opportunities to contest and advance policies in their interest. While going some ways to protect the rights of small fishermen, it is evident that the multiple levels of government, entrenched administrative procedures and inequalities between "big business" and rural, often poorly educated, small-scale fishers perpetuate an unequal relationship and inhibit economic growth. However, the collaborative partnerships built between state agencies, businessmen, international and local NGOs and civil society groups in the fisheries sector provides a blueprint for future reforms that promote more equitable access to, and sharing of, resources in other sectors. Such partnerships are also a means to achieving greater government accountability and a gateway to the participation of more vulnerable groups in society. Partnerships between the government and the civil society sector are also key to overcoming the multiple institutional legacies of military rule that continue to impede reform.

LIVING WITH INSTITUTIONAL LEGACIES

In the-lead up to the 2015 election, analysts made regular warnings about the NLD's low technical capacity to manage the country's multifarious and fractious reform process. While these factors have indeed hindered progress, historical legacies and a lack of capacity also stagnates change. An increasingly active civil society sector works hard to lay bare the "politics of dispossession" around various projects (Einzenberger 2018; Leehey 2019), including intertwined tactics of "resistance and refusal" (Prasse-Freeman 2020). Others artfully use humour and satire (Chu May Paing 2020). And yet, while political participation has improved significantly since the 2010s there are, as Nicholas Farrelly (2020) relates, still indications that "powerful interests in Myanmar, including the NLD, are uncomfortable with serious academic scrutiny of their policies and actions." As the chapters in this volume highlight, there is extensive internal change occurring, but there is also an immense sense of frustration in the slow pace of reform and bureaucratic hurdles which obfuscate change.

Nowhere is this more evident than in the space of education. As Lall shows in Chapter 9, when looking at the progress of education reform under the NLD, the government appears to be "stuck in quagmires that don't have easy solutions". Unsurprisingly, one of the main challenges to transforming education in Myanmar is the limited resources and capacity of staff. Despite a surplus of funds and initiatives from development partners to support quality education and evidence-based planning, Ministry of Education staff, teachers and trainers have little time and energy to absorb such work. Like other sectors, transforming the education sector is also deeply inter-connected with issues related to belonging, national identity and the peace process. Overhauling the curriculum, for example, will be key to reversing the decades of Burmanisation imposed under military rule. Concurrently there is also a lack of guidance, authority and political will to recognise the role that ethnic armed organisations (EAOs) play in providing education. Lall concludes by highlighting the importance of better supporting mother tongue-based multilingual education and how its implementation can not only help to ensure equal access to education across the country, but also promote social cohesion.

The multiple challenges to reforming education in Myanmar raise a much broader issue regarding access to information, critical thinking and knowledge. The critical importance of "building a knowledge society" is well addressed by Missingham and Carroll in Chapter 10, who highlight the role of library and information studies in developing an informed and participative democracy. Myanmar's tertiary sector is undergoing an extensive review with a strong focus on improving research capabilities. The development of this sector is key to building better social, political and economic outcomes that benefit all members of society. As shown by the authors, there are many challenges which impede digital literacy to support twenty-first century learning, including basic issues like limited internet access and regular power outages. Positively, new partnerships between local and international universities are paving the way forward. The commitment and dedication of university staff dedicated to change is also key to this. However, equity issues are being brought to the forefront as the government now grapples with COVID-19 disruptions to face-to-face education. The impact of controversial internet shutdown in regions of unrest is further marginalising those in conflict-affected areas (Anonymous 2020).

Alongside education, other areas are proving slow to reform, bogged down in processes which obfuscate meaningful change. As Khin Khin Mra and Livingstone detail in Chapter 11, efforts to implement a national gender policy have also stalled under the NLD. The former government enacted the National Strategic Plan for the Advancement of Women 2013–

2022 (NSPAW) as Myanmar's first policy framework to comprehensively address women's rights. However, the implementation of this plan faces similar capacity constraints, funding shortfalls and coordination issues as those examined by Lall. Despite the best intentions of women's groups and networks, the lack of common aims between different organisations and actors has also fragmented women's voices and their impact on institutional and policy reform. Their study also reveals the ongoing gendered legacies of military rule and patriarchal power structures that remain deeply embedded in all levels of government. Informally, social and cultural norms also play a significant role, sidelining women from playing a stronger role in policymaking and institutional reform.

At the heart of this is a question of norms and the difficulty of tackling patriarchal power structures that are entrenched at all levels of society. And despite these critiques of the civil society sector, they remain the driving force behind change in Myanmar. The opening political space afforded by Myanmar's social and political changes has seen a blossoming of civil society networks around various issues, including the rights of women. As Aye Thiri Kyaw and Miedema explain in Chapter 12, with Aung San Suu Kyi at the helm there was a great sense of optimism for women's rights in the period after the 2015 election. Growing public awareness of gender inequality also converged with the global #MeToo movement which gained international traction in 2017 following the exposure of Hollywood producer Harvey Weinstein's longstanding exploitation and sexual abuse of women. The authors specifically address how the #MeToo movement has served as a platform for women's rights in Myanmar and how it has brought previously forbidden topics into the spotlight, including sexual abuse and harassment. The traction of the global campaign amongst feminist circles in Yangon also highlights the lightning-fast dissemination of information that has resulted from Myanmar's rapid uptake of mobile phone technology and how this can be used for social good. While others have written on the negative implications of the social media space (Kinseth 2018; Yan Naung Oak and Brooten 2019), these authors show how Facebook and Twitter have also functioned as an enabling environment for many, the anonymity of the virtual space encouraging people to speak out. And yet, while feminists in Yangon have been able to take advantage of the anonymity provided by these platforms, other marginalised groups in society may not be as well poised to do so.

LIVING WITH PLURAL IDENTITIES

Forging an inclusive national identity remains a key issue at the heart of Myanmar's transformation and its peace process in particular (Joliffe 2018; South and Lall 2018; Walton 2013). Peace discussions in Myanmar since independence have been anchored in demands from EAOs around an ethnofederalist arrangement that would provide autonomy and self-determination for ethnic nationalities on the basis of historical entitlement. After decades of conflict, the legacy of broken trust is paramount in negotiations between EAOs and the military, only further heightened ongoing land confiscations and natural resource extraction projects (Barbesgaard 2018; Gabusi 2018; Woods 2015, 2019). However, as Breen and He argue in Chapter 13, elite level discussions around the merits of ethnofederal arrangements do not necessarily reflect the views of ordinary people. Based on a series of deliberative surveys, they show that while people want ethnic identity to continue to be recognised, it should not necessarily form the basis for a federal arrangement. Instead, a form of territorial or regional federalism is preferred by some, with the boundaries being based on criteria like geographical continuity, economic resources and infrastructure. While the results slightly differed in areas with stronger EAO control, participants in the surveys overwhelmingly suggested that ethnofederalist arrangements were impractical in a country as diverse as Myanmar. They also believed that a territorial federalist arrangement might help to mitigate future conflicts and fears of secession, as well as the marginalisation of smaller ethnic groups, such as the Lahu or Palaung. However, giving voice to ordinary ethnic nationality peoples and embedding their rights within Myanmar's governance system is likely a long way off.

Despite long-standing fears of secession, the military's ideology around belonging and exclusion exemplified in the notion of "national races" or *taing yin tha*, also perpetuates the centrality of ethnicity/race in Myanmar's political arena (Cheesman 2017; Robinne 2019). There has been much discussion around how this Burmese term works both structurally and socially to the exclusion of groups like the Rohingya (Arraiza and Vonk 2017; Cheesman 2017; Islam 2018; Nyi Nyi Kyaw 2017; Pugh 2013; Zawacki 2013). However, as Fujimura explains in Chapter 14, the politics of national belonging and "native races" are complex entities, which have deep historical and multi-lingual trajectories. Tracing the way spoken and written language was used to create a sense of unity amongst the diverse religious and linguistic Karen community during colonial rule, she reminds us of the importance of attending to the multiple, multilingual histories of Myanmar. Her examination of the failures of the Sgaw Karen Baptist elite to reach the diverse population also speaks to contemporary debates about the persisting inability of the majority-Bamar government to engage non-Burmese speakers in a common understanding of citizenship and belonging. Indeed, while the NLD continues to cultivate an image of a party which represents people across lines of ethnicity in the lead-up to the next election, their message of "Collective Strength" will only fall on deaf ears if its diverse peoples aren't deliberately made to feel part of the "collective".

Balancing decision-making for the benefit of the nation while acknowledging the rights of each ethnic group is potentially the single most important challenge for the current government. As Peggy Brett shows, such issues are structurally embedded, including in access to citizenship. In Chapter 15 Brett examines the multiple ambiguities embedded in the 1982 Citizenship Law and the way they act as "hidden forms of exclusion", trapping already marginalised groups in a perpetual state of limbo. She argues that part of this limbo is embedded within the ambiguous logics of the Citizenship Law itself and the narrowly constrained procedures which prove eligibility for identity documentation. In Myanmar, the National Registration Card (NRC) is essential to everyday life, rights and political participation. Even though there are legislated pathways for determining citizenship, procedural implementation at a local level does not appear to support this reform. While the National Verification Card (NVC), for example, was introduced in 2016 by the NLD government as a pathway to citizenship, in practice it effectively functions to deny eligibility for citizenship. With few incentives for government staff to resolve the status of those with other forms of identification, many people face a situation where their citizenship status simply remains unresolved. Indeed, like the issues facing the education sector, changing the practices of embedded administrative processes appears to be very difficult and will only further marginalise minority religious and ethnic communities from the national polity unless deliberately addressed.

CONCLUSION

Three years after the NLD took power, the 2019 Myanmar Update asked participants to reflect on the state of "living with Myanmar". The conference theme was a response to the challenges that people in Myanmar continue to face in living with the legacies of colonialism, civil conflict and military rule. The lack of meaningful reform detailed in the most recent Myanmar Update volume which probed the theme *Myanmar Transformed?* (Chambers et al. 2018), have become more evident in the last two years. The formation of a new government in Myanmar, led by the NLD, was a crucially important milestone in the country's "transition" (c.f. Rhoads and Wittekind 2018). However, as this volume shows, there are many ways to measure and assess what is happening in the country.

Much commentary on Myanmar focuses on the negative – what is "absent". This simplistic analysis ignores the nuances that underpin what is means to *live with Myanmar*. As this volume attests, living with Myanmar has always been many things, reflecting the many diverse peoples who call the country their home. Despite the lack of progress on many fronts, what we want to highlight as we conclude here is the importance of ongoing engagement with Myanmar and its people. Part of the aims of this volume is to provide a platform for Myanmar scholars to publish their work. This is reflected in the history of the Myanmar Update volume series and the growth in contributions from scholars based inside the country, and the diversity of subject-matter since its inception in 1990 (see e.g. Chambers et al. 2018; Cheesman et al. 2012, 2014; Cheesman and Farrelly 2016; Skidmore and Wilson 2007, 2008). After decades of heavy restrictions, Myanmar's research community has built strong partnerships with foreign universities and scholars. These partnerships have seen resultant transformations to the quality and diversity of academic scholarship. This has included growth, albeit slow, in the research output from university academics, and a flourishing network of think tanks and civil society groups contributing to the development of a vibrant and resilient research sector (see also GDN-CESD 2020; Rodriguez 2020).

Building on this momentum, the following chapters are therefore of great importance in highlighting "where things are at" prior to both the 2020 elections which at the time of printing are still scheduled for November this year. Preparation for the elections has taken an unexpected turn as a result of the COVID-19 pandemic that has swept the world in 2020. Whilst the NLD has been working to remind the public of their focus on the long-term, structural issues with which they will need time to deliver meaningful change, the impacts of COVID-19 has also allowed them to focus on a message of solidarity and civic pride amidst what is a global economic downturn. Reinforcing the party's narrative of the importance of Suu Kyi to the country in times of crisis, the COVID crisis has given the State Counselor a platform from which to demonstrate her leadership skills and promote her image as "the mother of the nation". In the winner-takes-all electoral system (Bünte 2018), Suu Kyi is unlikely to be forced into a coalition government (Dunant 2020). However, while the NLD is likely to return to power, they may also face a more diverse parliament.

The litany of problems the country continues to face – from the beleaguered peace process to rural land disputes – leaves it vulnerable to challenges from other parties. Prior to the 2015 election there was general unity amongst the state and regional electorates focused on ending military rule. However, if the November 2018 by-elections are a litmus test for 2020, the NLD could have a tough fight on their hands in ethnic constituencies, especially in areas with active conflict. This should already be clear to the NLD – of the thirteen constituencies up for grabs in 2018, the NLD lost six, five of which were in ethnic states. As Morten Pederson suggests, if the NLD has one thing it can rely on, it is the "horizontal accountability imposed by free and fair national elections" (Pederson 2019, 237).

The second-largest party, the military-backed Union Solidarity and Development Party (USDP), has focused on a narrative committed to nationalism, patriotism and sovereignty. Led by U Than Htay, they have been campaigning on the line that it's "Time to Think", reminding voters of the NLD's failure to live up to their election promises, in contrast to their own previous successes between 2011–2016. Ethnic parties too will likely pick up some more votes, as they amalgamate (Swe Lei Mon 2020). While the NLD focuses on developing a foundation for stable economic development and careful planning sector-wide reform, these and other parties are banking on the fact that they might pick up some votes from segments of the population eager for tangible change.

In many ways the election will be an important test of how far the country has progressed on the path to democracy. The military's recent declaration that they might postpone elections in parts of war-torn Rakhine State is telling for how far the country still has to go (Shoon Naing 2020). And yet, as the diversity of issues presented in this volume attests, to focus on electoral processes as a symbol of the country's transformation overlooks the deeper aspects of the country's transition. COVID-19, for example, was unheard of when this volume began to be compiled and its full impact is likely to remain unknown for years to come. At the time of writing in August 2020, the country is yet to experience a major outbreak of the virus, yet the economic ramifications are likely to be significant, with economic growth forecasted to fall to just 0.5 per cent (Turnell 2020). There is also strong evidence to suggest that the gaps between rural and urban areas that Warr describes in Chapter 6 are likely to grow as a result of the impacts of the global crisis (Mi Chan 2020). But Myanmar is resilient and its people continue to find new and creative ways to cope in the face of adversity (Chu May Paing 2020). The population has endured great hardships and divisions. While many contentious matters remain, the adaptability of Myanmar's peoples gives some confidence that the future continues to hold promise.

Notes

1 Significantly this motion was put forward on the 26 January, the two-year anniversary of when U Ko Ni, a vocal advocate for constitutional reform, was assassinated (Crouch 2017b).

2 A/HRC/39/64, Report of the Independent International Fact-finding Mission on Myanmar, 27 August 2018.

3 International Court of Justice, "Application of the Convention on the Prevention and Punishment of the Crime of Genocide (The Gambia v. Myanmar)". Available at https://www.icj-cij.org/en/case/178 (accessed 10 August 2020).

4 Mandy Sadan's (2016) edited volume provides a detailed insight the 17-year ceasefire agreement in Kachin State and the reason for its collapse in 2011. The ceasefire effectively enabled the strengthening of the Tatmadaw's position over Kachin areas and people, tying ethnic armed elite to the state through lucrative joint ventures which benefited few. These ceasefires did very little to address people's grievances related to human rights abuses nor demands for greater political autonomy.

5 The AA's popularity has grown dramatically in recent years, built off grievances and mistrust towards the political dominance of the Bamar in Rakhine affairs and an extremely popular ethnonationalist campaign (see Nyi Nyi Kyaw 2020, 240–241).

References

Anonymous (2020). "Covid-19 gives Cover for Threats to Freedom of Information and Expression in Myanmar". *New Mandala,* 9 April. Available at https://www.newmandala.org/covid-19-gives-cover-for-threats-to-freedom-of-information-and-expression-in-myanmar/ (accessed 22 July 2020).

Arnold, M.B. (2019). "Why GAD Reform Matters to Myanmar". *East Asia Forum,* 24 August. Available at https://www.eastasiaforum.org/2019/08/24/why-gad-reform-matters-to-myanmar/ (accessed 22 July 2020).

Arraiza, J.M. and Vonk, O. (2017). "Report on Citizenship Law: Myanmar". Country Report RSCAS/GLOBALCIT-CR 2017/14.

Barany, Z. (2018). "Burma: Suu Kyi's Missteps". *Journal of Democracy* 29 (1): 5–19.

Barbesgaard, M. (2019). "'Ocean and Land Control-Grabbing': The Political Economy of Landscape Transformation in Northern Tanintharyi, Myanmar". *Journal of Rural Studies* 69 (1): 195–203.

Brooten, L., McElhone, J.M. and Venkiteswaran, G. (2019). *Myanmar Media in Transition: Legacies, Challenges and Change.* Singapore: ISEAS-Yusof Ishak Institute.

BBC (2016). "Myanmar's Aung San Suu Kyi to be given new 'PM-like' role". *BBC News,* 31 March. Available at https://www.bbc.com/news/world-asia-35928524 (accessed 30 July 2020).

Bünte, M. (2018). "Perilous Presidentialism or Precarious Power-Sharing? Hybrid Regime Dynamics in Myanmar". *Contemporary Politics* 24 (3): 346–360.

Chambers, J. and Cheesman, N. (2019). "Coming to Terms with Moral Authorities in Myanmar". *Sojourn* 34 (2): 231–257.

Chambers, J., McCarthy, G., Farrelly, N. and Chit Win (eds.) (2018). *Myanmar Transformed: People, Places, Politics.* Singapore: ISEAS Yusof-Ishak Institute.

Cheesman, N. (2017). "How in Myanmar 'National Races' Came to Surpass Citizenship and Exclude Rohingya." *Journal of Contemporary Asia* 47 (3): 461–483.

---------- (2019). "Routine Impunity as Practice (in Myanmar)". *Human Rights Quarterly* 41 (4): 873–892.

Cheesman, N., Farrelly, N., Wilson, T. (eds.) (2014). *Debating Democratization in Myanmar.* Singapore: ISEAS.

Cheesman, N. and Farrelly, N. (eds.) (2016). *Conflict in Myanmar: War, Politics, Religion.* Singapore: ISEAS-Yusof Ishak Institute.

Cheesman, N., Skidmore, M., Wilson, T. (eds.) (2012). *Myanmar's Transition: Openings, Obstacles and Opportunities.* Singapore: ISEAS.

Chu May Paing (2020). "Viral Satire as Public Feeling in Myanmar". *American Ethnologist,* 20 May. Available at https://americanethnologist.org/features/pandemic-diaries/pandemic-diaries-affect-and-crisis/viral-satire-as-public-feeling-in-myanmar (accessed 14 July 2020).

Crouch, M. (ed.) (2017a). *The Business of Transition: Law Reform, Development and Economics in Myanmar.* Cambridge: Cambridge University Press.

---------- (2017b). "In Memoriam: 'Saya' U Ko Ni, Myanmar's Advocate for Constitutional Reform". *Australian Journal of Asian Law* 17 (2).

---------- (2019a). *The Constitution of Myanmar: A Contextual Analysis*. Bloomsbury: Hart Publishing.

---------- (2019b). "Illiberalism and Democratic Illusions in Myanmar." *New Mandala,* 20 November. Available at https://www.newmandala.org/illusions-in-myanmar/ (accessed 22 July 2020).

Dunant, B. (2020). "The Myth of 'Coalition Government'". *Frontier Myanmar,* 27 July. Available at https://www.frontiermyanmar.net/en/the-myth-of-coalition-government/ (accessed 30 July 2020).

Einzenberger, R. (2018). "Frontier Capitalism and Politics of Dispossession in Myanmar: The Case of the Mwetaung (Gullu Mual) Nickel Mine in Chin State". *Austrian Journal of South-East Asian Studies* 11 (1): 13–34.

Egreteau, R. (2016). *Caretaking Democratization: The Military and Political Change in Myanmar.* Oxford: Oxford University Press.

Farrelly, N. (2020). "Reflections on the Future of Myanmar Studies." Available at https://www.newmandala.org/reflections-future-of-myanmar-studies/ (accessed 22 July 2020).

Ferguson, J. (2015). "Ethnicity, Belonging and the National Census in Burma/Myanmar". *Bijdragen Tot de Taal-, Land en Volkenkunde* 171 (1): 1–28.

Ford, M., Gillian, M. and Htwe Htwe Thein (2016). "From Cronyism to Oligarchy? Privatisation and Business Elites in Myanmar". *Journal of Contemporary Asia* 46 (1): 18–41.

Fuller, Thomas (2015). "Aung San Suu Kyi and Myanmar General Meet, Taking Steps Toward Sharing Power". *New York Times,* 2 December. Available at http://www.nytimes.com/2015/12/03/world/asia/myanmar-aung-san-suu-kyi-meets-president-army.html?mwrsm=Facebook&_r=1 (accessed 28 July 2020).

Gabusi, G. (2018). "Change and Continuity: Capacity, Coordination and Natural Resources in Myanmar's Periphery". In *Myanmar Transformed: People, Places, Politics,* edited by J. Chambers, G. McCarthy, N. Farrelly, and Chit Win. Singapore: ISEAS-Yusof-Ishak Institute, 137–160.

GDN-CESD (2020). *Doing Research – Myanmar.* Yangon: Global Development Network and Centre for Economic and Social Development.

Griffiths, M. (2018). "Networks of Reciprocity: Precarity and Community Social Organisations in Rural Myanmar". *Journal of Contemporary Asia* 49 (4): 602–625.

Harrison, A.P. and Kyed, H.M. (2019). "Ceasefire State-Making and Justice Provision by Ethnic Armed Groups in Southeast Myanmar". *Sojourn* 34 (2): 290–326.

Hedström, J. (2016). "A Feminist Political Economy of Insecurity and Violence in Kachin State". In *Conflict in Myanmar: War, Politics, Religion,* edited by N. Cheesman, and N. Farrelly. Singapore: ISEAS Yusof Ishak Institute, 67–89.

HRW (2018). *"Nothing for Our Land": Impact of Land Confiscation on Farmers in Myanmar*. Bangkok: Human Rights Watch.

Hunter, A. (2014). "Is Thein Sein Myanmar's Real Champion of Democracy?" *The Age*, 2 July. Available at https://www.theage.com.au/opinion/is-thein-sein-myanmars-real-champion-of-democracy-20140702-zstai.html (accessed 22 July 2020).

Islam, N. (2018). "Rohingya and Nationality Status in Myanmar". In *Citizenship in Myanmar: Ways of Being in and from Burma*, edited by A. South and M. Lall. Singapore: Chiang Mai University Press, Yusof Ishak Institute.

Jolliffe, K. (2018). "Peace and Reconciliation". In *Routledge Handbook of Contemporary Myanmar*, edited by A. Simpson, N. Farrelly, and I. Holliday. London and New York: Routledge., 359–370.

Jones, L. (2014). "The Political Economy of Myanmar's Transition". *Contemporary Asia* 44 (1): 144–170.

---------- (2018). "Political Economy". In *Routledge Handbook of Contemporary Myanmar*, edited by A. Simpson, N. Farrelly, and I. Holliday. London and New York: Routledge.

Kinseth, A. (2018). "Genocide in the Modern Era: Social Media and the Proliferation of Hate Speech in Myanmar". *Tea Circle*, 10 May. Available at https://teacircleoxford.com/2018/05/10/genocide-in-the-modern-era-social-media-and-the-proliferation-of-hate-speech-in-myanmar/ (accessed 20 July 2020).

Kyaw Yin Hlaing (2012). "Understanding Recent Political Changes in Myanmar". *Journal of Contemporary Southeast Asia* 34 (2): 197–216.

Kyaw Zeyar Win (2018). "Securitisation of the Rohingya in Myanmar". In *Myanmar Transformed: People, Places, Politics*, edited by J. Chambers, G. McCarthy, N. Farrelly, and Chit Win. Singapore: ISEAS Yusof-Ishak Institute, 251–266.

Leehey, J. (2019). "Silencing a Snakehead Fish: A Case Study in Local Media, Rural-Based Activism, and Defamation Litigation in Southern Myanmar". In *Myanmar Media in Transition: Legacies, Challenges and Change*, edited by L. Brooten, J.M. McElhone, and G. Venkiteswaran. Singapore: ISEAS-Yusof Ishak Institute, 151–176.

Lue Htar (2018). "Everyday Justice and Plural Authorities: Insights from Karen State about Land Disputes". *Independent Journal of Burmese Scholarship* 1 (2): 181–210.

Lwin Cho Latt, Hillman, B., Marlar Aung and Khin Sanda Myint (2018). "From Ceasefire to Dialogue: The Problem of 'All-Inclusiveness' in Myanmar's Stalled Peace Process". In *Myanmar Transformed: People, Places, Politics*, edited by J. Chambers, G. McCarthy, N. Farrelly, and Chit Win. Singapore: ISEAS Yusof-Ishak Institute, 231–250.

MacLean, K. (2018). "The Rohingya Crisis and the Practices of Erasure". *Journal of Genocide Research* 21 (1): 1–13.

Mark, S. (2016). "Are the Odds of Justice 'Stacked' Against Them? Challenges and Opportunities for Securing Land Claims by Smallholder Farmers in Myanmar". *Critical Asian Studies* 48 (3): 443–460.

---------- (2017). *Land Tenure Reform in Myanmar's Regime Transition: Political Legitimacy versus Capital Accumulation* (PhD dissertation). Rotterdam, The Netherlands: Erasmus University Rotterdam.

Mathieson, D.S. (2020). "Selling Dog Meat while Showing a Goat Head in Myanmar". *Asia Times,* 21 August. Available at https://asiatimes.com/2020/08/selling-dog-meat-while-showing-a-goat-head-in-myanmar/?fbclid=IwAR26TlHwKEql6RecStjRXvI18rvT3tw-w47TYzz80hlnQAn24SLxzp7yy6I (accessed 22 August 2020).

Maung Aung Myoe (2018). "Partnership in Politics: The *Tatmadaw* and the NLD in Myanmar since 2016". In *Myanmar Transformed: People, Places, Politics,* edited by J. Chambers, G. McCarthy, N. Farrelly, and Chit Win. Singapore: ISEAS Yusof-Ishak Institute, 201–230.

McCarthy, G. (2019). "Democratic Deservingness and Self-Reliance in Contemporary Myanmar". *Sojourn* 34 (2): 327–365.

Medail, C. (2018). "Forming an Inclusive National Identity in Myanmar: Voices of Mon People". In *Myanmar Transformed: People, Places, Politics,* edited by J. Chambers, G. McCarthy, N. Farrelly, and Chit Win. Singapore: ISEAS Yusof-Ishak Institute, 277–307.

Mi Chan (2020). "Myanmar's Economic Relief Plan Risks Excluding Vulnerable Populations". *New Mandala,* 12 May. Available at https://www.newmandala.org/myanmars-economic-relief-plan-risks-excluding-vulnerable-populations/ (accessed 22 July 2020).

Ministry of Planning and Finance (2018). *Myanmar Sustainable Development Plan (2018–2030).* Naypyidaw: Government of the Republic of the Union of Myanmar Ministry of Planning and Finance.

Moe Thuzar and Cheong, D. (2019). "Ethnicity, Citizenship and Identity in Post-2016 Myanmar". *Southeast Asian Affairs* 2019: 243–258.

Myat Thida Win, Belton, B. and Zhang, X. (2018). "Myanmar's Rural Revolution: Mechanization and Structural Transformation". In *Myanmar Transformed: People, Places, Politics,* edited by J. Chambers, G. McCarthy, N. Farrelly, and Chit Win. Singapore: ISEAS Yusof-Ishak Institute, 109–136.

Naw Betty Han (2019). "Standing with Mother Suu". *Frontier Myanmar,* 13 December 2019. Available at https:// frontiermyanmar.net/en/standing-with-mother-suu (accessed 28 July 2020).

Nyein Nyein (2020). "Myanmar Govt Declares Arakan Army a Terrorist Group". *The Irrawaddy,* 24 March. Available at https://www.irrawaddy.com/news/burma/myanmar-govt-declares-arakan-army-terrorist-group.html (accessed 12 August 2020).

Nyi Nyi Kyaw (2017). "Unpacking the Presumed Statelessness of Rohingyas". *Journal of Immigrant & Refugee Studies* 15 (3): 269–286.

---------- (2020). "Myanmar in 2019: Rakhine Issue, Constitutional Reform and Election Fever". *Southeast Asian Affairs* 2020: 234–254.

OHCHR (2018). "Report of the Detailed Findings of the Independent International Fact- Finding Mission on Myanmar (A/HRC/39/CRP.2)". 10–28 September 2018, Agenda Item 4. Geneva: United Nations Office of the High Commissioner for Human Rights. Available at https://www.ohchr.org/Documents/HRBodies/HRCouncil/FFM-Myanmar/A_HRC_39_CRP.2.pdf (accessed 10 August 2020).

Pedersen, M.B. (2019). "Myanmar in 2018: New Democracy Hangs in the Balance". *Southeast Asian Affairs* 2019: 225–241.

Prasse-Freeman, E. (2020). "Resistance/Refusal: Politics of Manoeuvre under Diffuse Regimes of Governmentality". *Anthropological Theory* (available online): https://doi.org/10.1177/1463499620940218 (accessed 28 July 2020).

Pugh, C.L. (2013). "Is Citizenship the Answer? Constructions of Belonging and Exclusion for the Stateless Rohingya of Burma". *IMI Working Papers Series,* 76. Available at https://www.compas.ox.ac.uk/wp-content/uploads/WP-2013-107-Pugh_Stateless_Rohingya_Burma.pdf (accessed 12 August 2020).

Rhoads, E.L. and Wittekind, C. (2018). "Rethinking Land and Property in a 'Transitioning' Myanmar: Representations of Isolation, Neglect, and Natural Decline". *Journal of Burma Studies* 22 (2): 171–213.

Robinne, F. (2019). "Thinking Through Heterogeneity: An Anthropological Look at Contemporary Myanmar". *Journal of Burma Studies* 23 (2): 285–322.

Rodriguez, E. (2020). "A Key Role for Think Tanks in Myanmar's Development". *Tea Circle,* 26 February. Available at https://teacircleoxford.com/2020/02/26/a-key-role-for-think-tanks-in-myanmars-development/ (accessed 22 July 2020).

Sadan, M. (ed.) (2016). *War and Peace in the Borderlands of Myanmar.* Copenhagen: NIAS Press.

Salai Thant Zin (2019). "NLD Sues Myanmar Cartoonist for Facebook Post Criticizing Party". *The Irrawaddy,* 20 September. Available at https://www.irrawaddy.com/news/burma/nld-sues-myanmar-cartoonist-facebook-post-criticizing-party.html (accessed 21 July 2020).

Schissler, M., Walton, M. and Phyu Phyu Thi (2017). "Reconciling Contradictions: Buddhist-Muslim Violence, Narrative Making, and Memory in Myanmar". *Journal of Contemporary Asia* 47 (3): 376–395.

Selth, A. (2018). "The Defence Services". In *Routledge Handbook of Contemporary Myanmar* edited by A. Simpson, N. Farrelly, and I. Holliday. New York: Routledge.

Shoon Naing (2020). "Myanmar may Postpone Election in War-Torn Rakhine State – Official". *Thomas Reuters,* 30 July. Available at https://news.trust.org/item/20200730093529-dwrsy/ (accessed 30 July 2020).

Skidmore, M. and Wilson, T. (2007). *Myanmar: The State, Community and the Environment.* Canberra: ANU E Press.

---------- (2008). *Dictatorship, Disorder and Decline in Myanmar.* Canberra: ANU E Press.

Smith, M. (2020). *Arakan (Rakhine State): A Land in Conflict on Myanmar's Western Frontier.* Amsterdam: Transnational Institute.

South, A. (2018a). "'Hybrid Governance' and the Politics of Legitimacy in the Myanmar Peace Process". *Journal of Contemporary Asia* 48 (1): 50–66.

---------- (2018b). *The Politics of Peace in Myanmar: Ethnicity, Conflict and Building a Legitimate State in Burma.* Copenhagen: NIAS Press.

South, A. and Lall, M. (2018). *Citizenship in Myanmar: Ways of Being in and from Burma.* Singapore: ISEAS and Chiang Mai University Press.

Swe Lei Mon (2020). "Ethnic Parties in Myanmar Seek Election Edge with Mergers, Alliances". *Myanmar Times,* 26 June. Available at https://www.mmtimes.com/news/ethnic-parties-myanmar-seek-election-edge-mergers-alliances.html (accessed 17 August 2020).

Thawnghmung, A.M. (2019). *Everyday Economic Survival in Myanmar.* Madison: Wisconsin University Press.

Turnell, S. (2020). "Debt Relief Boosts Myanmar's Covid-19 Recovery". *East Asia Forum,* 21 July. Available at https://www.eastasiaforum.org/2020/07/21/debt-relief-boosts-myanmars-covid-19-recovery/ (accessed 22 July 2020).

Wade, F. (2017). *Myanmar's Enemy Within: Buddhist Violence and the Making of a Muslim "Other".* London: Zed Books.

Walton, M.J. (2013). "The 'Wages of Burman-ness': Ethnicity and Burman Privilege in Contemporary Myanmar." *Journal of Contemporary Asia,* 43 (1): 1–27.

Walton, M.J. and Hayward, S. (2014). *Contesting Buddhist Narratives: Democratization, Nationalism, and Communal Violence in Myanmar.* Honolulu, HI: East-West Center.

Woods, K. (2015). "Intersections of Land Grabs and Climate Change Mitigation Strategies in Myanmar as a (Post-) War State of Conflict". *MOSAIC Working Paper Series,* 3.

---------- (2019). "Green Territoriality: Conservation as State Territorialization in a Resource Frontier". *Human Ecology,* 47: 217–232.

World Bank (2020). *Doing Business 2019: Training for Reform.* Washington DC: World Bank.

Yan Naung Oak and Brooten, L. (2019). "The Teashop Meets the 8 O'clock News: Facebook, Convergence and Online Public Spaces". In *Myanmar Media in Transition: Legacies, Challenges and Change,* edited by L. Brooten, J.M. McElhone, and G. Venkiteswaran. Singapore: ISEAS-Yusof Ishak Institute, 327–365.

Zawacki, B. (2013). "Defining Myanmar's Rohingya Problem". *Human Rights Brief,* 20 (3): 18–25.

Zhang, R. (2020). "To Suspend or Not to Suspend: A Cost-benefit Analysis of Three Chinese Mega-projects in Myanmar". *The Pacific Review,* (published online). Available at https://doi.org/10.1080/09512748.2020.1776757.

II

Parliamentary Life

2

PARLIAMENTARY LIFE UNDER THE NLD

Renaud Egreteau

An increasingly dominant view in Myanmar's policy circles suggests that the Union parliament – or *Pyidaungsu Hluttaw* – has been steadily marginalised under the leadership of the National League for Democracy (NLD). Since the pro-democracy party took control of both chambers of the bicameral body after the 2015 elections, the most sustained explanations relate to the latter's relatively timid output in lawmaking. This stands in stark contrast with the first post-junta legislature, dominated between 2011 and 2016 by the Union Solidarity and Development Party (USDP), which proved far more prolific in terms of legislative outputs (Kean 2014; Fink 2015; Egreteau 2017a). Growing criticism within Myanmar's political and civil society circles about the erosion of parliamentary power since 2016 has also being directed at the fledgling leadership of the new ruling party, and its charismatic patron Aung San Suu Kyi. Bill initiation has been dictated by the commanding heights of the NLD. Party discipline has, by and large, also been more strictly enforced by NLD whips in the two chambers. Lastly, unlike during the previous USDP term, personal rivalries have not translated into open, politically motivated confrontations between the executive and legislative organs of government. This suggests that the balance of power has resolutely shifted to the executive, and the State Counselor Office in particular, after 2016.

This chapter examines the functioning of the second post-junta Union legislature elected in November 2015. It interrogates whether the entrance in parliament of a large cohort of legislators drawn from pro-democracy forces – only 13 per cent of incumbent MPs were re-elected in 2015 – has translated into meaningful changes in legislative behaviour, lawmaking processes and the tentative control of the executive branch. How has parliamentary life been shaped under the dominance of the new ruling party? How have the three core functions of parliament identified by the most recent scholarship on legislative studies, the good governance community and Myanmar parliamentary leaders themselves (Beetham 2006) – representation, lawmaking and oversight – been performed since the NLD took control of the legislature? Building on ethnographic research carried out in the bicameral parliament after the 2015 polls, the paper discusses the attitudes of new Members of Parliament (MPs) towards representation, the relative effects of party discipline, the relations between the new executive and legislative organs – both controlled by the NLD – and the new trajectories of civil-military relations in the house, where a quarter of the seats are constitutionally reserved for the armed forces, or *Tatmadaw*. It posits that the NLD has made clear legislative choices that have affected the way parliamentary life and work have emerged since the inaugural session was held in February 2016. Under the NLD, priority has been given to representational activities and capacity-building, while lawmaking and budgetary control mechanisms have been tentatively streamlined. As such parliament has consolidated its position as core site for policy discussion and the representation of the people, despite enduring amateurism and a superficial scrutiny of the powers-that-be.

THE FIRST NLD-LED PARLIAMENT IN CONTEXT

The legislative elections held in November 2015 resulted in a startling, yet peaceful, alternation of power. Only 13 per cent of incumbent MPs elected in the previous polls held in 2010 and 2012 were returned. The NLD won a thundering victory, with some 58 per cent of the national vote collected (ICG 2016). Aung San Suu Kyi was re-elected to the *Pyithu Hluttaw*, along with 254 other NLD candidates. In the *Amyotha Hluttaw*, the party grabbed

135 seats and thus came to control about 59 per cent of the new bicameral legislature – a commanding dominance reflecting that of the USDP in the outgoing parliament. The USDP barely maintained 41 legislators, or 6.2 per cent. Rakhine politicians from the Arakan National Party (ANP) kept their share at 3.3 per cent but most other political forces lost a considerable number of seats. Several parties made their parliamentary debut, in particular the Shan Nationalities League for Democracy (SNLD), a longstanding ally of the NLD that had also boycotted the 2010 polls. This high legislative turnover marked a major step forward in Myanmar's democratisation efforts (Tin Maung Maung Than 2016). A series of by-elections held in April 2017 and November 2018 further consolidated these processes of peaceful alternation of power and parliamentary elite renewal.

Excited reports about the seemingly infinite possibilities for democratic change created by the NLD victory were bolstered by the convening of the new parliament on 1 February 2016 (Lewis 2016). With a commanding majority of seats, the NLD-led government could set the legislative agenda and easily ram through progressive laws, it was assumed. In most legislative votes, apart from those purported to amend the 2008 Constitution, a single majority can indeed ignore military-appointed lawmakers who hold (only) a quarter of parliamentary seats. As an illustration, Htin Kyaw, an old friend of Aung San Suu Kyi, was elected president of the Union by the assembly in March 2016. The vote went without a hitch despite the opposition of military MPs. Two weeks later, the first piece of legislation adopted by the NLD created a novel policy-influencing position not outlined in the constitution – that of "State Counselor". The army appointees could not prevent its adoption and stood up in protest when the bill was swiftly passed in each chamber. One brigadier general – a *Pyithu Hluttaw* legislator – publicly deplored the emergence of a Tocquevillian form of "tyranny of the majority".[1]

Under the leadership of Win Myint, the first Speaker of the NLD-led *Pyithu Hluttaw* (2016–2018), and Mahn Win Khaing Than, his counterpart in the *Amyotha Hluttaw* since 2016, the NLD attempted with more or less success to consolidate the parliament's internal structures, redefine a handful of legislative duties and responsibilities, and tentatively streamline the legislative process. As its USDP-led predecessor, the second post-junta legislature developed an extensive list of *ad hoc* parliamentary committees. At the end of the USDP legislature in January 2016, there were forty-three committees in both chambers. In the first week of February 2016, nineteen committees were established by the NLD in the *Pyithu Hluttaw* and sixteen in the *Amyotha Hluttaw*.[2] This reduction in number was a welcome move. Yet several elected MPs have continued to sit in two, if not three, committees or joint committees at the same time.[3]

Under the NLD, the legislature's administrative services were expanded. The function of permanent secretaries – a pre-1962 position already brought back into Union ministries by the USDP in 2015 – was introduced in the *Hluttaw* Office. More clerks were recruited to reinforce permanent staff assigned to legislative committees.[4] This has helped routinise the daily functioning of the legislature (Egreteau 2019). Like its predecessor, the NLD has welcomed the many opportunities offered by domestic and international donors for strengthening the capacity, expertise, and knowledge of both neophyte MPs and permanent parliamentary staff. The new legislative branch has also attempted to more resourcefully manage parliamentary time and negotiate with the government a workable legislative calendar. Whilst the daily timetable of plenary sessions and the order of legislative business have stubbornly remained last-minute statements, the *Pyidaungsu Hluttaw* under the NLD has established a more foreseeable calendar of meetings (see Table 2.1).

In particular, once significant changes were made to the fiscal year in late 2017, the NLD seemed to have indicated that it favored an emerging annual parliamentary calendar based on a monsoon "budget" session, one or two winter legislative session(s), and a post-Thingyan session.[5]

Table 2.1 – Session schedule of the NLD-controlled Union parliament (author's compilation, as of November 2019)

SESSIONS	DATES
First plenary session	1 February 2016 to 10 June 2016
Second plenary session	15 July 2016 to 7 October 2016
Third plenary session	16 November 2016 to 21 December 2016
Fourth plenary session	31 January 2017 to 17 March 2017
Fifth plenary session	18 May 2017 to 31 August 2017
Sixth plenary session	17 October 2017 to 24 November 2017
Seventh plenary session	15 January 2018 to 30 March 2018
Eighth plenary session	14 May 2018 to 21 June 2018
Ninth plenary session	23 July 2018 to 19 September 2018
Tenth plenary session	12 November 2018 to 21 December 2018
Eleventh plenary session	21 January 2019 to 15 March 2019
Twelfth plenary session	29 April 2019 to7 June 2019
Thirteenth plenary session	15 July 2019 to 20 September 2019
Fourteenth plenary session	4 November 2019 to ..

SHIFTING BASES OF REPRESENTATION

Changes in the social composition of leaders at different levels of government can be indicators of the degree of democratisation in a society transitioning from authoritarian rule to political pluralism. The high legislative turnover observed during Myanmar's second post-junta elections in 2015 was hailed as a promising, albeit cautious, sign of democratic transition with the old guards of ex-military rulers turned USDP politicians elected in 2010 being promptly pushed aside by a cohort of NLD civilian supporters and civil society activists. Moreover, the strong emphasis placed by the NLD on proximity to the citizen and constituency services has bolstered the representative role of parliament after 2016.

The sociological profiles of the new parliamentarians elected in 2015 is of interest. I draw here on the full list of 6,000-odd candidates that was made public, in Myanmar language, by Myanmar's Union Election Commission (UEC) in September 2015. The average age of civilian legislators in each chamber of the NLD-led parliament was 54.5 years at the time of its first session – or about three years younger than the previous parliament. The two new chambers have shown quasi-identical age pyramids. Both highlighted a balanced distribution of MPs of each age group, in comparison with the USDP legislature which counted more lawmakers in their sixties and fifties. The by-elections held in 2017 and 2018 did not much change that balance. More than three-quarters of elected MPs have attended domestic public universities or private colleges. In comparison with the rest of Myanmar's population, the continuing high proportion of legislators with educational credentials after 2015 reflects the consolidation of a distinctive political "elite" – old and new – in Naypyitaw.

Furthermore, the second post-junta polls saw the number of women MPs increasing twofold. Sixty-six women MPs were elected to both chambers in 2015, representing 10.1 per cent of the legislature (MacGregor 2016). However, with Aung San Suu Kyi herself being appointed State Counselor in April 2016, only two female MPs were appointed as committee chairs. In the *Pyithu Hluttaw*, the Banks and Financial Development Committee was to be chaired by Khin San Hlaing (Pale constituency), while May Win Myint, a longstanding NLD activist elected from Mayangone, presided over the Government's Guarantees, Pledges, and Undertakings Vetting Committee in the same chamber. In March 2019 however, the reformation of the Women and Children's Affairs in the *Pyithu Hluttaw* helped bring another female MP to the forefront with Khin Soe Kyi being appointed as chair (Htoo Thant 2019).

Intriguingly also, the two post-junta legislatures have showed similar ethnic distributions. Both the parliament dominated by the USDP and its successor have been comprised of about two-thirds ethnic Bamar or half-Bamar lawmakers. In fact, the ethnic make-up of both successive parliaments seemed to have closely mirrored the ethnic composition of Myanmar's general population. In the NLD legislature, 64.3 per cent of the civilian representatives declared being Bamar or half-Bamar. Elected legislators of Shan origins formed the second biggest group after the Bamar, at 6.5 per cent, followed by the Rakhine (5.7 per cent), the Chin and Zomi combined (4.7 per cent), and the Kayin (4.7 per cent).

While the USDP parliament boasted three Muslim MPs (representing the constituencies of Maungdaw and Buthidaung in Rakhine state), the NLD legislature does not have any Muslim representatives. Christian candidates, on their side, fared a little better in the 2015 elections, with thirty-three seats gained in the *Pyithu Hluttaw* and twenty-three seats in the *Amyotha Hluttaw*. They were mostly elected from the Kachin and Chin states. Christian lawmakers accounted for around 11 per cent of the NLD legislature, which was higher than the proportion of the Christian population of the country at around 4–5 per cent. The share of Buddhist elected MPs in the NLD parliament remained high at 88.3 per cent, compared to 88.6 per cent in the USDP legislature. Fostering ethno-religious diversity in the upper levels of government or having a "rainbow parliament" does not necessarily lead to more efficient governance in a multi-ethnic society. But enhanced representation has nonetheless proved to be an essential first step towards a broader social integration of ethno-religious minorities, particularly after protracted civil wars such as Myanmar's (Reilly 2001).

Lastly, the substantial majority of representatives elected in both 2010 and 2015 were involved in business, finance or commerce. In 2016, their share was a third of the civilian bloc, with 161 MPs (32.8 per cent). They were followed by professionals from the education sector: seventy-one new lawmakers (14.5 per cent) were teachers, school headmasters, university lecturers and rectors, and private tutors. Medical professionals, including pharmacists and veterinarians, formed 11.8 per cent of the NLD assembly, while the proportion of MPs whose occupations were linked to agriculture, farming and other rural professions reached 11.6 per cent. The biggest increase between the two post-junta legislatures was in the law sector.

In modern democracies, lawyers abound in elected assemblies. But in Myanmar, only twenty-seven MPs of the USDP-led parliament hailed from the law sector. In the following legislature, there were forty-four professionals (high grade pleaders, lawyers) from the legal sector, or 9 per cent.

MPs take on different roles while in office. But representation is typically the one they enjoy the most, worldwide (Blomgren and Rosenberg 2012). Myanmar, with its ongoing struggle to move past its decade-long authoritarian context, is no exception. Interviews I have carried out with freshly elected MPs after 2015 have routinely pointed to their willingness to spent time providing constituency services, highlighting local problems and state inefficiencies, and offering their constituents a voice in Naypyitaw – in particular those from rural and ethnic-based constituencies. Many constituents now seem to understand the significance and potential influence of an elected legislator.[6] MPs, particularly those sitting in the Union-level assembly, are increasingly perceived as important people, or "*lu-gyis*" (big men), leaders that can "make things happen" for the people they represent.[7] MPs also recognise they have become "punching bags" for disgruntled constituents.[8]

There have been caveats, though. Many freshly elected NLD legislators have proved either completely new to the party (many were awarded an NLD "ticket" only a few weeks before the 2015 polls) or to their constituency (a phenomenon known in political science as "*parachutage*"). Nonetheless, the new ruling party has since 2016 asked its 370-odd MPs to regularly commute to their home districts, emphasising dialogue with their constituents by organising frequent consultative meetings, and listening to grievances.[9] Clearly, the NLD has conceived the Union legislature as a key site of popular representation, encouraging citizens to send their complaints to committees, and urging its elected members to focus on constituency-based duties and activities, more than lawmaking or the oversight of government – functions controlled by the commanding heights of the ruling party. Whilst condescension and patronising behaviours of MPs reluctant to accept public exposure or criticism by their own constituents have still commonly been observed (Htin Kyaw Aye 2018), the NLD has arguably attempted to strengthen the legislature's representational function far more than its predecessor had been willing to do.

POWER TO THE EXECUTIVE

In most democracies, leaders of the executive tend to dominate all layers of political and policymaking power. The balance of authority between the legislative and executive branches thus typically tend to favour the government – including under parliamentary systems (Löwenberg and Patterson 1979). Legislatures and their members can nonetheless develop strategies and use various mechanisms to adjust that relationship and exert a stronger pressure on the executive. Under the NLD tenure, the balance of power has clearly shifted back to the executive with the legislature plainly letting the commanding heights of the NLD, the State Counselor Office, and the presidency dominate the legislative process. Besides, members of the NLD-run parliament have proved far less eager – or even encouraged – to use the full extent of their parliamentary oversight functions and push for more executive accountability, despite signs of institutional learning.

Executive-legislative relations under the NLD

The institutional framework established by the 2008 Constitution has outlined a hybrid form of presidentialism in which the executive branch is meant to take the lead in lawmaking (Crouch 2019). It is the government – not the legislature – that is constitutionally obliged to provide substance to legislative debates, initiate policy changes, and draft the most significant bills. Myanmar's executive-dominant framework has also been reinforced by the presence of unaccountable military representatives in most state institutions (including the legislature), and by the first-past-the-post voting system, which has long contributed to a "winner-takes-all" mentality in the country (Bünte 2018).

During the USDP legislature, the political and personal interests of the parliamentary and executive leaderships differed sharply, and in open sight. However, the rising contention between the supporters of the *Pyithu Hluttaw* Speaker, Shwe Mann, and the entourage of President Thein Sein fostered a rather healthy competition between the legislative and executive organs of the first post-junta transitional administration (Kean 2014; Fink 2015). These internecine struggles made parliament appear far more proactive and influential than it actually was. The NLD legislature has developed different patterns after 2016. Relatively high levels of party cohesion have helped concentrate power and decision-making in the commanding heights of the new ruling party. Legislative–executive relationships have thus proved far more stable and disagreements over the amendment or rebuff by parliament of government-initiated bills has seldom, if ever, led to any visible clash.

In his first two years as *Pyithu Hluttaw* Speaker, Win Myint has been the most active and vocal of the two NLD leaders in parliament. A "headmaster in his own backyard", smiled a former USDP legislator.[10] Yet he has seldom openly contested choices and decisions made by then President Htin Kyaw, or more crucially, State Counselor Aung San Suu Kyi. When he himself replaced Htin Kyaw as Union President in March 2018 and was succeeded in the *Pyithu Hluttaw* by T. Khun Myat, the balance of power between the legislative and executive branches did not evolve. Above the two speakers still stands the towering figure of the State Counselor. This has been denounced as a sign of parliamentary weakness by opposition parties – the USDP in particular – and many outside observers (Lun Min Maung 2017). But there is nothing wrong with this pattern. Being reactive and letting the government – or the ruling party leadership – initiate the lawmaking process is by no means a sign of abdication for a legislative body (Mezey 1979).

Cursory parliamentary scrutiny

The 2008 Constitution has catered for a framework which subjects Myanmar's post-junta executive – with the exception of the security sector, although there are constitutional provisions allowing for a budgetary control and cursory legislative scrutiny of the activities and funding of the defense services (Egreteau 2017c) – to a noteworthy degree of parliamentary oversight (Crouch 2019). Yet, in both successive post-junta legislatures, challenges in institutionalising legislative scrutiny of the executive and the courts have proved numerous.

Many factors have impeded the shaping of a meaningful parliamentary oversight. The lack of expertise of parliamentary representatives and staff is a first, major one. Despite regular and well-attended capacity-building programs and trainings, many a legislator elected in 2015 simply does not fully grasp the concept of legislative scrutiny. Scores of freshly elected MPs I have interviewed still construe it as merely serving as the opposition to the government and its legislative bills. They are also seldom aware of the multiple procedural and legal instruments they can use to push the executive branch – including the defence services – as well as the courts, for more accountability.[11] Budgetary control is a case in point. Focused trainings have helped legislative staff and MPs perform a more regular and valuable vetting of budgetary documents sent to parliament by various governmental and administrative agencies, the Supreme Court or the Office of the Auditor General.[12] Clerks and managerial officers in ministries have also received similar training in budget oversight. But only a limited number of backbenchers have proved daring – or interested – enough to ask for more, and push for a meticulous, thorough auditing, or the launch of a parliamentary investigation (Htin Kyaw Aye et al. 2017a).

Party discipline imposed by the NLD is another factor. The party – and its various whips in the house, such as Aung Kyi Nyunt and Myat Nyana Soe in the *Amyotha Hluttaw* or Khin San Hlaing in the *Pyithu Hluttaw* – have a key control over funding allocations and local patronage networks. Ambitious MPs logically prefer remaining quiescent instead of openly confronting the party's top brass. The various leaderships of the executive under the NLD have also offered strong, unexpected resistance to the monitoring by backbenchers of their policy decisions, budget and activities. Challenging and publicly contesting the authority of the powers-that-be is also not common to the Myanmar culture, underlined a septuagenarian NLD lawmaker, elected in 2015 for the first time.[13] Many MPs feel uncomfortable at the idea of questioning and monitoring high-ranking bureaucrats and administrative – if not military – officials. Getting a response from the Ministry of Health has remained arduous even for someone who has served for three decades in that same ministry, lamented a retired medical officer, now a NLD representative in the *Amyotha Hluttaw*.[14] It is similarly testing to deal with bureaucrats from the defense ministries, noted a retired lieutenant-colonel from the NLD.[15]

A third factor is the lack of interest in oversight showed by lawmakers themselves – including those of the opposition to the NLD in parliament. As in many legislatures across the globe, backbenchers prefer representational duties against other tedious legislative activities, such as bill scrutiny and budget vetting. Fourth is the paucity of resources at the disposal of the parliament. The number of parliamentary staff assigned to committees has increased since the advent of the NLD. They have steadily professionalised also. Yet institutional resources at the disposal of the executive branch (and the ruling party) continue to outweigh the resources that the legislative branch and its civilian members can enjoy.

Several efforts in oversight were made by the previous USDP legislature. Its members, for instance, focused on land-grabbing issues and launched in 2011 a parliamentary inquiry into the long-lasting practice of land confiscation by state and military authorities, or their proxies. These efforts are yet to be renewed by the NLD parliament. The parliamentary commission set up by the USDP to investigate land confiscation was indeed not reintroduced in the NLD house (San Thein et al. 2017). The new ruling party has taken the issue out of the legislative agenda, regretted one of its own legislators.[16] Another key illustration has been the political, communal and humanitarian crisis in Rakhine State, rekindled in 2017. The Union parliament had under the USDP attempted to play a visible role following previous episodes of communal violence in 2012 and 2013 (Chit Win 2016; Chit Win and Kean 2017). But under the NLD, it failed to impose more rigorous scrutiny upon the institutional management of the tragedy unfolding from 2017 at the borders with Bangladesh (Kean 2018). Strong legislative oversight is often expected after the occurrence of a major state-led crackdown. Debates in the legislature on the brutal repression launched against Rohingya militants and populations by Myanmar's security forces and the subsequent exodus of 800,000 refugees into Bangladesh have been minimal since 2017. Only local civil society organisations and the media, besides the international community, have played a significant role in the investigation of alleged misconduct and wrongdoings by the government and the security forces.

However, parliamentary questions and motions have remained a tool of choice for performing a tentative scrutiny of the executive, and the wider public sector, in the NLD-controlled legislature.[17] The pattern was already observed in the previous parliament, particularly among ethnic lawmakers (Farrelly and Chit Win 2018). Ministers and deputy ministers have flocked daily to the floor of both chambers since 2016 to answer questions about a wide range of issues. They included illegal mining and armed conflicts in the Kachin and Shan states, the national verification process of identity papers delivered to members of Myanmar's 135 "national races" (and only them), the extensive, illegal agricultural use of fertilisers, and deforestation.[18]

Many of these detailed questions have embarrassed the NLD government, but also the military establishment and the three Union ministries it constitutionally controls. Party leaders and ministers do not like being grilled in public (Ei Toe Lwin 2016). But emerging patron–

client interactions between the executive and legislative branches under the NLD – aimed at curbing parliamentary discontent – may prove counterproductive to the institutionalisation of an indispensable oversight culture in the country. The constitutional presence of the military in parliament has also served as a powerful obstacle to critical debate on security matters and the speakers have since 2016 relentlessly attempted to deflect potential legislative disruptions, such as theatrical stand-ups by military MPs and rude interjections that would threaten the "dignified" conduct of parliamentary business imposed by legislative procedures.[19] Nevertheless, a handful of cases have shed light on future possibilities for strengthening legislative oversight. In 2018, the Ministry of Construction was publicly reprimanded by the Union legislature for having overcharged for the renovation of parliamentary buildings in Naypyitaw. A legislative investigation carried out by MPs from the *Pyithu Hluttaw* forced the executive branch to reimburse funds that had been misappropriated. Ministerial officials were even demoted or retired after the scandal was revealed by the legislative branch (Htet Naing Zaw 2018a and 2018b).

A MINIMAL, YET TECHNICAL, LEGISLATIVE RECORD

When I once sat with him in March 2017 for a lengthy, yet very engaging discussion, the Deputy Speaker of the NLD-led *Amyotha Hluttaw* kept stressing that lawmaking was the core legislative function on which recently elected representatives spared no efforts.[20] Evidence has long suggested the opposite, with a domineering executive taking most initiatives and party whips vetting most of the bills submitted to either chamber since 2016. This is not necessarily a damaging pattern, given the flurry of hurriedly drafted bills discussed – and adopted – by the first post-junta legislature. Many of the 232 pieces of legislation passed between 2011 and 2016 have had positive impact on governance, including in fostering reforms (Turnell 2014). Yet several of them had to be subsequently revised, corrected or supplemented. Quite ironically, the Commission on Legal Affairs and Special Issues Assessment headed between 2016 and 2019 by the former speaker of the *Pyithu Hluttaw*, Shwe Mann, even recommended a thorough revision of about eighty laws previously passed by the USDP legislature, smiled a NLD legislator from Yankin constituency.[21]

During the initial plenary sessions of the NLD legislature, the two chambers focused on a handful of technical matters, passed minor socio-

Table 2.2 - Laws passed by the first NLD-led legislature (author compilation)

From March 2016 (Session 1) to September 2019 (Session 13)	Number of laws enacted
TOTAL	114 [100%]
Incl. new pieces of legislation and budget-related laws	56 [49%]
Incl. laws amending, or building upon, existing laws	49 [43%]
Incl. laws repealing existing laws	9 [8%]

economic reforms and developed various capacity-building programs aimed at enhancing the lawmaking process. Between April 2016 and September 2019, the new majority adopted 114 bills (see Table 2.2). They included the annual mandatory bills regarding the Union Budget, Tax and National Planning. Fifty-six of these laws were entirely new pieces of legislation – including on progressive issues such as the rights of children. They also concerned, among other subjects, taxation, transportation, tourism, business licenses and company registration, infrastructure (dams) and irrigation, as well as forestry and river conservation. In contrast, forty-nine of these new bills passed until the end of the 13th session in September 2019 merely supplemented or amended existing legislation. The election laws for the Union and state or regional assemblies, as well as the Anti-Corruption Law and the Union Judiciary Law were for instance amended by the NLD for the fourth time since 2011.

Only nine bills passed by the NLD house revoked either no longer relevant regulations, such as the Public Accountants Default Act (1850), the Dock Workers Act (1948) and the Yangon and Mandalay Municipal Laws (1984), or more significantly age-old repressive laws. The Emergency Provisions Law (1950) and State Protection Law (1975) – both long employed by Myanmar's successive governments to stifle dissent – were repealed in the early days of the NLD legislature.

During its first four years in power, the NLD leadership has thus quietly sought to improve the country's legal business, environmental and fiscal governance. New legislation on copyrighted work and commodities was passed in 2019 (Industrial Design [Copyright] Law No. 2/2019 and Trademark [Copyright] Law No. 3/2019). There were also attempts at strengthening governing institutions. Amendments were made to the Auditor General Law, the Civil Services Law and the Union Judiciary Law while the legislation on legal aid was (lightly) revised. A new bill seeking to consolidate parliamentary structures and mechanisms was discussed from July 2017 and eventually signed into law in February 2018 (Myanmar Parliamentary Union Law, No. 4/2018). The NLD also successfully opted for a (quite disruptive) change of fiscal period in 2017, despite strong opposition from the military and USDP legislators (Pyae Thet Phyo 2017).

Observers of Myanmar's parliamentary affairs have, however, continued to stress the low quality of drafting. The lack of thorough debate in the house (including in closed-door committees), from both lack of willingness and expertise from backbenchers, has also been deplored (Thet Tun 2017). There are considerable hurdles to a smooth, efficient lawmaking process. This is mainly due to the highly hierarchical top-down structure of the new ruling party, and of Myanmar politics in general. Nonetheless, efforts have been made under the NLD to increase coordination among branches of government before a bill is introduced in parliament. The latter has even been assigned a leading role and started to convene "joint coordination meetings" to oversee, and strengthen, pre-legislative scrutiny processes (Htin Kyaw Aye et al. 2017b). The fact that under the NLD an increasing number of civil society organisations have been allowed, if not encouraged, to add inputs to freshly drafted legislations before discussion in the house has similarly proved a positive development.[22] Many civil society groups have established working relationships with new MPs, so as to inform and lobby them on any particular policy issue of interest. Yet to get a chance to influence the drafting and revision of government bills, one still seems to need a careful cultivation of the core members of the NLD executive committee, or its whips and key committee leaders in the house, not its backbenchers.[23]

There is also mounting criticism over the reluctance of the NLD to promptly dismantle the many illiberal regulations that continue to be used by the state against common citizens expressing their discontent. Following intense public debate, the controversial Telecommunications Law passed in 2013 by the USDP legislature was brought back to the NLD-controlled parliament for discussion in July 2017. Its infamous article 66[d] on defamation had been frequently used to suppress dissent, including since the NLD took power. Yet only minor amendments to the law were passed a month later (Moe Myint 2017). Likewise, a new round of debate started in the NLD-controlled *Amyotha Hluttaw* on another contentious piece of legislation, the Peaceful Assembly and Peaceful Procession Law. First designed in 2011 by the USDP to regulate protests, the law was revised in 2016. New amendments were again discussed a year later following criticism from civil society groups. The initial draft bill adopted by the *Amyotha Hluttaw* in March 2018 was however, once more, soon faulted for failing to lift existing restrictions on public demonstrations. Interestingly, several NLD representatives have publicly expressed their disapproval, highlighting the first cracks in the parliamentary majority.

DISCIPLINING MPS

Soon after the polls held in November 2015, when convening the freshly elected candidates of her party Aung San Suu Kyi pulled no punches. She warned them that once they had taken their legislative oath, a strong, unrelenting discipline would be expected from them (AFP 2015). A quarter of their monthly 1-million *Kyat* stipend would serve to replenish the party coffers.[24] Corruption and misconduct would not be tolerated. And indeed, less than two years after the elections, several MPs from different stripes were under investigation for embezzlement of public funds, while dozens were facing complaints by constituents, colleagues or party chiefs (Nay Phyo Win 2018). In August 2019, the MP for Monyo constituency (*Pyithu Hluttaw*) was the first NLD representative found guilty of corruption charges (Toe Wai Aung 2019). He was charged under Article 56 of the Anti-Corruption Law, which has been amended three times by the NLD since it took control of parliament in 2016.

Discipline and cohesion are necessary for a ruling parliamentary majority. Most theories of comparative politics say that disciplined parties are a precondition for responsible party government (Bowler et al. 1999). Efficient legislative decision-making depends on the ability of the leadership to secure a unified voting bloc in parliament and mobilise its supporters whenever needed. Despite palpable resentment among NLD lawmakers, there has been no organised dissent in parliament since 2016. But interviews with MPs have showed that draft proposals and motions prepared by individual legislators are routinely dismissed by the house speakers or the party internal vetting committee. Backbenchers are strongly advised not to exert the full extent of their oversight duties by asking "tough questions" to NLD ministers. Worse, many new parliamentarians have been scolded by senior NLD officials as if they were unruly schoolchildren.

But discipline in the NLD-led parliament has so far not only worked because ambitious MPs do not want to jeopardise their chances for advancement or re-election in 2020. It has also worked because activists-turned-lawmakers sometimes simply do not master the art of politicking or else lack a proper knowledge of how to conduct rebellious legislative politics (Egreteau 2018). Without an acquaintance with parliamentary procedures or an understanding that ruling parties can sometimes benefit from tolerating some parliamentary dissent, novice lawmakers tend to remain quiet and avoid breaking legislative discipline. Many NLD backbenchers have thus accepted to toe the party line (The Economist 2017). "Maybe we are soldiers. For us, maybe it is not the time for democracy, we must stay in the Revolution!", smiled one of them to me.[25] In addition, Myanmar society has been traditionally shaped by Buddhism, which considers values such as obedience and discipline paramount. Seniority is highly respected and dissent from those younger is seldom accepted. Young NLD members who privately criticise the political stance and party management of Aung San Suu Kyi rarely confront her in public.

There are some political risks for the NLD, though. Unlike before the 2010 elections, when the NLD last experienced a severe party split over the boycott of an upcoming poll to be fully controlled by the military regime, resentment in the late 2010s seems to have been chiefly observed among young and new party members, not in the commanding heights of the NLD. The greater the resentment, the more likely novice politicians will look for alternatives or even jump ship. Condescending disciplinary measures and public scolding can provoke a severe backlash against the senior party establishment. Many social activists turned lawmakers in 2015 have disliked being treated as children by the NLD leadership (Ei Ei Toe Lwin 2017). Many have already made no secret of their willingness to leave parliamentary politics after just one legislative term. In the short term, the discipline imposed by the NLD hierarchy may not be damaging to the party and its objectives in parliament. But in the long run, the lash of discipline may well produce a generation of frustrated political activists who may consider leaving the NLD and legislative politics altogether. A high legislative turnover, in polls after polls, will not only deprive the NLD of its most dynamic members, it will also prove harmful to the consolidation and professionalisation of the still-fragile parliamentary bodies.

CIVIL-MILITARY RELATIONS IN THE HOUSE

One of the peculiarities of the 2008 Constitution is the reservation of seats for serving military officers in both chambers of the Union legislature. Under the USDP term, the 166 military appointees in parliament built relatively smooth relationships with their 470-odd civilian counterparts, many of them being retired army officers or former junta bureaucrats themselves (Egreteau 2016a). They seldom proposed new pieces of legislation, and were content with the occasional pre-legislative bill scrutiny and parliamentary question. They proved vigilant in warding off constitutional amendments in June 2015. With the advent of a second post-junta parliament dominated by a political movement openly opposed to its privileges, the *Tatmadaw* has strengthened its parliamentary delegation and expanded its involvement in lawmaking activities and legislative oversight (Maung Aung Myoe 2018). In a sense, although an Air Force officer vehemently denied it during an interview, military delegates have come to form the chief opposition to the new ruling party after 2016.[26]

That take-off in parliamentary activism has not proved without tensions. Directly appointed by the commander-in-chief of the *Tatmadaw*, military MPs now offer a solid, cohesive bloc, with significant legislative experience and knowledge about the intricacies of the legislative process (Min Than 2018). About two-thirds of the serving officers sitting in the first session of the NLD legislature in 2016, or 107 delegates, were in fact re-appointees of the previous USDP parliament (Egreteau 2016b). As of November 2019, the military delegation in parliament even included nine majors in the *Pyithu Hluttaw* and two in the *Amyotha Hluttaw*, who have been sitting continuously for the past nine years since their initial secondment in January 2011. Furthermore, unlike in the previous legislature, the *Tatmadaw* parliamentary team under the NLD parliament counts a substantial number of high-ranking officers. That included (as of November 2019) four major generals – two in each house – and seventeen brigadier generals – ten in the *Pyithu Hluttaw* (including a Navy Commodore) and seven in the *Amyotha Hluttaw*.[27]

Despite its seat reservations, however, the *Tatmadaw* cannot block ordinary legislation. Bills are passed by a simple majority vote. Lacking numbers, military MPs have thus started to rely on theatrical manoeuvres to visibly state their disagreement with the way the legislative business has been carried out by the new administration. During the early days of the first plenary session of the new parliament a NLD representative openly criticised alleged misconduct by local military authorities involved in the Letpadaung copper mine project, in the Sagaing region. The whole bloc of military appointees in the *Pyithu Hluttaw* stood up as one man. The protest move, executed silently, was startling.[28] The *Tatmadaw* replicated the same stand up ritual later in April 2016, when the State Counselor Bill, which has bestowed upon Aung San Suu Kyi greater policy powers, was introduced and subsequently passed. In a twist of irony, one brigadier general, a member of the joint bill committee, derided the swift passing of the law as "democratic bullying" (Han Thiha 2016). This type of theatrical performance has no direct impact over the legislative business, but it has bluntly shown that the most powerful institution of the country could be as unhappy as powerless in parliament, and may therefore seek in years to come other types of disruptive legislative strategies to re-assert its policy influence.

CONCLUSION

Observational evidence and the data collected in Naypyitaw over the past three years allows us to make four conclusions on how parliamentary life has emerged under the NLD. First, the new ruling party has since its victory in the 2015 elections put a clear emphasis on representational duties allowing, if not encouraging, its MPs to link more regularly and intimately with their constituents, instead of focusing on lawmaking and scrutiny – the two other core functions of a parliament. MPs of the new majority have been urged to organise myriad consultative meetings in their constituencies to collect grievances while committees in the house have increasingly worked on the collection and classification of complaints received from the public. Second, the role in government scrutiny of the NLD legislature has proved rather marginal since 2016. As in other transitioning societies, a continuing challenge for parliament is to overcome various traditional, political and structural disincentives for a stronger oversight of the executive, the courts and the public administration. Third, as seen through the lenses of budgetary control, the ritual of parliamentary questions, and a pre-legislative scrutiny increasingly grounded on civil society consultations, a process of legislative institutionalisation seems nonetheless to be emerging under the NLD. Steady capacity-building programs provided by the local and international community of donors and growing engagement with civil society have greatly helped develop forms of routinisation and bureaucratisation of parliamentary work since 2016. Fourth, in contrast with the previous USDP term, the mounting activism of military parliamentarians has illustrated how increasingly complex – and thus long-lasting – could the intrusion of the *Tatmadaw* into policymaking prove in the post-junta order.

The argument of a sudden parliamentary deficit under the NLD is thus quite misplaced. Not only has the 2008 constitutional framework structured a legislative-executive relationship that is meant to be heavily weighted in favour of the government (and the military); the hyperactivity showed by the previous USDP legislature has also proved misleading. The Union legislature under the NLD ought not to be construed as an institution that merely rubber stamps the decisions made by the State Counselor Office or the new ruling party. The new parliament and its leadership have, echoing the experiences of many other post-authoritarian legislatures, made choices according to the nature and objectives of the new dominant party. Clearly since 2016, the emphasis has been put by the NLD on representational duties and capacity-building efforts. This idea was to shape the legislative institution as a key post-junta site for the representation of the people. True, the *hluttaws* are yet to become a place where open, uncensored public debate is held, with daring parliamentary leaders and proactive backbenchers developing a meaningful oversight and thorough scrutiny of draft legislation. But parliament has not been "neutralised" by the highly disciplined NLD machine or the unremitting intrusion into civilian affairs of the armed forces. This may be taken as an early sign of a much needed institutionalisation, if not consolidation, of parliament in Myanmar.

Notes

1 Read a gripping response to the military officer by one of the deputy directors of the *Amyotha Hluttaw* (Han Thiha 2016).

2 In March 2019, the *Pyithu Hluttaw* reinstated its Women and Children Affairs Committee, which had been intriguingly ditched in 2016. Discussion with the secretary of that same committee in the *Amyotha Hluttaw*, Naypyitaw, 21 November 2016.

3 Interview with a legislator sitting in *Amyotha Hluttaw*'s International Relations Committee (because he speaks English, he laughed) and its Natural Resources & Environment Committee, Naypyitaw, 20 November 2016.

4 Interview with Director General of the *Pyidaungsu Hluttaw*, Naypyitaw, 25 November 2016.

5 From 2018, Myanmar commences its fiscal year on October 1, instead of April 1 (Tin Htet Paing 2017).

6 Interview with a member of the *Pyithu Hluttaw*'s Committee for Citizen's Rights, Naypyitaw, 14 March 2017.
7 Interview with NLD *Pyithu Hluttaw* representative, Naypyitaw, 18 November 2016.
8 Interview with NLD representative from Sagaing Region in the *Amyotha Hluttaw*, Naypyitaw, 1 November 2019.
9 Although Union-level MPs have been urged to avoid bringing too many local affairs to the *Pyidaungsu Hluttaw* floor, and asking questions related to minor constituency issues (electricity breakdown, need for a bridge, etc.), leaving the latter to state and regional assemblies. Interview with a NLD *Pyithu Hluttaw* legislator from a rural constituency in the Irrawaddy delta, Naypyitaw, 8 June 2016.
10 Interview with author, Yangon, 12 February 2018.
11 Group interview with the Public Accounts Committee of the *Amyotha Hluttaw*, Naypyitaw, 1 November 2019.
12 Interview with a Myanmar consultant providing budget oversight training in Naypyitaw, Yangon, 4 November 2018.
13 Interview with author, Naypyitaw, 8 June 2016.
14 Interview with author, Naypyitaw, 13 March 2017.
15 Interview with author, Naypyitaw, 20 November 2016.
16 Interview with NLD member of the *Pyithu Hluttaw*'s Public Affairs Committee, Naypyitaw, 16 March 2017.
17 Interview with the Secretary of *Pyithu Hluttaw*'s International Relations Committee, Naypyitaw, 18 November 2016.
18 Interview with an *Amyotha Hluttaw* representative about to table a motion condemning unbridled deforestation in the Irrawaddy delta, Naypyitaw, 2 November 2019.
19 Interview with Chair of the Hluttaw Rights Committee in the *Amyotha Hluttaw*, Naypyitaw, 14 March 2017.
20 Interview with author, Naypyitaw, 14 March 2017.
21 Interview with author, Naypyitaw, 16 March 2017.
22 Interview with a civil society leader turned NLD legislator in the *Amyotha Hluttaw*, Naypyitaw, 30 October 2019.
23 Interview with a representative from a Myanmar NGO focused on gender issues, Yangon, 16 February 2018.
24 By comparison, Shan MPs from the SNLD give back 10 per cent to their constituency party branch and 10% to their headquarters. Interview with SNLD legislators from both houses, Naypyitaw, 9 June 2016.
25 Interview with a NLD *Pyithu Hluttaw* legislator from a rural constituency in the Irrawaddy delta, Naypyitaw, 8 June 2016.
26 Interview with a brigadier general sitting in the *Amyotha Hluttaw*, Naypyitaw, 10 June 2016.

27 There were none in the first delegation appointed in 2011. The highest ranking MPs were colonels.

28 Interview with an NLD representative from the *Pyithu Hluttaw*, Naypyitaw, 8 June 2016.

References

AFP (2015). "Suu Kyi Lays Down Law on Party Discipline to New Myanmar MPs". 28 November.

Beetham, D. (2006). *Parliament and Democracy in the Twenty-First Century*. Geneva: IPU.

Blomgren, M. and Rozenberg, O. eds. (2012). *Parliamentary Roles in Modern Legislatures*. London: Routledge.

Bowler, S, Farrell, D.M. and Katz, R.S. eds. (1999). *Party Discipline and Parliamentary Government*. Columbus OH: Ohio State University Press.

Bünte, M. (2018). "Perilous Presidentialism or Precarious Power-Sharing? Hybrid Regime Dynamics in Myanmar". *Contemporary Politics* 24(3): 346–360.

Chit Win (2016). "The Hluttaw and Conflicts in Myanmar". In *Conflict in Myanmar: War, Politics, Religion*, edited by N. Cheesman and N. Farrelly. Singapore: ISEAS Publications, 199–220.

Chit Win and Kean, T. (2017). "Communal Conflict in Myanmar: The Legislature's Response, 2012–2015". *Journal of Contemporary Asia* 47(3): 413–439.

Crouch, M. (2019). *The Constitution of Myanmar: A Contextual Analysis*. Oxford: Hart Publishing.

Egreteau, R. (2016a). "Soldiers as Lawmakers? Assessing the New Legislative Role of the Burmese Armed Forces (2010-15)". In *Metamorphosis: Studies in Social and Political Change in Myanmar*, edited by R. Egreteau and F. Robinne. Singapore: NUS Press, 15–42.

---------- (2016b). "Myanmar Military Chief Revamps its Parliamentary Team". *Nikkei Asian Review*, 27 January.

---------- (2017a). *Parliamentary Development in Myanmar: An Overview of the Union Parliament (2011–2016)*. Washington DC/Yangon: The Asia Foundation.

---------- (2017b). "Myanmar Legislative Agenda Slowed by Parliamentary Schedule". *Nikkei Asian Review*, 6 May.

---------- (2017c). *Negotiating Parliamentary Oversight of the Security Sector in Myanmar*. Singapore: ISEAS Perspectives No. 37.

---------- (2018). "How Myanmar's Ruling Party Keeps its Lawmakers under Control". TeaCircle Oxford, 1 March 2018, available online at < https://teacircleoxford.com/2018/03/01/how-myanmars-ruling-party-keeps-its-lawmakers-under-control/> [accessed on May 22, 2019].

---------- (2019). "Towards Legislative Institutionalisation? Emerging Patterns of Routinisation in Myanmar's Parliament", *Journal of Current Southeast Asian Affairs* 38(3): 265–285.

Ei Toe Lwin (2016). "Don't Ask Tough Questions". *The Myanmar Times,* 7 October.

---------- (2017). "NLD Cracks the Whip on Slacker MPs". *The Myanmar Times,* 25 September.

Farrelly, N. and Chit Win (2018). "Disciplining Democracy: Explaining the Rhythms of Myanmar's First Hluttaw, 2011–2016", In *Public Policy in the 'Asian Century',* edited by S. Bice, A. Poole and H. Sullivan. London, Palgrave Macmillan, 87–117.

Fink, C. (2015). "Myanmar's Proactive National Legislature". *Social Forces* 82 (2): 327–354.

Han Thiha (2016). "Bullying, Democratic, or Otherwise". *The Myanmar Times,* 25 April.

Htet Naing Zaw (2018a). "Parliament Probes Hefty Door Polishing Bill". *The Irrawaddy,* 29 May.

---------- (2018b). "Construction Ministry Disciplines Officials for Inflating Costs". *The Irrawaddy,* 24 August.

Htin Kyaw Aye (2018). "The Hluttaw's Failure of Communication". *Frontier* [Myanmar], 6 December.

Htin Kyaw Aye, Win Win Aye and La Win Maung (2017a). *The Role of Committees in the Assessment of Government Budget.* Yangon: OMI Parliamentary Research Series No. 2.

Htin Kyaw Aye, Hla Myo Kyaw, Win Win Aye and Su Myat Phyo (2017b). *Floor Debate vs. Committee Coordination Meeting: Analysing a Change in Legislative Process.* Yangon: OMI Parliamentary Research Series No. 1.

Htoo Thant (2019). "Hluttaw Sets Up Women, Children's Committee". *The Myanmar Times,* 1 March.

International Crisis Group (ICG) (2016). *Myanmar's New Government: Finding its Feet?* Brussels/Yangon: Asia Report No. 282.

Kean, Tom (2014). "Myanmar's Parliament: From Scorn to Significance". In *Debating Democratisation in Myanmar,* edited by N. Cheesman, N. Farrelly and T. Wilson. Singapore: ISEAS Publications.

---------- (2018). "Hluttaw Struggles to Find Voice on Rakhine". *Frontier* [Myanmar], 15 March.

Lewis, S. (2016). "Burma's Parliament Opens in the Dawning of a New Democratic Era". *TIME Magazine,* 1 February.

Löwenberg, G. and Patterson, S.C. (1979). *Comparing Legislatures.* Boston: Little Brown.

Lun Min Maung (2017). "Checks and Balances Weaker under NLD". *The Myanmar Times,* 13 June.

MacGregor, F. (2016). "Small Steps, But Big Potential for New Female MPs". *The Myanmar Times,* 5 February.

Maung Aung Myoe (2018). "Partnership in Politics: The Tatmadaw and the NLD in Myanmar since 2016". In *Myanmar Transformed? People, Place, Polities*, edited by J. Chalmers, G. McCarthy, N. Farrelly and Chit Win. Singapore: ISEAS-Yusof Ishak Institute.

Mezey, M.L. (1979). *Comparative Legislatures*. Durham, NC: Duke University Press.

Min Than (2018). *The Tatmadaw in the Hluttaw*. Singapore: ISEAS Perspectives No. 73.

Moe Myint (2017). "Activists Deem Amendments to 66(d) 'Ineffective'". *The Irrawaddy*, 2 August.

Nay Phyo Win (2018). "30 MPs, Including Ministers, Under Investigation". *Democratic Voice of Burma*, 12 January.

Pyae Thet Phyo (2017). "Fiscal Period Rejected", *The Myanmar Times*, 24 October.

Reilly, B. (2001). *Democracy in Divided Societies: Electoral Engineering for Conflict Management*. Cambridge: Cambridge University Press.

San Thein, Pyae Sone and Diepart, J. (2017). *Transparency Under Scrutiny: Information Disclosure by the Parliamentary Land Investigation Commission in Myanmar*. Vientiane: MRLG Case Study Series #1.

The Economist (2017). "Democracy has Muzzled Myanmar's Parliament". *The Economist*, 1 June.

Thet Tun, M. (2017). "Making Better Laws in Myanmar". *New Mandala*, 16 October.

Tin Htet Paing (2017). "Amid Opposition, Myanmar Amends Fiscal Year". *The Irrawaddy*, 31 October.

Tin Maung Maung Than (2016). "Myanmar's General Elections 2015: Change Was the Name of the Game". *Southeast Asian Affairs* 2016: 241–264.

Toe Wai Aung (2019). "MP Charged under Anti-Corruption Law". *The Myanmar Times*, 26 August.

Turnell, S. (2014). "Legislative Foundations of Myanmar's Economic Reforms". In *Law, Society and Transition in Myanmar*, edited by M. Crouch and T. Lindsey. Oxford: Hart Publishing, 183–199.

3

PEOPLE POWER OR POLITICAL PRESSURE? DRIVERS OF RESPRESENTATIVE PERFORMANCE IN SOUTHERN SUB-NATIONAL PARLIAMENTS, MYANMAR

Nyein Thiri Swe and Zaw Min Oo

Representation is widely considered to be an essential role of parliaments (Johnson 2005; Ruedin 2012). The extent to which the composition of a parliament reflects the diversity of political opinion, women or marginalised groups in society is an important indicator of genuine representation (Inter-Parliamentary Union 2008). Exisiting scholarship demonstrates the importance of the role of political institutions, political parties and individual MPs, for evaluating an emerging democracy (Judge & Leston-Bandeira 2017). In Myanmar, the representational performance of both elected and military MPs is yet to be determined.

This paper explores the representation of both military and elected MPs in sub-national parliaments in Myanmar and how MPs themselves believe their representative performance contributes to the wider understanding of democratic norms in the public eye. We draw on scholars who apply performativity theory to the study of political institutions (Judge and Leston-Bandeira 2017; Lavi 2016). Performativity allows us to understand the constructed nature of politics and to see the ways in which MPs perform or "act" their role (Loxley 2007). As Judge and Leston-Bandeira (2017, 156) point out, "the 'picturing', 'aesthetic' or 'performative' aspects of representation are central" to assessing representational performance. In applying performativity theory to democracy and democratic institutions, Lavi (2016, 1) suggests that "democracy is not the source of acts and procedures but rather their 'performative effect,' a social fiction, perpetually constructed through social enactments, performances, and imagination." Following from Lavi's work, we explore the way that MPs in Myanmar construct and enact their roles in sub-national parliaments and how that influences their modes of representative performance.

In drawing on this work, we are particularly interested in exploring what constraints MPs face in their representative performance. We build off qualitative research which the authors conducted in three sub-national parliaments: in the Mon and Karen State parliaments and Tanintharyi region parliament in 2018. The rationale for the selection of these smaller parliaments for this study was that since they are among the smallest in the country, they provide a unique insight into the structural issues that impact the representative performance of MPs. There are a total of twenty elected MPs in Mon State and twenty in Tanintharyi region parliaments, and fourteen elected MPs in the Karen State parliament. Out of the fifty-four elected MPs, fifteen are appointed as regional ministers by the President and Chief Minister, therefore thirty-nine elected MPs remain in these three *hluttaws* after these appointments. In accordance with the 2008 Constitution, 25 per cent of MPs are military MPs appointed by the Commander-in-Chief (Constitution of the Republic of the Union of Myanmar, Article 161 (d)). We conducted key informant interviews using a semi-structured question guide with fifteen active elected MPs from these three state/region parliaments, seven elected MPs from the national parliament and three military appointed representatives in regional and national parliaments respectively. MP respondents were selected based on observation of debates, the quantity of questions and motions submitted, their current position held in the parliament (for example, deputy speaker, chairperson or secretary of parliamentary committee), and inclusiveness of the political party background (NLD, USDP and ethnic party).

Although we wanted to include the perspectives of military appointed MPs in regional *hluttaws* as part of the study, it was harder to obtain interviews with them. While field research for this study was conducted, fifty military MPs were replaced directly by the Commander-in-Chief in the regional and national *hluttaws* (UEC, Announcement No. 167, 168 & 169, 2018, EMReF 2018). As a consequence, new legislators from the military came and moved into the *hluttaws* and were reluctant to engage with the study (Union Election Commission 2018). Under this unstable situation, the official informed consent letter and interview appointment request letters we sent were completely neglected or refused by the majority of senior military officers and selected remaining military MPs from Mon State and Tanintharyi region. Only one military MP from the Karen State *hluttaw* was officially given permission to be interviewed by us. To try and rectify this situation, two informal, unstructured interviews with former military MPs from the national *hluttaw* and a regional *hluttaw* were conducted. As a result of these limitations, this paper focuses on the representative role of military MPs from the perspective of elected MPs and how they believe their performance is perceived by the public.

THE POLITICS OF REPRESENTATION IN MYANMAR

Myanmar conducted electoral polls on 7 November 2010 under the guidance of the military regime and the 2008 Constitution. The 2010 election chose MPs for two houses of parliament at the Union level and fourteen state and regional parliaments. While the pro-regime Union Solidarity and Development Party (USDP) won over 75 per cent of votes (Toshiro 2011, 6), the National League for Democracy party (NLD), the main opposition party, boycotted the 2010 elections but later participated in the 2012 by-elections (International Crisis Group 2015, 4).The NLD contested the 2015 general election with more than ninety other political parties (Lall 2016) and won a landslide victory, gaining 887 of the 1150 seats that were contested (Kyaw Sein & Farrelly 2016, 21). Nevertheless, in accordance with the 2008 Constitution, 25 per cent of parliament remains allocated to military MPs who are appointed by the Commander-in-Chief.

Since the end of colonial rule, Myanmar's military has played a powerful role in overseeing the political affairs of the country. Even though military rule formally came to an end in 2010, the 2008 Constitution guarantees their ongoing role in parliamentary affairs. According to Article 33 of the Pyithu, Amyotha and States and Regions election law, military MPs must make up 25 per cent of parliament and are directly nominated by the Commander-in-Chief of the military *Tatmadaw*. Despite the ushering in of various democratic institutions since 2010, the military-drafted constitutional requirement for MMPs effectively maintains their power over parliamentary and constitutional affairs, and the nation as a whole.

There are two types of legislatures in Myanmar, namely the Union parliament and the state and region parliaments. The Union parliament, the *Pyidaungsu Hluttaw* (national parliament), is bicameral. Where the *Pyithu Hluttaw* represents the people and townships, the *Amyotha Hluttaw* represents the states and regions (Constitution of the Republic of the Union of Myanmar, 2008, Article 74). Both *hluttaw*s form an electoral college consisting of three groups of law makers. These groups include the elected representatives to the *Amyotha Hluttaw*, the elected representatives to the *Pyithu Hluttaw*, and appointed military representatives to both *hluttaw*s (Constitution of the Republic of the Union of Myanmar 2008, Article 60).

According to the 2008 Constitution, there are seven states and seven regions in Myanmar. Each state or region has its own legislature or *hluttaw*, which is unicameral. There are two types of members in each *hluttaw*; elected representatives and appointed military representatives. The chief ministers, nominated by the president, are the heads of the state and regional governments. The number of seats in each state or region depends on the number of townships (each township constituency has two MPs), as well as ethnic representatives (Constitution of the Republic of the Union of Myanmar, Article 161). State and region *hluttaw*s in Myanmar undertake key functions in legislation, oversight, and representation on their respective matters in accordance with Schedule Two of the 2008 Constitution. The state and region legislatures are important pillars of Myanmar's political infrastructure; however, insufficient attention has been paid to their current performance and the structural challenges they face (EMReF 2017) with more attention having been placed on the Union *Hluttaw* (Egreteau 2016, 2017; Kyaw Sein & Farrelly 2016).

There is very little research on why MPs choose to participate in politics in Myanmar. We started our interviews with an introductory question to all MPs about when and how they came to participate in politics. We found three main themes that encouraged them to do so. First, for NLD members, opposing the autocratic military regime was the primary motivation for their participation (see also Jefferson, this volume). Second was their belief in Daw Aung San Su Kyi's leadership and what they saw as her unique ability to create change in Myanmar. Third, in the case of USDP members, the institutional drive especially from the Union Solidarity Development

Association (USDA) to become the Union Solidarity and Development Party (USDP) led to their involvement.[1]

In addition to these three reasons, the primary motivation for ethnic MPs from Mon and Karen states was in advancing the rights of their corresponding ethnic groups. For example, ethnic MPs described the way they had used their role to propose budgets and curriculum for their unique literature and culture in state schools. As one ethnic MP stated, "Now we can teach ethnic languages during school hours and support the ethnic language teachers' salaries" (Interview 4 & 9, 2018). However, this differed with the perspective of members of the Tanintharyi *Hluttaw*, where every contested constituency was won by the NLD. Tanintharyi region MPs instead emphasised the importance of bringing development to their region under the guidance of the NLD party and Daw Aung San Su Kyi's leadership.

As a whole, many MPs framed their duty in relation to their ability to represent all people in their constituency regardless of opposition (Interviews 4 & 14, 2018). MPs noted that their discussions in parliament are primarily aimed at promoting the particular needs of their state/regions and/or individual constituencies. One of the Mon MPs, for example, explained, "The first priority is for my constituency's needs, not the party, in the *hluttaw*" (Interview 9, 2018). This suggests that, while every party has their own guidelines, MPs sometimes see themselves as playing an individual performative role in their ability to represent people from their constituency, regardless of their party affiliation.

In assessing the representative performance of MPs, it is important to examine what MPs see as part of their duties and responsibilities. In the interviews we conducted, MPs described the growing importance of their performance through communication technologies, such as mobile phones and social media, to reach out to their constituents (All interviewed MPs, 2018). For those who had constituencies which included inaccessible or remote areas without access to these communication technologies, elected MPs described how a big part of their role was reaching out to local administrators from the various township or villages to inform them about national and parliamentary affairs. The challenges of connecting with remote areas was a common theme amongst MPs from Tanintharyi and Karen, in particular, who also spoke about the issues associated with conflict and mixed administration with ethnic armed organisations (EAOs) (see South 2018). In addition, many MPs spoke about the importance of responding to the needs of their constituents, including dealing with complaints and enquiries (see also Batchelor 2018, 43). One MP noted a significant gap between MPs' constitutional duties and the expectations of the people:

> The public send a lot of complaint letters to the *hluttaw* every day. The public is not clear with the *hluttaw* and the executive. Even with a minor family quarrel they send a complaint letter to the *hluttaw*. Hence, I am thinking to change the *hluttaw* name to the "complaints department" (Interview 14, 2018).

One of the military MPs from the Karen State *Hluttaw* viewed this instead as a positive development, noting: "receiving many complaint letters means that people rely more on the *hluttaw*" (Interview 12, 2018). In contrast to the past, he suggested, people's engagement with the parliament was an indication of their increased expectations of MPs and the *hluttaw* to be able to effect change or solve their problems.

The lack of experience constituents have with democratic institutions was a common theme across all interviews. This is not entirely surprising, given the long history of military rule. One of the key challenges identified in interviews by the elected MPs in this respect is the structure of the *hluttaw* and their dual role enshrined in the 2008 Constitution. According to the dual role structure, MPs can take on a *hluttaw* member role, as well as an executive role. In many cases, MPs are nominated to the executive body without a substitute in their place in the state and region *hluttaw*. Consequently, some members feel that their representational role is constrained due to their dual executive and *hluttaw* roles. The dual roles that MPs take on means that they also have very little time to engage with their constituents and respond to their concerns in meaningful ways.

The dual role position for MPs has been identified in previous research as a significant barrier to public engagement, especially in small *hluttaws* (EMReF 2017; Batchelor 2018, 38). All of the MPs interviewed in the study participated in more than one legislative committee. Most of the MPs said that the committees functioned well, but that there were challenges balancing these dual roles. One of the Tanintharyi MPs noted the difficulties of managing both committee and constituency work (Interview 15, 2018). He suggested that the work of the committees is important to the proper functioning of the *hluttaw*, but, as MPs are often working on one or more committees, they have less time to engage with their constituencies. There was an overwhelming sense from MPs that voters didn't understand these dual roles and instead only make requests for basic needs such as schools, roads and bridges. One of the MPs from Tanintharyi described the issues associated with this misunderstanding:

> If fishermen wanted to change the fishery laws as they are not consistent or practical, we could make more meaningful change for the political transition. However, since they are just concerned with short-term issues and development activities, we are unable to reach these kinds of reforms and therefore the real democracy (Interview 16, 2018).

Another representational issue that elected MPs identified is the power of the *Tatmadaw* over the legislative process. In contrast to those who fought to be elected, military MPs are constitutionally mandated to represent the interests of the *Tatmadaw* and Commander-in-Chief. In line with official policy, a military MP from the Karen State *Hluttaw* explained:

> We are here to safeguard the three main national causes (non-disintegration of the Union, non-disintegration of national solidarity, and perpetuation of national sovereignty) and the Constitution. That is our key objective (Interview 12, 2018).

Unlike the concerns raised by elected MPs in relation to representation, military MPs very rarely engage with the public and their activities are only visible when posted by the *hluttaw* or other media. Military MPs themselves acknowledge that they are restricted in engaging with the public, needing the permission of their superior officers (Informal interview 1, 2018). This lack of engagement with the public is viewed by elected MPs as a symbol of their loyalty to the *Tatmadaw* over and above the people and a detriment to the representational performance of the parliament. This perspective is reflected in comments by one Karen MP who stated, "they only represent the *Tatmadaw*" (Interview 4, 2018). However, elected MPs do not see this as a personal choice. Rather, military MPs are seen as severely constrained in their ability to act in the interests of the constituency. Two-thirds of those interviewed pointed out that military MPs do not have the opportunity to speak freely or offer their individual opinion because they are required to obey their senior officer's instructions "sitting or standing". This situation and the difficulty in changing the Constitution is seen to corrode the ability of parliament to freely represent the interests of the people, as MPs believe a democracy should.

WHAT IS PARLIAMENTARY REPRESENTATION?

According to Johnson (2005), members of parliament are responsible for representing the differences in a country or state, which may be rooted in geography, ethnicity, religion, political identification, gender, or other characteristics, and for considering these differences in the policymaking area. With a narrow understanding of representation, however, some MPs may only consider the particular needs of their constituency or ethnic group. Meanwhile, some MPs may have a broader understanding of representation which speaks to the needs of the entire state or *hluttaw* as well as the constituency.

Our research revealed different understandings of representation in the case of the state and regional MPs interviewed. Firstly, their representative function is primarily carried out in relation to the commitments they gave to voters to implement projects in their interests, especially in the development or healthcare sectors. They are also expected to solve the problems of their respective constituencies as members of parliament. This sentiment was described by one elected MP from Mon state:

> A representative who is elected by the people will examine the needs requested by the people. If those needs are important, they will ask respective cabinet ministers or chief ministers (to implement this) for them. If I cannot fulfill the people's requests, I will be shown the yellow card. But if it is not an actual need, I don't accept it (Interview 9, 2018).

Two-thirds of elected MPs who were interviewed in this research explained that their understanding of representation is based upon the separation of the three core functions of the legislature: representation, oversight and legislation. Overall, they usually define representation in terms of their ability to listen to the voice of the people; oversight as providing checks and balances over the executive body; and legislation as the enactment of laws. However, some MPs, especially from the Tanintharyi region *hluttaw*, see representation as a wide-ranging function and not only in terms of these three duties. This sentiment is instantiated in a quote from the secretary of the legislative committee from the Tanintharyi *Hluttaw*, who noted:

> Everything I have been doing in the parliament, including taking the responsibility and duties for oversight and legislation (for example, budget oversight, handling parliamentary committee affairs, making or amending laws as is necessary) is defined as representation, because all of these are done in the name of representing the people (Interview 1, 2018).

Representation is also considered more broadly depending on the current position held by each representative at the state and region *hluttaws*. *Hluttaw* speakers, deputy speakers, some MPs as well as *hluttaw* committee chairpersons consider their roles in multiple ways. One of the Mon state parliamentarians suggested there are three types of representation:

> One, representation for the constituency; two, representation for all Mon ethnic people and; three, representation for the Mon State *Hluttaw*. Representing the constituency is clear because people from my constituency voted for me. I am representing all Mon ethnic people because here (in the Mon State *Hluttaw*) the quantity of MPs from Mon ethnic parties is so few. So, I am a key person to represent ethnic affairs and issues. Representing the Mon State *Hluttaw* means that, although the *hluttaw* is formed with all representatives, my role is very important for the effective functioning of parliamentary affairs committees and the *hluttaw* office staff who are able to support those committees. Guiding those committees and managing office staff in order to link to all those things has become my task (Interview 7, 2018).

Another MP also provided a wide-ranging perspective on what representation entailed:

> It is simple. Representation is representation. In my constituency, there might be 50,000 people and 30,000 with the right to vote, and I won by 15,000 votes. But I represent all 50,000 people. Those 50,000 people are not able to speak out about their issues to the *hluttaw*. So, those people that voted for me gave me a leadership role to speak out for them instead. That's why "we" are working to have their (people's) voice reach out to the *hluttaw*. This is what representation means to members of parliaments or representatives of people (Interview 8, 2018).

In contrast, military MPs see themselves as representing the *Tatmadaw* in line with the guidance of the Commander-in-Chief. This revolves around the *Tatmadaw*'s six fundamental constitutional principles and the notion that the military should "be able to participate in the national political leadership role of the state" (Joseph & Min Zin 2012, 112). Defending the country's sovereignty has been the national mission of the *Tatmadaw* since its origin as the Burma Independence Army (BIA) in 1942. The Commander-in-Chief of the *Tatmadaw*, Senior General Min Aung Hlaing, has also reiterated the importance of this historical mission in several media interviews, noting that the duty of military MPs is to defend the country's national interests and the 2008 Constitution. Following comments made by Senior General Min Aung Hlaing, one of the military MPs stated: "'We' are like a third party (in the *hluttaw*). Thus, we have to check (parliamentarians) are not (negatively) interfering in constitutional matters and the three main national causes" (Interview 12, 2018). However, we also found that there are instances where military MPs were able to raise personal concerns by submitting motions or questions to the parliament specific to their constituency. In the *hluttaws* we examined, these included questions around rule of law in the region[2] and the establishment of rehabilitation centers for drug users.[3] The MMP colonel from Karen State who was also a medical doctor, described how the process for military MPs to submit questions works there:

> Among our military representatives, some MMPs also ask questions. In our military group (in Karen State) we have a senior person who is the security border affairs minister. For every question or motion, we need to ask permission from him. He normally allows us to ask questions or bring forward motions about things that are not directly related to the three main national causes and sovereignty. However, he often emphasises to us the importance of safeguarding the three national causes and the constitution (Interview 12, 2018).

However, even though there is some space for MMPs to submit questions, they tend not to, since the culture of the military does not encourage them to speak out (see also Maung Aung Myoe 2018).

In research on parliaments, scholars focus on how parliamentarians engage with citizens (Judge & Liston Bandiera 2017). However, Judge and Liston-Bandeira (2017, 154) point out that there is a "neglected institutional dimension of parliamentary representation: the representation of what parliaments 'are', what claims are made on their behalf and who are the makers of these claims." In the context of Myanmar, the performance of MPs in Myanmar's sub-national parliaments oscillates between performance of voluntary actions and actions determined by the relevant party/institutional policy. Elected MPs might sometimes act in parliament freely and voluntarily for their constituencies; however, they often face coercion through their institutional affiliation and are forced to work in line with party rules and regulations.

Even though elected MPs are less constrained than military MPs, institutional affiliation also plays a powerful role in dictating the representative role of MPs in Myanmar. Under Aung San Suu Kyi's leadership, for example, it has been widely suggested that NLD MPs are heavily restricted in their ability to act independently.[4] The oscillation between following party policy and other interests is demonstrated in the case of the "General Aung San Bridge" scandal in Mon state. The proposal to name the bridge after the famed Burmese independence hero linking Chaungzone township and Mawlamyine, led to a protest of 3,000 people (see Medail 2018). NLD MPs in the Mon state parliament supported changing the name of the bridge in keeping with local people's wishes to another name, "Yamanya", which refers to the ancient Mon kingdom in the Mon language. However, this motion was overridden by the Union *hluttaw*'s motion for naming it the "General Aung San bridge" in keeping with a proposal from the NLD representative, Mi Kon Chan in the lower house of the national parliament (*Pyithu Hluttaw*). In this case, protestors used "we" to refer to themselves in contradistinction to Mi Kon Chan, who they saw instead as representing the interests of the party, rather than Mon people (Lun Min Mang 2017). Whereas Mon state NLD MPs were seen as representing the interests of the Mon people over and above their party. The bridge saga demonstrates how the Mon state NLD MPs performed freely (voluntarily) in the interest of their own constituency despite the fact that the outcome was ultimately determined by the party at the Union level. This case also demonstrates the constraints elected MPs in Myanmar face within their own party in undertaking voluntary actions in the interests of their constituency.

MODES OF REPRESENTATION

Our research also found some differences in the modes of representation between elected and unelected MPs. The representative methods of the civilian MPs in the studied *hluttaws* often depended upon their political backgrounds, their understanding of representation, and especially their individual capacity. We identified four different methods used to carry out their representative activities: 1. By asking questions and putting forward motions in the *hluttaw* sessions; 2. By engaging or dealing with the regional executive members and ministers; 3. By coordinating with relevant stakeholders (eg. civil society organisations, government departments, political party fellows etc.); and 4. By applying each MP's own professional skills (eg. lawyer, general practitioner etc.). From these four representative methods, the first two methods are used by almost all MPs, except *hluttaw* speakers. However, the latter two methods were found to be utilised by MPs who have their own professional experience or skills in a relevant field of work. In some cases, we found that certain MPs are able to use all four types of representational styles. The following brief case study of a female MP from the Mon state parliament helps to illustrate the role that the professional skills and individual capacity of an MP can have in shaping representative performance in unique ways by using those different modes of representation.

Daw Khaing Khaing (Interview 8, 2018) is an attorney and founder of a law firm. She competed in the 2015 general election as per the invitation of the National League for Democracy (NLD). She became an MP in the Mon State *Hluttaw* as well as the chairperson of two parliamentary committees: the Legislative Committee and the Women and Child Rights Protection Committee. In terms of her representative role as an MP, she explained that she usually conducts field visits to her constituency twice a week in order to know the needs of her people. The people from her constituency are also able to send complaint letters to her about their unique needs and grievances through the *hluttaw* representatives' office. She manages her own Facebook page and personal account in order to stay active and update her activities to let people know what she has achieved in her responsibilities to the *hluttaw*. Moreover, she gives her mobile phone number to people when she meets them if they need to contact her. In this way, her constituents can report to her the problems they face in the township through multiple avenues, including through social media (Facebook messenger, comments box), mobile phone calls and letters. She reported that she received many kinds of complaints from her constituents, even at night for emergency issues like floods in the town. Whenever people requested help, she explained that she was happy to respond to their needs if their problems are deemed reasonable. If she found a case was incorrect or driven by personal interest, she would refuse it. She noted, "An MP is taking a leading role, so there is no need to follow whatever they ask. If people are wronged, however, an MP has to be able to point them in the right direction" (Interview 8, 2018).

Daw Khaing Khaing told us that she chooses to represent the people as an MP not only by asking questions on their behalf in the *hluttaw*, but also through counseling them to recover from their psychological wounds and in issues related to justice. She told us, for example, in a child sexual abuse case, most people usually forget about the victim. Similarly, she explained that female victims often do not want to report cases of sexual violence (see also Aye Thiri Kyaw and Miedema, this volume). Therefore,

Daw Khaing Khaing described how she saw it as part of her representative responsibility to provide care for victims. In these instances, as an MP and the head of the child rights protection committee, she explained how she is able to work in cooperation with the department of social welfare, relevant CSOs and NGOs, to help support the relief of victims' suffering (Interview 8, 2018). Because of her open attitude, she reported that many people from her township constituency and from other Mon townships such as Ye and Bilin report to her on related issues, especially with access to justice. In this way, she contended, she is "a justice icon in the *hluttaw*" (Interview 8, 2018). She strongly believed that people came to know her performance for being honest, effective, and being able to give an answer without giving any false hope to people. However, she added:

> The main problem is many people think that an MP is like a "*Nat*" (spirit), with unique powers to settle all issues. In fact, people need to understand MPs have no rights to do that. So, I always have to give a clear explanation about which matters can be addressed and which ones cannot (Interview 8, 2018).

Like Daw Khaing Khaing, in many of other interviews MPs suggested that there is a large gap in perceptions of their representative role between themselves and the public. As highlighted by Daw Khaing Khaing's quote, many MPs believe the public see them as "*nats*" or magicians – that they have the ability to solve any problem because they are democratically elected MPs to parliament. The MPs also perform the role of democratically elected MPs, which is why the public has this view, but in reality, they are restricted by the 2008 Constitution and their institutional rules and regulations.

The limited understanding the public have of MPs' power and responsibilities also limits their representational ability in affecting change for people and addressing key concerns of the electorate. One key issue, that MPs from Karen State raised, for example, was people's expectations for them to be able to address the many land confiscation cases that took place under military rule. Even though this issue is the responsibility of the General Administration Department (GAD), many people view parliamentarians as having some power or political sway to affect land restitution cases. One Karen MP explained that they have received thousands of letters sent by victims to the complaints and appeal letters review committee concerning land grabs. With the suggestion of the *hluttaw* committee, the letters were handed over to the executive body and the minister concerned instructed the land records department, GAD and forest department to handle them (Interview 19, 2016). However, the people in those departments were largely appointed by the previous USDP government and were sometimes implicated in the land confiscations cases, disrupting restitutive justice. The ability of people to seek justice regarding land confiscations that occurred under military rule is also hampered by the fact that, up until recently, the GAD was controlled by the military under the Ministry of Home Affairs (Saw and Arnold 2014).[5] This includes those currently serving with the region and township committees under the purview of the Central Committee on Confiscated Farmlands and other Lands (Interview 4, 2018). Since they were involved in the land disputes resolution committee, it was suggested in interviews that responses to the complaints letters sent to the *hluttaw* committee were delayed and not followed up, obfuscating restitutive justice. Referring to the many land grabs that occurred under military rule and their continued involvement in justice mechanisms, one MP remarked, "they (inter-departmental staff) are like a father and son. A father will never reveal his son's wrongdoings" (Interview 19, 2016).

The role that the military plays in influencing national politics was a common theme in the interviews we had. Myanmar's military Commander-in-Chief, Senior General Min Aung Hlaing, has stated in multiple interviews that Myanmar's democracy is very young and therefore the people still require the support of the *Tatmadaw* in understanding democratic principles and practice (eg. Wong 2015). In the interviews we conducted, elected MPs pointed out that MMPs play a powerful role in influencing small subnational parliaments, in particular. When voting for motions in the *hluttaw*, MMPs' votes are often needed to pass the motions as a result of the multiple roles MPs take on. For example, in Mon State, there are a total of twenty-three elected MPs including three ethnic ministers and eight military MPs. The executive body was formed with a total of thirteen people. It included six elected MPs, three ethnic ministers and two others, the chief auditor and chief judge. With only fourteen MPs remaining, the role of military MPs is therefore key to passing any legislation.

To give an insight into how this plays out, in the Mon State *Hluttaw*, elected MPs and the executive had a heated debate about cancelling the collection of toll gate fees (EMReF 2018). In line with the constitution, the *hluttaw* speaker passed a motion to vote on the fees, but all military MPs gave their votes to the executive who wanted to keep the tolls in place.

Elected MPs explained that they feel like the *hluttaw* faced a major loss in their ability to represent the desires of the people, because of the military MPs' votes. Although constituents from townships across different areas in Mon State wanted to remove the toll gate fee, the government continued to collect the toll gate fees due to to the voting block of the MMPs. There was a perception from some of the elected MPs interviewed that the military was trying to sew discord between the people and the government, since many people don't understand the functioning of the parliamentary process: "The public will criticise the government. Hence, we could say that the MMPs are playing (the people) based on the political situation" (Interview 7, 2018). Indeed, elected MPs saw the military's position in parliament as impeding its representative role, since they do not need to consider the views of the people. The example of the toll gate fees also demonstrates how MMPs use their leverage over the parliament to obfuscate democratic processes in the interests of the people.

PERFORMATIVITY IN MODES OF REPRESENTATION

Representational performance is key to a functioning democracy, especially in a pluralistic society like Myanmar. As other scholars have shown (Lavi 2016), the way MPs construct and enact their roles in parliament influences their modes of representational performance. In applying a performativity analysis to democracies, Lavi (2016, 7) highlights that they are a "product of the repetitive performance of a set of actions, procedures and institutions associated with it." Adapting the concept of democracy as a set of performative acts to the case of MPs in Myanmar's parliaments, elected MPs regularly perform for the people through their own styles and modes of representation. For example, after the NLD party won the election in 2015, Daw Aung San Suu Kyi and her elected MPs led a national effort to go around communities picking up trash, as a symbol of their commitment to changing Myanmar for the better. Performative acts like these are used regularly by NLD party members, and also by the members of smaller or opposition political parties, as a symbolic gesture to the public of their commitment to reform. Many opposition USDP party members, for example, are also seen performing social work in their communities, such as assisting with free clinics or building schools, as a way to reach out to constituents.

There are also linguistic elements to the performances of MPs. According to the interviews, NLD MPs are told to use particular phrases repetitively as a way to reinforce party messaging. This includes iconic slogans such as, "together with the people" (Interview 14, 2018). This slogan stems from the State Counselor's speech at the ceremony of the first anniversary of the NLD government in office in March 2017 (Kyaw Zwa Moe 2017). Since it became the NLD slogan, MPs often use this phrase as a way to demonstrate their intent to overcome the challenges of transforming Myanmar "together with the people" and to establish a democratic federal union (Chit Min Tun 2018). This is an example of a repeated performed claim about democracy in terms of "of the people, for the people" and "by the people". However, these performative aspects of representation have tended towards a form of "populist democracy" (Meny & Surel 2002) since elected MPs have faced structural and constitutional limitations to achieving full representative democracy.

In contrast to the NLD, the military tends to take a more paternalistic approach. Senior General Min Aung Hlaing's speeches, for example, during the 21st Century Panglong Conference and Armed Forces' Day celebrations (Pyae Thet Phyo 2016) and in interviews (e.g. Wong 2015), reiterate the importance of the *Tatmadaw*:

> People need to understand and practice democratic principles. In that respect, the *Tatmadaw* is providing support and participating in the parliamentary democracy according to the law (Thiha 2015).

Military MPs therefore also try to institute democracy through enactment. This type of repeated speech is also an attempt to shape the perception of the importance of the military's continued role in politics as constitutive of a "discipline flourishing democracy". This reminds people that the *Tatmadaw* still sees themselves as "above the people", rather than as their representatives.

CONCLUSION

Since the 2015 national election, Myanmar has seen significant changes to the membership of its parliaments. This chapter has given an insight into how elected and appointed MPs from Myanmar's sub-national parliaments understand and perform their representative roles in what is an emerging democratic system. We have shown how the individual and institutionalised dimensions of representation oscillate between voluntarism, where MPs may act individually for the concerns of their own constituency, and determinism, where they follow the party's rules and directions. Despite elected MPs' desire to represent their constituents' needs, we demonstrate how structural limitations and institutional constraints have limited their representative role.

One of the biggest challenges identified to representation is a constitutional issue. As the Constitution does not clearly separate between the legislature and administration in state and regional parliaments, elected MPs often maintain dual roles and find they do not have time to fulfill all their duties. This affects sub-national parliaments in particular, as taking a dual role in both the legislature and administration, the number of MPs is reduced in the *hluttaw* and the remaining MPs are very busy with their committee affairs and constituency work. A constitutional amendment to the current structure of the state/region *hluttaws* is therefore required to improve the effectiveness of the representation of elected MPs and to contribute to a more truly representative democracy in Myanmar.

Many of the MPs interviewed expressed the difficulties of meeting their constituency's needs as a result of these constraints. They also spoke about the difficulties of engaging with and representing communities who live in remote areas with poor communications infrastructure. Some MPs noted the difficulties in both representing their communities and also following the party line. This is most clearly demonstrated in the Mon State bridge saga. Although Mon State NLD MPs supported the use of a locally relevant name for the bridge, the central NLD party overruled this without consideration for local interests. This example demonstrates how party policy can also be a barrier to representation within a local context.

We have also examined the role of military MPs, their loyalty to the *Tatmadaw* and their role in the parliament as per the 2008 Constitution. Military MPs are a strong collective body within the sub-national parliaments and their voting power is crucial for the parliament and the executive. When a motion is being debated between elected MPs and the executive, gaining the votes of military MPs is vital, as the outcome depends on whether they support the executive or elected MPs. We have also shown how MMPs see the nation and the parliament in paternalistic ways, emphasising the importance of their role in parliament in overseeing the democratisation process. Both types of MPs note that people in Myanmar need more education and knowledge about democracy and politics, and consequently there is a need for deeper political engagement. Elected MPs suggest that people only care about their individualised local needs with little interest in broader laws, policies, political management and democratic norms (Interviews 2 and 6, 2018). Military MPs also believe that they are needed to participate in politics because of national security concerns and to help shepherd the people during this period of political and social change.

As Myanmar moves along the path to democratisation it will take time to address these representational constraints on MPs. Further research into sub-national parliaments, the public perceptions of these MPs and what aspects of their performance most influence those perceptions is necessary to better understand Myanmar's budding democracy and how it functions on the ground. These representational issues may lead to a widening gap between *hluttaw* representatives and the local people. But in turn, as another election comes up, it may also help to shape the representational role of elected MPs who are forced to prioritise local people's concerns if they want to be re-elected.

Notes

1. The USDA was formed by former military leader, Senior General Than Shwe, in 1993. According to a report from the Network for Democracy and Development (NDD)(2010), the military government-backed USDA claimed around 24 million people which included students and civil servants, often without them knowing about their membership. However, the USDA changed to the dominant Union Solidarity and Development Party to contest the 2010 election (NDD 2010, 58).
2. This question was asked by a military MP in the sixth regular first day meeting of the Mon State *Hluttaw*: 7 June, 2017. Retrieved from www.monhluttaw.com.
3. This question was asked by a military MP in the second day *hluttaw* special meeting in Karen State *Hluttaw* (1/2018), *Karen Hluttaw Journal* p. 6, 30 April 2018.
4. See for example https://www.economist.com/asia/2017/06/01/democracy-has-muzzled-myanmars-parliament (accessed 16 July 2020).
5. In 2019 the GAD was moved to sit within the civilian-controlled Ministry of Union Government Office.

References

Batchelor, R. (2018). *State and Region Governments in Myanmar.* Yangon: The Asia Foundation.

Butler, J. (1997). *Excitable Speech: A Politics of the Performative.* New York: Routledge.

Chit Min Tun (2018). "NLD Announce That Will Establish a New Democratic Federal Union Country". *The Irrawaddy* (Burmese), 27 September. Available at https://burma.irrawaddy.com/ news/2018/09/27/171092.html (accessed 5 Jan 2019).

Egreteau, R. and Robinne, F. (eds) (2016). *Metamorphosis: Studies in Social and Political Change in Myanmar.* Singapore: NUS Press.

Egreteau, R. (2016). *Caretaking Democratization: The Military and Political Change in Myanmar* Oxford: Oxford University Press.

_____ (2017). *Parliamentary Development in Myanmar: An Overview of the Union Parliament 2011–2016.* Yangon, Myanmar: Asia Foundation.

EMReF (2017). *Performance Analysis: State and Region Hluttaws (Local Legislatures) of Myanmar* Yangon. Enlightened Myanmar Research Foundation.

_____ (2018). "Two Ministers for Security and Border Affairs and 48 Military MPs Reshuffled." *State and Region Parliaments News Bulletin* 2(67). Available at https://emref.org/sites/emref.org/files/publication-docs/bulletin_67_eng_final.pdf. (accessed 27 Oct 2019).

_____ (2018). "The Motion to Remove Toll Gates in Mon State Gets Voted Down". *State and Region Parliaments News Bulletin,* 2 (64) (2018). Available at https://emref.org/sites/emref.org/files/publication-docs/bulletin_63_ eng_final.pdf (accessed 27 Oct 2019).

Inter-parliamentary Union (2008). *Evaluating Parliament: A Self-Assessment Toolkit for Parliaments.* Geneva, Switzerland: IPU.

International Crisis Group (2015). *The Myanmar Elections: Results and Implications.* Yangon/Brussels: International Crisis Group.

Johnson, K.J. (2005). *The Role of Parliament in Government.* Washington DC: The International Bank for Reconstruction and Development/The World Bank.

Joseph, B. and Min Zin (2012). "The Opening in Burma: The Democrats' Opportunity". *Journal of Democracy* 4: 104–119.

Judge, D. and Leston-Bandeira, C. (2018). "The Institutional Representation of Parliament". *Political Studies* 66 (1): 154–172.

Kyaw Myo (2018). "President Calls for Nationwide Revamp of Waste-Management Practices". *The Irrawaddy,* 5 June. Available at https://www.irrawaddy.com/news/burma/president-calls-nationwide-revamp-waste-management-practices.html (accessed 30 Dec 2018).

Kyaw Sein and Farrelly, N. (2016). *Myanmar's Evolving Relations: The NLD in Government.* Stockholm, Sweden: ISDP.

Kyaw Zwa Moe (2017). "The Path to a New Country: Looking Back on One Year of NLD Rule". *Irrawaddy,* 7 April. Available at https://www.irrawaddy.com/opinion/ commentary/the-path-to-a-new-country-looking-back-on-one-year-of-nld-rule.html (accessed 5 Jan 2019).

Kyi Pyar Chit Saw and Arnold, M. (2014). *Administering the State: An Overview of the General Administrative Division*. Yangon, Myanmar: Asia Foundation.

Lall, M. (2016). *Understanding Reform in Myanmar: People and Society in the Wake of Military Rule*. London: Hurst.

Lavi, L. (2016). "Ups and Downs: Thinking about Democratic Legitimacy from a Performative Perspective". Paper presented at the Western Political Science Association Meeting. Available at http://www.wpsanet.org/lavi liron ups and downs thinking.pdf (accessed 2 Jan 2019).

Loxley, J. (2007). *Performativity*. London & New York: Routledge.

Lun Min Mang (2017). "Local Residents Protest NLD MP's Bridge-name Proposal". *Myanmar Times,* 3 March. Available at https://www.mmtimes.com/national-news/nay-pyi-taw/25166-local-residents-protest-nld-mp-s-bridge-name-proposal.html (accessed 17 June 2020).

Macey, D. (2001). *The Penguin Dictionary of Critical Theory*. London: Penguin.

Maung Aung Myoe (2018). "Partnership in Politics: The Tatmadaw and the NLD in Myanmar." In *Myanmar Transformed: People, Places, Politics,* edited by J. Chambers, G. McCarthy, N. Farrelly and Chit Win. Singapore: ISEAS-Yusof Ishak Institute.

Medail, C. (2018). "Forming an Inclusive National Identity in Myanmar". In *Myanmar Transformed: People, Places, Politics,* edited by J. Chambers, G. McCarthy, N. Farrelly and Chit Win. Singapore: ISEAS-Yusof Ishak Institute.

Meny, Y. and Surel, Y. (2002). *Democracies and the Populist Challenge*. Basingstoke: Palgrave.

Network for Democracy and Development (2010). "Burma: A Violent Past to a Brutal Future: The Transformation of a Paramilitary Organization into a Political Party". *Burma Campaign UK,* 3 November. Available at http://burmacampaign.org.uk/reports/burma-a-violent-past-to-a-brutal- future/ (accessed 5 Sep 2019).

Pyae Thet Phyo (2016). "Tamadaw Chief Marks 71st Armed Forces Day". *Myanmar Times,* 28 March. Available at https://www.mmtimes.com/national-news/19671-tatmadaw-chief-marks-71st-armed-forces-day.html (accessed 27 Dec 2018).

Republic of the Union of Myanmar (2008). *Constitution of the Republic of the Union of Myanmar*. Naypyitaw, Myanmar.

Ruedin, D. (2012). "Individual Representation: A Different Approach to Political Representation". *Representation* 48(1): 115–129.

South, A. (2018). "'Hybrid Governance' and the Politics of Legitimacy in the Myanmar Peace Process". *Journal of Contemporary Asia* 48 (1): 50–66.

Thiha (2015). "Myanmar Army Chief Senior General Min Aung Hlaing on presidential ambitions and military role". *Channel News Asia,* 21 January. Available at https://consult-myanmar.com/2015/01/28/myanmar-army-chief-senior-general-min-aung-hlaing-on-presidential-ambitions-military-role/ (accessed 5 Dec 2018).

Toshiro, K. (2011). *Results of the 2010 Elections in Myanmar: An Analysis.* Tokyo, Japan: IDE-JETRO.

UEC (2018). "Substitution of Military Representatives of Region or State Hluttaws: Announcement No. 167, 168. and 169/ 2018". Naypyitaw, Myanmar: Union Election Commission, 6 November. Available at https://www.uec.gov.mm/news_preview_detail (accessed 30 Nov 2018).

Wong, M. (2015). "Myanmar to 'Wait and See' on Constitutional Change: Army Chief". *Channel News Asia,* 21 January. Available at https://www.youtube.com/watch?v=lQyN0OR8N5s (accessed 27 Dec 2018).

4

TIME CHANGING HANDS IN MYANMAR: ON FORMER PRISONERS' JOURNEYS INTO POLITICS

Andrew M. Jefferson

During a public lecture and panel debate in Stockholm in 2019, Nick Cheesman outlined an agenda for a reinvigorated critical Myanmar studies. Myanmar studies, he implied, needs to move beyond the familiar tropes used to characterise the country and its history, for example, Bamar versus minorities, liberal democracy versus military dictatorship, and so on. Cheesman invoked Wittekind and Rhoades (2018) to challenge scholars to move from a focus on isolation, decline, decay and inertia towards agency, interaction and everyday life. He spoke against a deficit-oriented approach and called for the production of more compelling historical narratives.

As a newcomer to Myanmar studies I identify with Cheesman's sentiment, echoing Mbembe's call to scholars of Africa to take the continent seriously on its own terms and cease ahistorical theorising couched only in terms of what it is not (Mbembe 2001). Cognizant of the fact that increased levels of access for research give increased possibilities and raise the stakes around what is feasible and desirable, this chapter seeks to contribute to a reinvigorated critical Myanmar studies through an analysis of the development of political consciousness in the lives of eight former prisoners now occupying positions of political authority in Myanmar.

The chapter draws on interviews conducted in 2017 as part of the Legacies of Detention in Myanmar[1] research project. This is a collaborative project that aims to explore the historical and contemporary role of detention in Myanmar and its significance for the reconfiguration of state and society, utilising an ethnographic sensibility (Schatz 2009; Shore et al. 2011; Stepputat and Larsen 2015).[2] Focused on a small sub-set of national and regional parliamentarians, I explore how they came to be who and where they are today, and I argue that the interruptions and disruptions that characterise and constitute their lives are best understood as links rather than breaks. The analytic lens developed and demonstrated has implications for how we think about change in Myanmar, a topic preoccupying many scholars and commentators as previous *Myanmar Update* volumes and other works testify (Chambers et al. 2018; Cheesman et al. 2012, 2014; Cheesman and Farrelly 2016; Crouch 2014, 2016; Egreteau and Robinne 2016; Lall 2016; Simpson et al. 2018; Slater 2014).

This chapter covers both processes of political subjectification, that is journeys into politics and, to a lesser degree, perspectives on punishment. It is structured as follows. First, I situate the study in the light of some of the recent literature on politics and transition in Myanmar. Second, I introduce the methodology and some of the challenges facing scholars engaged in studies featuring imprisonment. Third, I present and discuss in some detail the disrupted life trajectories of two of the former prisoners I interviewed. Analytic commentary is provided, invoking material from some of the other interviews where relevant. In a penultimate section I discuss the surprisingly orthodox views that were expressed about the role of prison in contemporary society. Finally, in a conclusion, I re-emphasise the importance of attending to personal and socio-political trajectories as mutually constitutive if we want to make sense of the political in Myanmar today.

PEOPLING THE POLITICAL

Unsurprisingly, politics and transition are common themes within the discourse of academics and other commentators on Myanmar. Indeed, of late Myanmar has become almost the paradigmatic example of a country in transition attracting the attention of development actors and scholars keen to make a contribution. Rather than taking the meaning of these themes for granted, this chapter indirectly subjects them to critical interrogation through an examination of journeys into politics.

Cheesman's (2016) afterword to *Conflict in Myanmar* usefully anticipates some of the issues that this chapter points towards. This chapter takes up Cheesman's call for "attention to be directed to the political, so as to better articulate and understand what we mean when we say that people are talking and acting politically" (2016, 355). The orientation is to the acquisition of political consciousness as developed through current politicians' trajectories of participation in a range of lifelong social practices (Dreier 2003). Rather than focusing on institutions, the peace process, civil-military relations, governance structures, ethnicity, citizenship and belonging (the more traditional realm of the political as exemplified in, for example, *Myanmar Transformed* (13–15), the orientation of this chapter is avowedly, deliberately and unapologetically towards the person, though always the person-in-practice (Jefferson and Huniche 2009). The focus is on how the political is populated or occupied by particular actors or put more empirically: how do particular people become drawn to the political?

Inspired by Holland and Lave (2001), I am drawn to thinking of the political as constituted by actors engaged in contentious social practice, qualified perhaps, as Cheesman would have it, by a shared purpose or an investment in the relationship between contesting parties or as "a manner of relating to difference" (2016, 354).[3] This qualification points to the idea of thinking of politics as participation in contentious and contested social practice, or perhaps by way of shorthand as struggle. Certainly, the people whose lives I report on in this chapter are recounting tales of struggle. The promise of the political may remain unfulfilled, but not for want of trying.

Like many contemporary Myanmar scholars, I come to Myanmar interested in dynamics of transition and change, in my case, seen through the prism of prison[4] and inspired by Ian Hacking's perspectives on histories of the present and the "making up" of people (Hacking 1986, 2002). This approach to history is about interrogating the present in terms of how it came to be, rather than tracing lines of causality or inferred progress from past to present or interrogating the past through the knowledge of the present. It resonates with our research project's desire to make sense of legacies of detention in Myanmar and to situate prisons and those affected by prisons within their unique historical trajectories.

Inspired by anthropologist Lorna Rhodes, prison scholars have been writing for some time now not about dynamics of rupture and revolution but about the way prisons in the global south persist and mutate (Martin et al. 2014). We have used this language of persistence and mutation to try to capture the subtle shifts that characterise changes that occur in prisons (and states) alongside the things that stay the same; the shifts that counter tales of stubborn intransigence and inertia in the face of external intervention. This orientation lends itself to the Myanmar context as it provides a lens that is attentive to the current moment's unfolding dynamic as informed by, but not fully determined by the past.

The analysis I share here pertains mostly to the changed participation in changing practice of eight contemporary parliamentarians who were once in prison. It is mostly about people and their way into politics. But these tales of people and their disjointed trajectories can be used to think more broadly about life in Myanmar and the changes occurring there. The insights gained from examining personal trajectories can be transposed onto the broader canvas of persisting and mutating social processes in Myanmar. Thus, we can usefully ask what insights gained from analysis of lives unfolding over time can offer us when thinking about Myanmar's ongoing struggle to make history. Specifically, I propose that in the same way that the interruptions and disruptions in people's lives should be understood as links rather than breaks, we should resist the language of rupture to talk about the ongoing socio-political shifts in Myanmar.

I am not the first to make this argument. For example, Egreteau and Robinne (2016) propose the term "metamorphosis" to capture the changes that have taken place over the past couple of decades. Others too are well aware that media, policy debates and likely grant applications using familiar tropes of authoritarian to democracy; conflict to peace; state-building and so on do not fully capture the gradual, variegated unfolding of personal, institutional, provincial and national histories in the making. For example, writing just after the NLD election victory in 2015, Chit Win and Farrelly (2016) examined the "turbulent transformation" occurring between 2011 and 2015.[5] They urged analysts to "appreciate the complexity, contradiction and ambiguity of the processes of change, and to treat both old and new with adequate care" (2016, 37). Similarly, Egreteau and Robinne (2016) draw attention to the complexity of the processes of social and political change that are underway and the plurality of "transformative powers." They note the "deep-seated, incremental and observable transformations" that are laced with "elements of resilience, if not (frustrating) persistence" (2016, 4). And Chambers and McCarthy reference the "mutations, continuities, fractures" (2018, 8) of the field.

More specifically, as the scope for research in Myanmar has widened of late there is evidence of growing interest in parliamentary processes and also parliamentarians (Egreteau and Joelene 2018; Holliday and Su Mon Thazin Aung 2018; Nyein Thiri Swei and Zaw Min Oo this volume). Often this is related to tracing the progress of democratisation. My orientation is not the make-up of the legislature; parliamentary procedures; the balance of power in committees; the relationship between the upper and lower houses or national and regional parliaments, or the limits of democracy. I am not focusing on parliamentary life (Egreteau 2017; this volume) or "drivers of representative performance" (Nyein Thiri Swei and Zaw Min Oo this volume[6]) or the broader political developments associated with the stalled peace process (Lall this volume). My entry point is politicians rather than politics, subject-making rather than state-making but always with a sense of the interplay between such practices and the way "intimate identities" and "enduring struggles" intersect (Holland and Lave 2004). According to Egreteau (this volume) the elections of 2015 featured a high legislative turnover with only 13 per cent of incumbents returned to parliament and a number of MPs who were both new to the party and new to their constituencies. This current chapter provides a person-centred analysis that explores how a specific subset of these parliamentarians, those who were imprisoned, ended up there.

METHODOLOGICAL CHALLENGES AND PRAGMATIC SOLUTIONS

As part of the Legacies of Detention in Myanmar research project, eight interviews were conducted with four members of the national parliament, three members of Yangon regional parliament and one member of the National League of Democracy's (NLD) party apparatus. Interviews were recorded and run to a total length of 12.5 hours. All interviewees were male, which was not a deliberate choice but a result of outsourcing the selection of interviewees and a failure to specify that gender representativity would have been desirable. Two of the interviews were conducted in people's homes, one in an office, another in a community centre and four in the back room of a restaurant hired for the purpose.

Almost a year passed between the germination of the idea for this study and the interviews. Accessing members of parliament to talk about matters of prison and politics was not at first straightforward. I was even told by one reputable NGO that it would be impossible as MPs were not permitted to talk to foreigners without permission. The sensitivity of the topic may have played a role, though my experience conducting research on imprisonment and its consequences in other contexts (e.g. Tunisia, Nigeria, Sierra Leone) suggests that people are not necessarily reluctant to talk about such things provided the groundwork is done to create conditions for trust by demonstrating credibility and legitimacy. In my experience structural conditions associated with prisons being closed, and secure institutions featuring a general suspicion of outsiders' motives hinders more than individual sensitivities. Given Myanmar's history, I anticipated access might be a challenge. In the end *Justice for All* (JFA), our research partners, were able to identify relevant people for me to interview and arrange the interviews. Translation, in all cases, was provided by Kyaw Lin Naing of JFA.

In preparatory notes, written a few days before the interviews, I noted my desire to trace some of the "ideas about imprisonment held by people involved in politics today who know prisons from the inside, who have experienced incarceration on their own bodies" (from notes 5.10.17). In these notes, I did not in fact include an emphasis on people's *journeys into politics* which nonetheless became the main focus of the interviews and effectively the focus of this chapter.

My research guide was, in fact, structured around three themes: journey into politics, prison experience, and perspectives on contemporary punishment. In retrospect, I was trying to do too much and the data is somewhat limited by this. I certainly cannot claim to have conducted in-depth biographical interviews or collected detailed personal histories. Each theme could have been a research topic in its own right. Nevertheless, what became clear is that the three themes do speak to one another. Another important lesson was that while it might be tempting to think of former political prisoners involved in politics as a bloc with a common story and potentially common platform,[7] even a relatively superficial glance at the data reveals this to be a gross oversimplification. What became clear in the interviews is that there is no single narrative. There is no common route into politics evidenced in the eight interviews. While there are common themes – most of the men became initially politicised as university students or younger; many talk of the influence of their political seniors or older family members; there are repeated references to the significance of loyalty and sacrifice – their trajectories and declared influences are profoundly singular.

In what follows I present and analyse accounts of the disrupted lives of two of the men I interviewed. Where relevant I invoke details from the other six interviews. Inevitably the analysis presented here is partial and incomplete as I cannot do full justice to the narratives that emerged through the interviews themselves and most certainly not to the lives of the people interviewed.

CASES OF LIVES INTERRUPTED: FROM SPEAKING AND RUNNING TO WORDS OUTPOURING

The first interview took place in the politician's home. We sat together in his living room, my interpreter and I on a sofa and Tun Lin Kyaw[8] on a chair pulled up opposite. Behind us was a wall adorned with photographs of protests and to the left a portrait of our host together with Aung San Suu Kyi, apparently on the campaign trail. A filing cabinet with some folders and books was on the left and to the right a bookshelf filled with a range of books mostly in Burmese. At the far end of the room was a bed. Family members, young and old, drifted through the living room as we interacted.

Tun Lin Kyaw's interest in politics began during school and developed further during his university studies in the early 1980s. He described how he was a good student, but at the same time that he was getting distinctions for his assignments he was becoming increasingly critical of the government of the day. This puzzled his friends. As his knowledge broadened Tun Lin Kyaw looked abroad and was angered at how Burma was falling behind its neighbours in terms of development. He saw political leaders doing nothing for the country and he became disillusioned with the way the students were being squeezed and controlled. The more he learned the more he was disenchanted with the ruling party and the discrepancy between what he read about politics and history and what he saw in terms of policy and practice.

The legacy of student protest was strong in his account: "If you look at history the revolution has always come from the students", he said. He referred back to 1962, when the government bombed the student union office and over 100 people died: "Those memories are always fresh in our mind."

Early experience of practicing law added to his disillusionment, frustration and distress. He expressed how he hated the government, and the community of students and lawyers of which he was a part began to talk about these issues, always conscious of possible surveillance. He began to agitate in public, speaking out against the government at bus-stops. Strikingly for me, he described how he would "speak and run", explaining to people that the government was not working for their interests but only for their own.

Within a year or so of his graduation the student movement that included the protests of 8 August 1988 was picking up steam and Tun Lin Kyaw and his already graduated friends were in the background cautiously encouraging the students. When the NLD was formed later that year he joined and was given a youth leadership position. In the aftermath of the landslide election victory in 1990 he was arrested and sentenced to ten years in prison, the majority of which he served.

Seven months after his eventual release he was rearrested in a preemptive move, suspected of planning a protest scheduled for 9 September 1999 (9.9.99). He was held incommunicado for six weeks in a military intelligence facility. He did not provide details of this period, but it is not unreasonable to assume that he was subject to abuse and probably tortured during his time in prison at the hands of military intelligence. On release he reported to the leadership of the NLD and said he would continue to be supportive but would rest because of health issues. He experienced continued harassment from the authorities and was not as active politically as he had been previously. Instead he turned his attention to his elderly mother, left the city for the village, and temporarily became a monk. This immediate post-prison experience was a time when he needed a break to recuperate. His brother had died while he had been in prison but Tun Lin Kyaw had not been told. The tenor of the narrative shifted somewhat at this point, becoming quieter and sadder.

Having already jumped from 1990 to 1999 (his time in prison), the interview jumped from 1999 to 2007 and the run up to the so-called Saffron Revolution where Tun Lin Kyaw continued to be quietly supportive while still subject to harassment (military intelligence were always in the neighbourhood; they instructed his landlord to evict the family). Tun Lin Kyaw's wife was pregnant at the time and he chose to prioritise family ahead of open political activity, though this was no easy choice.

Three months after the birth of their baby his wife suggested they move to her mother's village because of the ongoing harassment they faced. His wife and child went, however Tun Lin Kyaw did not. He got more actively involved in politics for a while but after six months he followed them and then moved back and forth between the village and Yangon. As his child got older, he began to observe some changes; it became easier, he said, likely referencing the gradual opening towards democracy initiated by the military regime at this time. He spoke of how he again became more active and got involved enlightening and educating people, in some ways echoing the language he used to describe the speak and run tactics of his early activism as a student. It was at this time that his political allies proposed he stand for election. He could not contain his excitement and could not resist the call. By this time his son was around seven years old and so he negotiated with his wife and she agreed he should stand and so, at the end of 2014, he went to Yangon to fill in the candidate form. At this point he poignantly showed me a photo of the family.

Tun Lin Kyaw had become very excited, at this stage of the interview, in stark contrast to how he had sounded at the time when he mentioned his brother's death. He went on to speak of how during the 2015 national election campaigning he spoke very angrily and passionately because "they have oppressed us for many years and have done many bad things to us. When I speak I am pouring out..." he said. This marks the crescendo of his narrative: all the excitement with which he began the interview is back as he speaks about his voice pouring out on the campaign trail. Finally, the conditions are right for his anger and passion to be displayed and put to use. This corresponds with his move from underground to overground, from invisible to visible, and from the confines of the private sphere in the country to the public sphere of the city.

Tun Lin Kyaw had begun the interview enthusiastically and I had been immediately struck by his passion framed as it was by the photos on the wall. But as he had described what was a 24-year hiatus in his political activism his tone had saddened, reflective of how his voice was quietened and his body and spirit fatigued.

This tale can be characterised as one of the honing of a political consciousness forged through activism; hostility to a government he perceived as failing the people; incarceration; and post-prison adjustment.[9] It's the story of a journey from student activism under conditions of repression, to family life under similar circumstances, to a re-immersion in politics within a slowly changing political landscape. Tun Lin Kyaw's early political activism was limited to agitation and awareness-raising. After his ten-year incarceration (and his expulsion from the party) he limited himself to moral support rather than full involvement. Only very slowly as his child got older and the socio-political climate changed did he rediscover his drive to "open people's eyes". And only when the call came in 2014 to submit candidacy papers and run for office did his full passion re-emerge.

This account teaches us something of what matters and under what conditions things came to matter for one particular figure under changing carceral conditions through changing times. Carceral legacies infuse the account. We see the prison, mentioned only cursorily, that left Tun Lin Kyaw sick and tired and grieving. The relative absence of the concrete prison is striking but we might also note the salience of other sites of constraint: the bus-stop where he "spoke and ran", the home and neighbourhood where he and his family were harassed, and the village where he sought refuge. We can also identify carceral practices beyond the prison and his everyday life: the isolationism of government that left the country lagging behind its neighbours and its people at its mercy; we can think of the surveillance, control, harassment, and the threats of eviction and imprisonment that set limits and informed life choices. And we can note the climate of fear and suspicion as well as the sense of constraint that curtailed his activism and thwarted his passion.

Constraints and limits also feature strongly in the second narrative I will present and discuss.

REPOSSESSING TIME

My interview with Aung Kyaw Hlaing, a Yangon regional parliament member, took place in a restaurant rather than a living room but was no less personal for that. In the tale, as I reconstruct it below, we learn about two fundamental themes, one pertaining to the times in which people in Myanmar have lived and people's relative value in those times, and the second about the almost casual inevitability of his drift into politics. These themes emerge from an account featuring tales of hardship, sacrifice, duty and loyalty that begins as a tale of youthful frustration and anger at the lack of job opportunities.

Aung Kyaw Hlaing never expected to go into politics but his disenchantment with the way the country was governed stretches back a long way. It was in 1981, as a young adult, that he first identified a driving desire to overthrow the one-party system under which he observed Myanmar suffered for twenty-six years.[10] The suffering of Myanmar was represented in the narrative by his own struggles as a young person to find his way in life and carve out a career pathway. In a sense, he personifies the country's struggle. He described how under the socialist party everything was ruled by the party and party personnel. There was no chance to get work, no opportunities for people not members of the socialist party. However skilled or well-qualified one was, party-listed people would get the jobs. Aung Kyaw Hlaing emphasised, with very specific examples, that it was not his lack of knowledge that prohibited him but his non-party status. He expressed very strong emotions at not being able to bribe high-ranking officials as he applied for every job available saying, "whenever I think about it at the time, I got very angry, I wanted to kill people."

Resentment and frustration were key themes in the early part of the interview whereas the latter part featured a lighter tone and much laughter. In fact, there was even some laughter as the early part of the conversation concluded and we talked of how even when right, one could be wrong, in a situation where the common catchphrase of recruiters was "*kan ma pyaw nè*" (don't speak if not told to); "*khaing ta lôk*" (work as ordered); and "*kaw yin la*" (come when called).[11] This authoritarian mantra had certainly caused him offence as a young man, rendering his complaints mute.

Most striking was his account of how those in power would say dismissively "when your time comes do whatever you want. Now is our time." This is both poignant phrasing and a stark statement of control and entitlement. The authorities believed that the time belonged to them and that the system would endure, he explained. But Aung Kyaw Hlaing believed eventually the system would change, though it is unclear from where his hope sprang.

The structure of the tale is instructive. Having begun with 1981 as the marker of his sense of hostility to the regime he proceeded to ground this sense of hostility in the pre-history of the 1960s referring back to the coup of March 2 1962; the nationalisation of industry of 1964; the seizure of public property, as well as government experts' attempts to distract attention from real problems. He also specifically flagged the UN's inclusion (in December 1987) of Burma in the list of least developed countries, as a precursor to the 88 movement. He became involved at the frontline of the 88 movement. And while he clearly identified 1981 as the beginning of his overt desire to oppose the regime, Aung Kyaw Hlaing's move to the frontline is not presented as a radical awakening but rather a slow dawn. "If you were in my place would you not go?" he asked rhetorically implying, as in many places in the conversation, that his activism came naturally. I asked whether he was a leader in the 88 movement. His response was non-committal and modest. In his own words:

> Protests were nationwide... 40 million population... all came onto the street; even transgender people who came out as a group; each department came out, even police were protesting, people from hospitals, young people, student unions and student councils. I did not lead all these people, but my role was a leading role.

Interestingly, Aung Kyaw Hlaing does not sharply distinguish between himself and those he led. He was simply one of many, though one with a particular role. On 28 September 1988, the day after the founding of the NLD, he became a party member registering at 44 University Avenue, firm in the belief that the leaders could "change our politics".

Aung Kyaw Hlaing had no political ambitions when joining the party but he had longed as a citizen for a genuine democracy and saw it as his duty as a citizen to help bring that about. That was what led him to join and ultimately to run for election. I asked, why him, suggesting that not everyone who has a sense of duty ends up fulfilling it through political office but once again he played down any sense of drama about this. He did however emphasise that it was not a given outcome. It was a result of the sacrifices he made between 1988 and 2010, his "non-stop work for the party" and his "loyalty to party, colleagues and to self". What did he do for the party? What kind of sacrifices? I ask.

> I talked to people, formed committees, formed offices around the country, with signboards of party; tried to raise public awareness about party policy and principles of democracy and contrasting dictatorship with democracy.

Contrasting the early part of the interview when his persistent search for work was never rewarded, he reiterated that "in a dictatorship you will not get what you work for". On the other hand, he continued, "In a democracy you get the fruit you have worked for".

As if reminded of his own introductory remarks he returned to the theme of his younger self, weaving incidents from the more distant past into narratives of later times, describing again how it was impossible to get a job:

> Even if I sell ice on the street the dictatorship would ask for my property to be grabbed... My family were always intimidated by the government. I had friends who worked in different government departments but if I had gone to them they would have been dismissed. We were considered the fruit that is not good to eat.

Aung Kyaw Hlaing went on to describe how one could be arrested without doing any wrong without proper evidence, mentioning his five arrests and how his four children were left alone with their mother. "What would they eat while I, as sole bread winner, am arrested? This is the sacrifice. If this is not sacrifice what is sacrifice?"

The above narrative can be interpreted as essentially about how Aung Kyaw Hlaing moved from a situation where it was not "his time", to a situation where his time finally came, from a situation characterised by no opportunities and little sense of value to a situation where he became able to contribute to the creation of an anticipated flourishing democracy. Pointing in this direction is the image of the rotten or unripe fruit. His description of how he and others opposed to the regime were considered as the fruit that were not good to eat, but came to occupy a position where the fruits of democracy could be harvested is a potent image of gradual transition. In a democracy, as he explained, there is the opportunity to harvest the fruit one has worked towards. This contrasts with his experience living under dictatorship when even when qualified he was denied access to the potential fruit of his own actions. When analysed in this way, this account documents a journey from rotten/unripe, unworthy and disenfranchised to loyal participating citizen. This time is Aung Kyaw Hlaing's time and he is no longer a fruit that is not good to eat but a gardener in the democratic orchard. Along similar lines, in another interview, Myo Min Naing described to me how it was a belief that futures were lost (but might be regained) that informed his involvement in student union activities as strategist, implementer and later youth leader, after the events of August 1988.

One of the most striking facets of the interview material is the way in which lives and voices were repeatedly interrupted as Tun Lin Kyaw and Aung Kyaw Hlaing and others made their way towards a position in the world of formal politics. Even looking back over relatively long periods of time (often decades) the interviewees do not offer smooth, airbrushed accounts of early aspirations being met or ambition fulfilled. Rather the interviews in the main are stilted tales of multiple interruptions. Careers and family lives were put on hold, or never got started; university education was disrupted and sometimes only completed decades later. At the level of the everyday, lives were interrupted through actively participating and organising protests and strikes, secretly distributing pamphlets and posters, speaking out and recruiting activists, being harassed, arrested and imprisoned, being forced underground, joining or leaving a political party and so on. Sacrifices were made; bonds of loyalty created and sustained. The interviews then offer glimpses of lives disrupted but they are never purely negative; they are productive. Prison, at least for those who survived it, was in some ways educative, in some ways provided "family", and for some contributed to future career pathways.[12] So, I hesitate to characterise the interruptions and disruptions as rupture per se, that is as only an expression of brokenness (*rup* etymologically means break). The prefixes *inter*[13] and *dis*[14] are important. The breaks the interviewees speak about are not voids, gaps, abysses or black holes into which they and their lives disappeared. They have rather the nature of temporal markers in the narratives, signifying a shift from one mode of life to another. They are links as much as breaks and as such imply continuity as much as discontinuity.

Dates can be seductive to the analyst. They seem so concrete; they serve potentially to fix a narrative temporally, to bring some order to a tale. On some occasions during the interviews I reacted with astonishment at what seemed like extremely long periods of time spent in prison. But mostly if someone told me they were in prison from say 1989–1996 and 1999–2007 I simply failed to grasp what this calendrical marker might mean in experiential terms.[15] As I began to try to draw up timelines of journeys into politics such periods appeared as more or less empty. And yet as I revisited the narratives I realised this would be a faulty characterisation. Time in prison was clearly not, or not only, a "pause or break in continuity in a sequence or activity";[16] for these men it was in fact a formative time that not everybody expressed regret about. Another parliamentarian, Hla Myo Myint, described, for example, how his time in prison (twenty years over a twenty-three-year period) was his time "in politics". For him the protest movement, the prison experience, and later the party (NLD) were all part of doing politics. In his narrative it is not distinctions that stand out, but fusions. For example, being in prison was being political and being a member of the party was not that different from being part of the movement. He is now able to speak out within the parliament whereas previously he had only been able to protest outside, but the theme of speaking, of voice, is strong and consistent in both settings. This tale also emphasises continuity. Twenty years out of a twenty-three-year period might be understood as a kind of hiatus but for him this time was his time of political education, a time in which his horizon was broadened rather than narrowed

In another interview, Ni Aung Thein documented a journey from what we might call amateur to professional, a shift from uninformed student activism to educated political action. At one point Ni Aung Thein noted the value of the informal apprenticeship of the underground movement and reflected explicitly on the benefits of prison for his political subjectification: "For six years as a student activist I did not know what politics was. I never regret living in prison because living in prison changed my life and my thoughts". At age eleven, he reported, he participated in the protests of 1988 "shouting this and that but I knew nothing about politics". So, for Hla Myo Myint and Ni Aung Thein prison does not break time, it does not discontinue their history, it does not take them out of time. Prison time becomes incorporated into the history – not necessarily in an orderly, optimal fashion but nevertheless it becomes a part of a trajectory; it makes a contribution to the moulding of subjects, potentially changing their modes of participation in future non-carceral practices though in non-determined ways.

ATTITUDES TO PRISON TODAY

One way I thought prison might have changed those with whom I spoke was with regard to their attitudes to punishment and the role of prison in society. Somewhat naively, I now realise, I expected attitudes to punishment to be somehow related to or informed by harsh experiences of imprisonment such that a critique of imprisonment might emerge. But there was little evidence of any kind of desire to revolutionise the criminal justice system despite personal experience of injustice and suffering. The interview with Tun Lin Kyaw is instructive in this regard.

As already noted, Tun Lin Kyaw was arrested and imprisoned five times and I was interested to learn about what his time in prison might mean for his views on imprisonment today. His point of departure was that during the dictatorship prison was used for political prisoners, whereas under conditions of rule of law prisons should be reserved for proper criminals. Of course, it is not true that prisons were exclusively used for political prisoners during the dictatorship; there were other types of prisoners too, but a relatively common distinction between political prisoners and (other kinds of) law breakers is explicit here. He elaborated on how under conditions of rule of law the purpose of prison should be to correct the offender, implying the necessity of a just justice system rather than the one that he faced which involved the police arriving at his home and planting false evidence. Like many of the interviewees he did not elaborate much on his experience in prison, stating: "If I am to talk about the situation at Insein it will take seven days". Thus, it was not a part of his experience that was deliberately silenced; rather there was simply too much to tell.

I asked, probably somewhat sceptically, whether he believed prisons are important in a democratic society and he replied that many democratic countries, USA, UK, France, Switzerland, Italy, for example, have prisons. He threw the question back at me: are prisons not needed for rapists and murderers? I hesitated before replying with a question about whether he could ever imagine a world where prison was not necessary. "Why are prisons everywhere?" I asked. He laughed and began to explain patiently how if everyone felt equally obliged to follow the law there would be no need for prison but, he asked, "can everyone follow the law?" And, invoking potent international references he asked what we would do with "the Taliban, Bin Laden, ISIS, etc. without prisons". He laughed again. He seemed to think the idea of a world without prisons was ridiculous. Religion too was invoked in support of the prison:

> Every person adheres to some kind of religion. We are not so powerful as Gods. The Gods proscribe certain behavior, but still rules are broken. Criminal activity is universal. If everyone follows what they believe, if they follow their own Scripture, we wouldn't need prison...

The lesson is clear: in a perfect world prison would not be needed but that world is not here and not now. Three central arguments are used to push back against my apparently ridiculous hints that prison might be unnecessary: we need prisons for a. the worst types of criminals; b. terrorists/enemies of the state/threats to civilization, and c. because laws will always be broken/crime is universal. These are universalist tropes for justifying prison. And yet it is not the case that his own specific experience has played no role in his contemporary perspective:

"Are your views on prison affected by your own experience in prison?", I asked directly. "Yes", he answered, "because we call prison as hell; we have experienced prisons and we don't want others to suffer like us, so my view on prison changed. Prison should be a correctional training centre."

So, his experience has indeed affected his view of prison. They should be used for correction, that is for more than just punishment or containment.

In fact, most answers to questions about the role of prison in society parroted relatively well-rehearsed discourses on criminal justice from other parts of the world: prisons are a necessary part of dealing with crime, a key instrument of criminal justice. They are needed for the worst of the worst. Or they should be correctional centres, places where criminals can be rehabilitated and learn skills and be prepared for life back in society. The prison was taken for granted. Experience of prison, even terrible experiences, did not result in any radical questioning of the place or role of prison in society. If there was rule of law, or if people lived according to law, it was claimed, we would not need prison.[17] There was little evidence of the idea of crime as a social and political construction. Their own experience at the hands of the criminal justice system has not led to a questioning of its legitimacy, only perhaps the legitimacy of the regime misusing it. There is no radical disavowal of the prison evident in the material, rather a taken-for-grantedness, an assumption of its necessity, which is in fact a rather universal assumption. This seems to be informed by a clear operational distinction between the reasons political prisoners were in prison and the reasons criminals were in prison. While they had been charged and convicted of crimes under law they did not identify as or with criminals. But while here we do seem to find evidence of the work of distinction rather than the development of solidarity between imprisoned people, the rather orthodox attitudes expressed can also be seen as expressions of continuity. To embrace a relatively orthodox position on the role of the prison is consistent with accounts of lives where ordinariness and everydayness trump incidents of high drama and radicalism.[18]

CONCLUSION: MYANMAR LIVES

The ambiguity of this sub-heading is deliberately alluding both to the fact that this chapter has been about people's lives but also that the country does in fact live. Myanmar is alive and on the move. Lives are rarely problem-free or smooth; they are rather, laced with contention, friction and conflict. To live is to struggle, we might say. The lives of the formerly imprisoned politicians I had the privilege to interview bear witness to this. They also bear witness to the way struggle is always situated within ongoing trajectories where local and historical time is not carved up or broken but woven together as people and the country move through and in time as new possibilities for becoming emerge.

This chapter has considered the "making up" of people (Hacking 1986), that is, the way the parliamentarians came to be who and where they are today as well as the way intimate identities are redrawn via subjects' embodied participation in changing – and often contentious – social practice. Additionally, I have observed how lives, like institutions, both persist and mutate as they unfold and the world slowly changes with and around them.

I have focused on individuals' stories but these are also socio-political stories. The analysis has been person-centred but the material and analysis have implications for how we think not only about subject-making but also about state-making and history-making. As Jean Lave and Dorothy Holland (2001) have argued, "intimate identities" and "enduring struggles" are mutually constitutive. The implication is that we should resist the language of rupture to talk about the ongoing socio-political shifts in Myanmar, but further work is clearly required to consider more intensively the implications of thinking in terms of links rather than breaks in the context of the country's ongoing trajectory.

The interweaving of different types of disruption and interruption demonstrated in this chapter confirms the need for an approach to research on "Living in Myanmar" that traces personal and socio-political trajectories beyond single sites. It is not the space of prison (the cell) and the space of politics (parliament) but the development of a penal and political consciousness across and through and beyond such spaces (in and through time) that should be of interest and hence recommends itself for ongoing and future study. The eight accounts I gathered all attest to the fact that prison experience is somehow incorporated into people's life experience. The prison experience is woven into narratives about journeys into politics. This is to say that lives are not made sense of by reference to singular events or experiences alone. This suggests we should avoid granting undue weight to singular events (positive or negative) in our explanations of the changing political landscape too.

To close I would like to draw attention back to the almost incidental remark made by Tun Lin Kyaw as he observed how as his son got older he began to notice what he referred to as "some changes; things got easier". The world had changed. But there had been no rupture, no "sense of an ending" (Grounds and Jamieson 2003). There is no justification to be found in this narrative (or the others) for grand claims about political revolution or a radical transformation. Rather what we see is a slow mutation, a subtle changing of circumstances, that enabled this particular individual to reconnect with his earlier political identity as an active activist. His story and the other stories I have drawn on in this chapter are tales of struggle. The struggle continues. My hope is that the analysis shared in this chapter might help us to better understand and make sense of the way people in Myanmar forge lives and futures under their so often highly compromised and politically charged circumstances, and how we might understand the changes occurring in the country as time changes hands. By so doing I hope to have made a modest contribution to a reinvigorated critical Myanmar studies that foregrounds agency, interaction and everyday life, as intimated at the start of this chapter.

Notes

1 See https://legacies-of-detention.org/ (accessed 28 May 2020)._I wish to acknowledge the role played by Liv Gaborit and Tomas Martin in the conceptualisation of the research project and its ongoing implementation. Ideas developed here owe much to ideas initially germinated in collaboration. I also thanks members of the JFA team for helping facilitate access and Kyaw Lin Naing for interpretation. Additionally, I'm grateful to Justine Chambers and an anonymous reviewer for insightful editorial comments. A very early version of this chapter was presented in Birmingham UK at the second annual conference for Carceral Geography in December 2017. The work is supported by a research grant from the Danish Foreign Ministry.

2 Much has been written about the challenges of doing prisons research often with a focus on the negotiation of access, and the presentation of self under conditions over which the researcher does not have full control (Drake et al 2015, Jefferson 2015, Jewkes 2014 Liebling 1999, Rhodes 2001, Rowe 2014). The Legacies project was designed in such a way that while access to prison was desirable (and was achieved by Liv Gaborit and Tomas Martin) it was not essential. Much can be learned about prison life from a distance. Applying an ethnographic sensibility and settling for the 'closest possible vantage point' is an option when a prison presence is not possible. See Gaborit (In Press) for a fuller discussion of this in relation to Myanmar.

3 Cheesman follows Mouffe (1993) and Chakrabarty (2002) in distinguishing between politics and the political in this fashion.

4 The notion of 'prison as prism' points to the fact that prisons are vital loci of the state-subject relationship and that analyses of them can serve as an important lens on social and political practices more generally.

5 Of specific note, but beyond the scope of this chapter, is their call for a 'democratisation of *thinking*' about politics (my emphasis) and their quite circumspect descriptions of the changes that have taken place since 2011.

6 Nyein Thiri Swei and Zaw Min Oo (this volume) claim that styles of political representation depend on political background, understandings of representation and individual capacity, implying an interest in the intersection between personal narratives and political action.

7 Undoubtedly, I was seduced by this idea when I devised this preliminary study.

8 All names are pseudonyms.

9 This post-prison adaptation involved both changing personal circumstances and changing political circumstances.

10 It is likely no coincidence that 1981 was the year of a general election that saw the sole legal party, the Burma Socialist Programme Party re-elected.

11 I'm grateful to Nick Cheesman and Kyaw Lin Naing for linguistic clarification here.

12 A cautionary note is necessary here: this is a select group of former prisoners, a group each of whom had the skills, personal resources and connections to end up as candidates in elections and to be voted (or in one case appointed) into a position of authority. There are many who did not survive and many whose experience of imprisonment had overwhelmingly negative consequences.

13 Defined at https://www.dictionary.com/browse/inter- as 'a prefix occurring in loanwords from Latin, where it meant "between," "among," "in the midst of," "mutually," "reciprocally," "together," "during" (intercept; interest).

14 Defined at https://www.dictionary.com/browse/dis- as "a Latin prefix meaning 'apart,' 'asunder,' 'away,' 'utterly,' or having a privative, negative, or reversing force".

15 See in this connection the forthcoming dissertation of Liv Gaborit that addresses the experiences of former prisoners in Myanmar based on extensive fieldwork.

16 Source: www.dictionary.com

17 See Cheesman (2015) on the long-sheld conflation between rule of law and law and order in Myanmar

18 A deeper analysis of legislators' perspectives on punishment as well as public perceptions of punishment (and justice) would be a valuable future endeavour.

References

Chakrabarty, D. (2002). "The In-Human and the Ethical in Communal Violence". In *Habitations of Modernity: Essays in the Wake of Subaltern Studies*. Chicago & London: University of Chicago Press.

Chambers, J., McCarthy, G., Farrelly, N., and Chit Win (eds) (2018). *Myanmar Transformed? People, Places, Politics*. Singapore: ISEAS–Yusof Ishak Institute.

Cheesman, N. (2015). *Opposing the Rule of Law: How Myanmar's Courts Make Law and Order*. Cambridge: Cambridge University Press.

_____ (2016). "Myanmar and the Promise of the Political". In *Conflict in Myanmar: War, Politics, Religion*, edited by N. Cheesman and N. Farrelly. Singapore: Institute of Southeast Asian Studies.

Cheesman, N. and Farrelly, N. (eds) (2016). *Conflict in Myanmar: War, Politics, Religion*. Singapore: Institute of Southeast Asian Studies.

Cheesman, N., Farrelly, N. and Wilson, T. (eds) (2014). *Debating Democratization in Myanmar*. Singapore: Institute of Southeast Asian Studies.

Cheesman, N., Skidmore, M. and Wilson, T. (eds) (2012). *Myanmar's Transition: Openings, Obstacles and Opportunities*. Singapore: Institute of Southeast Asian Studies.

Crouch, M. and Lindsey, T. (2014). *Law, Society and Transition in Myanmar*. Oxford and Portland, Oregon: Hart Publishing.

Crouch, M. (2016) "Legislating Reform? Law and Conflict in Myanmar", in Cheesman, N. and Farrelly, N. (eds.) *Conflict in Myanmar: War, Politics, Religion*. Singapore: Institute of Southeast Asian Studies.

Drake, D., Earle, R. and Sloan, J. (eds) (2015). *The Palgrave Handbook of Prison Ethnography. Houndmills*. Basingstoke: Palgrave Macmillan: 169–186.

Dreier, O. (2003). *Subjectivity and Social Practice*. Aarhus: Center for Health, Humanity, and Culture, Department of Philosophy, University of Aarhus.

Egreteau, R. (2017). *Parliamentary Development in Myanmar: An Overview of the Union Parliament 2011–2016*. Yangon: Asia Foundation.

Egreteau, R. and Robinne, F. (eds) (2016). *Metamorphosis. Studies in Social and Political Change in Myanmar*. Singapore: NUS Press.

Egreteau, R. and Joelene, C. (2018). "Legislature". In *Routledge Handbook of Contemporary Myanmar*, edited by A. Simpson, N. Farrelly and I. Holliday. Oxford: Routledge.

Gaborit, L.S. (2019), "Looking Through the Prison Gate: Access in the Field of Ethnography". In *Cadernos Pagu 55*. Available at https://doi.org/10.1590/18094449201900550005 (accessed 29 July 2020).

Grounds, A. and Jamieson, R. (2003). "No Sense of an Ending: Researching the Experience of Imprisonment among Republican Ex-Prisoners". *Theoretical Criminology* 7 (3): 347–362.

Hacking, I. (1986). "Making Up People". In *Reconstructing Individualism: Autonomy, Individuality and the Self in Western Thought* , edited by T. Heller et al. Stanford: Stanford University Press, 161–171.

_____ (2002). *Historical Ontology.* Cambridge, MA: Harvard University Press.

Holland, D. and Lave, J. (eds) (2001). *History in Person. Enduring Struggles, Contentious Practice, Intimate Identities.* Santa Fe, Oxford: SAR Press, James Currey.

Holliday, I. and Su Mon Thazin Aung (2018). "The Executive". In *Routledge Handbook of Contemporary Myanmar,* edited by A. Simpson, N. Farrelly and I. Holliday. Oxford: Routledge.

Jefferson, A.M. (2015). "Performing Ethnography: Infiltrating Prison Spaces". In *The Palgrave Handbook of Prison Ethnography,* edited by D.H. Drake, R. Earle and J. Sloan. Basingstoke: Palgrave Macmillan, 169–186.

Jefferson, A.M., & Huniche, L. (2009). "(Re)Searching for Persons in Practice: Field-Based Methods for Critical Psychological Practice Research". *Qualitative Research in Psychology* 6 (1–2): 12–27.

Jewkes, Y. (2014). "An Introduction to 'Doing Prison Research Differently'". *Qualitative Inquiry* 20 (4): 387–391.

Lall, M. (2016). *Understanding Reform in Myanmar: People and Society in the Wake of Military Rule.* London: Hurst.

Lave, J. (2011). *Apprenticeship in Critical Ethnographic Practice.* Chicago: University of Chicago Press.

Liebling, A. (1999). "Doing Research in Prison: Breaking the Silence?" *Theoretical Criminology* 3: 147–173.

Martin, T.M., Bandyopadhyay, M. & Jefferson, A.M. (2014). "Sensing Prison Climates: Governance, Survival, and Transition". *Focaal - Journal of Global and Historical Anthropology* 68: 3–17.

Mbembe, A. (2001). *On the Postcolony.* Berkeley: University of California Press.

Mouffe, C. (1993). "Introduction: For an Agonistic Pluralism". In *The Return of the Political.* London & New York: Verso.

Rhodes, L. (2001). "Toward an Anthropology of Prisons". *Annual Review of Anthropology* 30: 65–83.

Rowe, A. (2014). "Situating the Self in Prison Research: Power, Identity, and Epistemology". *Qualitative Inquiry* 20 (4): 404–416.

Schatz, E. (ed.) (2009). *Political Ethnography: What Immersion Contributes to the Study of Power.* Chicago: University Of Chicago Press.

Shore, C., Wright, S. and Pero, D. (eds) (2011). *Policy Worlds: Anthropology and Analysis of Contemporary Power* Vol. 14 edition. New York: Berghahn Books.

Simpson, A., Farrelly, N. and Holliday, I. (eds) (2018). *Routledge Handbook of Contemporary Myanmar.* Oxford: Routledge.

Slater, D. (2014). "The Elements of Surprise: Assessing Burma's Double-Edged Détente". *South East Asia Research* 22 (2): 171–182.

Stepputat, F. and Larsen, J. (2015). "Global Political Ethnography: A Methodological Approach to Studying Global Policy Regimes". *DIIS Working Paper* 01.

Stokke, K., Khine Win and Soe Myint Aung (2015). "Political Parties and Popular Representation in Myanmar's Democratisation Process". *Journal of Current Southeast Asian Affairs* 34 (3): 3–35.

Wittekind, T. and Rhoades, E. (2018). "Rethinking Land and Property in a 'Transitioning' Myanmar: Representations of Isolation, Neglect, and Natural Decline". *Journal of Burma Studies* 22 (2): 171213.

III

Economic Life

5

MACRO-FINANCIAL REFORMS IN MYANMAR UNDER THE NLD: PLANS, PROGRESS AND PROSPECTS

Sean Turnell and Nyein Ei Cho

For much of its modern history, an unstable macro-economy has been Myanmar's constant companion. Excessive extractions from the State, mostly as a consequence of the resource demands of the country's security organs, fuelled persistent and growing budget deficits, rising debt, price inflation and monetary instability, a dysfunctional (and crisis-prone) financial system, and an insatiable dependence on the money-printing of Myanmar's central bank. Of course, many other economic maladies plagued Myanmar under its five decades of military rule, but foundational to all of them was this inherent macro-financial instability.

Given this, and understanding its consequences, the civilian government that took office in Myanmar in March 2016 assigned to the task of achieving macro-financial stability a priority that transcended other economic policy objectives. Accordingly, from its first year in office public spending across just about all sectors of the economy was trimmed, revenue enhancement policies introduced, restrictions imposed on borrowing from the central bank, the exchange rate fully liberalised, and the foundations laid for the full funding of budget deficits via a functioning bond market. Meanwhile, in an effort to bring stability to the banking sector – and to finally transform it into a mechanism for the proper aggregation and allocation of capital – various prudential banking regulations were introduced, along with other measures designed to stimulate competition and expand product offerings.

Of course, policy intentions and successful policy *implementation* are very separate things, and not all of the reforms outlined above have brought about the results hoped for or, indeed, been free of opposition (explicit or otherwise). Accordingly, in this chapter we not only outline the policies introduced under the National League for Democracy (NLD) government since 2016, but explore the extent that they have achieved the ends sought. Finding that stability in macro-financial terms has been largely achieved, at least in the short term, the paper concludes both with an account of a reassessment on the need for a mild fiscal stimulus in Myanmar, and some thoughts on the longer term macro-financial challenges.[1]

PLANNING FOR STABILITY

Stabilising Myanmar's chronically unstable macro-economy was foundational in the economic policy planning of the NLD-led government that took office in March 2016. This was reflected in the NLD's election manifestos, the brief "12 Point" policy program released soon after the government took office and then, much more comprehensively, in the government's "Myanmar Sustainable Development Plan" (MSDP) that was published in August 2018 (but in effect on the macro front much before then).[2] In the MSDP, the quest for macroeconomic stability was given broad expression in its Goal 2, "Economic Stability and Strengthened Macroeconomic Management", Goal 3, "Job Creation and Private Sector-Led Growth", and more specifically in subsequent strategies to:

- Effectively manage the exchange rate and balance of payments (Strategy 2.1)
- Reduce inflation and maintain monetary stability (Strategy 2.2)
- Increase domestic revenue mobilisation through a fair, efficient and transparent taxation system (Strategy 2.3)
- Strengthen public financial management to support stability and the efficient allocation of public resources (Strategy 2.4)

- Enhance the efficiency and competitiveness of State Economic Enterprises (Strategy 2.5)
- Increase broad-based access to financial services and strengthen the financial system overall (Strategy 3.5)

Reigning in excessive government spending was an early policy objective of the NLD Government, a fact that was reflected in its first Budget after coming into office in March 2016, and in every budget since. As Table 5.1 below reveals, Myanmar's budget deficit dramatically declined in the 2016/17 financial year, and has maintained a distinctly parsimonious stance throughout the government's tenure.[3]

Table 5.1: Government spending, revenues and budget deficit

	2015/16	2016/17	2017/18	2018/19	2019/20*
Government Exp. (%GDP)	23.9	21.3	19.7	20.7	21.2
Tax Revenue (%GDP)	6.1	6.5	6.7	7.0	7.2
Total Government Revenue (%GDP)	19.5	18.8	17.1	17.3	17.4
Budget Deficit (%GDP)	-4.3	-2.5	-2.7	-3.5	-3.8

Source: * IMF (2019a)

Table 5.1 also reveals that the source of Myanmar's fiscal turnaround is not just a function of much tighter spending (which reached a low point in 2017/18, but remains in the latest financial year well below previous government benchmarks), but also from greater tax revenue across the period. The latter phenomenon, a function of certain critical tax reforms (some of which, such as the creation of the Large Taxpayers' Office, are the work of the previous Thein Sein administration), partially offsets falls in other government revenue sources, but especially income from state-owned enterprises (SOEs). With the notable (but unreliable) exception of the Myanmar Oil and Gas Enterprise (MOGE), Myanmar's SOEs have long been a serious drain on the country's finances. Dramatic reform of such entities, manifest in some important personnel moves in August 2019, has become an elevated government priority.[4]

Yet, and notwithstanding the growth of tax revenue in Myanmar in recent years, comprehensive taxation reform in Myanmar remains both an urgent need but a work-in-progress. At just over 7 per cent of GDP, Myanmar is one of the lowest taxing countries in the world. Policies to address this have been rolled out since 2016, including (in 2019) the dull-sounding but critically important Tax Administration Law, under which a range of specific tax changes have been given legal force. Meanwhile, a tax reform unit was established within the Internal Revenue Department (IRD), members of which are working on a number of initiatives, including the transformation of Myanmar's commercial tax arrangements (along the way to something resembling a Value Added Tax, VAT), the introduction of more comprehensive income tax arrangements (which nonetheless would exempt the vast bulk of Myanmar's working population), and the implementation of a uniform (revenue) tariff to replace the myriad of bespoke tariffs that presently raise little revenue, even as they distort prices and resource allocation. Naturally, taxation policy in every country involves overtly political calculations, and in this Myanmar is no exception. Accordingly, and despite the heroic efforts of some policy-makers, progress on this front might be expected to be moderate, especially in the lead-up to the November 2020 elections.

Finally, on the spending side of the equation the tighter purse-strings have also been accompanied by changes in structural allocations. Defence spending across the period of the NLD government (2016 to the present) rose in nominal terms by just 2.9 per cent which, inflation adjusted, represents a reduction in such spending in real terms. By contrast, spending on education (up 34.3 per cent across the same period) and health (up 30.4 per cent) have considerably increased their share of overall government allocations, in both nominal and real terms.[5] Of course, in both of these areas such increased spending comes atop a very low base. Myanmar for a long time was one of the few countries in the world that spent more on its military than education and health combined, and thus spending in both of these areas – critical to "human capital" formation as well as fundamental concerns of equity and justice – continues to fall well short of need.

LOOSENING UP

For a variety of reasons, but prominent among which included the political and human rights regression in Rakhine State and other locations (that greatly deterred foreign investment, especially from the "West"), economic growth in Myanmar slowed in 2017. While still high by global standards (Myanmar remained throughout amongst the fastest growing economies in the world), the retrenchment in growth amidst the increasingly successful efforts in fiscal restraint caused something of a rethink – and a decision to engage in a mildly expansionary fiscal policy, primarily via increased capital expenditure, and guided through the creation of the so-called "Project Bank".[6] A mechanism to prioritise infrastructure according to socio-economic returns and financial sustainability, the Project Bank's establishment was an effort to bring sound economics, as well as environmental and social considerations, into a process that hitherto had been little more than random and arbitrary. Likewise, however, it was also an effort to deliver a boost to growth – both directly in terms of greater government spending, and indirectly via the "crowding in" of facilitating private investment, and (hoped-for) elevated private sector efficiencies and profits.[7]

Significantly, this stimulus enjoyed the support of the World Bank and the IMF – the latter noting that "fiscal policy should aim at promoting spending to achieve the Sustainable Development goals", while maintaining progress in the elimination of CBM money-financing, as well as accelerating taxation reforms for greater revenue mobilisation.[8] The World Bank noted likewise in its June 2019 assessment of Myanmar's economy, while noting that the Project Bank offered medium to long-term benefits via "improved quality of project entry, greater transparency, and possibly providing medium-term budgetary commitments to execute priority projects" (World Bank 2019, 36).[9]

Electricity tariff reform

Uniting both the need for on-going budgetary prudence, along with the creation of space for a mild fiscal stimulus, was the Myanmar Government's decision in June 2019 to increase electricity tariffs. Hitherto unchanged since 2014, and accounting for less than 60 per cent of generation and distribution costs, Myanmar's low (the lowest in the region) electricity tariff rates not only drove increasingly severe budget losses (an implicit subsidy in excess of over K1.2 trillion[10]), but were highly regressive.[11] Of course, set below cost such low tariffs were also a certain impediment to private sector investment in the sector – investment desperately needed if Myanmar's cities are ever to avoid the "blackouts" and "brownouts" still characteristic in many areas.

The June 2019 tariff increases resulted in increased electricity prices for consumers for usage above 30 kilowatt-hours (which jumped as much as 275 per cent – prices for consumption below 30 kilowatt hours remaining the same), as well as businesses (the tariffs on which increased, with no exceptions, by up to 66 per cent).[12] The saving to the national budget from the electricity price increases amounted to over K600 billion for the first year alone, with the "surplus" funds allocated to the 2019/20 budget to increase spending on health, education, and to repair and extend the national electricity grid itself.[13]

STOPPING THE PRINTING PRESSES, BUILDING A BOND MARKET

In the absence both of sufficient tax revenues or a bond market to otherwise finance Myanmar's budget deficits, for much of Myanmar's modern history recourse was made to borrowing from the central bank – in popular parlance, "printing money". Such an approach to public finance, more or less anywhere and everywhere historically, has been the fuel of inflation and monetary instability. This has certainly been the case in Myanmar, whose relatively high inflation rates (especially as compared to peers and neighbours in Southeast Asia) and volatile informal exchange rates was taken as a defining characteristic of its economy broadly.

To rectify this, and to eliminate what has been in essence the "original sin" of macro-economic policy making in Myanmar, early in its tenure the government revealed its timetable for the complete elimination of borrowing from the central bank:

Financial Year	CBM Financing Proportion of Budget Deficit
2017/18	30%
2018/19	20%
2019/20	10%
2020/21	0%

Meanwhile Table 5.2 reveals what actually happened:

Table 5.2: Central Bank, and bond financing

	2015/16	2016/17	2017/18	2018/19	2019/20
CBM Financing (%GDP)	22.3	8.7	3.5	0.8	0.4
Bonds Comp. Tender (% of total)	0	13.7	28.3	48.0	54.3

Source: CBM (2019), IMF (2019a)

Clearly the government has been running ahead of its financing reform timetable. That said, a certain flexibility with respect to the zero bound might be advisable. Public finance in Myanmar is not just chronically deficient; sources of revenue are also seasonally volatile and "lumpy", thus often requiring short-term fixes beyond that which can be covered by Treasury Bill sales (more on which below). Accordingly, and given the widespread acceptance globally for what is euphemistically called "quantitative easing", it might pay Myanmar not to be too doctrinaire on this front.

Of course, it is the growth of the bond market, but especially the competitive sale of such bonds to the private sector (by far the preferred, and least macro-disruptive of all the options for financing budget deficits) that is the most important in the "good" story of Myanmar's improving public financial management. As Table 5.2 reveals, such competitive sales now account for over half of all bonds sold, and it is a ratio that should only improve in the future given the opening up of Myanmar's insurance sector to new domestic and foreign entrants. Elsewhere in Southeast Asia (notably Vietnam), foreign life insurance companies (which build up through the course of their business ever-increasing local currency liabilities – that must be matched by stable local-currency assets – such as government securities) are the largest source of demand for government bond issues.[14] The latter is an almost unmatched example of the synergies between micro (particular market) and macro-economic reform.

Finally, lest concerns be raised that Myanmar's increasing use of bond-funding could lead to an excessive build-up of debt, Table 5.3 below reveals that the country's public indebtedness continues to be very mild.

Table 5.3: Myanmar's domestic and external public debt

	2015/16	2016/17	2017/18	2018/19	2019/20
Domestic Public Debt (%GDP)	20.5	20.9	20.9	21.5	22.5
External Public Debt (%GDP)	15.9	15.6	13.8	15.3	14.4

Source: CBM (2019), IMF (2019a)

EXCHANGE RATE REFORMS AND EXTERNAL PUBLIC DEBT

The highly divergent official and informal exchange rates of Myanmar's currency, the *Kyat,* were for many decades the most visible symbol of the country's economic mismanagement. For over four decades formally fixed in terms of the IMF's Special Drawing Rights at an effective exchange rate of around K6:$US1, informally the *Kyat* traded at rates many hundreds of times below this metric.[15] Of course, these informal rates were "illegal", but they were the only exchange rates that mattered to all but a handful of well-connected people who could buy foreign currency at the formal fixed exchange rate. In short, and beyond generating a machine of extraordinary opportunities for corruption, Myanmar's fixed exchange rate was, for long, an absurdist farce.

Much of this changed, however, in April 2012 when the Thein Sein government announced that henceforth the *Kyat* would be determined via a "managed float".[16] In practice still hemmed in by a number of restricting conditions, this decision nevertheless largely brought an end to Myanmar's dual exchange rate regime. Fully floating the *Kyat* came with the NLD government which, in April 2018, removed the trading band that had been part of the managed float apparatus, along with some other foreign exchange restrictions.[17] The move was then codified within the MSDP which, according to Strategy 2.1.1, asserted that what was needed was to "allow the *Kyat* to float more freely in response to market supply and demand'".

As can be seen in Figure 5.1, the market exchange rate of the *Kyat* (up until April 2012 the informal rate, afterwards a *unified* rate) has been volatile. This is not unexpected, and to a large extent is not anything to be particularly concerned about. As principally an energy and agricultural exporter, Myanmar's terms of trade are subject to the swings and roundabouts of global commodity prices, and an exchange rate that compensates for these (exchange rates of commodity-producing countries tend to move inversely to commodity prices) accordingly acts as something of a "cushion" to such movements in terms of trade revenues.

Noteworthy in Figure 5.1, however, was the particularly pronounced fall in the value of the *Kyat* across roughly the calendar year 2018. This prompted considerable press (and social media) commentary in Myanmar (much of it confused), but the phenomenon was very largely a global one

Figure 5.1: *Kyat*/$US1 (market) exchange rate

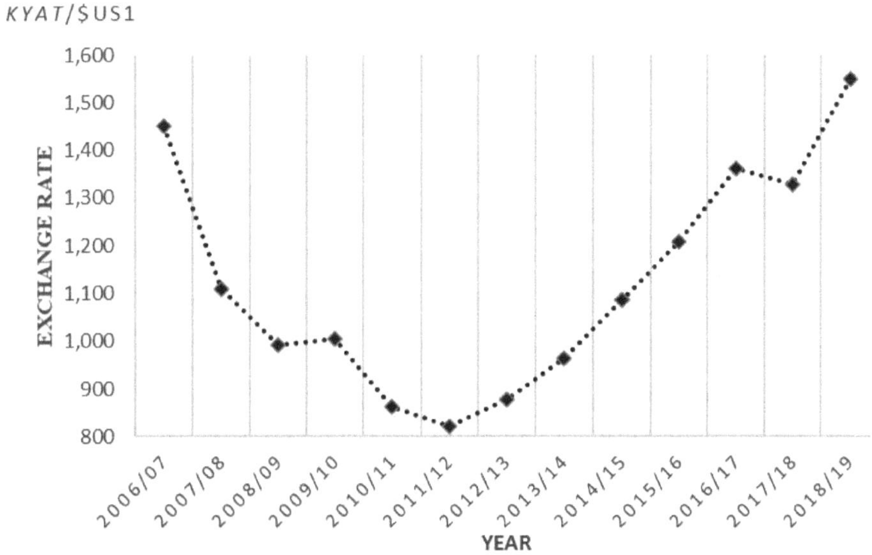

Source: IMF (2019a)

in that it was simultaneously experienced by most emerging and frontier market currencies in terms of their price against the US Dollar (indeed, in many ways the whole episode could more justifiably be described as a rise in the value of the $US, rather than a fall in other currencies). The *Kyat's* fall was slightly more pronounced than most (the *Kyat* fell by around 2–3 per cent more than peer currencies in the region), reflecting the country's higher perceived risk, political (reporting on the terrible events in Rakhine and elsewhere being at something of a peak at this time) as well as economic.

Of course, in the longer term, currencies tend to move according to their relative spending power, and thus reflect differential inflation rates. Accordingly, what might be described as the chronic weakness of the *Kyat* is a function of Myanmar's higher inflation compared to its peers and neighbours, and as compared to the US itself (Table 5.4). Naturally, all of this in turn underlines for yet more reasons the importance of prudent and plausible macro-financial management.

Table 5.4: Relative inflation rates, Consumer Price Index, end of period, (% change)

	2018	2019*
Cambodia	1.6	2.6
Indonesia	3.1	3.6
Myanmar	8.6	7.2
Thailand	0.4	1.9
United States	2.0	2.7
Vietnam	3.0	3.2
Emerging Economy Average	5.0	4.7

*As at October 2019 Source: IMF (2019b)

Meanwhile, Myanmar's external trade itself has remained remarkably strong, whatever the ups and downs of its exchange rate and other variables. As can be seen in Table 5.5, this improving performance (significantly driven by rising garment exports from Myanmar, primarily to Europe) drove Myanmar's current account deficit (which reflects income as well as trade flows) to historically low levels.

Table 5.5: Current Account Deficit (CAD/Foreign Direct Investment (FDI)

	2013/14	2014/15	2015/16	2016/17	2017/18	2018/19
CAD (%GDP)	-3.5	-6.2	-7.4	-5.5	-2.6	-1.8
FDI Approvals ($USm)	4097.1	8.010.5	9,486.1	6,649.8	5,718.1	3,548.2

*As at end July 2019. Sources: World Bank (2019, 2020), DICA (2019)

Less impressive has been the record of foreign direct investment (FDI). An area for unrealistically high expectations (and coming off never-to-be-repeated inflows from the sale of telecommunications licenses, 2014–2016), the violence and displacement in Rakhine and other places in Myanmar had a significantly dampening effect on FDI from the "West" especially, as investor cohorts were scared off at the prospect of possible renewed sanctions, consumer boycotts, and "brand damage" generally.[18] Myanmar's FDI had recovered somewhat by June 2019, with Singapore (over 60 per cent of the total) and greater China (mainland China and Hong Kong SAR) by far the largest investors (World Bank 2020, 26–27). In the longer term, the magnitudes of FDI to Myanmar will remain uncertain – boosted by possible factory relocations from China as a consequence of their "trade war" with the United States, and its rising labour costs, but also impeded by Myanmar's continuing conflicts and their international implications.

SAFEGUARDING THE BANKS

Implementing Basel

Myanmar's Financial Institutions Law, promulgated by the Thein Sein government in January 2016, was "state of the art" when it came to prudential bank regulation. This was no surprise perhaps, given that it was largely written by the World Bank. Yet, despite all this, bank regulation in Myanmar remained, in the absence of implementing regulations, both severely deficient and little more than a fig-leaf for practices as venerable as they were problematic for the stability of the financial system.

In July 2017, however, the Central Bank of Myanmar (CBM) issued (under Notifications 16-19/2017) four new prudential regulations designed to genuinely implement the Financial Institutions Law of 2016.[19] These four new regulations, consistent with international banking standards known as the "Basel Accords", covered capital requirements, asset classification and provisioning, large exposures, and liquidity ratios:

Capital adequacy (CBM Notification 16/2017)20

Ensuring that banks have sufficient capital (in essence owners' funds, or their "skin in the game") is the cornerstone of modern banking regulation. Expressed as a percentage of risk-weighted assets, the capital-to-assets ratio (CAR) was set in this Notification by the CBM at a minimum of 8 per cent overall. The CAR is divided into two tiers, however. Tier 1, which comprises the highest quality capital (in large part common equity) and which must be at least 4 per cent of risk-weighted assets, and Tier 2 or so-called "supplementary capital" (lesser quality and/or ess certain commitments of owners funds, usually via more esoteric financial instruments), which must not comprise more than 4 per cent of the overall CAR minimum.

On the denominator side, assets are classified (weighted) according to the risk of the counterparty granted the loan, or issuing the debt instrument. The default risk-weighting, accorded to general private sector or individual borrowers, is 100 per cent. Some assets enjoy lower risk weights, in accordance with generally accepted perceptions of risk (for example, claims on the central bank, claims on OECD governments, or loans backed by cash or gold bullion, enjoy a zero risk weighting – requiring no capital to be set aside).

Liquidity Ratio requirement (CBM Notification 19/2017)

Banks need to have liquid assets in sufficient quantities so that they can make payments when required. Liquid assets can take a number of forms, but the common feature they must share is that they can be readily converted into cash (currency) without undue loss or delay. Given Myanmar's long history of financial crises, ensuring that banks have sufficient liquidity is especially important. There is, after all, nothing quite so panic-inducing as a bank's apology to its customers that they have run out of money.

Notification 19/2017 declared that henceforth banks would have to maintain a Liquidity Ratio, expressed as the percentage of Net Liquid Assets as a proportion of Volatile Liabilities, of 20 per cent. This new Liquidity Ratio applying to Myanmar's banks was not regarded by the industry as controversial. Banks are required to report their liquidity position daily, and the new Liquidity Ratio came into immediate effect on 7 July 2017.

Large exposures regulation (Notification 18/2017)

Being exposed to any one borrower, or a related party of borrowers, is clearly dangerous for a bank should such counterparties default. Accordingly, banking regulators everywhere impose limits on the individual size and aggregate number of defined large exposures banks take on. In the past (under the Financial Institutions Law of 1990, for instance) Myanmar too has long had such large exposure limits. However, in this same past such limits were routinely ignored.

Notification 18/2017 imposed large exposure limits on Myanmar's banks – against a single counterparty or group of related counterparties – of no more than 10 per cent of core capital. This measure has not been seen as controversial, but in practice a number of Myanmar's banks remain in breach.

Asset classification and provisioning (CBM Notification 17/2018)

The regulations relating to asset classification and provisioning were the most contentious of the prudential measures announced in July 2017.

Taking up provisioning first (the less controversial component), the new requirements were once more rather standard and pedestrian – and designed simply to ensure that banks recognised loans and other assets that have become doubtful or "bad". These provisioning requirements (very much in keeping with international banking standards), were far tougher than the *practice* that has long prevailed in Myanmar, but were otherwise unremarkable.

More remarkable, in the context of Myanmar's banking environment, were sections 11 and 12 of Notification 17/2017, which touched upon an especially peculiar feature of Myanmar banking – that is, the overwhelming use of overdrafts as the primary mechanism through which credit has been granted. Driven by poorly designed (former) regulations that had long inhibited Myanmar's banks (regulations that prohibited banks from lending on terms of more than one year, and only on real-property as collateral), overdrafts made against real estate take up 75 per cent+ of the "typical" bank loan portfolio. Very short-term funding financing very long term assets, in short – and a recipe for trouble even in the best of contexts.

Notification 17 addressed this by applying three requirements (initially to be met within a year):

1. For two consecutive weeks every year, all overdrafts have to be repaid *in full*.
2. Should all or any part of such overdrafts not be repaid, then they must be classified as impaired, and provisioned accordingly.
3. Overdrafts that were *really* long-term loans in disguise (i.e., constantly revolving overdrafts) must be converted into term loans with a maximum maturity of three years. Interest payments on these loans have to be made at least on a quarterly basis, with "reasonable" amortisation payments likewise required every quarter.

Notification 17 alarmed many of Myanmar's banks and, after a delay occasioned by a seeming disbelief amongst many bankers that the CBM was (for the first time in its history) serious about implementing its prudential rules, a concerted campaign followed that (while giving some ground on the over-reliance on overdrafts) exerted great pressure over what was asserted as "unrealistic deadlines".[21]

In the wake of this push-back from the banks, and an understanding of the sheer scale of the actions required, the CBM issued a follow-up Directive (No.7/2017) on 24 November 2017, that extended the transition time for the conversion of overdrafts into term loans. According to the new schedule, the maximum proportion of a bank's total outstanding loan portfolio that could be in the form of overdrafts was to be adjusted thus:

As at July 6, 2018 – 50 per cent
As at July 6, 2019 – 30 per cent
As at July 6, 2020 – 20 per cent

Notwithstanding these revised timetables, in late 2019 a majority of Myanmar's banks were still struggling to meet the requirements of Notification 17. These included most of Myanmar's largest banks, some of which remain far from being compliant.

Of course, once compliant, Myanmar's banks will need much greater levels of capital (not least on account of the non-performing loan write-offs that will have to take place amongst "converting" overdrafts). Where will this capital come from? Some *may* come from foreign banks taking equity positions in local banks (more below). In the likely event this does not deliver much, however, the issuance of subordinated debt by some of the banks will help.

Allowed by the CBM's "Subordinated Debt Directive" (Directive 3/2019, 24 January 2019), banks in Myanmar may now issue debt instruments "subordinate to depositors and to the general creditors" that will count as supplementary (Tier 2) capital. To count in this way as regulatory capital, such debt must also have an initial minimum maturity of at least five years (once maturity dips below five years, successive annual deductions of 20 per cent must be made to the value of a subordinated debt issue as regulatory capital). Subordinated debt will provide part of the answer to the capital shortage of the strongest and largest of Myanmar's banks.[22] For other banks its issue will neither be sufficient nor, indeed, possible.

One understandable, if unfortunate, consequence of the emphasis on the repair and safeguarding of Myanmar's private banks was that, (necessarily) distracted by the need to fix their balance sheets, they began to greatly restrain new lending. As can be seen in Table 5.6, the growth of bank credit to Myanmar's private sector began to decline in 2017/18, and fell still further in the two subsequent financial years. Given that access to credit is consistently listed as the number one problem Myanmar's businesses face (ahead even of problems of unreliable electricity supplies and poor infrastructure) this decline of growth in available finance has been no trivial matter.

Table 5.6: Bank credit, deposits

	2015/16	2016/17	2017/18	2018/19	2019/20
Bank Credit Private Sect. (% chge)	34.5	33.8	23.8	14.0	13.5
Bank Deposits (%GDP)	35.6	40.3	43.3	59.6	59.4

Source: CBM (2019), IMF (2019a)

LIBERALISATION OF PERMITTED LENDING ACTIVITIES OF LOCAL BANKS

In order to stimulate private sector credit growth, even as the banks engaged in the prudent reconstruction of many of their activities, the CBM initiated a number of liberalising measures. These centred upon a relaxation of hitherto strict collateral requirements upon bank lending, loan tenors,[23] as well as measures to give at least *some* greater freedoms to banks in terms of the interest rates they charged and paid:

- Directive 7/2017[24] – allowed banks to make medium term loans (up to three years tenor) based on credit analysis, cash flow, and overall risk-based assessment rather than simply collateral assurance. This is a profoundly important reform that, if coupled with further liberalisation measures with respect to interest rates priced for risk, would do much to deliver to Myanmar the system of capital accumulation and allocation it needs.

- Directive 1/2019 – allowed banks to charge a higher interest rate (16 per cent) on loans without collateral. This measure improved the ability of Myanmar's banks to price for risk – although not completely nor, indeed, sufficiently. The same directive also redefined collateral to comprise: *"land and buildings, gold and gold products, diamond and precious stones, saving certificates, government treasury bonds, fixed deposits (part-time deposit accounts), securities, negotiable instruments, pledges, and credit guarantee including loans issued subject to the types of mortgages prescribed by the CBM from time to time."* This redefinition is, of course, an important step in reinforcing Directive 7/2017 (above).

  Myanmar has long had administratively fixed deposit and lending rates, a policy that (up until this reform) disallowed banks from "pricing for risk", and thus denying many smaller borrowers access to credit. The hitherto maximum lending rate of 13 per cent, and the minimum deposit rate of 8 per cent gave Myanmar's banks a 5 per cent margin on their borrowing and lending, and little room for profitable lending against macroeconomic instability and inflation (both of which, of course, have been chronic in Myanmar).

Myanmar desperately needs full interest rate liberalisation, but this current move at least is a moderately positive step. Despite the urging of the World Bank, IMF, Asian Development Bank, as well as various economic reformers within the Myanmar government, as yet there is limited political appetite for full interest rate liberalisation amongst key policy-makers.[25]

- Directive 2/2019 – allowed banks to make long-term housing loans, up to a limit of 5 per cent of a bank's total portfolio (subject to CBM approval on a "case by case basis" if longer than three years). Whether this reform, welcome and interesting in the abstract, will do little to change banking habits in Myanmar, or do much to stimulate investment in housing, remains to be seen.
- Directive 14/2019 – Raised the maximum interest rates that banks can charge on credit card balances (effectively unsecured personal loans) from 13 to 20 per cent.

REINVIGORATION OF STATE-OWNED BANKS

Myanmar has four large state-owned banks, the two most important of which are the Myanmar Economic Bank (MEB, a broad-based state-owned commercial bank that accumulates a lot of deposits, but does little lending to private businesses and individuals), and the Myanmar Agricultural Development Bank (MADB – an institution that functions mostly as an allocation mechanism for credit to farmers, but which collects no deposits and does nothing in the way of credit analysis or other regular banking activity).

In late 2018 the Ministry of Planning and Finance (the banks' owner) approved a restructuring program for the MEB/MADB. Utilising a $US100 million loan taken on for the purpose from the World Bank, and guided by Rabobank Advisory Services from the Netherlands (a division of the world's largest and most highly rated agricultural bank), the MEB and MADB are to be effectively merged over time, revitalised in terms of core banking systems, processes, and given expanded outreach via the application of modern technologies (not least via mobile-phone based financial applications).[26]

EXPANDED ALLOWABLE ACTIVITIES, AND MORE FOREIGN BANKS

There are thirteen licenced foreign banks in Myanmar. Commencing initial operations in 2015, up until late 2018 the scope of activities foreign banks could undertake was severely limited – in essence, to just providing financial services to foreign investors, and to local banks.

In November 2018, however, under CBM Notification 6/2018, foreign banks were permitted to lend to local businesses (although not yet to local individuals, or to take deposits from local retail customers). The interest rate applying to such loans is the set rate applying to collateralised loans from local banks, and currently fixed at 13 per cent p.a. (as noted above).

The CBM's decision to allow foreign banks to lend to Myanmar enterprises, more or less on an equal footing with domestic banks, is a deeply significant reform – but which was followed up in July 2019 with an announcement that a new round of foreign bank licences would be granted by years' end. Interestingly, this announcement also allowed foreign banks in Myanmar to operate as either branches of their foreign parent (as was the case for the incumbents), or as Myanmar subsidiaries (Khine Kyaw 2019).[27] The latter classification raises the possibility (still to be tested) that foreign banks could directly compete with local banks for public deposits. In which case, Myanmar's commercial banking sector could become a significantly more competitive arena.

PERMITTING FOREIGN EQUITY INVESTMENT IN LOCAL BANKS

In late January 2019, the CBM issued a letter granting foreign banks and financial institutions in-principle authorisation to buy equity (up to 35 per cent) in local banks.[28] This equity threshold, at and below which a bank (and any company) can still be classified as a Myanmar entity, is consistent with the new Myanmar Company Law and Regulations (the latter put in place August 2018).

Allowing foreign equity in local banks allows for a potentially quick and (relatively) easy way for Myanmar's banks to access (desperately needed – see Notification 17 above) capital, and in turn grow and prosper. It is a strategy adopted in many other countries, especially in developing Asia. Along the way such foreign bank investors also usually bring in the latest technologies, as well as cutting-edge methodologies and management practices.

NEW GOVERNANCE DIRECTIVES

In a bid to improve "governance" in Myanmar's banks, on 25 March 2019 the CBM issued four directives designed to bring the sector closer to international norms, and away from practices that traditionally honoured such matters in the breach. The directives:

No. 9/2019 – Directive on Directors of Banks (Fit and Proper Persons)
No. 10/2019 – Directive on External Auditors of Banks
No. 11/2019 – Related Parties Directive
No. 12/2019 – Directive on Acquisitions of Substantial Interest

Of course, these directives targeted the broader business norms that, in turn, lay behind some of the prudential anomalies identified earlier (poor auditing allowing breaches on lending to related parties, for instance, the 'ever-greening' of non-performing loans to favoured borrowers, and the selection of unqualified directors not up to the task of bank oversight...). As always, implementation and genuine compliance will be critical – and almost certainly gradual and partial.

CONCLUDING THOUGHTS AND PROSPECTS

A stable macro-economy is a necessary, if not sufficient, condition for economic growth and development – anywhere and everywhere. This truth, more or less universally acknowledged, was (and is) central to the economic policy framework that it has been the intention of Myanmar's current government to construct and implement. And, notwithstanding difficulties elsewhere, as well as opposition (intentional and otherwise) to its stabilising measures, this objective has been largely achieved.

Mission accomplished then? Alas, not yet. Myanmar's ongoing macro-financial circumstances continue to face a number of headwinds, any or all of which could set affairs back. Myanmar's banks remain fragile and structurally ill-equipped to aggregate and allocate capital; taxation arrangements continue to yield insufficient revenues, and are inefficient; government spending is excessive in some unproductive areas (not least in defence, an expenditure category over which the civilian government cannot determine); meanwhile, even the external environment, mostly well beyond the Myanmar government to influence, has mutated in ways that are not conducive to a poor country trying to reform and re-integrate with the global economy. Yet, as has been outlined here, critical foundations have surely been laid, and an environment in which for five decades macroeconomic instability was an absent concern of government seems impossible to imagine for the future.

As the MSDP acknowledges, macroeconomic stability is an "indispensable prerequisite" for its central vision of Myanmar as a peaceful, prosperous and democratic country. The stakes remain enormously high.

Notes

1 This assessment, and others in this chapter, is based upon the authors' work on macro-financial policies in Myanmar, and other places. In the case of Sean Turnell, this is in the role of Special Economic Consultant to the State Counsellor of Myanmar, Daw Aung San Suu Kyi, as well as earlier appointments at the Reserve Bank of Australia, and other international organisations. With respect to Daw Nyein Ei Cho, this reflects her work in financial services reform at the Myanmar Development Institute in Naypyitaw, and in other financial sector roles.

2 The most comprehensive of these pre-election manifestos, *Economic Strategy and Priorities: Stabilisation, Liberalisation, Institutionalisation,* was compiled by the NLD Economic Committee, in Yangon and across 2014/15. It declared that:

> The NLD will deliver fiscal prudence, while creating the financial space necessary for an expanding economy. Better revenue mobilization, budget prioritization, and greater efficiency in public spending will be the focus, underpinned by observing budget transparency and a rules-based fiscal framework. Under NLD stewardship, any budget deficits will be kept to less than 5% of GDP.
>
> The reduction of unnecessary government expenditure will be a priority, as will the privatization of appropriate state owned enterprises according to open and transparent processes. A significant source of extra revenue will also come from the proper accounting of Myanmar's foreign exchange earnings, especially from the sale of off-shore gas, jade and other natural resources.

While extolling the *economic* benefits of democracy:

> Being a democracy brings the application of the most powerful engine of economic growth known to human history – a system based on individual rights and freedoms that aligns incentives, allows spontaneous solutions to problems, promotes technological advance and the delivery of public services according to demand, and expands both choice and opportunity. In short, democracy and the focus on individual rights are both the ends of policy, and the vehicles through which our country may escape poverty, and achieve the prosperity our people deserve.

3 The (estimated) increase in the deficit for 2019/20 reflects the Government's desire to deliver something of a mild fiscal course-correction, on the basis that the initial tightening had been somewhat over-done, and on a growing understanding that the ability of Government agencies to properly execute spending plans was decidedly poor (World Bank 2019,20).

4 In particular, the appointment of Dr Min Ye Paing Hein as the Deputy Minister of the Ministry of Industry, and with a specific mandate of reforming some of the critical SOEs. For some of the reporting on this appointment see Nan Lwin (2019).

5 Spending data here sourced from Myanmar Budget Data Dashboard, https://mmbudgets.info/#/ (accessed 6 June 2020).

6 For more on the decision of government to institute a mild fiscal stimulus, see the Statement of Myanmar's President to the Finance Commission meeting, June 18, 2019, on the President's homepage, <http://www.president-office.gov.mm/en/?q=briefing-room/news/2019/06/18/id-9397> (accessed 29 September 2019).

7 The most important driver of these private sector gains being widely regarded as those resulting from greater access to reliable electricity, along with improved ports and rural roads.

8 This assessment of the IMF's executive Board is contained in a press release preface (April 12, 2019) to the IMF's 2018 Article IV Staff Report (IMF 2019).

9 The World Bank's reference here to project execution reflects its understanding that one of the reasons for Myanmar's modest government spending is less about the outcome of deliberate policy, but about an inability of some ministries to actually implement their spending plans.

10 That is, around $US800 million at current exchange rates (K1,540:$US1).

11 The World Bank (2019,42) estimated that the richest 20 per cent of Myanmar households received over 60% of the subsidies because of their greater usage of electricity. Of course, many households in rural Myanmar have no access to the electricity grid at all, and so enjoy no benefit at all from the tariff subsidies.

12 Details of the full spectrum of revised rates can be found at the website of the

Ministry of Electricity and Energy, at <https://www.moee.gov.mm/en/ignite/page/640> (accessed 29 September 2019). For a taste of the broad (and highly positive) reaction to the tariff increases, see Nitta (2019).

13 Statement by U Maung Maung Win, Deputy Minister of Planning and Finance, to the 5th Macroeconomic Management Sector Coordination Group Meeting, September 18, 2019, Naypyitaw. For an overview of the meeting, see <https://www.mopf.gov.mm/my/content/budget-news>. (accessed 28 September 2019). See also Myat Thura (2019).

14 For more on this role of foreign insurance companies in Vietnam and the lessons from it for Myanmar see Turnell and Vu (2018).

15 In 2006, against the official exchange rate of $US1:K6, the informal exchange rate reached $US1:K1,450. For more on this, and the round-tripping corruption it inspired see Turnell (2014: 369-386).

16 For background to this decision see Turnell (2014,370–371).

17 For more on Myanmar's new exchange rate arrangements, see the dedicated section of the website of the CBM, at <https://www.cbm.gov.mm/content/3908> (accessed 28 September 2019).

18 Representative of which might be the decision of the global coffee chain Starbucks to invest in Myanmar – and then back out of the decision in 2018. See Zin Thu Tun (2018).

19 The Central Bank of Myanmar was granted formal independence from control of the Ministry of Planning and Finance (MoPF) in 2013. However, these prudential notifications (which will, and already have had, macro-economic implications) were introduced with the understanding and cooperation of MoPF, as well as other government agencies, but most especially the National Economic Coordination Committee (NECC). Two members of the CBM sit on the NECC, as does the MoPF Minister (U Soe Win) and Deputy Minister (U Winston Set Aung), the Minister of Commerce (U Than Myint), the Deputy Minister of Industry and former Executive Director of the Myanmar Development Institute, Dr Min Ye Paing Hein), and a number of independent individuals. The NECC is chaired by the State Counsellor, Daw Aung San Suu Kyi, which gives its deliberations a certain force – right across the many portfolios that come under its purview.

20 This, and all other CBM Notifications discussed here, are available at the central bank's website, at <https://www.cbm.gov.mm/content/fiml-regulation> (accessed 29 September 2019).

21 For a flavour of this pushback, which absorbed many pages and much airtime in Myanmar's media in this period, see Downing (2019).

22 At the time of writing a couple of Myanmar's largest and best-run banks had submitted proposals for subordinated debt issues to the CBM.

23 Under past regulations, Myanmar's banks had long been restricted to lending

only on land as collateral, and for terms not exceeding one year. Of course, it was such restrictions that stimulated the practice of Myanmar's banks lending more or less purely in the form of ever-revolving real estate-backed overdrafts – to the great cost of the sector's long term stability.

24 This, and all other CBM Directives discussed here, are available at the central bank's website, at <https://www.cbm.gov.mm/content/fiml-regulation> (accessed 30 September 2019).

25 Seemingly on the basis of fears that bank interest rates in Myanmar would then soar, crippling indebted firms (and ultimately thus the banks too) and undermining economic growth. Such fears are understandable perhaps in a country in which monetary instability (as noted) has historically been the order of the day. Yet, in the absence of an ability to flexibly price for risk, it is hard to imagine how Myanmar's entrepreneurs, especially the newest, will ever be able to source the capital they need to.

26 One of the authors of this paper (Sean Turnell), is involved in this project.

27 As was the case with the selection of the thirteen existing licensed foreign banks in Myanmar, the German consultancy firm Roland Berger won the tender to establish the process for choosing the new entrants (Irrawaddy 2019).

28 Letter dated January 29, 2019 (MaBaMa/Bank Scrutiny/1 [1/2019], January 29, 2019).

References

Central Bank of Myanmar, Directives (Full Series), 2017 – 2019. Available at: https://www.cbm.gov.mm/content/2882 (accessed 24 September 2019).

Central Bank of Myanmar, Notifications (Full Series), 2016 – 2019. Available at: https://www.cbm.gov.mm/content/fiml-regulation (accessed 24 September 2019).

Directorate of Investment and Company Administration (DICA) (2019). *Yearly Approved Amount of Foreign Investment,* August. Available at: https://www.dica.gov.mm/sites/dica.gov.mm/files/document-files/country_yearly.pdf (accessed 20 September 2019).

Downing, J. (2017). "Bankers Warn of Economic Disruption Unless Rules Deadline Eased". *Frontier,* 25 September. Available at: https://frontiermyanmar.net/en/bankers-warn-of-economic-disruption-unless-rule-deadline-eased (accessed 22 September 2019).

Government of the Union of Myanmar (2017). "Myanmar Companies Law", Pyidaungsu Hluttaw Law no.29/2017, Naypyitaw.

Government of the Union of Myanmar (2019). "Tax Administration Law", Pyidaungsu Hluttaw Law no.20/2019, Naypyitaw.

International Monetary Fund (IMF) (2019a). *Myanmar: Staff Report for the 2018 Article IV Consultation,* 25 February. Washington DC: IMF. Available at: https://www.imf.org/en/Publications/CR/Issues/2019/04/10/Myanmar-2018-Article-IV-Consultation-Press-Release-Staff-Report-and-Statement-by-the-46748 (accessed 23 September 2019).

_____ (2019b). *World Economic Outlook, 2019.* Washington DC: IMF. Available at: https://www.imf.org/external/datamapper/PCPIEPCH@WEO/OEMDC/USA/THA/MMR/IDN/KHM/LAO/VNM (accessed 22 September 2019).

Irrawaddy (2019). "German Firm to Advise Central Bank of Myanmar on Licensing Foreign Lenders". *The Irrawaddy,* 21 August. Available at: https://www.irrawaddy.com/business/german-firm-advise-central-bank-myanmar-licensing-foreign-lenders.html (accessed 24 September 2019).

Khine Kyaw (2019). "Myanmar to Award More Foreign Bank Licences this Year". *The Irrawaddy,* 27 July. Available at: https://elevenmyanmar.com/news/myanmar-to-award-more-foreign-bank-licences-this-year (accessed 24 September 2019).

Ministry of Planning and Finance (2019a). *Myanmar Sustainable Development Plan.* Available at: https://www.mopf.gov.mm/en/page/planning/foreign-economic-relations-ferd/692 (accessed 23 September 2019).

_____ (2019b). "Insurance Market Liberalization for Foreign Entities". Announcement No.1/2019. Naypyitaw: Ministry of Planning and Finance, 2 January.

Myanmar Development Institute (2019). *Macroeconomic and Fiscal Analysis of Myanmar.* Naypyitaw: Myanmar Development Institute.

Myat Thura (2019). "Budget for 2019/20 Slashed by More than K400 Billion". *Myanmar Times,* 16 September. Available at: https://www.mmtimes.com/news/budget-2019-20-slashed-more-k400-billion.html (accessed 22 September 2019).

Nan Lwin (2019). "Myanmar Appoints Ex-World Bank Economist as Deputy Minister". *The Irrawaddy,* 16 August. Available at: https://www.irrawaddy.com/news/burma/myanmar-appoints-ex-world-bank-economist-deputy-minister.html (accessed 21 September 2019).

National League for Democracy (2015). *Economic Strategy and Priorities: Stabilisation, Liberalisation, Institutionalisation.* Yangon: Unpublished internal NLD economic policy manifesto.

Nitta, Y. (2019). "Myanmar Hikes Electricity Rates to Fund Grid Investments". *Nikkei Asian Review,* 26 June. Available at: https://asia.nikkei.com/Business/Energy/Myanmar-hikes-electricity-rates-to-fund-grid-investments (accessed 24 September 2019).

Turnell, S. (2014). "Burma's Economy and the Struggle for Reform". In *Burma Myanmar: Where Now?* edited by M. Gravers and F. Yitzen. Copenhagen: Nordic Institute of Asian Studies.

Turnell, S. and Vu, H. (2018). *Foreign Banks and Insurance Companies in Financial*

Sector Reform in Myanmar and Vietnam. Washington DC: United States Agency for International Development. Available at: https://www.nathaninc.com/wp-content/uploads/2018/08/FgnBksInsCosInFinSectorReformMyanmarVietnam.pdf (accessed 28 September 2019).

World Bank (2019a). *Myanmar Economic Monitor June 2019: Building Reform Momentum.* Washington DC: World Bank Group. Available at: https://www.worldbank.org/en/country/myanmar/publication/myanmar-economic-monitor-reforms-building-momentum-for-growth (accessed 24 September 2019).

World Bank (2019b). *Myanmar Economic Monitor December 2019: Resilience Amidst Risk.* Washington DC: World Bank Group. Available at: https://www.worldbank.org/en/news/press-release/2020/01/15/myanmars-growth-resilient-despite-global-slowdown (accessed 15 January 2020).

Zin Thu Tun (2018). "Starbucks Suspends Move to Myanmar". *Myanmar Business Today,* 24 September 6 (39). Available at: https://www.mmbiztoday.com/articles/starbucks-suspends-move-myanmar (accessed 28 September 2019).

6

POVERTY AND INEQUALITY IN MYANMAR: 2005 TO 2017

Peter Warr

Are the people of Myanmar becoming economically better off over time, and if so, to what extent? To assess changes in standards of living, measures of average levels of consumption per person provide a useful start, but a poor ending. The distribution of consumption across the population is also important. Do the poor benefit, in absolute (inflation-adjusted) terms, when average consumption grows? If so, do they benefit relative to their wealthier neighbours, or are the gains from growth concentrated disproportionately among the rich? Answers to these two very different questions can be provided by measures of absolute poverty incidence and inequality, respectively. These statistical measures are highly relevant for the design of economic and social protection policies when the objective is the achievement of inclusive economic growth. Not surprisingly, indicators of poverty incidence and inequality feature prominently in the international Sustainable Development Goals (SDGs).[1] These indicators are therefore important for monitoring progress in the achievement, or otherwise, of the SDGs.

Information on poverty incidence and inequality in Myanmar is difficult to obtain and the data available are often imperfect. The commonly used measures require household survey-based data on the distribution of consumption (or incomes) across the population and not just average levels. Because household-level surveys are so costly, small and imperfect samples are almost always used to estimate the characteristics of large and diverse populations.[2] In the case of Myanmar, information of this kind has been particularly scarce and even moderately reliable data sets have become available only quite recently. This chapter provides a critical summary of the statistical data currently available for Myanmar on these matters, covering the period 2005 to 2017.

With the advent of a more democratic form of government, following the November 2015 elections, the Myanmar people expected to see profound social and economic reforms (Chambers and McCarthy 2018). Reforms are ongoing (Warr 2016), but economic reforms primarily intended to boost growth also have the potential to increase economic disparities among households. The experience of the period preceding most of these reforms provides a baseline against which subsequent, post-reform analyses of poverty and inequality can be compared.

Examining the factors influencing the levels of poverty incidence and inequality and their changes over time can contribute to the development of a policy framework for achieving poverty-reducing economic growth while inequality is kept at a low to moderate level. In particular, it is important to know the extent to which changes in poverty and inequality can be influenced by public policy and which policy measures are likely to be more effective than others. The discussion below of the currently available studies on Myanmar will demonstrate that research of this kind remains largely an aspiration, rather than a reality.

The chapter begins with a non-technical summary of the analytical issues involved in measuring poverty and inequality. The Myanmar data sources used in this study are then described. The following sections then summarise the findings from existing studies on three economic variables, covering the period 2005 to 2017: levels of average consumption expenditures; the headcount measure of poverty incidence; and the Gini coefficient of inequality. This discussion does not present research findings based on new data, but critically reviews the information currently available. The following section then summarises the findings of a recent study estimating the impacts on the above three variables in relation to the May 2008 Tropical Cyclone Nargis, which devastated parts of Myanmar. The final section concludes.

MEASUREMENT OF POVERTY AND INEQUALITY[3]

Measure of welfare

Measures of poverty and inequality normally focus on the distribution of either real household consumption expenditures or real household incomes, measured per person or per adult equivalent within the household. Consumption expenditure is generally the preferred indicator of current welfare because income includes savings, which is relevant for future use, but not current household welfare. In the case of Myanmar, the available data – described in the following section – measure consumption expenditures at the household level, but not income levels. The word "real" means that the money value of expenditure is adjusted to allow for inflation. It is best to understand "real consumption" in terms of the quantity of goods and services consumed, rather than their monetary value. "Per adult equivalent" means that total household expenditures are divided by the number of "adult equivalents" in the household, a measure of household size that weights children less heavily than adults because their consumption requirements are considered smaller.[4]

As indicators of economic welfare, the resulting measures are far from perfect. For example, whether household consumption or income is used as the basis for these calculations, the primary focus is on the goods and services that the household is able to purchase with its own money. Neither measure, income or expenditure, includes the value to the household of services provided in kind, by local, state or national governments, without involving monetary payment. When some payment does occur for these goods or services, only the value of that payment is counted and this amount may be far below the value to the household of the good or service provided. Despite this point, it would be incorrect to say that the consumption or income measures are based exclusively on monetary outlays. In the case of rural households in particular, consumption or income is always adjusted for the value of home-produced food, in addition to purchased food, although other household-produced goods and services are generally ignored.

In Myanmar, as in virtually all countries conducting similar surveys, the unit of observation is the household, meaning that data on consumption expenditures are recorded for the household as a unit, not the individual. No information is collected on the distribution of consumption *within* the household. Consequently, the resulting measures of poverty incidence and inequality are based solely on the distribution of expenditures *between* households. In the subsequent discussion it will be assumed that the *real value of household expenditures per adult equivalent* is the welfare measure being used.

The cumulative distribution of expenditures

The core statistical concept is the cumulative distribution of expenditures per adult equivalent, illustrated in stylised form in Figure 6.1.[5] For each household the value of expenditures per adult equivalent is calculated and the households are then sorted by this variable, ranging from those for which real expenditure per adult equivalent is the lowest to the highest.[6] These data are displayed on the horizontal axis of the diagram. The cumulative distribution then shows, on the vertical axis, the percentage of the population belonging to households for which (the logarithm of) real expenditure per adult equivalent is *less than* the amount shown on the horizontal axis.

Figure 6.1. The cumulative distribution of expenditures and the headcount measure of poverty incidence

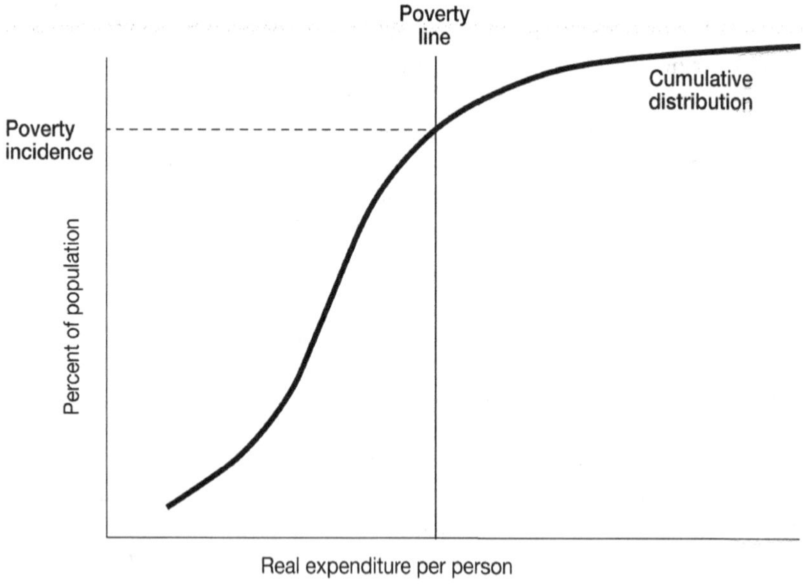

Source: Author's construction

The poverty line

The poverty line is a level of real expenditure per adult equivalent deemed necessary for a household to be capable of attaining a "decent" standard of living. Although some studies implicitly attribute a scientific meaning to it, this author's view is that the poverty line is a value judgment, rather than a scientific concept – an arbitrary level of real expenditure per person, used for statistical convenience to distinguish households that are "poor" from those that are "non-poor". It involves an opinion – a judgment about the level of expenditure required for a household to achieve a "decent" standard of living, given the economic environment that the household faces. According to this view, arguments about what the "true" poverty line is, or should be, are misguided.[7] Statistical agencies establish these poverty lines based on their own value judgement of what "true" poverty is. The approach of this study is to take them as given, recognising that they are value judgments, and then to analyse their implications for changes in poverty incidence over time. The vertical "Poverty Line" shown in Figure 1 represents one such possible poverty line.[8]

Recognition that the poverty line involves an arbitrary judgment has an important implication. Since poverty incidence depends on the poverty line, a discussion of whether the "true" level of poverty incidence in a particular country at a particular time is, say, 20 per cent or 40 per cent is meaningful only in relation to the poverty line that is being used. Different agencies use different poverty lines, reflecting different value judgments about the appropriate division between "poor" and "non-poor" households. Unless the poverty line is made explicit, arguments about the "true" level of poverty incidence are meaningless.

In comparing poverty incidence over time, the crucial point is that the purchasing power of the poverty line must be *held constant*. The purchasing power of the poverty line should be understood in terms of the actual quantity of goods and services it can buy – its real value. This real value is held constant by adjusting the monetary value of the poverty line to allow for changes over time in the prices of goods and services. This makes it possible to study systematically changes in the proportion of households with real expenditures falling below this real threshold, holding constant the value judgments underlying the poverty line. That is, while the absolute real value of the poverty line is arbitrary, its adjustment over time to allow for inflation is not arbitrary.

Poverty incidence

In Figure 6.1 the percentage of individuals belonging to households with real expenditures below the poverty line is shown by the vertical intersection between the poverty line and the cumulative distribution. This measure is known as the headcount measure of poverty incidence.[9] Because the cumulative distribution of expenditures is upward-sloping by construction, it is necessarily the case that the higher the poverty line, the higher the measured headcount level of poverty incidence.

Inequality

Whereas poverty incidence is concerned with *absolute* purchasing power, discussions of inequality are interested in the *relative* purchasing power of different households.[10] There are many statistical measures of inequality but all share the feature that if the real purchasing power of every household increased (or decreased) by the same proportion, say by doubling, measured inequality would not change. In contrast, if all real expenditures doubled but inequality remained constant, poverty incidence would necessarily decline. The cumulative distribution of real expenditures would shift to the right, but the real value of the poverty line would remain constant.

The most commonly used inequality measure is the Gini coefficient, illustrated in Figure 6.2, which is based on a Lorenz curve of expenditures, a modified form of the cumulative distribution discussed above and resting on the same underlying data. Households are arranged along the horizontal axis, sorted by expenditure per adult equivalent, from the poorest (left hand side of the axis) to the richest (right hand side). The position of a particular household on the horizontal axis depends on the percentage of all households whose expenditure per adult equivalent is *lower than* that particular household. The vertical axis shows, for each household on the horizontal axis, the cumulative percentage of total expenditure of all households whose expenditure per adult equivalent is lower than that household. If all households had the same levels of expenditure per adult equivalent, all households would lie on the diagonal dotted line labelled "Complete equality". Otherwise, if expenditures are distributed unequally, the graph of all households must lie somewhere below this diagonal.

Figure 6.2. The Lorenz curve and the Gini coefficient of inequality

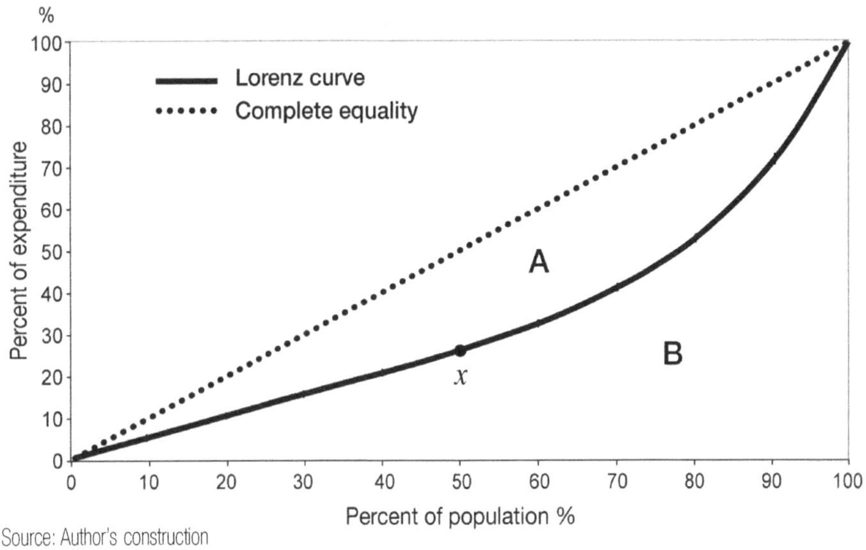

Source: Author's construction

Consider household *x*, which happens to lie in the centre of the horizontal axis, meaning that half of all households are poorer than *x*. By construction, all households poorer than *x* must account for less than half of all expenditures, so on the vertical axis, household *x* must take a value below 50 per cent. The Lorenz curve is the graph of all such households in the sample. The greater the degree of inequality, the further the Lorenz curve is from the diagonal. This is the basis for the Gini coefficient, given by the area A / (A+B). The index varies between the hypothetical values of 0 and 1, where 0 represents complete equality and 1 is the value the index would hypothetically take if a single household had all the expenditure. Neither of these two extremes is ever observed empirically and measured Gini coefficients always lie in the interval between 0 and 1. The Gini coefficient is sometimes expressed as a percentage, in which case it varies between 0 and 100. The higher the number, the greater the inequality.

Sampling error

Because of the cost of conducting detailed household surveys, mean expenditures, poverty and inequality at the population level are almost always estimated through sample surveys, covering only a small fraction of a country's heterogeneous population. These samples produce estimates of population statistics that inevitably involve error. Statisticians endeavour to minimise sample bias, such that the statistically expected value of sample-based estimates is equal to their true population values, but because of limited sample sizes, random sampling error is unavoidable. Sample estimates have a variance. The smaller the sample, the higher the sample variance and therefore the less reliable are the sample-based estimates of the true population parameters. Therefore, when sample-based estimates change over time, it is reasonable to ask the likelihood that these changes could have arisen by chance, due to random sampling error. The smaller the sample and the greater the within-sample variation, the greater is the sampling variance and the less reliable are the population estimates based on the sample. In practice, this means that when sample variances are large, measured changes over time are not necessarily statistically significant, in turn meaning that measured changes of this size could have arisen purely by chance, due to random sampling error. Statisticians have developed tests of significance designed to estimate the probability that this could have occurred.

MEASURING POVERTY INCIDENCE AND INEQUALITY IN MYANMAR

Household Income and Expenditure Survey (HIES), 1989 to 2004

Data on household expenditure have been collected in surveys conducted by the Myanmar government at least since 1989. A survey known as the Household Income and Expenditure Survey (HIES) was undertaken in intermittent years, including 1989, 1997, 2001 and 2004.[11] Based on these surveys, various issues of the *Myanmar Statistical Yearbook* published average values of household consumption expenditures and their commodity composition, arranged by socio-economic and geographical groups, for the above years. These published average consumption data were expressed on a per household basis, rather than per household member or per adult equivalent. Nevertheless, no estimates of poverty incidence or inequality, based on these data, were ever published. These measures may have been calculated by government officials, but if so, they were considered secret, presumably because of their political sensitivity. That is, the published summaries reported data about household level averages of real consumption expenditures but not their distribution across households. The distributional information contained in these data sets was unique but to the best of the present author's knowledge, no external researcher has ever received access to these data and no analysis of their implications for poverty or inequality has been published. It is not clear whether any of the original raw data sets still exist.

Integrated Household Living Conditions Assessments (IHLCA), 2005 and 2010

In 2004/05 and 2009/10 the United Nations Development Program (UNDP) conducted two moderately large household surveys, in conjunction with the Myanmar government, and published detailed estimates of poverty incidence based on the data collected.[12] No inequality measures were included and inequality was not discussed. These two surveys were known as the Integrated Household Living Conditions Assessments (IHLCA). Unlike the earlier HIES data described above, these household-level data were made available to qualified researchers for independent analysis.[13]

The detailed sampling procedures have been documented in IDEA and IHLCA (2007a, b, c) and IHLCA (2011a, b, c). The full survey included roughly 18,000 households in 2005 and a similar number in 2010, with data collected throughout the country. Approximately half of the sample was a panel, meaning that it covered the same households in each of the two years. Panel data are useful for statistical analysis of the causes of changes in the distribution of household expenditures, but the discussion in this paper will relate to the full sample.[14] The statistical methods used by government statistical agencies and other researchers to estimate poverty incidence vary widely.[15] The IHLCA reports estimate poverty incidence based on household expenditures on: (i) food consumption expenditures, including estimates of the value of home-produced food; (ii) non-food consumption expenditures, including clothing and other apparel, home appliances, house repair, education, travel and other household personal services; and (iii) housing expenditures, represented by yearly user costs, approximated by actual rental value, in the case of rented housing, or estimated rental value in the case of owner-occupied housing.

The expenditure data collected were based on recall of expenditures and the actual collection and recall periods are important. The 2005 and 2010 data were each collected in two rounds: December 2004 and May 2005; and December 2009 and May 2010, respectively. For non-food items the recall period was six months. For food items the recall period was seven days for some items[16] and thirty days for others.[17] Two important omissions from the IHLCA calculations were health-related expenditures and expenditures on household consumer durables. The proportion of expenditure allocated to these items may vary with the level of household income, so measured inequality and changes in it could be affected by their omission. The raw household survey data collected in the IHLCA survey include actual expenditures on these two items and the ownership of consumer durables. Warr and Aung (2019) and Aung and Warr (2020) amend the data used by the IHLCA team to include these two items, but since these amendments do not change estimated poverty incidence and inequality markedly they will be ignored in the present discussion, which focuses on the published IHLCA data.

Myanmar Poverty and Living Conditions Survey (MPLCS) 2015

The World Bank undertook a relatively small sample survey in 2015, again in conjunction with the Myanmar government, called the Myanmar Poverty and Living Conditions Survey (MPLCS 2015) and published detailed estimates of poverty incidence and inequality for that year. The earlier IHLCA data sets were largely disregarded in the subsequent reports, World Bank (2017a and 2017b). The design of the 2015 World Bank survey essentially discards the previous two surveys conducted by UNDP and begins again.[18] The sample size of the MPLCS was 3,648 households, one-fifth the size of the earlier IHLCA samples, limiting the reliability of the national estimates obtained and eliminating the capacity of the data to produce estimates of poverty incidence at the state or division level. The MPLCS survey also abandoned the panel component of the earlier IHLCA surveys.

The above sampling decisions are not explained in the World Bank reports, but their implication is that while it is possible to use the earlier 2005 and 2010 data to study the causes of the changes in poverty incidence and inequality that occurred over that short interval, the subsequent discontinuity in the data impedes any similar study covering the interval between 2010 and 2015. It is not possible to comment on the sampling or commodity details of the MPLCS survey because these details have not been published. The household-level data collected by MPLCS 2015 have not yet been released for independent analysis.

Myanmar Living Conditions Survey (MLCS) 2017

Most recently, in June 2019, the World Bank, in association with UNDP and the government of Myanmar, released summary results from a medium-sized 2017 survey, called the Myanmar Living Conditions Survey (MLCS). The findings are summarised in UNDP/World Bank (2019a and 2019b). The sample size was 13,730 households, almost four times the size of the World Bank's earlier MPLCS survey and three-quarters of the size of the UNDP's two IHLCA surveys. There is apparently no panel component. Details of the sampling methods have not been published and the household-level data have not yet been released for independent analysis.

Table 6.1 summarises the characteristics of the above four surveys conducted between 2005 and 2017. The UNDP's two IHLCA surveys, 2005 and 2010, used a common sampling methodology, but the World Bank's 2015 MPLCS survey and the UNDP/World Bank 2017 MLCS survey used sampling methods that differed from this and from each other. Comparison of the findings from these studies is precarious at best. The changing design of the surveys themselves, compounded by the standalone nature of the reports based on each of them, makes this comparison difficult. Nevertheless, if conclusions are to be drawn about changes in economic welfare over time, based on statistical data available on Myanmar, this is the exercise that must now be attempted. The important point is that we are discussing statistical estimates of real consumption, poverty and inequality, based on imperfect information and these estimates must be viewed critically.

Table 6.1. Household expenditure surveys: 2005 to 2017

Name of survey	Year	Source	Sample size (households)	Level of representation	Timing of data collections	Panel data exist	Household data available
Integrated Household Living Conditions Assessments (IHLCA-I)	2004 / 2005	UNDP/ GoM	18,634	National; Rural/Urban; State/Region	Nov, Dec 2004; May 2005	Yes (9,102 households)	Yes
Integrated Household Living Conditions Assessments (IHLCA-II)	2009 / 2010	UNDP / GoM	18,609	National; Rural/Urban; State/Region	Dec 2009; Jan, May 2010	Yes (9.102 households)	Yes
Myanmar Poverty and Living Conditions Survey (MPLCS)	2015	World Bank/GoM	3,648	Nationa; Rural/Urban; Agro-zone	Jan-April 2015	No	No
Myanmar Living Conditions Survey (MLCS)	2017	UNDP/ World Bank/GoM	13,730	National; Rural/Urban; State/Region	unstated	No	No

Note: UNDP - United Nations Development Programme. GoM - Government of Myanmar.
Table Source: Author's compilation, from IDEA and IHLCA (2007a, b, c), IHLCA (2011a, b, c), World Bank (2017a) and UNDP and World Bank (2019b).

MEAN CONSUMPTION EXPENDITURES

Estimated levels of real consumption expenditures, based on the above survey data, are summarised in Table 6.2, for the period 2005 to 2017.

Table 6.2. Estimated mean consumption, poverty incidence and inequality, 2005 to 2017

Variables	2005	2010	2015	2017	Change 2005 to 2017
Mean real consumption[a]					
National	1,950	1,977	2,243	2,628	34.8%
Urban	2,205	2,144	2,625	3,475	57.6%
Rural	1,875	1,944	2,175	2,286	21.9%
Poverty incidence (%)[b]					
National	48.2	42.4	32.1	24.8	-23.4
Urban	32.2	24.8	14.5	11.3	-20.9
Rural	53.9	48.5	38.8	30.2	-23.7
Gini coefficient of inequality[c]					
National	0.256	0.220	0.317	0.303	0.047
Urban	0.315	0.262	0.366	0.318	0.003
Rural	0.212	0.188	0.280	0.263	0.051
Memo item: Median real consumption[a] National	1,711	1,860	2,006	2,181	27.5%

Notes: a Real consumption measured as Kyat per adult equivalent per month, 2017 prices. 'Adult equivalent' calculations use the weights recommended in Deaton and Zaidi (2002). 'Change' means percentage change from 2005 to 2017.
b Based on 2017 UNDP/World Bank (2019b) poverty line. 'Change' means absolute change from 2005 to 2017.
c Gini coefficients are expressed above as proportions, where the possible values range from 0 to 1. Higher values mean greater inequality. Gini coefficients are sometimes expressed as percentages, in which case the above values are multiplied by 100. 'Change' means percentage change from 2005 to 2017.
Table Sources: a Data for 2005 and 2010 from Warr and Aung (2019), updated to 2017 prices using consumer price index data from World Bank, World Development Indicators. Data for 2015 from World Bank (2017a); data for 2017 from UNDP / World Bank (2019b).
b Data for 2005, 2020 and 2015 from World Bank (2017a); data for 2017 from UNDP / World Bank (2019b).
c Data for 2005 and 2010 from Warr and Aung (2019); data for 2015 from World Bank (2017a); data for 2017 from UNDP / World Bank (2019b).

Between 2005 and 2010, the mean value of real consumption expenditures barely changed in Myanmar, increasing by only 1.4 per cent over the entire five years. Taking into account the size of the sample and the estimated sample variance, Warr and Aung (2019) show that, in statistical terms, this small change was not significantly different from zero. The 2005 to 2010 period can therefore be regarded as one of no growth. Between 2010 and 2015, mean expenditures increased by 13.4 per cent, roughly ten times the increase over the previous five years. Over the full decade the change was 15 per cent, an annual compound growth rate of just under 1.5 per cent. This story was roughly similar for urban and rural areas. In urban areas measured mean expenditures actually declined (by 2.8 per cent) between 2005 and 2010, then increased by 22.5 per cent over the following five years. In rural areas the corresponding changes were 3.7 and 16 per cent, respectively. Over the full decade urban and rural real expenditures increased by 19 and 16 per cent, respectively.

Although the estimated annual rate of growth of real consumption over this decade was only slight, average living standards apparently did improve. Figure 6.3 summarises supporting evidence on this point, using data on assets owned by households, drawn from World Bank (2017a). The data sources include the three household expenditure surveys for 2005, 2010 and 2015 mentioned above, together with the 2014 census. Ownership of mobile phones, rice cookers, motorcycles, electrical fans and television sets all increased significantly. In addition, the use of electric lighting and tin roofs both expanded and reliance on thatched roofing declined correspondingly. Based on the data available, there was an improvement in average living standards, starting from very low levels of asset ownership in 2005.

According to the UNDP / World Bank reports relating to the 2017 survey, average real consumption increased by a further 17 per cent between 2015 and 2017.[19] Overall, these data sets indicate that average real consumption in Myanmar increased by 35 per cent between 2005 and 2017, but fully half of that estimated increase occurred over the two years between 2015 and 2017. If correct, these findings reveal a positive economic impact from early economic reforms.

Figure 6.3. Myanmar: Asset indicators, 2005 to 2015

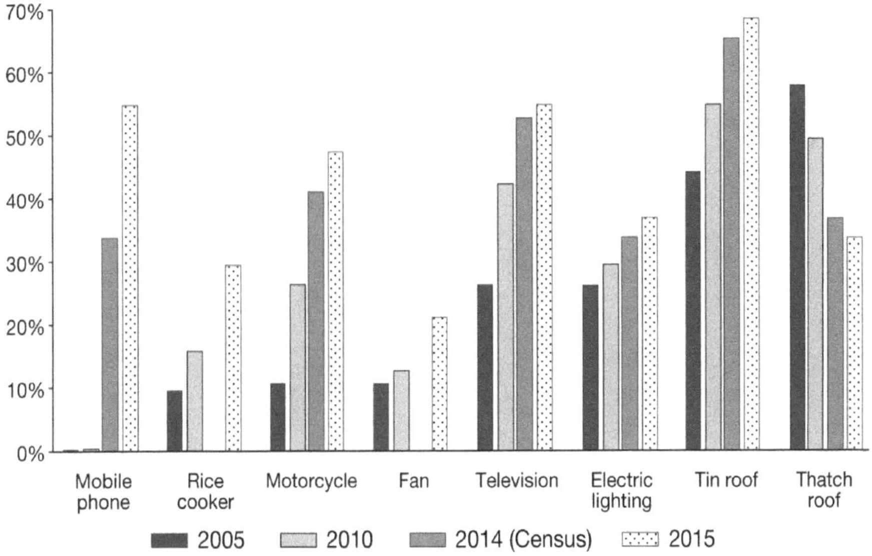

Source: Author's compilation, based on data from World Bank (2017a).

An important further point can be extracted from this information: the radical difference between the story for urban and rural areas. In urban areas estimated average real consumption increased by 58 per cent over the full twelve years but two-thirds of that change occurred over the two years between 2015 and 2017. In rural areas, estimated real consumption rose by only 22 per cent over the full twelve years and only a quarter of that change occurred over the two years from 2015 to 2017. The implication is clear. The gain in estimated real consumption that occurred between 2015 and 2017 was heavily concentrated in urban areas and the gap between urban and rural consumption levels widened. In 2005 the ratio of average real consumption per adult equivalent between urban and rural areas was 1.18. A decade later, in 2015, it was 1.21 and in 2017 it was 1.52. Therefore, the recent gains in estimated real consumption at the national level were heavily concentrated in urban households.

POVERTY INCIDENCE

Drawing upon the household expenditure surveys described above, in conjunction with the World Bank's (2017) poverty line, Figure 6.4 illustrates the calculation of poverty incidence for 2005 and 2017, holding the real purchasing power of the poverty line constant. In this illustrative graph,

Figure 6.4. Myanmar: Poverty incidence 2005 and 2017

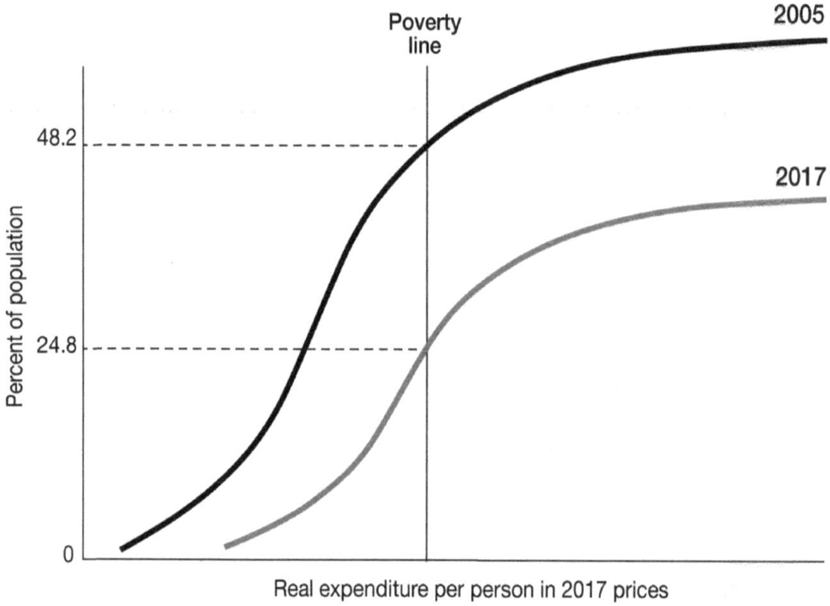

Source: Author's construction, based on UNDP / World Bank (2017) poverty line

levels of expenditure in 2005 and 2017 are both expressed in 2017 prices. According to the estimates described above, over this twelve-year interval almost one-quarter of the population (23.4 per cent) belonged to households that moved from levels of real expenditure per adult equivalent below the poverty line to levels above it.

Revising the poverty line

In its first report on poverty incidence in 2015 (World Bank 2017a), the World Bank presents calculations of poverty incidence based on the UNDP (2007) poverty line. The report then emphasises what it says is the necessity of revising these poverty lines. It generates a new, higher poverty line based on World Bank (2014) and compares the resulting poverty incidence with those obtained using the earlier UNDP poverty line. A subsequent report (World Bank 2017b), focuses on this issue again, producing a still higher real poverty line and a third series of poverty estimates.

The reasons given for this emphasis on raising the real value of the poverty line are said in World Bank (2017a and 2017b) to relate to changes in living conditions within Myanmar. But if living conditions change, measured poverty incidence will presumably change accordingly, given the poverty line. That is what the measurement of poverty incidence is intended to reveal. The suggestion that a change in living conditions necessitates a change in the real value of the poverty line does not make sense. This aspect of the two World Bank reports remains mysterious. In any case, as shown above, "living conditions" in Myanmar changed far more rapidly between 2015 and 2017 than they had during any previous interval and the 2019 reports covering this interval apparently saw no necessity to change the poverty line again.

The World Bank's calculation of the 2017 poverty line takes account of expenditure on some commodities not captured by the early UNDP poverty line, such as mobile phones, but this is a relatively minor point. The principal change is in the overall level of the poverty line, not the inclusion of a handful of new commodities. The real value of the World Bank (2017) line is roughly 30 per cent higher than the UNDP (2007) line. Figure 6.5 shows the resulting levels of poverty incidence for Myanmar estimated from each of the three poverty lines mentioned above: UNDP (2007), World Bank (2014) and World Bank (2017). In the construction of this diagram, for each poverty line its nominal magnitude was adjusted over time in the same way, using the consumer price index. Of course, a higher real poverty line necessarily produces a higher estimated level of poverty incidence. In addition, when changes in poverty incidence are being studied over time, holding the poverty line constant but at different alternative values, we are studying changes in different regions of the cumulative distribution of expenditures. Accordingly, the resulting changes in measured poverty incidence should not be expected to be identical. Nevertheless, Figure 6.5 shows that the resulting pattern of changes in poverty incidence over time is similar, regardless of which poverty line is used.[20] It is unclear what the revision of the poverty line achieved, or why the World Bank was so insistent upon it.

Figure 6.5. Myanmar: Poverty incidence, 2005, 2010 and 2015, based on varying poverty lines

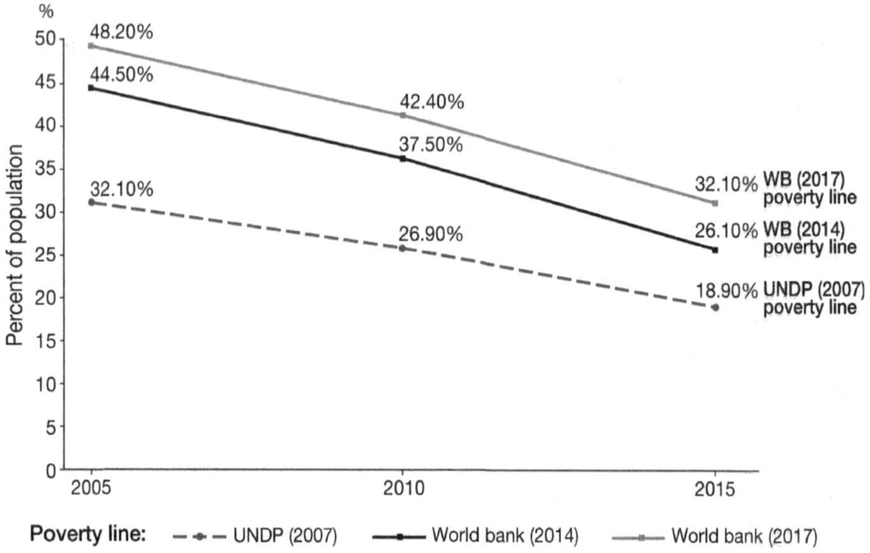

Source: Author's compilation, based on UNDP (20007), World Bank (2014) and World Bank (2017) poverty lines

In its vast literature on global poverty, the World Bank has emphasised the relevance for the world's poorest countries of an international poverty line of US$1.90 per day, measured at 2011 purchasing power parity (PPP),[21] updated in October 2015 from the previously recommended US$1.25, also at PPP.[22] It is therefore relevant to compare the poverty lines recommended for Myanmar with this yardstick. The poverty line recommended in World Bank (2017b) is 1,303 *Kyat* per adult equivalent per day (1,241 *Kyat* per capita per day), in January 2015 prices.[23] At the January 2015 market exchange rate of 1,025 *Kyat* per US$, this converts to US$1.27 per day. The World Bank's 2011 PPP conversion factor for Myanmar is 3.767, similar to the conversion factors for neighbouring poor countries Laos and Cambodia.[24] The recommended poverty line for 2015 therefore converts to US$4.78 per day at 2011 PPP, roughly two and a half times the World Bank's recommended international poverty line for poor countries. This discrepancy is acknowledged in the World Bank (2017b) report, but not explained.[25]

An explanation may lie buried in the World Bank's 2017 *East Asia and the Pacific Update* report, which cites poverty incidence in Myanmar, using the

$1.90 international poverty line (at 2011 PPP), as 6.5 per cent. In addition, it reports poverty incidence in Myanmar, using a poverty line for "lower middle-income countries" of US$3.20 (at 2011 PPP), as being 30.2 per cent, comparable with the Bank's estimated poverty incidence for Myanmar in 2015 of 32.1 per cent. Other World Bank documents show that the Bank's internal classification of Myanmar, which has potential implications for its lending policies, was amended in 2014 from "low income" to "lower middle-income".[26]

"Lower middle-income" is a broad statistical category used by the World Bank for countries with Gross National Income per capita (Atlas method) ranging between US$996 and US$3,895. In 2015 the World Bank's estimate of Gross National Income per capita in Myanmar moved from just below, to just above this arbitrary lower threshold, reaching US$1,190 in 2015. Myanmar is far from typical of most countries in this "lower middle income" category, which also includes Indonesia, Bolivia and Ukraine. Of course, the World Bank's definition of the "lower middle-income" category of countries and its US$3.20 recommended poverty line for all such countries, are both arbitrary.

The desire for consistency with this change of Myanmar's internal World Bank classification may help explain the Bank's eagerness to raise Myanmar's poverty line to one that the World Bank arbitrarily uses for all countries in this income category. If this explanation is correct, the World Bank's eagerness to change Myanmar's poverty line was motivated by the desire for consistency with its own internal operating procedures, having nothing to do with understanding poverty and its causes in Myanmar or with finding effective policy solutions, and the explanation provided for this change was misleading.

Poverty profile

The reports World Bank (2017a and 2017b) and UNDP/World Bank (2019a and 2019b) provide comprehensive descriptions of the characteristics of the poor in 2015 and 2017. For example, as Table 6.2 indicates, in both years estimated poverty incidence was higher in rural than in urban areas. From Table 6.3, poverty incidence in 2015 varied significantly by geographic region. It was highest in the Coastal Zone, followed by the Hills and Mountains regions, then the Dry Zone and lowest in the Delta region, which includes the largest city, Yangon. The incidence of poverty also varied with the education of the household head. The better educated, the lower the average level of poverty incidence. Young couples with children had the highest incidence of poverty and couples with no children the lowest. The more children, the higher the average level of poverty incidence and finally, households whose head was between 35 and 44 years of age, presumably coinciding with the largest average number of dependent children, are the most likely to be poor. Similarly, poor households are less likely than the non-poor to possess legal title to land that they cultivate or to their dwelling, and less likely to own a bank account. In addition, the profile for 2017 shows that poverty incidence is highly concentrated among agricultural workers without land.

This description of poverty at a particular time is called a poverty profile. Its findings are interesting but unsurprising in light of earlier work on poverty in developing countries.[27] However, this form of analysis has two central defects. First, there is almost no attempt to compare the findings for any one year with those from earlier years. For example, the poverty profile for 2017 makes almost no comparison with the profile for 2015. Indeed, the format of the two profiles is so different that the reader is precluded from making this comparison.[28] The 2017 findings are described in standalone form, as though the 2015 reports, let alone the earlier reports for 2005 and 2010, did not exist.

Second, the deeper analytical weakness of these profiles is that they describe correlation and not causation. For policy purposes, what is needed is knowledge of the causes of poverty and changes in it, so that these causes can be addressed. The two World Bank reports dealing with the 2015 findings and the two UNDP/World Bank reports dealing with the 2017 findings describe the poor but make no attempt to explain why people are poor, or why poverty changes over time.

To illustrate the difference between correlation and causation in this context, suppose, hypothetically, that poor people were found to be less likely than the non-poor to consume ice cream or to wear brand-name clothing. No one would imagine that non-purchase of these items caused poverty. Obviously, the causation runs in the opposite direction. Saying that poor people do not purchase these commodities would reveal nothing about why they were poor. Policies to facilitate their purchase might be popular, but they would not assist poor people to exit poverty.

Now, what about education? Does inferior education cause poverty or does poverty cause families to skimp on the education they are able

Table 6.3. Poverty profile, 2015 (percentage of group population who are poor)

Geographic Region		Education of head		Family structure		Number of children		Age of head (yrs.)	
Category	Poverty Incidence	Category	Poverty incidence	Category	Poverty incidence	Category	Poverty Incidence	Category	Poverty incidence
Hills and mountains	40.0	Tertiary	4.5	Three Generations	34.9	0	16.7	15 – 34	29.8
Dry zone	32.1	High school	11.8	Couple with young children	38.1	1	22.5	35 - 44	36.0
Delta region	26.2	Middle school	21.4	Couple with older children	20.4	2	34.3	45 – 59	31.7
Coastal zone	43.9	Primary school	32.6	Couple with no children	13.6	3+	52.7	60+	30.2
		Below Primary	42.8	Others	14.8				
		Monastic school	32.7						
		None	49.7						

Note: Poverty incidence is measured as percentage of group population. Table Source: Author's compilation from World Bank (2017b).

to give their children? Both effects presumably operate, but if we are to know how improved education might affect poverty incidence we need to separate these two causal links. We need to know how improved education affects poverty, net of any reverse effect. Similarly, does non-possession of a bank account cause poverty, or the reverse? Again, both effects probably operate. A poverty profile merely describes the poor. It doesn't explain why they are poor.

To design policies that can reduce poverty it is necessary to know its drivers – what causes changes in poverty incidence – and not just its correlates. A poverty profile may superficially appear to provide an explanation for poverty, but it really doesn't. Simply knowing that being poor is correlated with something else reveals very little about how poverty might be reduced. Indeed, if the poverty profile was interpreted in that incorrect way, the results could be harmful to the cause of poverty reduction. A rigorous analysis of the drivers of poverty reduction is needed, but in the case of Myanmar this analytical work has not yet been done.

INEQUALITY

Based on the available data, each of the standard measures of inequality declined between 2005 and 2010, increased between 2010 and 2015, then declined between 2015 and 2017, reaching a level in 2017 exceeding the 2005 level. Inequality in 2017 was higher than earlier levels measured in Myanmar, but not high relative to levels in other Southeast Asian countries, as shown in Table 6.4. Inequality is higher within urban areas than rural areas, as shown in Table 6.2, but an analytical point that will be important for subsequent discussion is that measured inequality at the national level depends not only on inequality within sub-groups, such as urban and rural areas, but also on inequality between these groups. The discussion of mean consumption levels above revealed that inequality between urban and rural areas apparently increased between 2015 and 2017, even though estimated inequality declined within each of these areas.

Table 6.4. Measures of inequality, Myanmar and neighbouring countries

	Gini coefficient (%)	Ration of top 10% to bottom 10%
Myanmar 2005	25.6	3.9
Myanmar 2010	22.0	3.4
Myanmar 2015	31,7	7.4
Myanmar 2017	30.0	6.5
Thailand 2012	39.4	10.9
Vietnam 2012	38.7	11.6
Indonesia 2009	35.6	8.3

Note: Data for 2005 and 2010 from Warr and Aung (2019); data for 2015 from World Bank (2017a); data for 2017 from UNDP / World Bank (2019b)
Table Source: Author's compilation from World Bank (2017b)

THE POVERTY AND INEQUALITY IMPACT OF CYCLONE NARGIS

In May 2008 coastal and near-coastal areas of Myanmar suffered the effects of a massive tropical cyclone. The areas directly affected, as identified by post-cyclone satellite imagery, contained about 14 per cent of the country's total population (Tripartite Core Group 2008). Within this area, the cyclone killed an estimated 138,000 people and obliterated public and private assets on a vast scale (Guha-Sapir et al. 2016). In those regions of the country directly affected by the cyclone, virtually all standing crops and stored food stocks, along with most capital goods such as vehicles and other machinery, were destroyed, along with many buildings, and in coastal farming areas, salt-water inundation reduced soil fertility (Larkin 2010). Steinberg (2013, 46) cites estimates of property damage equivalent to 27 per cent of annual GDP and describes Cyclone Nargis as "the single most devastating disaster to strike Burma/Myanmar in recorded history."

It would seem that Cyclone Nargis might explain at least some of the puzzling decline in recorded inequality that occurred between 2005 and 2010. A recent long-term historical study by Walter Scheidel (2017) has argued that over several millennia of human history substantial reductions in economic inequality have almost always resulted from only two types of events: man-made disasters such as warfare, revolution and state collapse; and natural disasters such as mass epidemics, earthquakes, volcanic eruptions, tsunamis and unexpected climatic disruptions. Sheidel argued that disasters reduce inequality by destroying the assets owned by better-off people, leveling the distribution of economic welfare among the survivors.

Warr and Aung (2019) developed a statistical methodology for estimating the impact that an exogenous event (in this case, the cyclone) had on the distribution of consumption, including its effects on poverty incidence and inequality. The method is to use panel data – in this case, those contained in the 2005 and 2010 UNDP survey data described above – to estimate a hypothetical distribution of household consumption expenditures in 2010 representing the counterfactual situation in which the cyclone did not occur. The impact of the cyclone was then measured as the difference between this hypothetical distribution of consumption (without the cyclone) in 2010 and the observed distribution of consumption (with the cyclone) in the same year, as recorded in the 2010 survey data. This analytical exercise was possible only because of the existence of the panel component within the UNDP surveys. Within this panel component (roughly half the total sample), the same households were surveyed in both 2005 and 2010.

The findings were that the estimated impact of the cyclone was to reduce average real consumption within the directly affected region by 14.9 per cent and at the national level by 6.4 per cent, compared with what it would otherwise have been in 2010 if the cyclone had not occurred. Similarly, the cyclone increased poverty incidence within the directly affected area by an estimated 12.9 per cent of that population and at the national level by 2.8 per cent of the total population.

The estimated effects on inequality were surprising and not at all straightforward. First, and contrary to Scheidel's argument, the cyclone *increased* inequality within the population directly affected. The reason was that the *absolute* loss of consumption was, on average, largest among better-off households, as Scheidel contends, but the *proportional* loss was larger for the poor. Scheidel's argument regarding effects on inequality logically requires that the disaster harms the rich more than the poor in proportional terms, and not just in absolute terms.[29]

Second, the estimated impact on overall inequality at the national level combines two components: within-region changes in inequality, and between-region changes. As described above, the within-region component was an increase in overall inequality because the Cyclone-Nargis affected region experienced an increase in inequality and there was no impact in the non-affected region.[30] The between-region component depends on whether the region negatively affected was initially better-off or worse-off than the rest of the population, unaffected by the cyclone.

Cyclone Nargis reduced average consumption within the affected region by 13 per cent, but this region, including the business centre and former capital, Yangon, was the wealthiest part of Myanmar, both before and after the cyclone. In 2005, before the cyclone, average consumption expenditures within the region subsequently affected by Cyclone Nargis were 35 per cent higher than the non-affected regions, and in 2010, after the cyclone, average consumption expenditures within the affected region were still 12 per cent higher than in the non-affected regions, despite the damage caused by the cyclone. Accordingly, the impact of the cyclone was to reduce between-region inequality.

The reduction in between-region inequality was so large that it outweighed the increase in within-region inequality. That is, Cyclone Nargis did contribute to a reduction in national inequality within Myanmar, accounting for about one-fifth of the observed decline. But this did not occur for the reason suggested by Scheidel's argument. The within-region impact of the cyclone was the opposite of his prediction, at least in the short term. Inequality declined at the national level because the cyclone just happened to impact the part of the country that was initially the best-off.

CONCLUSIONS

National-level household surveys of Myanmar's population for 2005, 2010, 2015 and 2017 make it possible to study changes in average real consumption, poverty incidence and inequality over the twelve years spanned by these four surveys. The availability of these household-level data, and their use for research purposes, is unprecedented for Myanmar. This chapter has reviewed critically the data contained in these surveys and the calculation of poverty and inequality that can be derived from them. Because the sample surveys are relatively small, the findings from them should be viewed with caution and even some skepticism. The data indicate that over the twelve years ending in 2017, mean real (inflation-adjusted) consumption per person in Myanmar increased by 27 per cent and median real consumption increased by 35 per cent. At the same time, measured poverty incidence almost halved, but inequality increased significantly.

The two five-year intervals 2005 to 2010 and 2010 to 2015 were very different. Average real consumption expenditures were virtually stagnant during the first period but rose by 13 per cent during the second. Nevertheless, poverty incidence declined by similar amounts – 6.5 per cent of the population in the first period and 6.2 per cent in the second. In the first period, this combination of outcomes was possible because national-level inequality declined markedly. In the second period the reduction in poverty incidence occurred in spite of an increase in inequality that exceeded the decline in the first period, a combination of outcomes that was possible only because of the large increase in average consumption that occurred between 2010 and 2015.

The decline in measured inequality between 2005 and 2010 and the subsequent increase between 2010 and 2015 both remain largely unexplained. According to one recent study, the negative impact of Cyclone Nargis in May 2008 explains about one-fifth of the decline in inequality between 2005 and 2010 (Warr and Aung 2019). Other factors must explain the rest (Aung and Warr 2020).

The available data also indicate that between 2015 and 2017, average consumption increased far more rapidly and poverty incidence declined more rapidly, on an annual basis, than it did over the preceding decade. If these statistical estimates are roughly accurate, they indicate welcome progress in the post-2015 period. Inequality is a different story. Until now, public policy discussions within Myanmar have focused on poverty incidence with little attention to inequality. At the early stages of economic development some increases in inequality may be inevitable, and perhaps even appropriate, though that is a matter of opinion. But if inequality continues to increase it seems certain to become a focus of policy attention within the near future.

The data indicate that since 2015 economic gains have occurred in both urban and rural areas, but that these gains are heavily concentrated on the former. The findings of this chapter reveal a widening gap between the economic welfare of Myanmar's urban and rural populations. The recent political experience of neighbouring Thailand demonstrates that unchecked disparities of this kind can become seriously destabilising.

Notes

1 They are SDG Goal 1 (No poverty) and Goal 10 (Reduced inequality). For more details, see https://www.undp.org/content/dam/undp/library/corporate/brochure/SDGs_Booklet_Web_En.pdf (accessed 27 November 2019).

2 The exception to 'almost always' is that census data, in principle covering the entire population, can sometimes be used to supplement and check the results of the more frequent and less costly sample surveys.

3 Readers wishing a fuller discussion of the measurement of poverty and inequality are referred to Houghton and Khandker (2009), available online.

4 In most recent studies, the calculation of 'adult equivalent' uses the weights recommended in Deaton and Zaidi (2002).

5 Figure 1 is a stylized representation designed to illustrate the method of calculating poverty incidence. It is not intended to provide an accurate representation of the full cumulative distributions of expenditures for Myanmar. The same point applies to Figures 2 and 4, below.

6 The data are normally expressed as the logarithm of consumption, to compress the numerical spread of the household consumption data without affecting its ordering.

7 Some authors disagree with the perspective expressed here. See, for example, Reddy and Pogge (2005).

8 When expenditures are measured as their logarithm, then of course the poverty line must also be calculated as its logarithm.

9 Other measures of poverty incidence are used, including the poverty gap and poverty gap squared measures, but they tend to move in the same direction as the headcount measure.

10 The discussion of inequality in this chapter focuses more narrowly on the distribution of purchasing power. In a broader sense, inequality also relates to the distribution across individuals of wealth, assets and political power.

11 This survey may have been undertaken in some additional years, unknown to the author. UNDP/World Bank (2019b) states that this survey was conducted every six years, beginning in 1989 and ending in 2012, but this information is incorrect.

12 For brevity, these two surveys will subsequently be referred to as the 2005 and 2010 surveys.

13 Warr and Aung (2019) is one such study using the raw household level data, including the panel component.

14 The research value of panel data derives from the fact that the households are the same in different years of the sample. This facilitates analysis of the impact of external variables affecting the households, because these impacts are not compounded in the data with changes in the characteristics of the particular households contained within the sample, as is the case when the sample changes over time.

15 As noted above, poverty lines can differ, but a deeper statistical problem, affecting both poverty and inequality estimates, is that the household level data themselves are often constructed differently. Statistical agencies in some countries use household expenditures as the basis for their calculations which others use incomes. Moreover, the items included in the calculation of income or expenditure also differ widely. Warr et al. (2017) make this point by comparing poverty and inequality measurement in the eight poorest Association of Southeast Asian Nations (ASEAN) countries, including Myanmar. No two ASEAN countries include the same items in their definitions of household incomes or expenditures.

16 The 7-day recall items were: (i) pulses, beans, nuts and seeds; (ii) meat, dairy, eggs; (iii) fish and other seafood; (iv) roots and tubers; (v) vegetables; (vi) fruits, (vii) spices and condiments; and (viii) other food products, including dried rice noddles, cake, vermicilli biscuits and tofu, alcoholic beverages and food and beverages consumed outside the home.

17 The 30-day recall items were: (i) rice and other cereals; (ii) oils and fats; (iii) milk products; (iv) other food items such as green tea leaves, betel leaves, coffee, and potato chips.

18 The subsequent reports, World Bank (2017a and 2017b) similarly focus almost entirely on the 2015 data, largely ignoring the findings of the two earlier surveys.

19 Levels of asset ownership are reported for 2017, but in a format that does not support comparison with the earlier years.

20 The reductions in aggregate poverty incidence over the full decade, calculated from the World Bank (2014) and World Bank (2017) poverty lines, were 18.4 and 16.1 per cent, respectively.

21 The use of purchasing power parity (PPP) exchange rates takes account of the fact that US$ 1, converted at the market exchange rate, does not purchase the same quantities of goods and services in all countries. It typically purchases more in poor countries than in richer countries, mainly because labour costs are lower in the former and services, in particular, are correspondingly cheaper. The PPP conversion factor is the ratio of the PPP exchange rate, expressed as local currency unit per US$, to the market rate. See Houghton and Khandker (2009).

22 See http://www.worldbank.org/en/topic/poverty/brief/global-poverty-line-faq (accessed 20 June 2019).

23 In comparison, median expenditures per adult equivalent in 2015 were 1,644 kyats (World Bank 2017b) and mean expenditures were 1,933 kyats (author's calculation, using mean expenditures in December 2009 prices from World Bank (2017a), as in Table 3 above, adjusted for changes in the consumer price index).

24 Calculated from https://data.worldbank.org/indicator/ny.gdp.pcap.pp.cd (accessed 20 June 2019).

25 The report states (p. 29) that at US$ 1.90, 2011 PPP, poverty incidence for Myanmar in 2015 "was estimated at 6.5 per cent" (roughly one fifth of the 32.1 per cent level estimated in the report). The subsequent discussion dismisses the relevance for Myanmar of the U$1.90 international poverty line, but provides no coherent reason.

26 See the Excel file OGHIST, downloadable from the World Bank website: https://datahelpdesk.worldbank.org/knowledgebase/articles/906519-world-bank-country-and-lending-groups (accessed 21 June 2019).

27 Numerous examples can be found in the World Bank's poverty website: https://www.worldbank.org/en/topic/poverty

28 An exception to this statement is the case of education. Comparison of the 2015 and 2017 profiles is possible in this case because the data are presented in a similar format. The comparison reveals that the decline of poverty between 2015 and 2017 was highest among households for which the household head was better-educated.

29 A reduction in measured inequality requires the rich to lose relative to the poor. That is, in the case of a negative shock like the cyclone, the proportional loss to the rich must exceed the proportional loss to the poor.

30 This was an assumption of the analysis. As Warr and Aung (2019) describe, some indirect price effects could have occurred, deriving from reduced food production in the directly affected region.

References

Aung, L.L. and P. Warr (2020). "Explaining Changes in Inequality: Myanmar, 2005 to 2010." *Working Papers in Trade and Development*. Arndt-Corden Department of Economics, Crawford School of Public Policy, Australian National University, 2020/06, May. Available online at: https://acde.crawford.anu.edu.au/sites/default/files/publication/acde_crawford_anu_edu_au/2020-05/acde_td_wp_aung_and_warr_2020_6_0.pdf. [Accessed 25 May, 2020].

Central Statistical Organization (2005 and subsequent years). *Selected Monthly Economic Indicators*. Nay Pyi Taw, Myanmar.

Chambers, J. and G. McCarthy (2018). "Myanmar Transformed?" In *Myanmar Transformed? People, Places, Politics*, edited by J. Chambers, G. McCarthy, N. Farrelly and Chit Win. Singapore: ISEAS–Yusof Ishak Institute, 3–20.

Deaton, A., and S. Zaidi (2002). *Guidelines for Constructing Consumption Aggregates for Welfare Analysis* (LSMS Working Paper. 135). Washington, DC: World Bank Publications. Retrieved from: https://openknowledge.worldbank.org/handle/10986/14101

Guha-Sapir, D., R. Below and P. Hoyois (2016). The International Disaster Database. Centre for Research on the Epidemiology of Disasters, Catholic University of Louvain, Brussels, Belgium. http://www.emdat.be/database [Accessed: December 29, 2016].

Houghton, J. and S.R. Khandker (2009). *Handbook on Poverty and Inequality*. Washington DC: World Bank. Available online at: http://documents.worldbank.org/curated/en/488081468157174849/pdf/483380PUB0Pove101OFFICIAL0USE0ONLY1.pdf [Accessed 28 November 2019].

IDEA International Institute and IHLCA Project Technical Unit (2007a). *Poverty Profile: Integrated Household Living Conditions (IHLCA) Survey in Myanmar (2009–2010)*. Nay Pyi Taw: Ministry of National Planning and Economic Development.

IDEA International Institute and IHLCA Project Technical Unit (2007b). *Quality Report: Integrated Household Living Conditions (IHLCA) Survey in Myanmar (2009–2010)*. Nay Pyi Taw: Ministry of National Planning and Economic Development.

IDEA International Institute and IHLCA Project Technical Unit. (2007c). *Technical report: Integrated Household Living Conditions (IHLCA) Survey in Myanmar (2009–2010)*. Nay Pyi Taw: Ministry of National Planning and Economic Development.

IHLCA Project Technical Unit (2011a). *Poverty Profile: Integrated Household Living Conditions (IHLCA) Survey in Myanmar (2009–2010)*. Nay Pyi Taw: Ministry of National Planning and Economic Development.

IHLCA Project Technical Unit, IHLCA (2011b). *Quality Report: Integrated Household Living Conditions (IHLCA) Survey in Myanmar (2009–2010)*. Nay Pyi Taw: Ministry of National Planning and Economic Development.

IHLCA Project Technical Unit (2011c). *Technical Report: Integrated Household Living Conditions (IHLCA) Survey in Myanmar (2009–2010)*. Nay Pyi Taw: Ministry of National Planning and Economic Development.

Larkin, E. (2010). *Everything is Broken: Life Inside Burma*. London: Granta Publishers.

Reddy, S.G. and T.W. Pogge (2005). "How *Not* to Count the Poor". Version 6.2. Available at: https://papers.ssrn.com/sol3/papers.cfm?abstract_id=893159 [Accessed 28 November 2019].

Rogers, B. (2012). *Burma: A Nation at the Crossroads*. London: Rider Books.

Scheidel, W. (2017). *The Great Leveler: Violence and the History of Inequality from the Stone Age to the Twenty-First Century*. Princeton, N.J: Princeton University Press.

Steinberg, D.I. (2013). *Burma/Myanmar: What Everyone Needs to Know* 2nd ed. London: Oxford University Press.

Tripartite Core Group (2008). *Post-Nargis Joint Assessment, Vols I, II and II, Yangon, Myanmar*.

United Nations Development Programme/World Bank (2019a). *Myanmar Living Conditions Survey 2017, Key Indicators Report*, June, Yangon. Available at: http://documents.worldbank.org/curated/en/739461530021973802/pdf/127618-REVISED-14-12-2018-18-51-31-KIMLCSEnglishFinalOctlowresolution.pdf [Accessed 24 November 2019].

United Nations Development Programme/World Bank (2019b). *Myanmar Living Conditions Survey 2017, Poverty Report*, June, Yangon. Available at: https://www.worldbank.org/en/country/myanmar/publication/poverty-report-myanmar-living-conditions-survey-2017 [Accessed 24 November 2019].

Warr, P. (2016). "Myanmar's Opening to the World Economy". In *Managing Globalization in the Asian Century*, edited by H. Hill and J. Menon. Singapore: Institute of Southeast Asian Studies, 333–357.

Warr, P., Rasphone, S., and Menon, J. (2017). "Two Decades of Rising Inequality and Declining Poverty in Laos". *Asian Economic Journal* 32: 165–185.

Warr, P. and L.L. Aung (2019). "Poverty and Inequality Impact of a Natural Disaster: Myanmar's 2008 Cyclone Nargis". *World Development* 122: 446–461.

World Bank (2017a). *An Analysis of Poverty in Myanmar, Part 1, Trends Between 2004/05 and 2015*. Yangon: Ministry of Planning and Finance and World Bank Group.

World Bank (2017b). *An Analysis of Poverty in Myanmar, Part 2, Poverty Profile*. Yangon: Ministry of Planning and Finance and World Bank Group.

7

MYANMAR'S RURAL ECONOMY AT A CROSSROADS

Ikuko Okamoto

The agricultural sector, the backbone of Myanmar's economy, has long been a stagnant sector. However, in the past four to five years, the sector's position in the national economy has started to change rapidly. In 2014/2015, for the first time in its history, the GDP share of the agricultural sector began to decline such that it became lower than that of the manufacturing sector (CSO 2017). While about 70 per cent of the population still resides in rural areas (CSO 2017), the number of people employed in the agricultural sector also decreased. From 2000 to 2010, it was between 70 per cent and 78 per cent, but it shrank to less than 60 per cent after 2011 (ILO Stat). The share of agricultural exports has also been decreasing consistently from 17.4 per cent in 2009/2010 to 11.8 per cent in 2016/2017 (CSO 2017).

The economic reforms of President Thein Sein since 2011 contributed to these changes in the agricultural sector. Despite many people's pessimistic expectations for any fundamental change, especially at the initial stages of the reforms, the government promoted industrialisation led by foreign direct investment as a key economic development strategy. As a result of other social and political changes occurring at the time, several longstanding controls and regulations were relaxed, from which the agricultural sector was not immune. The NLD government which took power in 2016 followed in the same direction of economic management, while prioritising the agricultural and rural sectors in its policies. This has led to major transformations in various aspects of Myanmar's rural economy.

While deregulation and a broad policy aimed at opening up the economy to foreign investment had been a target of the transition to a market economy under the military regime in the late 1980s, liberalisation in the 1990s and 2000s remained partial. The government controls and regulations rooted in the previous socialist regime were maintained in many respects, partly because the military government at the time wanted to capture the benefit for themselves and partly because they did not have much confidence in allowing the market to work freely. Therefore, it took more than twenty years for the Myanmar government to becoming fully committed to economic liberalisation, which led its departure from the socialist legacy that had long undermined the sound functioning of open market mechanisms.

The purpose of this chapter is to provide a comprehensive overview of how Myanmar's agricultural policies, namely, on production, land, and marketing, have changed since 2011 and how rural residents have responded to these changes. The regime change in 2011 not only shifted the way the economy was managed, but also opened up political space in the country. The progress of national reconciliation in favour of democratisation significantly improved Myanmar's position in the international community and allowed the country to finally become less isolated. As a result of the changing political landscape, it also became possible for scholars to conduct a much wider range of research on Myanmar's rural economy based on large-scale field surveys.[1] This was not previously feasible under the military government, which was facing strong international pressure and, thus, was reluctant to have outsiders investigate the real status of the country. This chapter is based on the author's long-term engagement with the country, including observations made from research conducted between 2013 and 2019,[2] to capture the current status of Myanmar's rural economy.

This chapter is organised as follows. The first section summarises the major changes to agricultural policies since 2011. It then goes on to examine the transformation in the rural economy as a result of these policy shifts. The final section then details some immediate challenges faced by Myanmar's rural sector.

CHANGES IN AGRICULTURAL POLICIES SINCE 2011

There have been two significant changes to agricultural policies since 2011. The first was weaker government control, which has been especially evident in rice-related issues. Rice was effectively a "political" crop during the socialist and military regimes, because both governments believed a sufficient supply of rice at a low price was necessary to assure their political stability and to contain people's potential discontent. This belief came from historical memories shared by government authorities of times when a sudden hike in rice prices triggered social unrest or intensified existing unrest – as occurred in 1967, 1974, and 1988 (Okamoto 2017). Thus, the government set rice policies that would maintain the stability of the rice supply at a sufficiently low price with the goal of curbing social unrest.

Three major policy tools were used to increase rice supply while keeping the price low (Okamoto 2017). First, the government intervened in the domestic and export rice markets. The socialist government introduced a compulsory system of purchasing paddy at a fixed price, often below the market price, to secure an adequate amount of rice for nationwide rationing. This system was maintained under the military government, although it was scaled down to cover the rationing for public servants only. Rice exports were also monopolised by the governments, aiming to keep the domestic price low regardless of the export market conditions.

Second, farmers were mandated to cultivate crops according to the government's yearly compulsory cropping plan. The cropping plan for rice was strictly enforced and monitored to assure an increase in rice production. In the early 1990s, this cropping plan functioned very effectively in expanding the double cropping of rice as well. Because the policy to increase rice production was largely politically motivated, this cropping plan was not formulated with consideration for farmers' profitability. For example, farmers in the dry zone and in mountainous areas suffered when the government introduced the "regional" rice self-sufficiency policy, which even forced farmers to cultivate rice in fields not categorised as "paddy land". In some of the areas in the delta, farmers sometimes needed to launch double cropping of rice according to the plan although they knew they would face losses because their fields were prone to salinity problems in the summer season.

Third, the nationalisation of farmland, under which farmers were considered tenants of the state and were entitled only to tillage rights, contributed to the enforcing of marketing and production policies mentioned above. Farmers were not allowed to transfer, mortgage, or inherit their titles freely, and if they failed to meet their annual quotas to produce or sell paddy to the government, their tillage rights could be revoked.

However, all these policy measures were relaxed in the early 2010s (Okamoto 2017). First, new farmland legislation was introduced in 2012 by enacting two laws – the Farmland Law (FL) and the Vacant, Fallow and Virgin Lands Management Law (VFVL). These laws were designed to develop business opportunities through improved use of farmland (Boutry et al. 2017). Farmers were the target of FL; they are now entitled to stronger land rights, although these are not yet defined as "property rights". The stipulations of these rights are: (1) farmers can sell, purchase, mortgage, lease, exchange, donate and inherit tillage rights; (2) land use certificates are issued to prove ownership of the rights; and (3) a land use certificate can be used as collateral to borrow money from formal financial institutions.

On the other hand, VFVL is an extension of the 1991 Management of Cultivable Land, Fallow Land and Waste Land (Woods 2010), which encourages large-scale agricultural development by the private sector. The primary intention of this law is to provide incentives to private enterprises to invest in land not registered as any type of farmland. As will be discussed in the next section, its 2018 amendment that required registration of those who had used this unregistered land on a customary or de facto basis has caused controversy.

Moreover, cropping control was relaxed in the early 2010s and farmers no longer had to strictly follow the yearly cropping plan. This was an especially big relief for farmers in areas where wet-land rice cultivation is not suitable as a result of the agro-environment, including because of the availability of irrigation, the condition of the soil, or economic viability.

Although the phrase "freedom of crop choice" appeared in the Ministry documents (MOALI 2011), it was true that the government still hesitated to grant complete freedom to change the type of crops produced (i.e., from seasonal to perennial crops) on a specific category of land. This hesitancy was reflected in the Farmland Law that required farmers to obtain permission from the appropriate authority to change crops to cultivate.[3] Nevertheless, as is shown in Figure 7.1, the actual pressure on cropping paddy was dramatically reduced.

Figure 7.1: Gross sown area and share of area under paddy

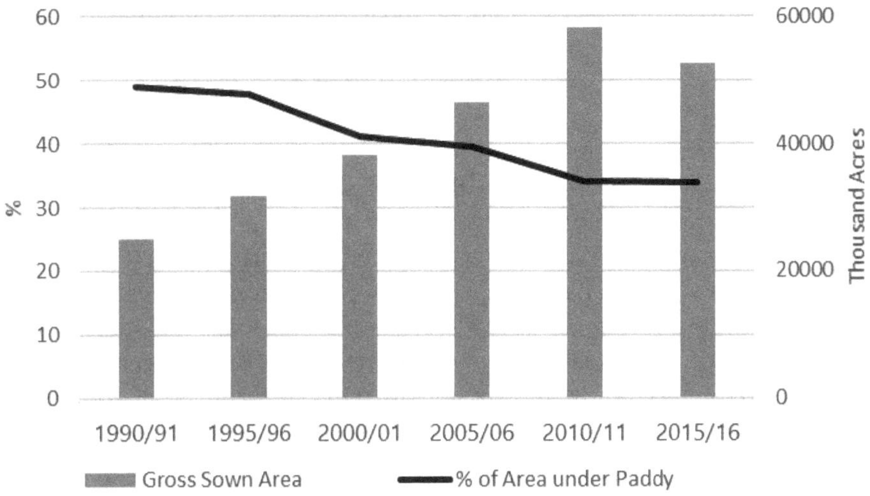

Source: CSO 2010; CSO 2017

The government's compulsory purchase of paddy was suspended much earlier in 2003. As a result, the government's monopoly on rice exports was gradually relaxed and fully opened to the private sector by 2012. This was an effort to revive Myanmar's status as a major rice exporter. In its effort to promote private exports of rice, the government even encouraged the private sector to establish a specific type of company for rice exports.[4] This change in the rice export system indicates that the government found it more realistic to develop commercial production of rice aimed at larger exports rather than to maintain subsistence-oriented or domestic market-oriented rice production.

The other major change in the agricultural policy under the Thein Sein government was shifting policy focus from "quantity of production" to "quality of people's lives". Socialist economies typically set economic targets regarding quantity, and this policy continued under the military regime in the 1990s and 2000s. However, the Thein Sein government stopped treating people simply as a means of production to achieve the economic goals set by the government. Rather, the quality of people's lives became the target of economic policy. This is a fundamental change in economic management. In line with this, the government set a poverty reduction goal for the first time in its history. Poverty was to be reduced from 25.6 per cent in 2010 to 16.1 per cent in 2015.[5] This was a significant change in policy rhetoric since previous governments tended to avoid even using the word "poverty" in their policies.

An increase to the supply of credit in rural areas was highlighted as one of the first priority areas as a way to reduce poverty. Limited access to financial services – or underdevelopment of the rural financial market – has been considered as one of the major causes of rural poverty and low agricultural productivity in Myanmar (Dapice et al. 2009). The rural population mainly depended on informal loans at usurious interest rates for their daily living as well as for agricultural production. To overcome this problem, while increasing the per acre amount of crop loans provided by the Myanmar Agricultural Development Bank (MADB), the government also diversified formal credit sources besides MADB in rural areas. Microfinance organisations (MFIs), cooperatives and government-supported village credit schemes (called "*Mya Seinn Yaung*") offered relatively reasonable credit compared to the existing informal credit sources. Among these various sources, the entry of MFIs was quite remarkable after the enactment of the Microfinance Law in 2012 (Turnell 2018). More than 160 MFIs were established by 2017.[6] These organisations are both international and local with differences in targets and in the areas covered.

CHANGES AFTER THE SHIFT OF AGRICULTURAL POLICIES: STANDING AT THE CROSSROADS

The agricultural policies that generated distortions in the market were almost completely removed under the Thein Sein government and consolidated under the NLD government. The next question relates to how and to what extent these new agricultural policies actually changed Myanmar's rural economy.

Commercially oriented agriculture with low return

Since 2011, the percentage and the absolute area under paddy production has decreased with the relaxation of government pressure to cultivate rice. Instead, farmers have started to choose crops according to market conditions. Since Myanmar farmers share high expectation that the production for export markets would provide them higher incomes, the area under export-oriented crops (e.g., pulses and maize) is increasing (Table 7.1). Good examples are pulses and beans primarily for the Indian market, and rice and maize for the Chinese market, which will be discussed in more detail later.

Table 7.1: Changes in sown acre (per cent)

	2010/11	2011/12	2012/13	2013/14	2014/15	2015/16	2016/17
Paddy	-0.2	-5.6	-4.6	0.6	-1.5	0.6	-0.7
Maize	7.2	5.7	2.5	4.5	4.1	2.8	3.9
Sesame	-2.9	0.8	-2.6	3.1	-4.8	4.4	-1.6
Matpe	3.1	3.3	1.6	-0.5	-0.4	3.2	4.0
Pedisein	4.2	-2.1	-1.0	3.3	4.5	3.1	0.9
Vegetable	3.2	-0.7	0.6	2.2	2.2	0.5	0.6

Source: CSO 2015; CSO 2017

When the author was doing fieldwork in 2018 and 2019 in Bago region, an interesting phenomenon was observed that indicated the spread of commercial production of rice among farmers. Most farmers in the area sold their entire paddy, not only the summer paddy but also the monsoon paddy, which they used to keep for their home consumption. They then purchased rice in the market for their home consumption. This is because they chose to cultivate the variety[7] that major export companies prefer to purchase, of which taste they do not like for their daily consumption. In other words, rice has become a genuine cash crop for farmers in this area. Previously, the typical behavioural pattern of Myanmar rice farmers has been to do their best to keep paddy for their own consumption (*wunsa*) and seed for the next season, fearing a price hike in the rainy season when they would have to buy rice in the market.

Commercialisation of agricultural production may indicate that farmers are receiving larger incomes from farming than before. However, this is not the case. Table 7.2 shows an estimate of agricultural income, and Myanmar ranked the lowest income level, although the figures are for 2009–2010. Another recent study presented the estimated gross profit[8] of households (not per capita) as US$840 per year for a medium-sized farm in the delta (Boughton et al. 2018a) and the average was US$1,100 per year in the case of the dry zone (Mather et al. 2018). Given that the average household size is four (Ministry of Immigration and Population 2015), these figures suggest that farmers continue to face low returns from their crops.

Table7.2: Agricultural GDP per agricultural population ($ per year)

Malaysia	8324
Thailand	1698
Indonesia	1431
Philippines	951
Vietnam	728
Cambodia	659
Myanmar	207

Source: Haggablade et al. 2014.

There are several causes for the low return. Some are on the revenue side. First, there is a limited improvement in the yield for most of the crops. For example, it is indicated that Myanmar's average paddy yield was simply half of the potential yield (Boughton et al. 2018a, 10) and it is the lowest among Asian countries (World Bank 2016a, 23). While pulses and beans are important export crops for Myanmar, they also suffer from a lack of improvement in yield (Boughton et al. 2018b, 13). The causes of low yields are low utilisation of improved varieties and quality seeds, low level of inputs such as chemical fertilisers and the impact of climate change,[9] especially on rain-fed crops (Ame Cho et al. 2017; Boughton et al. 2018a; Mather et al. 2018).

Second, limited export options are causing price instability for some crops. Figure 7.2 indicates the composition of agricultural exports. Pulses and beans account for the dominant share of agricultural exports, with Myanmar being the second-largest exporter of beans and pulses after Canada (World Bank 2016a, 60). Rice and maize also increased in amount after 2010.

The problem lies in the limited export destinations for these major export crops (World Bank 2014; Okamoto 2017; Boughton et al. 2018b). For example, India is Myanmar's major export destination for pulses and beans (especially black gram and pigeon pea) and accounts for 90–95 per cent of total exports. China is an important market for both rice and maize, and accounts for 60–70 per cent and 90 per cent of total Myanmar's exports, respectively.[10] Dependence on a single market or a few markets is extremely risky for any country because the prices fluctuate widely according to changes in the market situation or the trade policies of the partner countries.

Figure 7.2 Changes in agricultural exports and the share of crops

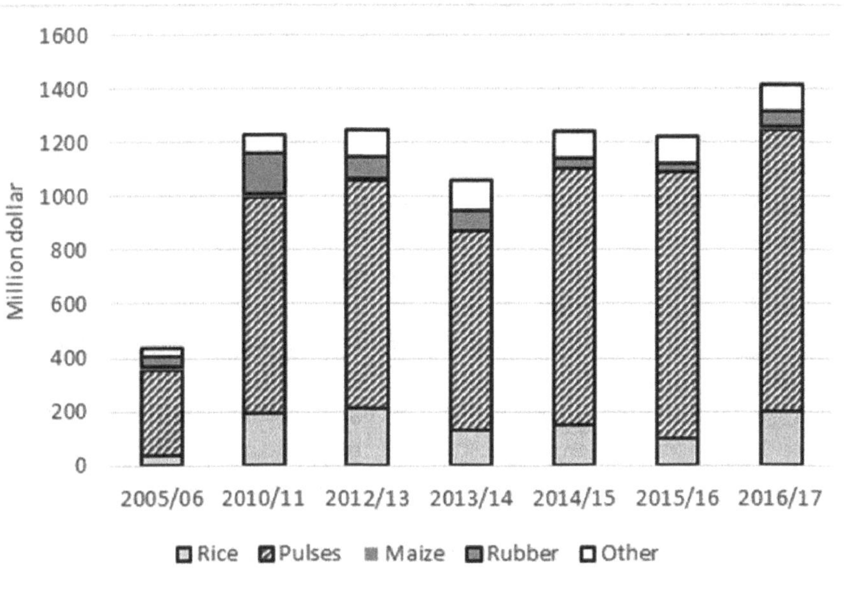

Source: CSO 2017

In the case of pulses and beans, the prices of Myanmar's pulses (mainly black gram and pigeon pea) in 2012 fell by 50 per cent compared with those of 2011 because of the increasing domestic supply of these pulses in India. In August 2017, the Indian government suddenly announced that it would set an import quota on pulses from Myanmar to raise its domestic price for pulses.[11] Consequently, the prices of these pulses in Myanmar plunged to 40 per cent compared to the price in the same month in the previous year (MOALI, MIS data).

A similar price collapse occurred with rice in 2014. China's announcement that it was banning imports of rice from Myanmar via the border led to a 17.5 per cent plunge in domestic rice price from three months earlier. Maize also faced an import quota from China, and a domestic bumper crop led to a price decrease of 11 per cent in 2016 (MOALI, MIS data).

In addition to the price risk arising from limited export markets, the lack of infrastructure development especially in the area of logistics (e.g., roads) has been a hurdle to Myanmar's agricultural produce becoming competitive in the exports markets, thus pushing down the potential profits for farmers. A good example is the transport cost of exporting rice to be exported to China via the border, which is reportedly higher than sending it by shipping to Africa (World Bank 2014).

The reason for the low rate of return lies on the production cost side as well, especially the increasing cost of labour (Belton et al. 2017; Boughton et al. 2018a; Myat Thida Win et al. 2018). As shown in Table 7.3, the real wages of agricultural labour have increased quite rapidly after 2010, though Myanmar's wage level is still low compared with its neighbouring countries (World Bank 2016a, 14). Due to the high dependency on wage labourers for cultivation, especially for planting and harvesting, which has been a major feature of Myanmar's agriculture until quite recently, rising wages for labourers would, *ceteris paribus,* directly lead to reduction of profit for farmers.

In response to the increasing labour cost, some farmers changed their rice cultivation method from transplanting to broadcasting, which can lower the yield if it is not accompanied with a sufficient amount of fertiliser.[12] Another option for farmers is to utilise agriculture machinery for some operations, which will be discussed in more detail below. However, neither of these strategies are necessarily considered as a viable option for every farmer. The location and the condition of the field, the choice of a suitable variety for the specific area, the difference in cropping patterns and financial constraints to purchase inputs are additional factors that influence choice of coping strategy against the increasing labour cost.

Table 7.3: Changes in real wages

Delta	
2011-13	2013-16
8%	32%
Dry Zone	
2012-14	2014-16
20%	15%

Source: Belton et al. 2017, Myat Thida Win et al. 2018

Accelerated technological change: The substitution of labour with mechanisation

The spread of agricultural mechanisation is the most striking change observed in recent years (Boughton et.al. 2018a; Myat Thida Win et.al 2018; Belton and Filipski 2019). Initially, wide-scale use of the power tiller started after the loss of cattle due to Cyclone Nargis in 2008. Furthermore, sporadic climate changes such as unexpected rain urged some farmers to use machinery to shorten the operational time to avoid crop damages in both the delta and dry zones. The tightening of the rural labour market, which led to the rapid increase in the labour wage, added to the momentum.

The accelerating speed in the use of machinery after 2013 is notable. Myat Thida Win et al. (2018, 116) reported findings in the delta in 2016 that were extremely different from the results of the survey conducted by the World Bank in 2013, which reported very low use of machinery. The percentages of farmers using machines for various purposes were 94 per cent for land preparation, 50 per cent for harvesting (combine harvester) and 38 per cent for threshing in 2016. The case of the combine harvester is the most striking since its usage increased from none to 50 per cent in just three years. A similar trend was observed in the dry zone. Due to the different cropping patterns in the dry zone from that of Delta, the usage of the four-wheel tractor showed the most impressive growth, approximately 30 per cent between 2013 and 2017, while the combine harvester increased by 8 per cent in the same period (Belton and Filipski 2019, 6).

Three factors are identified for this accelerated spread of machinery. First was the relaxation of financial constraints on the purchasing side. Myanmar's rural credit market is still underdeveloped, and the majority of the rural population has limited access to credit. When the size of the required loan is large, such as for expensive combine harvesters or four-wheel tractors, this is even more true. However, in 2013, a hire-purchasing system introduced by dealers and banks allowed buyers to pay the cost in installments with interest if they can pay the down-payment (Myat Thida Win et al. 2018).

Second, the prices of machinery became more affordable due to the overall increase in supply imported from China and Thailand. Filipski et al. (2018, 5–6) found a continuous decrease in the price of water pumps and two-wheel tractors between 2007 and 2017. In the case of the water pump, the price decreased by US$49 per year, while that of the two-wheel tractor decreased by US$153 per year.

Third, a rental market for the machinery has developed. As Myat Thida Win et al. (2018, 119–121) and Belton and Filipski (2019, 6) illustrate, a majority of farmers rent machinery (approximately 90 per cent), both in the delta and the dry zone, especially for high-cost machinery like the combine harvester and the four-wheel tractor. The development of the rental market makes the machinery usage scale-neutral. Without the rental market, the usage might be limited to those with better economic status, such as large landholders, for example. Again, both Myat Thida Win et al. (2018) and Belton and Filipski (2019) show that there is no significant difference in the usage of machines between farmers with small, medium, or large land holdings.

Mixed impact of the new rural credit policy

Policies that increased the rural credit supply was one of the major priorities in stimulating the rural economy, but it has yielded a somewhat mixed outcome. On the positive side, interest rates for informal loans are decreasing due to the overall increase in the credit supply. For example, Belton et al. (2017) reported that in the dry zone, the average monthly interest rates of informal loans were down by between 1.3 per cent and 5.2 per cent per month from 2012 to 2017. Lu Min Lwin and Khun Moe Htun (2016) reported a decrease of approximately 1 per cent between 2011 and 2016 in the delta.

On the negative side, one concern is related to Myanmar Agricultural Development Bank (MADB) loans. The MADB loan still heavily prioritises paddy production. For example, 94 per cent of the total MADB crop loan in 2016/2017 went to paddy. The next crop for which loans are allocated is pulses but this accounts for only 3 per cent of crop loans (MOALI 2018). Farmers who produce cash crops with relatively larger costs, such as vegetables and fruits, but do not have access to government loans, must seek other credit sources including informal loans. Even if farmers are eligible to take MADB loans, there are certain setbacks, such as the ceiling of ten acres, inadequate timing of disbursement that does not match farmers' real cash flow or cropping calendars, and complex and sometimes inefficient procedures (Boutry et al. 2017, 235–236). All these factors have led farmers to seek informal credit sources.

The second concern is the risk of over-indebtedness. The rapid increase in MFIs has led to keen competition to obtain customers in some areas, as new MFIs tend to initiate operations in easily accessible areas. A typical example is the case of Bago Township where twenty-seven MFIs were in operation in 2017.[13] Concerns regarding over-indebtedness of clients are increasing among MFIs because this can eventually lead to large-scale default which would make their operations difficult.[14]

In fact, the accumulation of debt is one of the major reasons for farmers' loss of land (Aung Hein et al. 2017; Boutry et al. 2017, 245–246). Aung Hein et al. (2017, 3) found that indebtedness accounted for about 40 per cent of the reasons for disposal of land from 1988–2016. Before the new FL was enacted, land was not recognised as "collateral" but was merely sold "informally" to obtain cash to repay the debt. However, since the land title can now be used as collateral for the loan from formal financial institutions, it is highly probable that the disposal of land due to indebtedness can proceed faster because the informal lenders may take advantage of the more secure land titles as collateral (Boutry et al. 2017, 134). This is reminiscent of the bitter history of the agricultural sector after the world economic crisis in the late 1920s, when the landless class increased rapidly due to default on the debt from the *Chettiers,* or Indian moneylenders, who were lending money to farmers and taking land as collateral (Furnival 1957).[15]

The third concern is limited outreach. For example, though the majority of MFIs aim to achieve financial inclusion for all economic classes, the poorest of the poor tend to be excluded. This is not necessarily because the MFIs are reluctant to lend them to maintain the organisation's financial sustainability, but because the poor themselves are afraid of not being able to make regular payments or feel the lending system is too complicated and demanding. The author found such a case in 2013 in a village in the delta. The majority of landless people continued to depend on wage payment advances, which they can get from farmers by promising that they will work for labour-intensive operations such as transplanting or harvesting. For this poorer class, borrowing from informal moneylenders is not easy due to a lack of economic creditworthiness or collateral, either. Thus, although advance wage payments are normally accompanied by implicit, but high interest rates, the flexibility and easiness is attractive for these poorer classes as a last resort to meet their credit needs for daily expenses including consumption (Okamoto 2015b).

Ambivalent impact of new land legislation

The introduction of new land laws in 2012 aimed at encouraging investment in farmland, included land previously not used for agriculture. Unfortunately, several unwanted consequences resulted from the new legislation.

First, there is a lack of institutional backup for enforcing of the law and implementing the process (Mark 2016, 451; Boutry et al. 2017, 127–147). There were several problems due to the hasty process of delivering land certificates, such as discrepancies in boundaries, areas, and the holder's name on the certificate. Small farmers could be excluded from the list due to differences in the registration process among villages and inability to make a claim. Exclusion of small famers from the process also occurred due to administrative costs related to registration being too prohibitive for them.[16] Further, although the major purpose of securing the title is to provide tools to resolve land conflicts (both within and outside the village), the land management body often has insufficient capacity to do so.

Second, as Mark (2016) argues, the new farm-related laws are in fact adding another "layer" of laws to those enacted by the past four regimes. Various stakeholders, including farmers, came to use not only the current laws but also old laws and notifications from the previous regime to defend their titles. This causes ambiguity, contradictions and even conflicts regarding the land. Mark (2016) further states that the ambiguity caused by these layers of laws often works against (small) farmers *vis-a-vis* the military, large private companies or administrative agencies. The latter group uses these laws selectively and strategically to their advantage to establish their land rights if there are conflicts with the farmers about the targeted land.

This treatment of laws and regulations can be a serious threat, especially in the mountainous and hilly areas, such as Shan, Chin, or Kachin States, where customary communal land tenure systems are still dominant. These tenure systems are not properly recognised under the current legal framework and a high possibility remains that farmers from these communities could lose access to this land (Woods 2010; Mark 2016; Boutry et al. 2018).

After the amendment of the VFVL in September 2018, there has been an increasing concern about this issue. The amendment would require farmers that are utilising land on a community tenure basis or de facto ownership basis – categorised as "virgin, fallow or vacant land" – to apply to a land management committee by March 2019 or they will be regarded as trespassers and will face punishment. Any cases of legal action following this particular new amendment is not reported yet. However, the ambiguity of the rights that apply to non-registered land, especially in the ethnic minority areas, is starting to cause some land disputes (e.g. in Kachin State[17]). There continues to be a high possibility that the new amendment will work against those who have been cultivating the land over the long term either on communal tenure or de facto basis.

The third issue is related to the previous discussion. Along with the continuous low return from agricultural production together with the economic structural changes described earlier, there is a clear tendency to regard land not as a factor of production, but rather as an "asset". In other words, some land is becoming a target for speculation regardless of its actual utilisation status. This often leads to the problematic "land grabbing".

The increasing importance of rural non-farm livelihood

Partly due to the low-return agricultural production and partly due to the new expanding economic opportunities in both rural and urban areas, the non-farm sector is increasingly gaining importance in the livelihood of rural people. This is clearly evident by the increase of rural enterprises, both related and unrelated to agriculture. For example, Belton et al. (2017, 14–16) report that agricultural machinery rental services have increased by 450 per cent; motorised transport increased 447 per cent; retail shops 190 per cent; food services 117 per cent and construction-related services 80 per cent between 2007 and 2017 – based on their surveys in the dry zone. Boughton et al. (2018a, 11) estimated that the non-farm business provides around 20 per cent of income sources and employment. However, these enterprises remain basically self-operated and do not hire workers, so this sector has not yet had a substantial impact on employment creation in rural areas.

Migration from rural areas has also rapidly increased since the early 2010s (Aung Hein et al. 2016; Htoo, K. and A. M. Tun 2016; LIFT 2016; World Bank 2016b; Prichard et al. 2017; Belton and Filipski 2019), signifying the increasing importance of non-farm income. The World Bank (2016b) reports that 20 per cent of the households in the delta and 25 per cent in the dry zone had at least one family member who migrated domestically or internationally. The number of domestic migrants is much larger than that of international migrants, comprising 91 per cent and 78 per cent of the total migrants in the delta and dry zones, respectively (World Bank 2016b, 20–28). Contrastingly, international migration accounts for a larger share in border states, such as Chin, Rakhine, Shan and Mon (Aung Hein et al. 2016, 94; LIFT 2016, 31; Prichard et al. 2017, 34). The industries migrants engage in are diverse, but migrants have a large share of non-farm jobs such as casual labourers in manufacturing, construction, wholesale and retail (Aung Hein et al. 2016; World Bank 2016b).

The dominant reason behind migration is employment, accounting for more than 70 per cent of migrants in the case of the delta and dry zones (World Bank 2016b). The motivations underlying migration to find employment can be broken down into three subcategories: shock management, risk management of household income and seeking upward economic mobility. Migration is a common response to unexpected shock, such as disasters, crop failure and illness of family members. Migration as risk management for household income is meant to deal with volatility by diversifying income sources. Thus, this type of migration can occur even if the income from new jobs is almost at the same level as the income at the home village. The last category, seeking upward mobility, is to earn a higher income or better working conditions and a better lifestyle than the migrant can get in their home area. Thus, the migrants in this category are not necessarily from poverty-stricken households but can be equipped with assets and capital. Those who migrate overseas typically fall into this category, as it normally costs much more to migrate internationally. Following these three motivations, different economic classes in the rural areas are migrating, either domestically or internationally, with different time spans.

Improving welfare with widening disparities

With all these economic transformation in rural areas, the important question is whether the welfare of the rural population has improved. According to the latest country poverty profile, the poverty rates of rural areas showed a consistent decrease between 2004/2005 and 2017 (Figure 3). Although the poverty rate of the rural areas remains high, because 87 per cent of the poor lived in rural areas in 2017 (World Bank 2019, 6), it is clear that the share of the population living below the poverty line is quickly decreasing.

General improvement in the economic status can also be confirmed through other related indicators (Boughton et al. 2018a; CSO et al. 2018; Prichard et al. 2018; World Bank 2019). Possession of consumer goods including small home appliances has been increasing since 2015. One of the most striking indicators is the spread of mobile phone ownership. Seventy-seven per cent of rural households owned mobile phones in 2017. This figure is now close to that of urban households, which is 82 per cent. Considering that the percentage gap in ownership between the urban and rural population was almost 30 per cent in 2014, there has been a remarkable increase in mobile phone ownership in rural areas.

The general increase in home appliances is made possible by improved access to electricity. Although access to public grids was still constrained even in 2017, users of solar systems have increased, especially after 2014 (CSO et al. 2018, 48–53). Sanitation has improved as well. The percentage of people with access to safe drinking water has increased from 70.6 per cent (dry season) and 80.6 per cent (rainy season) in 2015 to 79.4 per cent (dry season) and 86.9 per cent (rainy season) in 2017. Likewise, the share of the population without toilet facilities decreased from 13 per cent to 6 per cent between 2015 and 2017. A positive trend is also found in the area of education. School enrolment rates in rural areas increased from 87 per cent to 94 per cent for primary school, 47 per cent to 68 per cent for middle school and 20 per cent to 39 per cent for high school between 2010 and 2017 (CSO et. al. 2018, 111).

Despite these positive signs of welfare improvement, there remains a serious concern that needs special attention: the increasing disparities among the different geographical conditions (rural-urban and among the different regions) and among the different economic classes (landholding and landless class) within rural areas.

Increasing economic disparity between urban and rural areas is clear from Figure 7.3. The poverty rate in urban areas in 2017 was about one-third of that in the rural areas. Among the regions, poverty also shows distinct geographic concentration. Coastal (Rakhine and Tanintharyi) and hill and mountain regions (Chin, Kachin, Kayah, Kayin and Shan) show the highest poverty rates, compared to the dry zone (Mandalay and Sagain) and the delta regions (Ayeyarwady and Bago). Average poverty rates in

2017 were 32.2 per cent and 31.1 per cent for coastal, hill and mountain regions, while it is 24.8 per cent and 24.4 per cent for the dry zone regions and delta regions (World Bank 2019, 8).[18] Reflecting this difference in economic conditions, all other welfare indicators for welfare, such as asset holdings, including home appliances, furnishing items and transportation, sanitation and education were much lower for rural areas, especially in coastal, hills and mountain regions, than in urban areas (CSO et al. 2018).

Figure 7.3: Changes in poverty rate estimated based on 2015 living conditions

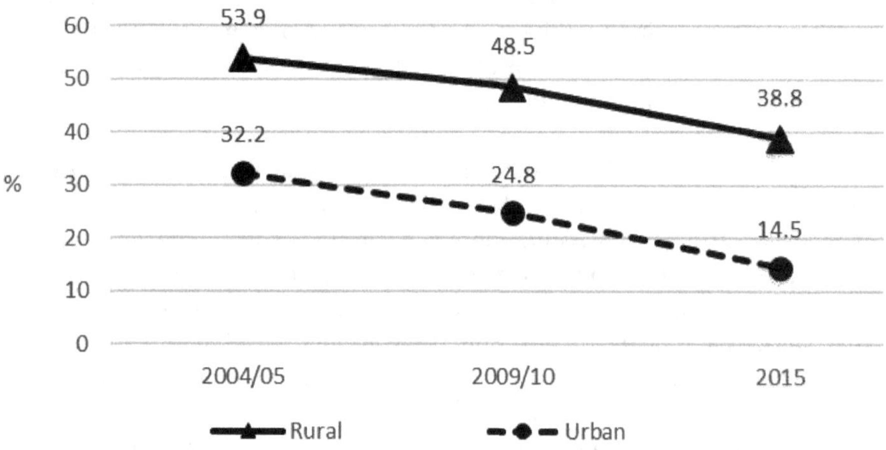

Source: World Bank 2017a, 25; World Bank 2019, 7

Several studies prior to 2011 have indicated that a large pool of the landless classes in rural Myanmar that depend on agricultural wage labour are in the poorest class in the country (Okamoto 2008; Dapice 2009; Fujita 2009). Seemingly, this has yet to change and the landless might be further disadvantaged. Despite the recent momentum towards income diversification into non-farm income sources in rural areas, these classes are left behind and tend to stay within the agricultural sector as wage labourers (World Bank 2017b; Boughton et al. 2018a; World Bank 2019). Consequently, "the welfare of the poorest 10 per cent in the population has not changed as remarkably as the welfare of the average households" (World Bank 2017b, 20). Moreover, this landless class faces food and nutritional insecurities (Rammohan and Prichard 2014).

IMMEDIATE CHALLENGES TO MYANMAR'S RURAL SECTOR

Myanmar's rural sector is entering a new phase. The economic reforms since 2011 have triggered a transformation in various aspects of the rural economy. The relaxation of longstanding government intervention in the agricultural sector, which focused on increasing rice production, gave farmers more freedom in crop choices and marketing channels. However, this freedom did not necessarily bring higher profit from agricultural production to farmers because of the lack of improvement in yield and price instability. Combined with the expansion of the non-farming sector in general, it has led to an acceleration of out-migration of the rural population, pushing the substitutions of labour with machinery for some agricultural operations. Injection of capital into the rural economy and a new legal framework concerning land usage also generated some new problems such as over-indebtedness and land speculation. Alongside this transformative process, economic disparity is increasing between regions, between urban and rural areas and within rural areas more than ever.

A very rapid diversification of livelihoods away from agriculture is occurring in Myanmar. However, it should be noted that this process in itself is not new or unique to Myanmar. In the case of Southeast Asian countries, the same process began back in the 1960s and 1970s (Hart 1994; Rigg 1998; Rigg and Vandergeest ed. 2012). The striking difference between the experience of these countries and that of Myanmar lies in the speed of transformation. As reflected in the speed of agricultural mechanisation such as the spread of combine harvesters between two and three years, several changes have been happening at an accelerated pace. The speed of transformation itself can generate new problems and requires government and policymakers to respond quickly to remedy any unexpected consequences from this process.

Myanmar's economic goal is to achieve development through industrialisation. Under industrialisation policies, one of the major roles of the agricultural sector is to supply food at a low price to keep wages low. Another role is to increase the purchasing power of the rural population to provide a market for industrial goods and services. An increase in agricultural productivity and an improvement in the rate of return of agricultural production is indispensable for meeting these goals. With the rapid speed of economic transformation in rural areas, the policies that improve productivity and profitability along with a clear agenda to check the increasing disparities must be formulated and implemented quickly.

In 2018, the Myanmar government launched a comprehensive strategic plan called the "Agricultural Development Strategy" (MOALI 2018). This puts a clear emphasis on the improvement of the well-being of the rural population (Boughton et al. 2020). However, experience tells us that when developing the rural sector, merely allowing the market to function is not a sufficient condition for either improving people's welfare or reducing inequality. Therefore, at this stage, *implementation* of concrete policy agenda to tackle these challenges is crucial. For that purpose, institution-building and developing human capacity must go hand-in-hand, in both the public and private sectors, and cannot lag behind the on-going transformation of the country as a whole.

Notes

1 For example, LIFT, the World Bank, a team of Michigan State University researchers supported by USAID, and migration studies funded by IOM and the University of Sydney have all conducted large-scale surveys.

2 The author did several stints of fieldwork to examine the current status of rural financial market between 2013 and 2019 (three times in Kaungyidaung, Ayeyarwady region, and twice in Daik-Oo, Bago region). As a part of the survey, the author investigated the recent changes in farm management.

3 The requirement to obtain permission to change crops is also written in the Land Use Certificates (often referred to as "Form 7") provided to farmers. Whether or not these conditions are strictly enforced needs further investigation.

4 These companies are known as Rice Specialising Companies and are intended to build a comprehensive supply chain from production to export by incorporating a sort of contract farming (see Okamoto 2015 for details).

5 These are the figures utilised in President Thein Sein's speech, but later estimates made by the World Bank suggest that actual poverty incidents were much higher than this.

6 Internal document of the Financial Regulatory Department.

7 *Hmawbi 2* is the variety the exporters want to purchase, while farmers like to consume *Shinthuka* or *Pawsan Hmwe*. Rice has been mainly marketed according to the shape and type (e.g., *Emata, Meedon,* etc.) since the colonial period, not according to the specific variety in Myanmar. However, a mixture of the varieties decreases the quality of milled rice, thus some exporting companies started to purchase specific varieties in order to maintain high milling quality.

8 See the detailed data for the rate of return in Ame Cho et al. (2017) and Mather et al. (2018). Estimation is for 2015/16.

9 For example, according to Cornish et al. (2018), the average rainfall during the monsoon season has not changed, but the number of rainy days declined by 56% between 1951 and 2016, from 156 days to 69 days.

10 Data for rice is based on UN Comtrade (accessed on 20 January 2019), while data for maize is based on *Global New Light of Myanmar* (21 July 2018).

11 See Boughton et al. (2018b, 14–15) for a detailed discussion on the impact of Indian policies and the response from the Myanmar side. The author found that in the village of Bago in 2018, some farmers changed the dry season crop from black gram to rice in response to the price collapse. It is reported that the Indian import of pulses is considered the lowest in 2018–2019, since 2000–2001 (*Reuters,* 18 July 2018). In the case of Myanmar, the quota for black gram is 300,000 tons per fiscal year and 200,000 tons for pigeon peas. For the 2016–2017 fiscal year, Myanmar exported a total of 185,000 tons of pigeon peas, 562,000 tons of black beans and over 400,000 tons of mung beans to India (*Myanmar Times* 24 August 2017).

12 This paragraph is based on the author's survey in Kaungyidaung in 2017.

13 Internal memo distributed in the meeting of MFIs held in Bago.

14 Author's interview with a microfinance organisation in November 2018.

15 In fact, this experience was the major motivation for the socialist government to introduce the land nationalisation while forbidding tenancy in the early 1960s (Boutry et al. 2017, 98).

16 According to Mark (2016, 450), nine million land usage certificates have been issued as of January 2016.

17 In Kachin State, the Chinese companies set up a banana plantation on the land that is leased by local residents. However, the contracts are insecure and the residents are afraid of losing their land (*Irrawaddy,* 4 December 2019).

18 According to the state-wise poverty rates in 2017, the highest is 58.0% (Chin), followed by 41.6 % (Rakhine) and 36.6% (Kachin), while the lowest is 13.2 (Mandalay and Tanintharyi) and 13.7% (Yangon). Also note that because of the population density, Ayeyarwady has the largest number of the poor among the states.

References

Ame Cho, Belton, B. and Boughton, D. (2017). "Crop Production and Profitability in Ayeyarwady and Yangon". *Food Security Policy Research Paper No.66*. East Lansing: Michigan State University. Available at: https://ageconsearch.umn.edu/record/264387/files/FSP%20RESEARCH%20PAPER%2066.pdf (accessed 26 May 2020).

Aung Hein, Lambrecht, I., Kyaw Lwin, and Belton, B. (2017). "Agricultural Land in Myanmar's Dry Zone". *Food Security Policy Project Research Highlights No.8*. East Lansing: Michigan State University. Available at: <http://foodsecuritypolicy.msu.edu/uploads/resources/Research_Highlights_8.pdf> (accessed 26 May 2020).

Belton, B., Filipski, M., Hu, C., Aung Tun Oo, and Aung Htun (2017). "Rural Transformation in Central Myanmar: Results from the Rural Economy and Agriculture Dry Zone Community Survey". *Food Security Policy Research Paper No. 46*. East Lansing: Michigan State University, 2017. Available at: http://foodsecuritypolicy.msu.edu/resources/rural_transformation_in_central_myanmar (accessed 26 May 2020).

Belton, B., and Filipski, M. (2019). "Rural Transformation in Central Myanmar: By how much, and for whom?" *Journal of Rural Studies* 67 (1): 166–176.

Boughton, D., Nilar Aung, Belton, B., Filipski, M., Mather,D., and Payongayong E. (2018a). "Myanmar's Rural Economy: A Case Study in Delayed Transformation". *Food Security Policy Research Paper 104*. East Lansing: Michigan State University. Available at: https://www.canr.msu.edu/fsp/publications/researchpapers/RP104_for_pdf_temporary_Recent%20Transformation.pdf (accessed 26 May 2020).

Boughton, D., Haggblade, S., and Dorosh, P. (2018b). "The Challenge of Export-led Agricultural Growth with Monopsonistic Markets: The Case of Myanmar's Pulse Sector and Trade with India". *Food Security Policy Research Paper 105*. East Lansing: Michigan State University. Available at: https://www.canr.msu.edu/fsp/publications/researchpapers/RP105_for_pdf_temporary_Myanmar%20Pulse%20Sector.pdf (accessed 26 May 2020).

Boughton, D., Okamoto, I., Mark, S., Tin Htut Oo, Theingi Myint and Ardeth Maung Thawnghmung (2020). "Agriculture and the Rural Economy: The Struggle to Transform Rural Livelihoods".In *Myanmar: Politics, Economy and Society*, edited by A. Simpson and F. Farrelly. London: Routledge.

Boutry, M., Allaverdian, C., Mellac, M., Huard, S., U SanThein, Tin Myo Win, and Khin Pyae Sone (2017) *Land Tenure in Rural Lowland Myanmar: From Historical Perspectives to Contemporary Realities in the Dry Zone and the Delta*. Yangon: GRET. Available at: http://www.gret.org/publication/land-tenure-in-rurallowland-myanmar/ (accessed 26 May 2020).

Boutry, M., Allaverdian, C., Tin Myo Win and Khin Pyae Sone (2018). *Persistence and Change in Hakha Chin Land and Resource Tenure: A Study on Land Dynamics in the Periphery of Hakha*. GRET: Yangon. Available at: https://www.gret.org/publication/persistence-and-change-in-hakha-chin-land-and-resource-tenure/?lang=en (accessed 26 May 2020).

Central Statistical Organization (CSO) (2010). *Statistical Yearbook 2009*. Nay Pyi Taw: Myanmar Ministry of Planning and Finance.

_____ (2015). *Statistical Yearbook 2015*. Nay Pyi Taw: Myanmar Ministry of Planning and Finance.

_____ (2017). *Statistical Yearbook 2017*. Nay Pyi Taw: Myanmar Ministry of Planning and Finance.

_____ (2018). *Myanmar Agricultural Statistics (2007–2008 to 2016–2017)*. Nay Pyi Taw: Central Statistical organization, Ministry of Planning and Finance in collaboration with Ministry of Agriculture, Livestock and Irrigation, Ministry of Natural Resources and Environmental Conservation.

Central Statistical Organization (CSO), UNDP and WB (2018). *Myanmar Living Conditions Survey 2017: Key Indicators Report*. Nay Pyi Taw and Yangon: Myanmar Ministry of Planning and Finance, UNDP and WB.

Cornish, P., Birchall, C., Herridge, D., Denton, M., and Guppy, C. (2018). "Rainfall Related Opportunities, Risks, and Constraints to Rainfed Cropping in the Central Dry Zone of Myanmar as Defined by Soil Water Balance Modelling". *Agricultural Systems* 164: 47–57.

Dapice, D., Valley, T. and Wilkinson, B. (2009). *Assessment of the Myanmar Agricultural Economy*. Cambridge, MA: Harvard Kennedy School, Ash Centre for Democratic Governance and Innovation.

Filipski, M., Belton, B., and van Asselt, J. (2018). "Mechanization in the Dry Zone". *Food Security Policy Project Research Highlights No.13*. East Lansing: Michigan State University. Available at: http://foodsecuritypolicy.msu.edu/uploads/resources/Research_Highlights_12.pdf.

Fujita, K. (2009). "Agricultural Laborers in Myanmar during the Economic Transition: Views from the Study of Selected Villages". In *The Economic Transition in Myanmar after 1988: Market Economy Versus State Control*, edited by K. Fujita, F. Mieno and I. Okamoto. Singapore: NUS Press and Kyoto University Press, 246–280.

Furnival, J.S. (1957). *The Political Economy of Burma*, 3rd edition. Rangoon: Peoples' Literature Committee & House.

Haggblade, S., Boughton, D., Cho, K.M., Denning, G., Kloeppinger-Todd, R., Wong, L. (2014). "Strategic Choices Shaping Agricultural Performance and Food Security in Myanmar". *Journal of International Affairs* 67 (2): 55–71.

Hart, G. (1994). "The Dynamics of Diversification in an Asian Rice Region". In *Development or Deterioration: Work in Rural Asia,* edited by B. Koppel, Ja Hawkins and W. James. Boulder and London: Lynne Rienner, 47–71.

Htoo K. and Htun, A.M. (2016). "Rural-Urban Migration around Yangon City, Myanmar". *Food Security Policy Projects Research Highlights No. 5.* Michigan State University. Available at:http://foodsecuritypolicy.msu.edu/uploads/resources/Research_Highlights_5.pdf (accessed 26 May 2020).

International Labor Organization (ILO) (2017). *Myanmar: Employment and Environmental Sustainability Fact Sheets 2017.* Available at: https://www.ilo.org/asia/publications/issue-briefs/WCMS_624758/lang--en/index.htm (accessed 26 May 2020).

Livelihoods and Food Security Trust Fund (LIFT) (2016). *Qualitative Social and Economic Monitoring: Round 5 Report.* Yangon: LIFT. Available at: http://www.lift-fund.org/sites/liftfund.org/files/publication/QSEM%205%20%28English%29%20LOW%20RES%20FINAL.pdf (accessed 26 May 2020).

Lu Min Lwin and Khun Moe Htun (2016). "Credit Access and Utilization in Agriculture and Aquaculture in the Ayeyawarady Delta". *Food Security Policy Project Research Highlights* No. 3. Available at: http://foodsecuritypolicy.msu.edu/uploads/resources/Research_Highlights_3.pdf (accessed 26 May 2020).

Mark, S. (2016). "Are the Odds of Justice 'Stacked' Against Them? Challenges and Opportunities for Securing Land Claims by Smallholder Farmers in Myanmar". *Critical Asian Studies* 48 (3): 443–460.

Mather, D., Nilar Aung, Ame Cho, Boughton, D., Belton, B., Kyan Htoo and Payongayong, E. (2018). "Crop Production and Profitability in Myanmar's Dry Zone". *Food Security Research Paper 102* East Lansing: Michigan State University. Available at: https://www.canr.msu.edu/fsp/publications/researchpapers/FSP%20Research%20Paper%20102.pdf (accessed 26 May 2020).

Ministry of Agriculture and Irrigation (MOAI) (2011). *Myanmar Agriculture in Brief 2011.* Yangon.

Ministry of Agriculture, Livestock and Irrigation (MOALI) (2018). *Agricultural Development Strategy.* Nay Pyi Taw: Ministry of Livestock, Agriculture, and Irrigation.

Ministry of Immigration and Population (2015). *The 2014 Myanmar Population and Housing Census: Highlights of the Main Results.* Available at: http://www.dop.gov.mm/sites/dop.gov.mm/files/publication_docs/census_highlights_report_-_english_clean.pdf (accessed 26 May 2020).

Myat Thida Win, Belton, B. and Xiaobo Zhang (2018). "Myanmar's Rural Revolution: Mechanization and Structural Transformation". In *Myanmar Transformed? People, Places and Politics,* edited by J. Chambers, G. McCarthy, N. Farrelly and Chit Win. Singapore: ISEAS.

Nyien Nyien (2019). "Chinese-Backed Banana Plantations in Myanmar's Kachin State Prompt Fear of Environmental Damage, Land Loss". *Irrawaddy*, 4 December 2019. Available at: https://www.irrawaddy.com/news/burma/chinese-backed-banana-plantations-myanmars-kachin-state-prompt-fear-environmental-damage-land-loss.html?fbclid=IwAR1Xn5KG-nhULsCw2tsDl2GT1G9aT5buiCJwi8E7XolC050pCrGfI8DpoBc (accessed 20 December 2019).

Okamoto, I. (2008). *Economic Disparity in Rural Myanmar: Transformation under Market Liberalization*. Singapore: NUS Press.

_____ (2015a). "Rice Export and Contract Farming: Lessons from the Rice Specializing Companies". In Japan International Cooperation Agency "Report for Economic Reform" (Agricultural and Rural Working Group), prepared for Japan International Cooperation Organization. Available at: http://libopac.jica.go.jp/images/report/12238812_01.pdf (accessed 26 May 2020).

_____ (2015b). "Summary of Survey Findings for a Village in the Ayeyarwady Region". In Japan International Cooperation Agency "Report for Economic Reform" (Agricultural and Rural Working Group), prepared for Japan International Cooperation Organization. Available at: http://libopac.jica.go.jp/images/report/12238812_01.pdf (accessed 26 May 2020).

_____ (2017). "Agriculture". In *Routledge Handbook of Contemporary Myanmar*, edited by A. Simpson , N. Farrelly and I. Holliday. London: Routledge, 192–201.

Pritchard, B., Dibley, M., Rammohan, A., Htin, Z.S., Nay, S.M., Thwin, T., Pan Hmone, M., Htet, K., Vicol, M., Aung, A.M., Linn, K.K., Hall, J. (2017). *Livelihoods and Food Security in Rural Myanmar: Survey Findings*. Sydney: University of Sydney.

Pritchard, B., Dibley, M., Rammohan, A., Htin, Z.S., Khay, S.M., Thtet, M., Vicol, K., Horton, M., Welch, J. (2018). *Food and Nutrition Insecurity in Rural Myanmar under Conditions of Rapid Livelihood Changer: Survey Findings from the 2015-18 Australian Research Council Project*. Sydney: University of Sydney. Available at: https://feedingmyanmar.wordpress.com/publications/ (accessed 26 May 2020).

Rammohan, A. and Prichard, B. (2014). "The Role of Landholding as a Determinant of Food and Nutrition Insecurity in Rural Myanmar". *World Development* 64: 597–608.

Rigg, J. (2012). "Rural-urban Interactions, Agriculture and Wealth: A Southeast Asian Perspective". *Progress in Human Geography* 22(4): 497–522.

Rigg, J. and Vandergeest, P. (2012). *Revisiting Rural Places: Pathways to Poverty and Prosperity in Southeast Asia*. Honolulu: University of Hawaii Press.

Turnell, S. (2018). "Microfinance in Myanmar: Unleashing the Potential". In *The Business of Transition: Law Reform, Development and Economics in Myanmar*, edited by M. Crouch. Cambridge: Cambridge University Press, 122–147.

Woods, K. (2010). "Community Forestry in Cease-Fire Zones in Kachin State, Northern Burma: Formalizing Collective Property in Contested Ethnic Areas". Paper presented at CAPRI Workshop on Collective Action, Property Rights and Conflict in Natural Resources Management, Siem Reap, Cambodia, 28 June–1 July.

World Bank (2014). *Myanmar: Capitalizing on Rice Export Opportunities*. Available at: http://www.bankinformationcenter.org/wp-content/uploads/2014/10/Myanmar-Capitalizing-on-Rice-Export-Opportunities.pdf (accessed 26 May 2020).

_____ (2016a). *Myanmar: Analysis of Farm Production Economics*. Washington DC: World Bank..

_____ (2016b). *A Country on the Move: Domestic Migration in Two Regions of Myanmar*. Yangon: World Bank.

_____ (2017a). *An Analysis of Poverty in Myanmar: Part One – Trends Between 2004/05 and 2015 (Vol. 2) (English)*. Washington, D.C.: World Bank Group. Available at: http://documents.worldbank.org/curated/en/556581502987486978/An-analysis-of-poverty-in-Myanmar-part-one-trends-between-2004-05-and-2015 (accessed 26 May 2020).

_____ (2017b). *An Analysis of Poverty in Myanmar (English)*. Washington, D.C.: World Bank Group. Available at: http://documents.worldbank.org/curated/en/829581512375610375/pdf/121822-REVISED-PovertyReportPartEng.pdf (accessed 26 May 2020).

_____ (2019). *Myanmar Living Condition Survey 2017 Report 3 – Poverty Report (English)*. Washington, D.C.: World Bank Group. Available at: http://documents.worldbank.org/curated/en/921021561058201854/Myanmar-Living-Condition-Survey-2017-Report-3-Poverty-Report (accessed 26 May 2020).

8

TEN YEARS OF FISHERIES GOVERNANCE REFORMS IN MYANMAR (2008–2018)

Yin Nyein, Rick Gregory and Aung Kyaw Thein

Fishing is a vital economic activity in Myanmar, particularly in the coastal regions and states. The fishery and livestock sectors are considered to be the most important after agriculture in meeting the protein needs of the population, enhancing food security, and providing employment and livelihoods in rural communities. In 2018, the livestock and fisheries sectors were estimated to account for a total of 8 per cent of annual GDP (Department of Planning 2018). Freshwater fisheries governance in Myanmar from the British colonial period onwards has focused consistently on revenue generation, resulting in a gradual reduction in small-scale fisher access to traditional fishing grounds and fuelling natural resource degradation and declines in fisheries' production. In recent years this situation has triggered demands from small-scale fishers for more equitable access and sustainable resource use, through co-management.

Over the last ten years, freshwater fishery governance has steadily improved through structural changes and interactive processes. Through persistent lobbying, collaboration, engagement and trust-building by NGOs and CSOs, regional and state parliaments have promulgated freshwater fisheries laws in Rakhine, Mon, Bago, and Ayeyarwaddy regions that encapsulated pro-poor policies and created a legal basis for community fisheries co-management. Three interactive processes supported these reforms. Firstly, the civil society movement strengthened significantly, and in many areas, small-scale fishers demanded improved access to their traditional fishing grounds and recognition of their fishing rights. Secondly, the democratic transition created uncertainty for bureaucrats, policymakers, and the private sector who had previously controlled the fishery resource rents unchallenged. This opened the door for multi-stakeholder engagement initiatives and proactive engagement by small-scale fisher groups, associations and partnerships. Thirdly, the establishment of inter-state/regional experience exchange platforms through the establishment of fishery partnerships, contributed to improvements in fishery laws and governance mechanisms. This supported the exchange of experiences between small-scale fishers but also introduced an element of competition amongst the different partnerships striving to achieve better policies and governance arrangements.

The fisheries sector in Myanmar can be categorised into three sub-sectors, each having separate legislation; freshwater fisheries[1] (inland fisheries); marine fishery (off-shore and in-shore/coastal fisheries); and aquaculture. National statistics suggest that during 2017–2018, the total production of fish from Myanmar was 5.88m metric tons, with freshwater fish accounting for 1.59m metric tons, marine fish production accounting for 3.15m metric tons, and aquaculture accounting for 1.13m metric tons. According to official government sources more than half a million (0.57m) metric tons of fish and fisheries products were exported to other countries generating a total value of USD 711.72 million (Department of Fisheries 2018). The fisheries sector is also an important generator of employment and wealth along supply chains in domestic and export markets and the processing of fish is an important source of income for many people, particularly women. In many lowland inland areas, people continue to rely on wild fish caught from the country's extensive and diverse freshwater fisheries for domestic food consumption and income generation.

This paper examines freshwater fisheries governance reforms between 2008 and 2018. It draws on the authors' collective experience working as consultants in this field as part of a project implemented by the Network Activities Group aimed at improving the fishery governance system in in Myanmar since 2009.[2] The authors also carried out qualitative interviews with fishermen, parliamentarians (including speakers and chairperson of the Bill Committee), and Chief Ministers of the Ayeyarwaddy region, Bago region and Mon State over a one-month period between November–December 2018 to assess how these reforms are viewed in the contemporary era.

In this paper we demonstrate that there are several challenges to the successful implementation of the new freshwater fishery laws and pro-poor policies. First, the revenue collection and socio-economic development goals of the state and regional governments continue to contradict each other. Second, the effectiveness of local government staff to operationalise laws and implement new policies remains limited, due to conflicting interests and lingering uncertainty over union and state-level roles and responsibilities. Finally, there is limited institutional and financial capacity of small-scale fisher organisations to implement co-management mechanisms, when many of their members remain poorly educated and shackled to local bonded market chains. Despite these challenges, the recent freshwater fisheries sector governance reforms in Myanmar are regarded as a significant success and provide lessons and guidance for the improved governance of other economic sectors. As we show, these lessons include: approaches to the incorporation of pro-poor policies into legal frameworks; the role of democratically elected MPs in law-making processes; the role of NGOs and CSOs in lobbying for pro-poor policies and supporting law-making processes by government; the role of partnerships and networks in widening perceptions and improving stakeholder communications; and the importance of cooperation with other countries in the region, who can articulate lessons learned based on their own national context and experience.

FRESHWATER FISHERIES LAWS AND POLICIES UNDER DIFFERENT POLITICAL REGIMES

Freshwater fish production has played a critical role in trade and commerce since ancient times. Under the ancient Burmese dynasties, two types of fisheries existed – public lease fisheries and private/hereditable lease fisheries. People managing public lease fisheries paid a fixed rate of tax on their fish production as well as rent for use of the resource. Private and hereditable lease fisheries only paid tax based on production, but this tax rate was not fixed and was decided by local tax officers (Reeve et al. 1999).

When Britain seized the lower part of Burma in 1852, they established an administrative system that looked to increase revenue collection (Schendel 1991). Under the Burma Fishery Rules of 1864, the ownership of leasable fisheries passed from individual to State control. This was considered necessary at the time in order to collect revenue from the leasable fisheries, more systematically. Under the Burma Fishery Act of 1875, a new fishery tax system abolished the principle of fair taxation for all resource users. The introduction of an auction system for fishery leases created many negative consequences for the people engaged in the sector, as well as changing the traditional structure of the relationship between fishermen and lease fishery owners. The customary owners of lease fisheries were referred to as *Innthugyi* and *Innthargyi,* similar sounding words which had two distinct meanings. *Innthugyi* means "governor of the '*Inn*'", and *Innthargyi* means large-scale fisher who worked on the lease fisheries. The first hereditary lease owners were often referred to as *Innthugyi* and were amongst the wealthiest and most influential people in Delta society (U Khin 1948; Ba Thaw 2011). The name *Innthugyi* implies authority and influence and reflected the superior-subordinate relationship with village communities, gradually becoming a basic social element of Burmese rural society. Many *Innthugyi* acted as community decision-makers and provided remuneration and social welfare for their respective village communities (Reeve et al. 1999). The system introduced under the British created a new elite class, eroding these traditional "patron-client" relations between *Innthugyi* and their respective communities (c.f. Scott 1972). Under the British, the new lease purchaser, *lelan gaung,* controlled multiple fisheries and sub-leased the fishing grounds to *Innthugyi* or local fishers, with the proviso that all fish caught must be purchased by them. The new auctioning system effectively turned fishers into sub-tenants of an elite class who had the financial capital to bid for the leases, sometimes at exorbitant rates. Under the new conditions, local fishers found themselves under increasing pressure from moneylenders and traders who crowded in to take advantage of the new system. In 1905, a Fisheries Act (Act III of 1905) was drafted to strengthen the country's fishery laws and included guidance on the rights of fishers, lease arrangements, the protection of fishery resources, and official powers. Although there were significant provisions in the new Act that sought to better protect fisheries, the main focus of the Act was on increasing revenue.

During the post-independence period (1947–1962) the colonial taxation system remained largely unchanged in this sector (Thaw 2011), making the fishery resources taxation system introduced under the 1905 law the longest continuous taxation system in Myanmar's history. In the quasi-Socialist period (1962–1988), the 1974 Constitution abolished the leasing rights system, placing the State as the ultimate owner of "all-natural resources above and below the ground, above and beneath the waters and in the atmosphere." The 1974 Constitution also proclaimed that "all-natural resources shall be developed, extracted, exploited and utilized". During this period, the People's Pearl and Fisheries Cooperation (PPFC), and local cooperatives managed all of the most productive freshwater fishing grounds in Myanmar. They also allocated some leases through a selective allocation system rather than through an auction-based system as existed under the colonial government. The fishery taxation system deteriorated during this period due to a lack of transparency, nepotism and structural corruption. One positive aspect of the quasi-socialist era was that local fishing communities were allowed access to fishing grounds for a seven-month period annually, since the national corporations and cooperatives were only permitted to operate for five months during the most productive fishing seasons each year (San Aung 2010).

During the subsequent military period (1988–2007) the Fishery Department was given full authority to collect revenue from the country's fisheries. The 1991 Union Freshwater Fisheries Law replaced the 1905 Fishery Act and provided a new legal basis for the introduction of tender fisheries. This new way of generating fishery revenue allowed for the renting out of river and creek areas, through an auction system, and a permission system to the use of large-scale stationary fishing gear to individuals. These new fishing concessions added to the general erosion of small-scale fisher access to traditional fishing grounds, leading to increased household hardship in many fishing communities. During this period, it was common for influential large-scale businesses or military personal to be awarded leases or tenders, to resell them to local businessmen and brokers under a system broadly known in Myanmar as "crony capitalism" (Ford et al. 2016, 16) who then on-sold the leases or tenders at a profit, to smaller-scale businessmen and eventually to small-scale fishers (San Aung 2013). In order to access customary fishing grounds, local fishers now had to navigate a cascade of transactions that could culminate in

Figure 8.1: Fishing Rights Access and Bonded Fisheries Market Chains during the Military Government Period, (1988–2007)

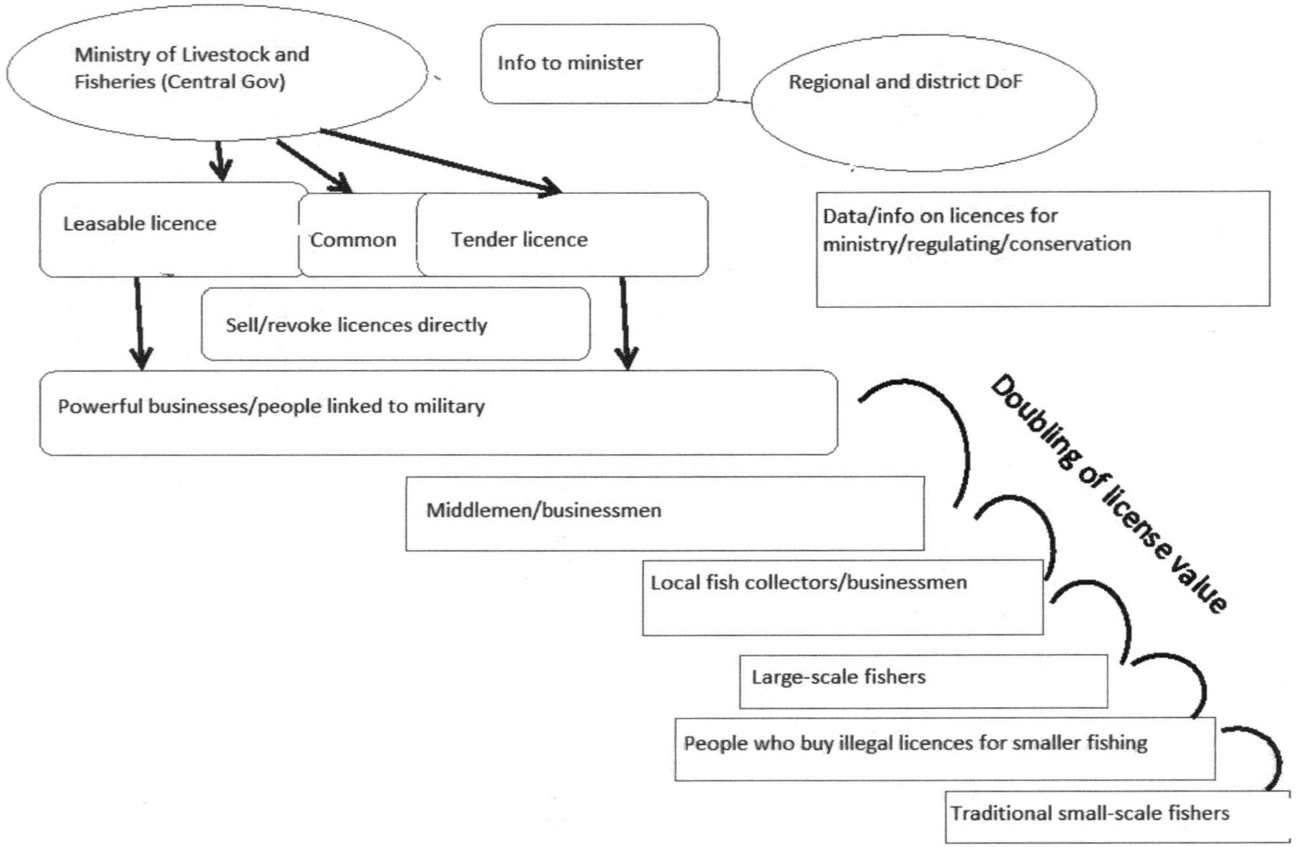

them paying ten to fifteen times the cost of the original lease or tender (Yin Nyein 2015) (see Figure 8.1 left). Those who could not afford to pay these fees in cash had no choice but to fish illegally or to borrow money from local businessmen in exchange for selling their fishery produce at a lower than market price (Yin Nyein 2015).

Up to this point in history, freshwater fisheries governance in Myanmar had consistently focused on maximising revenue generation, fuelling the systematic extraction of natural resources, leading to grave consequences for many small-scale fisher families living in rural communities. Through the steady erosion of their fishing rights and the tightening of bonded market chains the livelihoods and socio-economic conditions of many small-scale fishers deteriorated to the point where they became widely recognised as one of the poorest segments of Myanmar society. The extractive nature of this system of governance led inevitably to conflicts over natural resource access as fishers became ever more desperate to secure fishing grounds and fish supplies in order to sustain their livelihoods. In some cases, these conflicts turned violent and there are reports of physical altercations, sometimes resulting in the death of individuals (e.g., Soe Sandar Oo and Htoo Aung 2012). During these years of international isolation, the desperate plight of the country's small-scale fishers received little, if any, international attention.

Over the decades of successive military governments in Myanmar, access to land and natural resources like freshwater fisheries become heavily contested. Powerful political and economic vested interests, a lack of democratic institutions, corrupt practices and resource use conflict all contributed to the over-exploitation of fisheries resources, accelerated environmental degradation, and harsh, sometimes slave-like fisher labour conditions. Inappropriate natural resource governance frameworks included disjointed legal frameworks and destructive informal practices had significant negative repercussions on both the environment and those that relied on freshwater areas for their livelihoods. The vast majority of citizens lost trust in the government's institutional functions, often seeing them as a threat to their livelihoods rather than a source of protection (Yin Nyein 2015; Campbell 2019). The lack of coordination and collaboration amongst the natural resources-related line departments, private sector, development actors, and other resource users also contributed to conflict and resource exploitation, entrenching poverty and undermining stability for economic development.

CHANGING FISHERIES GOVERNANCE DURING THE DEMOCRATIC TRANSITION PERIOD

In 2008 Myanmar's military government introduced a new constitution which saw all natural resources including fisheries, land and forests recognised as being owned by the State. Resource access rights were assigned by respective government departments, with the military-controlled General Administration Department retaining custodial rights to maximise their value to the nation's citizens. The Department of Fisheries, now under the Ministry of Agriculture, Livestock, and Irrigation, was the primary agency responsible for fisheries management and revenue collection.

Four months before the new constitution was passed, Cyclone Nargis devastated the Ayeyarwaddy Delta, killing an estimated 140,000 people, destroying livelihoods and causing enormous damage to infrastructure in the region. Coastal fishing communities were hit particularly hard by the disaster. In response, from 2008–2010 a tri-partite collaboration between the Myanmar Government, the United Nations and ASEAN implemented a successful recovery effort that rebuilt communities and livelihoods throughout the affected areas. Although Western sanctions were not lifted until after the 2011 government commenced its reform process, this successful relief collaboration helped to improve relations between the Myanmar Government and neighbouring Southeast Asian governments in particular (TCG 2010).

Civil society organisations and local NGOs were also allowed to proliferate during this period, playing a significant role in recovery efforts. Many international organisations involved in the post-disaster recovery efforts established a permanent presence in Myanmar that allowed for regular dialogue with government. In the fisheries sector this change exposed government staff to international fisheries norms, ushering in a number of significant policy changes which later took place under the civilian government (TCG 2010).

Under the 2008 Myanmar Constitution, the administration of freshwater fisheries had been decentralised to state and regional governments and parliaments. Schedule V of the 2008 Constitution grants to the regions and states, "the right to collect revenue from fresh water fisheries and marine fisheries within the permitted range of territorial waters" (MOI 2008). The decentralisation of freshwater fisheries governance from the Union to the state and regional level had significant consequences for fisheries governance as it provided local governments with the full authority to promulgate new freshwater fishery laws relevant to their local context. The decision to allow this may have been to try and encourage states and regions to take control of revenue collection from fisheries, on behalf of the Union government. Thus, revenue collected from fishing activities was now divided between the Union and the states and regions, with freshwater fisheries and inshore (*kan ni*) fisheries revenue going to the region/state, and offshore (*kan way*) fishing revenue going to the Union. Taxes from the fisheries sector collected by the states and regions include: tender fishing licenses, leasable fisheries (*inn*) licenses, and fishing implement (fishing gear) licences.[3]

Among the coastal regions and states, the Ayeyarwaddy and Bago Regions have extensive freshwater fishery areas and revenue generated from this sector stands as the second-largest source of income for both regions. In the Ayeyarwaddy Region in 2012, for example, fishery revenue contributed close to 39 per cent of total revenue at almost 4.5 billion Myanmar *Kyat* (Aung 2013). Other coastal regions/states such as Rakhine, Tanintharyi, Yangon and Mon have less extensive freshwater fishing grounds with local fishing communities depending more on the coastal and marine fisheries.

In drafting new freshwater fisheries legislation, most states and regions simply copied the 1991 Union Freshwater Fishery Law and made few amendments. Their main concern was drafting a fishery law that created a legal basis for decentralised collection of revenue from the fisheries sector (San Aung 2013). However, the Ayeyarwaddy Region Freshwater Fishery Law passed in 2012 recognised some of the rights of small-scale fishers who had been overlooked in the Union-level fisheries legislation. As a result, several large tenders and leasable fisheries licenses were sub-divided to make them more accessible to small-scale fishers. Fishing ground demarcation was also improved (Yin Nyein 2015). The 2012 Law also recognised some of the rights of "flooded area fishers" (i.e. small-scale floodplain fishers) and allowed for sixteen types of small-scale fishing gear to be used on a tax-free basis. In the same year, Rakhine State became the first state/region to abolish their tender fisheries and in 2014 promulgated a freshwater fisheries law that departed from the conventional Union level format by including a chapter dedicated to community fisheries organisations and co-management.

Encouraged by Rakhine's initiative and the broader social and political changes occurring in the country, by 2015 other regional governments begun widescale consultation processes with stakeholders from the fisheries sector. In particular, there was a growing recognition of the need to implement legislation that encouraged fisheries community co-management, increased fishing ground access for small-scale fishers, and strengthened natural resource conservation. This created a degree of uncertainty for the powerful *Innthargyi* and Department of Fisheries staff, who had enjoyed close and longstanding relationships. In contrast, the confidence and influence of small-scale fishers grew as a number of CSOs and NGOs (including the Network Activities Group and Pyoe Pin) helped organise networks and associations of community fisheries organisations aimed at asserting their collective rights.

Emboldened by the landslide victory of the National League for Democracy (NLD) in the 2015 election, small-scale fishers in several states and regions sensed a growing opportunity for further fisheries governance reform. Several MPs elected in 2015 picked up on and supported their constituent demands for fisheries governance reform, in many cases providing them with grass roots experience of political canvassing for the first time. In April 2018, the Ayeyarwaddy Region, which had piloted the community co-management of some tender fishing grounds since 2012, passed a new freshwater fishery law that as with Rakhine in 2014, included a section dedicated to community fisheries co-management (LIFT 2014a). In the same year, Bago Region also amended its freshwater fishery law to include a dedicated section on community organisations and co-management (BFP 2018). The 2014 Mon State Fishery Law, (which encompassed freshwater and coastal fisheries) introduced a novel fishery co-management governance mechanism. Although the 2014 Fishery Law initially did not explicitly include a co-management mechanism at the community level, the fishery law did support the creation of a state-level Fishery Management Committee. Chaired by the Regional Minister and composed of members from the Department of Fisheries and other relevant departments, it became the authority charged with implementing the new fishery law (Mon State Parliament 2014). Significantly, this committee created two seats for private sector and fishing representatives. In February 2018, the Mon State Fishery Law was then amended to include a dedicated section on fishery co-management. Of all the coastal states and regions in Myanmar, by 2018, only Yangon and Tanintharyi Region retained a freshwater fishery law that did not include a community co-management section.

In advance of the new freshwater fishery law, from 2016 onwards the Ayeyarwaddy Regional Government piloted a fisheries policy that offered all leaseholders and tender fisheries below a value of 4,000,000 *Kyat* (US$3,000) or that had a history of conflict, to community-based organisations at the auction floor price. This dramatic shift in policy sent shockwaves through the Ayeyarwaddy fisheries sector and in 2017 a series of peaceful public demonstrations were held in the regional capital Pathein, with groups in favour and against the new policy and draft law. Most, but not all, *Innthargyi* were against the new policy as it loosened the control that they had over the sector. Virtually all small-scale fishers, who vastly outnumbered the *Innthargyi*, were in favour of the new policy as it secured their access rights to fisheries at a lower price. Broad support from the Ayeyarwaddy's fishing community helped ensure that the Regional Parliament continued to back the retention of the new policy and the development of the new law.

Figure 8.2 on the next page highlights the main freshwater fisheries governance reforms that took place in the Ayeyarwaddy during the decade (2008–2018).

In 2014, Mon State and Tanintharyi Region enacted fishery laws that covered both freshwater fisheries and inshore marine fisheries. Although Schedule II of the Constitution only granted regional and state governments legislative power for fresh-water fisheries, Mon State and Tanintharyi Region drafted laws that included inshore fisheries by referencing Schedule V of the Constitution which allowed for the states and regions to collect revenue from coastal fisheries. At the time, this was seen as controversial and possibly unconstitutional and there were policy debates on the legality of these freshwater/coastal fishery laws. This culminated in the July 2015 Amendment to the Constitution that supported the devolution of coastal fishery legislative powers to the states and regions. In this regard, there were two supporting factors. Firstly, the Union government had limited interest in coastal fisheries since revenue collection powers had already been decentralised under the 2008 Constitution. Secondly, Mon State and Thanintharyi Region had limited freshwater fishing grounds and most of the local fisher communities depended on coastal fisheries resources. The amendment therefore balanced fisheries administrative powers more evenly across the states and regions.

Figure 8.2: Ayeyarwaddy Region Fishery Governance Reform (2008–2018)

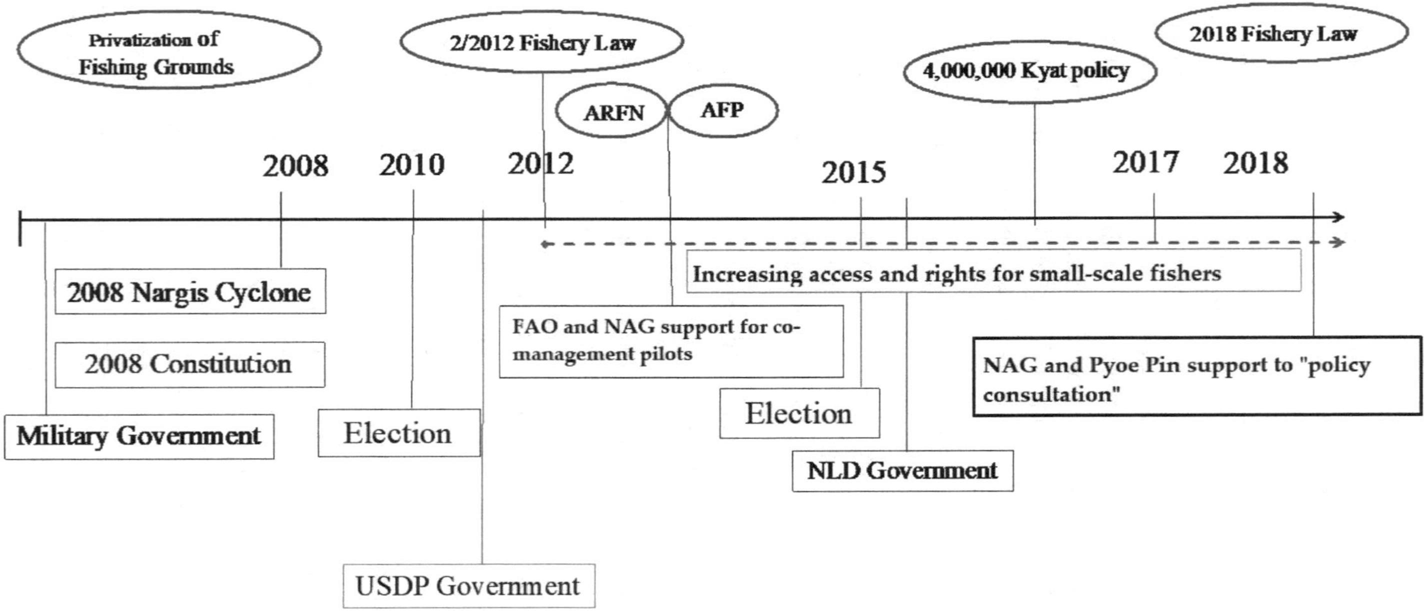

THE SMALL-SCALE FISHER RIGHTS MOVEMENT

As a result of Myanmar's political reforms, small-scale fisher networks proliferated between 2011–2018, including the Ayeyarwaddy Small-scale Fisher Network (ARFN), which played a crucial role in lobbying and campaigning for fisheries governance reform and in facilitating communication between community representatives. In Ayeyarwaddy, the early small-scale fisheries movement sought to abolish the tender and leasehold fisheries system altogether, and to provide open access to fishing grounds for all resident fishing communities, similar to the freshwater fisheries reforms that had occurred in Cambodia in 1999 and 2004 (Kurian et al. 2006). These early demands were unsuccessful for several reasons. Firstly, revenue from fishing leases and tenders is one of the few sources of significant income for the Ayeyarwaddy Regional Government. Secondly, the small-scale fisher organisations were small and there was limited communication or collaboration between them. Thirdly, the fish collectors and *Innthargyi* remained powerful and influential at all levels of decision-making and were able to block any attempts at reforms that threatened their business interests. The small-scale fisheries movement, supported by several CSOs and NGOs who had worked with fishing communities since the Cyclone Nargis relief operation, was therefore unsuccessful initially in its demands and this contributed to an increase in tension, law violations, and conflict with business operators in 2011–12.

In order to counter the power and influence of the *Innthargyi,* the small-scale fishers organised larger representative bodies in their respective townships and thereby strengthened their collective voice and actions. The Network Activities Group played a major role in facilitating this collectivisation. With improving access to mobile phones and telecommunications, small-scale fisher organisations were now able to access information more easily, as well as social and political updates. The growing communications infrastructure also allowed them to network and communicate better with each other, making them a more powerful lobby group. In 2014, the Ayeyarwaddy Region Fisher Network (ARFN) was established, accelerating and intensifying collective advocacy actions for fishing rights. With the formation of the ARFN, there was a transformation in their approach as the collective advocacy actions changed from demanding the complete abolition of the tender and leasehold system, to increasing resource access for small-scale fishers through community involvement in co-management with government. The piloting of community fisheries co-management approaches by NGOs and UN organisations at the time, in particular, helped to provide an important foundation for the ARFN to push for more inclusive and pro-poor fisheries policy and legislation (MFP 2015; Chan et al. 2018).

The policy shift towards community co-management of fisheries and the strengthening of small-scale fisher rights that has now taken place in all of Myanmar's coastal states and regions did not happen spontaneously. As mentioned above, since 2012 several NGOs (primarily NAG and Pyoe Pin) and a number of international organisations (including the UN's Food and Agriculture Organisation) have promoted and piloted community fisheries co-management approaches and lobbied tirelessly for the improved rights of small-scale fishers. The formation of fisher networks and fisheries partnerships facilitated inter- and cross-state/regional communications and collaboration and proved to be an effective mechanism for change. For example, the Rakhine Fisheries Partnership (RFP), formed in 2012, brought together parliamentarians, civil society, the Department of Fisheries, lawyers, members of the private sector and representatives of fisher communities, to discuss necessary changes in Rakhine fisheries governance and management to offset recent declines in productivity. The Partnership, supported by Pyoe Pin and NAG, also guided public consultations, participatory development and the enactment of Rakhine State's 2014 Freshwater Fisheries Law, which was the first law to include a section dedicated to community fisheries organisations and co-management. The successful outcome in Rakhine also provided a template for organisations focusing on fisheries governance reform. These inclusive processes challenged the long-established vested interests in the fisheries sector, leading to positive changes in both legislation and stakeholder informal behaviours. The success of the Rakhine model was recognised and taken up by stakeholders in other coastal states and regions including Ayeyarwaddy, Bago, Mon and Tanintharyi, and contributed significantly to an improving dialogue on fisheries and natural resource governance and conflict reduction. The participation of the Thai and Cambodian governments and NGO staff in partnership meetings and the organisation of study tours also helped to build confidence in the validity of the fisheries community co-management approach (AFP 2018). Despite these successes, policy, institutional and community changes are still required if fisheries governance and co-management in Myanmar are to continue to progress.

REMAINING AND FUTURE CHALLENGES

At the policy level, two issues related to decentralised powers have affected the success of Myanmar's fisheries reforms. Firstly, although the 2008 Constitution allows for political, administrative and fiscal decentralisation, it does not mandate the relevant institutional structures necessary to implement full decentralisation. For example, although the Ayeyarwaddy Region has its own constitutionally sanctioned authorities to enact their new fishery law, the regional government lacks the full authority to "control" the Department of Fisheries (DOF). Secondly, although the constitution allows regional and state governments to collect revenue from fisheries, they do not have the authority to use or manage the funds collected. The revenue collected goes to the Union Government account, with subsequent budget allocations dependent on state and regional annual plans. The system therefore limits the power of the regional and state governments and their ability to implement the new policies and influence the performance of the Department of Fisheries officials.

At the institutional level, the tension between revenue generation verses sustainable fisheries management and rural development continues to challenge the performance of government institutions. The Department of Fisheries' primary focus remains on revenue collection and may require institutional reform if it is to effectively implement the new laws. The decentralisation of fisheries governance and the close involvement of NGOs and CSOs in supporting the development of fisheries legislation and policies at the state and regional level may have left some in the Department of Fisheries feeling circumvented and disarmed. Incentive policies that could motivate staff and enhance research and extension activities in government-led projects are currently lacking. Information and statistics on fisheries are unreliable and there is an urgent need to develop an improved framework for fisheries data collection, natural resource conservation and sustainable management, as well as socio-economic support. Building the next generation of government fishery officers who have the capacity and motivation to lead the sustainable development of the sector is crucial but is likely to take some time.

The General Administration Department's role remains critical in terms of influence over natural resource distribution and conflict resolution. At the village level, the elected village head under the GAD has access to higher government authorities and therefore has the capacity to influence decisions on access and the use of resources, including land registration and land use. Fisher communities are often located in remote areas lacking infrastructure such as roads and electricity, and are often unattractive posts for qualified professionals. This limits the capacity of many communities to engage in new approaches or technologies, including post-harvest product development from which they could improve their livelihoods.

To date, at the community level the initial impact of the new fisheries laws and co-management policies has been generally positive although in some areas community fisheries resource access remains recaptured by old or new elite groups. Old elite groups might include *Innthargyi* or fish collectors/moneylenders, whilst the new laws and policies allowed for the emergence of new elite groups such as community leaders or rice farmers who pretend to be fishers. For example, in the Ayeyarwaddy a number of "fake groups" have emerged, looking to take advantage of the new governance arrangements. Under the fishery policy in Ayeyarwaddy, fishers can organise themselves into fisher groups and can submit proposals for the purchasing of leases/tenders under a value of 4,000,000 *Kyat*. However, the criteria for group membership is not yet robust enough to prevent non fishers or occasional fishers, from forming groups. For example, in one village in Bogalay Township, a group of rice farmers formed a "fisher group" and were awarded fishing rights at the auction floor price and then promptly resold these rights to individual fishers in their village, at a profit. In other cases, community fisheries' organisational powers have been undermined by their members' ties to traditional bonded market chains, denying them the chance to co-manage fisheries resources effectively and market their produce freely. However, in many villages of the Delta, the new law and policies have been successful in improving fisher access rights and re-balancing the relationships between small-scale fishers and local *Innthargyi*.

Since many fishermen have only a basic education it is often difficult for them to be successful in their first application attempts to fisher rights and this often requires support and facilitation by a local organisation. Although the new freshwater fishery laws state that Department of Fisheries officials should support the establishment of community fishery groups, including the application process, this aim is often hampered by inadequate organisational capacity, and working cultures and practices that tend to focus on individual business initiatives rather than community collaboration. Successful community fisheries co-management requires long-term planning and investment. In Myanmar, the annual allocation of fishing rights to individuals and communities leads to short-term management planning and fishing practices. This issue is further complicated by the Department of Fisheries policy of increasing the auction floor prices by 10 per cent a year, threatening to put fishing ground access beyond the reach of community fisheries organisations or disqualify them from bidding, once the fishery value threshold for communities of 4,000,000 *Kyat* has been exceeded.

To give these policies a reasonable chance of success, NGOs and CSOs are actively leading the capacity building of community fisheries organisations and some are developing quickly. To date, however, fishery management planning and practices have been weak, particularly in the conservation side of resource management.

CONCLUSIONS

The changes in freshwater fisheries governance that have occurred in Myanmar from 2008–2018 are perhaps the most profound sectoral changes to have occurred since the British colonial period. The new laws and policies have significantly impacted the lives of literally millions of rural people in the coastal states and regions. The freshwater fisheries governance model that has emerged in Myanmar provides key lessons for how changes to legislation can occur and how these processes can be facilitated for politically contested natural resource issues, to achieve fairer and more equitable distribution of natural resources.

At the heart of this story is the growing collaboration between fisher communities, parliamentarians, fisheries departments and ministries. The establishment of multi-stakeholder fisheries partnerships has been a catalyst to create an environment and space conducive for local actors to influence change in both formal and informal institutions, leading to more equitable access to natural resources and better state-citizen relations across the country. To a large extent, the partnerships created have owned and driven the reform process across the states and regions. The stakeholder relationships continue to act as catalysts for broader change and inclusion that will be critical for a successful and complete democratic transition as the years pass by.

The role of facilitating NGOs has been to work "behind the scenes", providing politically smart support, brokering, and often timely technical inputs that have been both flexible and adaptive. It is a process that has achieved remarkable results, transforming the rules of the game to be more inclusive, open and fairer for millions of people. An example of this approach is illustrated by NAG and Pyoe Pin Programme's work in Rakhine State and Ayeyarwaddy Region that began with political economy studies of the fisheries sector. This was followed by the mobilisation of fisher associations/networks and the formation of coalitions of interested partners, who worked together to draft a freshwater fisheries law that was acceptable to all stakeholders in the sector, and which introduced legislation that provided a legal basis for community fisheries co-management (LIFT 2014a, b; Christie and Green 2018).

To date, however, the governance reforms that have been achieved in Myanmar's fisheries sector have generally not been duplicated in other sectors. For example, the forestry sector saw a new Union-level Forestry Law enacted in 2018, but this has not expanded the space for community co-management, beyond that established by the 1995 Community Forestry Instruction. Experience from the forestry sector shows that a lack of a comprehensive and complete legal framework can be used as a reason to delay policy and change implementation, including community co-management, especially when these changes are perceived to be against vested interests (Kyaw Tint et al. 2011). Explicit recognition of the importance of natural resource co-management at the state and regional level, as has been achieved in the fisheries sector, is crucial.

The NLD government continues to promote a democratic reform agenda but with a bureaucratic administration that is accustomed to command and control as experienced under previous regimes. It will take time and new incentives to transform and adjust the behaviour of government departments to conform to the federal democratic transition dreamt of by the majority of society in Myanmar. The NLD policy states that it is people-centred and aims to achieve inclusive and continuous development. It also aims "to establish an economic framework that supports national reconciliation, based on the just balancing of sustainable natural resource mobilization and allocation across the States and Regions".[4] As other chapters in this volume demonstrate, there are significant risks that structural changes in the country could at best be delayed or at worst disrupted during this key transitional period. Without strategic support for economic reform both politically and technically, it is likely that economic growth will be either marginal or exclusive, and that the country will see political breakdown. Without further political and administrative reform, states and regions will also continue to struggle to deliver services, responsibilities will be unclear, and the control of the central authorities will be maintained, thereby discouraging the country's democratic efforts and increasing tensions between different stakeholders. In the context of Myanmar's long-term civil conflict, the management of resources is also key to achieving peace. A failure to secure a lasting peace both at the community level and the country level will threaten long-term security, stability and prosperity.

The fishery reforms that have been implemented over the last decade in Myanmar provide a strong example for reform in other sectors. As this chapter shows, although challenges remain, the reforms in the fisheries sector are able to meet the challenges facing the current decentralisation process within the framework of the 2008 Constitution and also reveal practical lessons for further administrative and fiscal reform. The economic and social future of Myanmar will be determined by whether opportunities for reform like this are seized or missed.

Notes

1 According to the Myanmar Freshwater Fishery Law (1991): "Freshwater fisheries water means waters, pond, course, river, steam and lake which is of permanent or temporary nature in which fish live and thrive and which is situated within inland boundary along the seacoast of Myanmar. This expression also includes a leasable fishery, reserved fishery, fishery waters in which rights of fishery are permitted under a license, reservoirs, water in an area belonging to any Government department, inland tidal places, waters on an island, crocodile nets and turtle banks in which crocodile and turtle lay their eggs and brackish waters. Furthermore, water on the inland- side of the straight line drawn from one extreme end of one bank to extreme end of the river mouths and creek mouths continuous to the sea are freshwater fisheries waters" (MLF, 1991: 2).

2 See for example Gregory et al. (2018) and Yin Nyein (2015, 2018).

3 Revenues are managed on an annual basis, with the fishing season beginning on 1st of April and ending on 31st of March of the following year.

4 See http://www.myanmarembassy.sg/commercial/economic-policy/ (accessed 22 July 2020).

References

ACIAR (2016). *Myanmar Fishery Partnership Overview*. Canberra: Australian Centre for International Agricultural Research. Available at http://pubs.iclarm.net/resource_centre/MFP-01-Overview.pdf (accessed 21 July 2020).

Ayeyarwaddy Region Parliament (2012). *Ayeyarwaddy Freshwater Fishery Law*. Pathein: Ayeyarwaddy Region Parliament.

_____ (2018). *Ayeyarwaddy Freshwater Fishery Law (2018)*. Pathein: Ayeyarwaddy Region Parliament.

Ba Thaw (2011). *Leasable Fisheries in Myanmar*. Yangon: Aye Chan Myat Press.

BFP (2018). *Public Consultation Report on Bago Region Fresh-Water Fishery Law*. Bago: Bago Fishery Partnership.

Bago Region Parliament (2014). *Bago Region Fishery Law*. Bago: Bago Region Parliament.

_____ (2018). *Bago Region Fishery Law*. Bago: Bago Region Parliament.

Christie, A. and Green, D. (2018). *Adaptive Programming in Fragile, Conflict and Violence-Affected Settings.What works and under what conditions? The Case of Pyoe Pin, Myanmar*. Yangon: ITAD and Oxfam. Available at https://www.itad.com/wp-content/uploads/2018/07/A4EA-Case-of-Pyoe-Pin-final-version-12-July-2018.pdf (accessed 21 July 2020).

Department of Fishery (2018). *National Fisheries Statistics 2017-2018*. Naypyidaw: Department of Fishery, Myanmar.

Department of Planning (2018). *National Statistics 2018*. Naypyidaw: Department of Planning, Myanmar.

Dickenson-Jones, G., Kanay De, S. and Smurra, A. (2015). *State and Region Public Finances in Myanmar*. Yangon: MDRI-ECSD, Asia Foundation & ICG.

FAO (2006). *The Union of Myanmar General Economic Data*. Yangon: Food and Agriculture Organization of the United Nations. Available at http://www.fao.org/fi/oldsite/FCP/en/MMR/profile.htm (accessed 21 July 2020).

Ford, M., Gilian, M. and Htwe Htwe Thein (2016). "From Cronyism to Oligarchy? Privitisation and Business Elites in Myanmar," *Journal of Contemporary Asia* 46(1): 18-41.

U Khin (1948). *Fisheries in Burma*. Rangoon: Supdt., Govt. Printing and Stationery, Burma.

Kurien, J., Nam So, and Sam Onn Mao (2006). *Cambodia's Aquarian Reforms: The Emerging Challenges for Policy and Research. Inland Fisheries Research and Development Institute, Phnom Penh, Cambodia*. Phnom Penh: Inland Fisheries Research and Development Institute.

Kyaw Tint, Springate-Baginski, O. and Mehm Ko Ko Gyi (2011). *Community Forestry in Myanmar: Progress and Potentials*. Yangon: ECCDI.

LIFT (2014a). *Learning Together in the Ayeyarwaddy Delta*. Yangon: LIFT.

LIFT (2014b). *The LIFT Qualitative Social and Economic Monitoring Study.* Yangon: LIFT.

Ministry of Information (2008). Constitution of the Republic of the Union of Myanmar. http://www.burmalibrary.org/docs5/Myanmar_Constitution-2008-en.pdf (accessed 21 July 2020).

MLF (1991). "Myanmar Fresh-Water Fishery Law." Yangon: Government of the Union of Myanmar.

MSFP (2018). *Public Consultation Report on Mon State Fresh-Water Fishery Law.* Mawlamyaing: Mon State Fishery Partnership.

Mon State Parliament (2014). *Mon State Fishery Law.* Mawlamyaing: Mon State Parliament.

——— (2018). *Mon State Fishery Law.* Mawlamyaing: Mon State Parliament.

Rakhine State Parliament (2014). *Rakhine State Fishery Law.* Sittwe: Rakhine State Parliament.

Reeves, P., Pokrant, B. and McGuire, J. (1999). "The Auction Lease System in Lower Burma's Fisheries, 1870–1904: Implications for Artisanal Fishers and Lessees." *Journal of Southeast Asian Studies* 30(2): 249–62.

San Aung (2010). *Tender Process Analysis in Pyapon District.* Yangon: Network Activities Group.

_____ (2013). *Analysis on Tender and Leasable Fisheries in Ayeyarwaddy Region of Myanmar.* Yangon: Network Activities Group.

Scott, J. (1972). "The Erosion of Patron-Client Bonds and Social Change in Rural Southeast Asia." *Journal of Asian Studies* 32(1): 5-37.

Schendel, W. V. (1991). *Three Deltas: Accumulation and Poverty in Rural Burma, Bengal and South India.* New Delhi: Sage Publications.

Soe Sandar Oo and Htoo Aung (2012). "Ayeyarwady Fish Rights Violence Escalates, Two Killed," *The Myanmar Times,* 15 October. Accessed at https://www.mmtimes.com/national-news/2437-ayeyarwady-fish-rights-violence-escalates-two-killed.html (accessed 21 July 2020).

Tripartite Core Group (2010). *Post-Nargis Periodic Review IV.* Accessed at https://reliefweb.int/sites/reliefweb.int/files/resources/B0F06845E98A406949257776001A4A56-Full_Report.pdf?fbclid=IwAR2dhE_lYZH186PP_9qFL0FAEyTz4n22bj7T-88X96wIbqDagGuOvbW5pTk (accessed 21 July 2020).

TWP (2018) "Rakhine Fisheries Partnership Short Documentary Film – TWP." Available at https://twpcommunity.org/meetings/bangkok-june-2015/rakhine-fisheries-partnership-short-documentary-film (accessed 21 July 2020).

Yin Nyein (2015). "Enforcing Rights to Fishing through Collective Actions of Small-Scale Fishers." Master Thesis. Geneva: Graduate Institute of International and Development Studies.

_____ (2018). "Democratization, Decentralization and Fishery Governance Reform in Myanmar." Master Thesis. Canberra: The Australian National University.

IV

Living with Institutional Legacies

9

REVIEWING REFORMS IN THE NLD'S FOURTH YEAR – EDUCATION, CITIZENSHIP AND PEACE

Marie Lall

The NLD-led government has faced many challenges since it assumed power in April 2016. This has included the need for constitutional, education, legal and land reform, the demand for capacity building in many sectors, further economic reforms, and an unfinished peace process. During the first 100 days of its administration, the NLD government completed a number of projects and policies initiated by the previous government, offering – contrary to expectations – more continuity than change.[1] Continuity across the reform process has been a good thing when it came to the policy work that had been completed earlier, allowing the ministerial administration to continue with their work. However, over the past two years there has been a gradual slowing of the reforms. As the NLD ends its fourth year in power the overall mood across Myanmar has changed from hope to stagnation. The list of challenges confronting the government seem almost unchanged from when the NLD took power. In many ways, the country appears to have stopped moving forward, stuck in quagmires that don't have easy solutions.

The transition from a military dictatorship to a more participatory democratic system was never going to be smooth – as could be seen for example in the Eastern European and former Soviet states (Turk 2014). Education plays a key role as countries move on from crisis and conflict, with the concept of "transition" capturing the change, reforms, innovation and development that occurs (Mitter 2002). In Myanmar issues pertaining to education reform are also deeply embedded in the peace process (Lall and South 2018) and questions of belonging and citizenship (South and Lall 2017).

A key issue for The NLD government has therefore been how to link the wider reforms with the peace process, since without a lasting and just peace, the reforms are unlikely to be sustainable. The lack of decentralisation means that ethnic states still do not have the required mandate to engage with issues specific to their state or their ethnic groups. This is underpinned by the lack of ethnic voices in parliament and in wider politics. Whilst the NLD did put up ethnic candidates in certain areas, they have not been able to speak up specifically for local and ethnic issues, as ethnic parties have done in the past.[2]

Political literacy remains low, and the issue of rights remains defined by ethnicity, with ethnic nationality communities becoming more vocal about the fact that little has changed for them when it comes to issues such as language rights. It should be clear that in order to reinforce peoples' belief in the government's commitment to equality, the freedom to maintain culture, language and literature has to be guaranteed. However, not much progress seems to have been made on that front.

Other problems include the lack of freedom of expression for the press, the lack of decentralisation of power even within ministries, the stagnating economic growth, the widening gap between urban and rural, rich and poor etc (Warr, this volume). Ministries are working towards change according to strategic plans that they have co-developed with development partners; however, many have reached a point where they cannot take any more capacity building, nor spend the aid money that has been allocated to drive reform. While ministries are supposed to drive change in all sectors, the lack of agency their officials are allowed means the direction of instructions remains top-down, begging the question of how Myanmar will ever move to a more participatory administration. The role of the international community is not blameless in these developments. The lack of coordination between development partners means that ministries are yanked in different directions and those in most senior positions are left with unbearable workloads to keep all the funders as well as the government happy.

In the context of the NLD's fourth year in power, this chapter examines the education reform process and its interlinkages with issues related to national identity and the peace process. This is based on the author's experience both as a researcher and consultant on Myanmar since 2005, working in country with national CSOs, Ethnic Armed Group Education Departments as well as the Ministry of Education during the reform process. The paper first discusses issues related to citizenship and national identity and the importance of education reform. It then goes on to examine the processes that have been put in place to reform Myanmar's education system at all levels and the various hurdles that challenge any potential progress. Before concluding, it looks at the importance of mother tongue-based multilingual education and why the lack of its implementation in Myanmar continues to hamper the peace process.

CITIZENSHIP, NATION AND THE POLITICAL COMMUNITY

A defining feature of Myanmar's reform journey has been contestations over narratives and understandings of citizenship and national identity. There has been a growing sense of Buddhism as part of the national identity that serves to discriminate and divide rather than unite (see Schonthal and Walton 2016; Schober 2017). An increasingly large number of Buddhists across different ethnic groups equate citizenship with religion, or seem to think that in order to be Myanmar one has to also be Buddhist.[3] This religious nationalism that reared its ugly head in 2012 has not been dealt with carefully and has alienated other groups with different religious identities (see Cheesman 2017a). Debates regarding citizenship and national identity across the press and social media have been galvanised by the crisis in Rakhine, but these issues resonate across other states and regions as well (see South and Lall 2017).

The unchecked rise of religious nationalism under the previous government means that the building of an inclusive understanding of citizenship for all remains a distant prospect (Walton and Hayward 2014; Cheesman 2017b). The treatment of Muslims, particularly the Rohingya, in Rakhine State makes this an urgent task (Islam 2017). The international community has taken a strong stand against the Myanmar government and the lack of progress for the hundreds of thousands of refugees across the border in Bangladesh. Indeed, Myanmar's image abroad has taken a severe knock in recent years[4] and there are voices calling for renewed sanctions. However, in Myanmar there has been support for the government's line on the Rohingya, and when the State Counselor Daw Aung San Suu Kyi found her name and portrait removed from the Oxford college where she had studied,[5] students and others demonstrated in Yangon to show their support to their leader and government.

Young peoples' views on identity and citizenship are of course shaped by education, in particular textbooks and schooling, and more recently by the use of social media. Even though education reforms are in full swing, narrow conceptions of citizenship are reinforced by decades of rote learning from textbooks whose contents are still not challenged (Salem Gervais and Metro 2012; Metro 2019). School-based history is key in framing the issues, and although both the curriculum and examination systems are being reformed, it will take time for teachers to change their pedagogy to allow critical thinking rather than regurgitation on examination papers. It is therefore pertinent to review the education reforms and how this process links in with the wider peace process, which underpins Myanmar's transition.

EDUCATION REFORMS AS A CASE STUDY

Most education reform literature is written from a dominant Western economic perspective (Wolf 2002), focusing on its role in producing future benefits, largely drawing on human capital theory (Hanushek 2013). Research has begun to highlight the limitations of the human capital theory approach (Marginson 2019); however, many fundamental questions about the role, and alternatives to human capital theory, remain unanswered (Kapur and Crowley 2008). Research on rates of return of education has shifted focus in developing countries from a focus on primary education to now also include the role of higher education (Psacharopoulos and Patrinos 2018). Much of this is supported by international aid agencies, which see the development of a strong economy with skilled young people accessing jobs as a pillar of any transition. Whilst developing the economy is certainly a key part in supporting the democratic transition in Myanmar, historical legacies of ethnic inequalities mean that the education reforms are yet to encompass more than simply a focus on quality and skills creation. As discussed in a number of her publications, Naidoo (2004 and 2007) points to the delicate balance between engaging with international organisations whilst accounting for local contexts and conditions in an education reform process.

At the time of writing the Myanmar government educates 9 million children in 45,600 schools with 320,000 teachers.[6] It is the largest provider of education services across the country, although it is estimated that another 300,000 students study in monastic schools and another 300,000 are provided for by ethnic systems.[7] Although access has improved, dropout rates remain high, particularly in grade 5 for children from poorer households and around 2.7 million children remain out of school. There is limited national data on learning outcomes and according to an early grade reading assessment conducted in 2015, too many children cannot read at the appropriate level,[8] pointing to a quality crisis.[9]

The NLD inherited the results of the Comprehensive Education Sector Review (CESR) spearheaded by the Ministry of Education and supported by international aid agencies/Development Partners (DPs) between 2012 and 2015. It also inherited the National Education Law (NEL) that had been drafted by the Education Promotion Implementation Committee in 2014, that led to widespread student protests ending with violent police suppression. The students had a list of eleven demands, ranging from increased government funding of education, to the role of student unions in higher education, to ethnic minority languages being used in schools. The NLD, then still in opposition, opposed the new education law, but would not endorse the student protests. On 26 March 2015, the Upper House voted to accept amendments to the National Education Law, without all the changes for which the students had protested (Lall 2016). However, the amendments have allowed for very limited decentralisation: the 330 township education offices now have increased responsibility for implementing and managing *some* parts of the budget, and states and regions can now recruit and deploy *some* of their own teachers. Teachers are now allowed the use of ethnic languages, *where necessary* alongside Burmese in the classroom (Article 43b). The revised curriculum also includes a 10 per cent allocation for local content, which *can* cover ethnic languages.

Education policy under the NLD government has not really changed much since they took power. This is reflected in the National Education Strategic Plan (NESP) of 2016, which was launched by the NLD government in February 2017 and is primarily based on the previous government's draft National Education Sector Plan. The main focus remains on access, completion, quality, and transparency. In order to achieve this, the plan proposes nine transformational shifts that are to be driven by the Ministry of Education.

Reforms within the MoE

In recent years Myanmar has seen the creation of new structures and institutions within the Ministry of Education to help support the reform process. The National Education Policy Commission (NEPC) was established first in September 2016 as a statutory body based on the National Education Law 2014 and the 2015 Amendment – "to provide education policies for the promotion of national development". The NEPC has twenty-one academic and educationalist members from various education sectors to provide practical policies for the attainment of the national education objectives. The role of these members is to advise on how to achieve quality education accessible to all and to provide policy recommendations so that Myanmar can achieve "international standards and develop human resources for a knowledge based economy and society."[10] The NEPC was designed to have an executive role in advising and coordinating higher education policy and legislation in the form of Myanmar's thirty-year Long-term Education Development Plan as well as coordinating with development partners (Channon 2017). The NEPC also oversees the National Curriculum Committee (NCC), the National Accreditation and Quality Assurance Committee (NAQAC) and the Rectors' Committee (RC).

The National Curriculum Committee (NCC) was formed in November 2016 with fifteen members to develop and review curricula so that they met international standards. The National Accreditation and Quality Assurance Committee (NAQAC) formed in January 2017 is composed of twenty members focusing on developing and implementing a comprehensive quality assurance system as well as assessing and providing accreditation to educational institutions and programmes. The Rectors' Committee, formed just over a year later in April 2018, has as members all Rectors and Principals of public higher education institutions. It also has a Central Committee of forty-four members and a Central Executive Committee of fifteen members elected from among its members. It is meant to coordinate the affairs of higher education institutions, help to enhance the quality of teaching, research and management in higher education institutions, give guidance to higher education institutions in the transition to autonomy and provide advice to higher education institutions for increasing revenues to support their development. These four institutions are supposed to support the MoE in delivering the reforms by bringing in non-ministerial experienced staff, but the MoE remains the main government institution that is responsible to deliver the nine transformational shifts on which the NESP is based.

However, the MoE's ways of working have been defined by decades of centralisation, with officials not empowered to make their own decisions. In order to transform Myanmar's education system, a change in working style and structure is needed. As part of supporting this aspect of the process, different development partners have offered targeted support to the MoE to try to change the ways in which the ministry and its staff work. In October 2017 the MoE established a Capacity Development Fund (CDF), in partnership with the Danish development cooperation (DANIDA) to strengthen MoE systems and build human resource capacity. The key challenge that had been identified was the limited professional training programs for new and existing staff that were needed to strengthen human resource development. So in order to enhance the capacity of senior managers to be able to support the NESP implementation efficiently and effectively, as well as strengthen the effectiveness of existing systems and procedures at national and sub-national levels, the CDF project put in place an *Education Management Training Programme* that included critical thinking and management seminars, as well as the development of a diploma in Education Management to be delivered by the Yangon University of Education (with the support of the UCL Institute of Education). The idea behind this project was that senior staff of the MoE, including Director Generals (DGs) and Deputy Director Generals (DDGs) would get the kind of training required, that they would not have been able to receive previously under Myanmar's unreformed Higher Education system. CDF and others also arranged for ICT and English trainings for more junior staff as part of a general capacity-building program.

Another large support program to the MoE is Australia's DFAT-funded My-Equip quality improvement program that aims to support the MoE in developing systems to measure education quality and evidence-based planning. The MoE has traditionally been focused on numbers not outcomes or standards, and monitoring and evaluation are relatively new concepts. Monitoring and evaluation has been formalised at the MoE through a dedicated department, which has however struggled with its mandate.[11] My-Equip now supports the MoE in general, and this dedicated department to develop and implement an education quality improvement system that assesses performance of education services against indicators and quality standards produces outputs to inform decision-making and enables learning and continuous improvement in the sector. The aim is to fill knowledge gaps – including quality assurance, monitoring, evaluation, and research. The project's focus is, according to DFAT, on "building capacity, systems and a culture in which decision-makers are empowered to make decisions within their level based on evidence".[12] Linked with this is the UNESCO-supported MoE's education management information system (EMIS), including work on data collection and reporting systems. The UNESCO CapEd program also provides broader capacity development training and support on education sector planning and budgeting.

Development partners agree that the whole education system needs a quality shift and are pouring support directly into the MoE. However, at the time of writing the various departments of the MoE no longer seem to have the capacity to absorb more funds and training, in part because there are not enough staff, but also because too much is being done at the same time and everyone appears to have to work on everything simultaneously (Lall 2020).[13]

Reforms to basic education

The reforms to Basic Education (that runs from Kindergarten to Grade 11 – soon to be Grade 12) are numerous and complex. They include access (including through alternative education for out-of-school children): formalising a Kindergarten (KG) year; moving to twelve-year schooling; overhauling the curriculum and the examinations system as well as teacher training to be able to deliver the new curriculum; and preparing the students for the new examinations system.[14]

Most at the MoE agree that the quality shift needed is stark. The policy documents such as NESP speak of skills-based and transitions to employment. Development partners are emphasising that some of the changes have been hampered by the interrelated nature of the system; for example, to implement a more child-centric approach (CCA) to education requires both different teacher training and a reformed examination system that does not rely on rote learning. There are also calls for more teachers teaching smaller class sizes in better equipped classrooms.[15]

One of the main reforms to basic education is the curriculum and textbook content, led by the Japan International Cooperation Agency (JICA) under the "Project for Curriculum Reform at Primary Level of Basic Education (CREATE)" that has been running since May 2014.[16] This has been the first major curriculum revision in twenty years and involved forty Japanese and overseas curriculum experts as well as over sixty Myanmar academics. The textbooks were reviewed and approved by the National Curriculum Committee. The new primary education curriculum now comprises nine subjects: Myanmar, English, Mathematics, Science, Social Studies, Morality and Civics, Life Skills, Physical Education, and Arts (Performing Arts and Visual Arts). In 2017 the new Grade 1 curriculum and its textbooks developed jointly by the MOE and JICA was introduced into schools. The announcement by the Ministry of Foreign Affairs (MOFA) stated that "approximately 1.3 million new Grade 1 primary school students across the country will learn with the new textbooks. [...] The textbooks are colourful with many pictures and designed in a way that learning is fun and linked with students' life."[17] The project also developed a detailed teachers' guide for each subject. In preparation for the introduction of the new Grade 1 curriculum, JICA supported a series of trainings, which were conducted by MOE for education officers from townships, districts, and states/regions, and the ministerial officials from the concerned departments at the central level. Following this, nation-wide in-service teacher training was conducted to introduce the new curriculum to teachers and JICA claims that through the in-service education and training (INSET), all primary teachers who teach Grade 1 from all schools, including monastic schools, private schools, and other schools that use the government were trained. At the time of writing, however, it is unclear how far the curricular reforms are engaging with issues of identity, equality and citizenship.

In parallel to JICA's efforts on the curriculum, UNESCO has focused on reforming teacher training. A new national Teacher Competency and Standards Framework had been written in 2016 as part of the Strengthening Pre-service Teacher Education in Myanmar (STEM) project.[18] The Teacher Competency and Standards Framework was, for the first time in Myanmar, articulating what is expected of teachers in their professional practice at various stages in their professional development. STEM continues its work with a focus on teacher empowerment through the UNESCO pre-service teacher education project by developing the curriculum for the new ECs degree. This work has been ongoing since 2015–2016, starting with a review of the curriculum used in ECs and the subsequent development of a Curriculum Framework for a competency-based curriculum for a four-year degree program, with primary and middle school teacher specialisation tracks.

In the summer of 2019, the UK's Department for International Development (DFID) started the five-year Myanmar-UK Partnership for Education (MUPE) program that addresses some of the interrelated issues in the education reform process. The five components focus on strengthening English and teacher education, assessment and education reform support, education provided by monastic and ethnic education providers, and education in conflict-affected areas, including Rakhine. There is also a separate component on evidence, evaluation and learning support.

Reforms to higher education

Within higher education reform the NLD's focus has been on the historical flagship universities in Yangon and Mandalay. Daw Aung San Suu Kyi's particular priority has been to restore Yangon University (YU) to its former "glory" as one of Asia's leading universities, asking both Britain and Australia to support YU's development. Drawing on Arnhold et al.'s (1998) educational reconstruction conceptual framework, Esson and Wang (2018) analysed the reformation process of Yangon University in 2013 and argue that efforts have failed to consider the ideological and psychological reconstruction of the university in the reform process.

As part of the broader reform process, undergraduates are being reintegrated on the main campuses of urban universities and autonomous flagship universities and their university charters now have a certain level of independent admission. These universities now face the challenge of developing their own research agenda. Curricula that have traditionally been passed down from the MoE to teach subjects will have to be revised, and courses supplemented with new and relevant material for which individual universities, rather than the MoE, are responsible. For the first time, universities and their staff have to engage with issues such as ethics, student engagement, international engagement and budgeting. High-level meetings are also focused on new ways of funding that could mean big changes for the way universities operate (Kandiko-Howson and Lall 2019).[19]

All of these efforts bode well for Myanmar's education system and its development. However, much of this is bogged down in bureaucratic report writing, workshops and meetings. The reality on the ground is an exhausted MoE, not much change in schools, an overwhelmed tertiary sector and a great sense of despair amongst parents and students who are still awaiting the qualitative shift they were promised in 2012 and again in 2015.

EDUCATION REFORMS AND ETHNIC STAKEHOLDERS

Things are not much better for Myanmar's ethnic stakeholders. As mentioned above, the peace process has largely stagnated and ethnic representatives have not had much of a chance to voice their opinions through the stalled political dialogue. Ethnic groups are therefore marginalised in the wider education reform process.

One of the key challenges facing the government since the reform process started in 2012 has been to reach a consensus on language education policies that meet the diverse needs and hopes of all groups and can help promote social cohesion, ensuring that all children have an equal opportunity to learn effectively across the country. The government has a stated commitment to "Education For All", as outlined in the NESP, and has promised to improve the quality of education, especially for ethnic nationality citizens and marginalised communities in remote conflict-affected areas. The five main system aspirations of the NESP are quoted as access, quality, equity, inclusion and efficiency (NESP 2016, 57). As such the reforms represented a window of opportunity to reverse decades of Burmanisation by engaging with the needs of the ethnic nationality communities, key to sustaining the wider peace process. This should have been a priority given the historic disparity of achievement of ethnic children in government schools, largely due to the language gap that children face when having to learn in Burmese despite their mother tongue being quite different. Research by Shalom in 2011 shows that ethnic nationality children, especially in remote and conflict-affected areas, cannot read or write Burmese at the same speed as their Bamar peers, and often drop out. Those who stay in the education system are often unable to join university due to poorer matriculation marks, resulting in a cycle of lifelong disadvantage for the individual, their family and the whole community.

Despite ethnic aspirations to see their languages recognised and formally included in the government education system, neither the peace process nor the education reforms have delivered (Lall and South 2018). Part of the problem has been the separation between the education reform process and the peace process (Lall 2016). Ethnic nationality representatives at the various 21st Century Panglong conferences run by the NLD confirm that neither language policy nor education is on the "peace agenda" despite this being a high priority issue for ethnic communities. The latest round of talks in July 2018, yielded fourteen new basic principles, among which is for the first time a reference to an "all-inclusive education system", a point which was not further clarified at the meeting.

The reforms have therefore not touched much upon the hopes and concerns of Myanmar's ethnic population.[20] Policy under the NLD government has not changed much with only Burmese being allowed as a means of instruction, although ethnic minority languages are now allowed as "classroom language"[21] to help explain concepts when necessary. Mother tongue-based multilingual education (MTB-MLE) is not presently Myanmar education policy.

The inequalities created by the lack of implementation of mother tongue-based multilingual education are life-long. Research shows that teaching in a second or third language [i.e. *not* the mother tongue] is very demanding, especially if coupled with additional issues, such as poverty, poor learning conditions and parents with little or no formal education (Ndaruhutse and Plantak 2011). In the end, children who don't understand the teacher drop out and educational performance and outcomes decline where children have limited or no access to school language outside school.[22] International best practice remains MTB-MLE.

There are however multiple views on and multiple practices of MTB-MLE across ethnic stakeholders. The Mon National Education Committee (MNEC), for example, has practiced a form of MTB-MLE for decades across its Mon national schools, with students transitioning to Burmese in the course of late primary/early secondary schooling. The Karen Education Department (KED) schools have promoted the mother tongue, yet not taught much Burmese (unless it was a mixed school), with children leaving proficient in Karen and English, however unable to integrate into the Burmese system (Lall and South 2013). More recently more Burmese is to be taught, especially since the KNU signed the National Ceasefire Agreement (NCA) and more Karen students are having to transition into Myanmar government schools. The Kachin Education Department (KIOED) used to have a similar system of MTB-MLE as the Mon, but since fighting resumed in 2011 and the difficulties associated with children transiting between KIOED schools and government schools, Burmese has been reduced in many Kachin schools with an even greater focus on Jingpaw and English. In Shan State the various systems tend to focus more on the mother tongue, with little if any teaching of Burmese (unless of course the school is mixed with a government or monastic school). Many children say they want their own teachers who can at least explain things in Shan. The issue in Shan is further complicated by the many non-Shan communities in these areas, some of whom have voiced that they prefer teaching to be in Burmese as this is the national language and Shan is not their mother tongue.[23] The PaO are a case in point who want to see their children taught in Burmese but with multi-lingual teachers who are able to explain the Burmese textbooks in PaO.

The government's answer: Local curriculum development

The government has decided to recognise Myanmar's diversity, not with the introduction of MTB-MLE, but with the introduction of a "local curriculum" of one period a day in KG, Grade 1 and Grade 2 that is locally developed and can be taught in an ethnic language.[24] The development of this Local Curriculum (LC) and the rollout is haphazard and uneven, privileging larger, more organised ethnic groups.[25] According to difficult--to-verify official data, there are around 20,000 ethnic language teachers teaching sixty languages across the country (Salem Gervais 2018). There remain, however, lots of challenges, starting with the salary and status of these teachers. Where requested, government funds were raised for a stipend for the teachers, but MMK 30,000 per month (approx. $US21) for ten months a year to cover the teaching of one period a day is often insufficient to attract and then retain ethnic language teachers.[26] State Education Offices have to approve the textbooks that are to be used in these lessons and Literature and Culture Committees (LCCs) of the different ethnic groups have faced the challenge in standardising materials that had been used across communities in summer or Sunday schools and that often had different scripts and varied spellings depending on religion and denomination. This has led to disagreements between community leaders, the splitting of communities and the creation of new LCCs who are in disagreement with each other. Other challenges include teacher training and whether these classes can be held during school hours or only after school. The timing of these classes is particularly important as parents find their children already overburdened and anything outside of school hours is not taken seriously. However, in multi-lingual communities like in Shan State, having classes in one language and not in the others means that they can only take place outside of school hours.

Reforming education for ethnic stakeholders – MoE-EAO partnerships?

In order to meet the government's stated commitments to "Education For All", as outlined in the NESP, through providing quality education that includes ethnic nationality citizens and marginalised communities in remote conflict-affected areas, the MoE has had to look at what education ethnic children are accessing in their ethnic states. As mentioned above, children from minority communities benefit greatly from education in the mother tongue, of the type provided by EAO education departments and ethnic parents have historically chosen to send their children to these schools as the children could understand the teachers and progress. It is well documented that EAOs' education departments and other non-state education actors have been fulfilling a crucial role for ethnic children in remote and conflict-affected areas by providing capacity and capability in basic education provision, especially in areas where there are either no government schools, or where government teachers refuse to serve for security issues (Lall and South 2018; South and Lall 2016). This is driven by a number of recognised reasons,[27] but primarily to make up for the deficits in government provision with quality-focused solutions, and to ensure the next generation are well-educated and will not lag behind the others in the country. Many EAOs are also heavily invested in transmitting their language and culture to the next generation. These ethnic education providers have provided these services under dire conditions with little or no funding, lack of government support, lack of government recognition, and in some cases in areas of military conflict. The lack of federalism across the country with no devolution in education decision-making has meant that the State Education Offices, whilst at times recognising the contribution and services provided, have lacked the guidance, authority or political will to provide active and systematic support.

In order for the MoE to implement a key component of the National Education Strategic Plan (NESP) as outlined in section 5.2.2, that is, "develop a partnership mechanism to support the participation of different education service providers in basic education reforms", the World Bank commissioned a research project that was undertaken in 2018–19 by Covenant consult (Myanmar Education Partnership Project – MEPP). This project aimed to identify the barriers to engagement as well as possible partnership models that the MoE and ethnic education providers could subsequently work on together. For EAO education departments the primary barriers to engagement are often related to political grievances over historic government policies of Burmanisation, discrimination, and centralisation. This has over the years led to widespread lack of trust, exacerbated by perceptions that the government/MoE does not recognise the value of MTB-MLE, or the roles and value of EAO school systems, and therefore does not recognise EAO teachers or students' qualifications. Further grievances relate to the lack of ethnic language-speaking local teachers in MoE schools. None of these barriers are easy to overcome, but the project allowed for limited discussions to take place between certain signatory EAOs and the MoE to see what partnerships might be possible. There is of course a significant difference between willing signatories (Mon and Karen), reluctant signatories (RCSS Shan) and non-signatories (SSPP Shan and Kachin).[28] If such partnerships could be developed, either based on recognition of the certificates and the ethnic teachers or a jointly agreed system of standards that enables easy student transfers, this would do much to build trust and confidence in the peace process.

CONCLUSION

The NLD reforms have not reached as widely or deeply as Myanmar citizens might have hoped in 2015. The example of education shows that the government is engaging with development partners, that there are lots of processes that have been engendered, but that there is little if any result on the ground – as yet. It also shows that while the priorities of development partners are heeded, various ministerial staff find themselves pulled in different directions through the lack of coordination (Lall 2021).

When looking at what these changes mean for developing a truly inclusive education system for all – as stated in the NESP as a policy priority and as a system that can support a sustainable peace process – the reforms have a long way to go. The engagement with ethnic systems has been an afterthought that is not integrated with the peace process. Issues pertaining to equality, identity and citizenship are not being engaged with. Long-term change will need a clearer vision than what has been on offer these past four years since a government trying to transform a nation is faced with two steep challenges: first to make the people believe in a future that is positive and possible, and second to follow that up with coherent action to fulfil that possibility.

Notes

1 Anonymous interviews - international government consultants.
2 Informal and anonymous conversations with NLD ethnic MPs in NPT between 2017 and 2018.
3 See Lall (2017) in South, A. and Lall, M. (eds.). The research on youth and citizenship uncovered that this view was not only held by Bamars but also by Mon, Shan and Rakhine who identify as Buddhist.
4 See for example https://www.businessinsider.com/aung-san-suu-kyi-loses-another-human-rights-award-2018-11; https://www.theguardian.com/world/2017/nov/27/aung-san-suu-kyi-loses-freedom-of-oxford-over-rohingya-crisis (accessed 28 May 2020).
5 See https://www.theguardian.com/world/2017/oct/19/oxford-college-drops-aung-san-suu-kyi-as-name-of-common-room (accessed 28 May 2020).
6 See https://dfat.gov.au/about-us/business-opportunities/Documents/my-equip-myanmar-education-quality-improvement-program-presentation.pdf (accessed 28 May 2020)
7 These are estimates that are published by the WB and DFID in some of their background information.
8 See http://documents.worldbank.org/curated/en/319981468060904888/ACS13261-REVISED-PUBLIC-Myanmar-Early-Grade-Reading-Assessment-IDU.pdf (accessed 28 May 2020)
9 DFID points to a more recent exercise in one of their unpublished documents (2019) stating: 'recent early grade reading assessments indicate that 10-15 percent of grade 2 students are unable to read a single word in a level-appropriate paragraph'.
10 See https://myanmar.ca/edu/ (accessed 28 May 2020).
11 Expressed by many participants at a training seminar at the department of Monitoring and Evaluation held in Naypyidaw in Jan 2019.

12 See https://dfat.gov.au/about-us/business-opportunities/Documents/my-equip-myanmar-education-quality-improvement-program-presentation.pdf (accessed 28 May 2020).

13 There is hope that the NESP mid-term review that took place in the summer of 2019 will allow for a reprioritisation and some streamlining of programmes within the MoE.

14 See details of the NESP here: https://www.britishcouncil.org/sites/default/files/myanmar_national_education_strategic_plan_2016-21.pdf (accessed 28 May 2020).

15 This is presented as 'new' yet was detailed in the pre CESR review of Lall and South (2013) Teachers' voice that highlighted exactly this issue. The problem was also detailed in a review of CCA in Monastic schools in 2010 Lall (2010) where teachers said CCA was impossible if the examination systems did not change and if they had between 50 and 100 children in a class.

16 In education JICA is also involved in enhancement of engineering education at Yangon Technological University (YTU) and Mandalay Technological University (MTU). This year JICA will expand their assistance to the TVET sector, and this project is the first major project to be undertaken. See https://www.jica.go.jp/myanmar/english/office/topics/press180315.html

17 https://www.jica.go.jp/myanmar/english/office/topics/press180315.html (accessed 28 May 2020).

18 See https://opendata.unesco.org/project/XM-DAC-41304-508MYA1000 (accessed 28 May 2020).

19 See https://www.universityworldnews.com/post.php?story=20190604151019822 (accessed 28 May 2020).

20 It is estimated that non-Burman communities make up around 30-40% of the population including Shan 9%, Karen 7%, Rakhine 4%, Chinese 3%, Indian 2%, Mon 2%, and other 5%. The official categories of 135 'national races' (taingyintha) recognised by the government are deeply problematic, representing arbitrary and often imposed identities (Cheesman 2017b).

21 Using any ethnic language in the classroom effectively would require recruiting local teachers, or teachers who have learnt an ethnic language. According to UNICEF, 70% of teachers working in ethnic areas do not speak local languages (Joliffe and Speers 2016: 37).

22 Based on a multi-country study of nearly 160 language groups by Smits, Huisman and Kruijff (2008).

23 Fieldwork across Shan State summer and autumn 2018.

24 The teaching of ethnic languages in government schools that started in 2013 is different from the development of this local curriculum, a more recent initiative that started in 2016. The LC initiative is broader as it encompasses cultural and local content that is relevant at state level.

25 It is also not accepted by all ethnic education stakeholders as the solution to ethnic linguistic and education grievances.
26 Ethnic language teacher salaries are extremely modest, at 30,000 to 80,000 MMK/month (20 to 50 USD), depending on their exact status, which the local community may supplement) for those who are not already in-service government teachers (who receive around 200 000MMK, depending on their exact position)
27 Not each ethnic education provider will have the same or all these motivations.
28 Lall et al. MEPP Policy Brief, World Bank

References

Arnhold, N., Bekker, J., Kersh, N., Mcleish, E.A., and Phillips, D. (1998). *Education for Reconstruction: The Regeneration of Educational Capacity Following National Upheaval*. Wallingford, Oxfordshire: Symposium Books.

Channon D. (2017). *Exploring the Dynamics of Higher Education Curriculum Change in Myanmar: A Case Study of Internationalisation in an English Department.* Unpublished EdD Thesis, UCL Institute of Education.

Cheesman, N. (2017a). "Introduction: Interpreting Communal Violence in Myanmar". *Journal of Contemporary Asia* 47 (3): 335–352.

_____ (2017b). "How in Myanmar 'National Races' Came to Surpass Citizenship and Exclude Rohingya". *Journal of Contemporary Asia* 47 (3): 461–483.

Esson, J. and Wang, K. (2018). "Reforming a University During Political Transformation: A Case Study of Yangon University in Myanmar". *Studies in Higher Education* 43 (7): 1184–1195.

Government of Myanmar (2016). *National Education Strategic Plan 2016–2021*. Nay Pyi Taw: Ministry of Education.

Hanushek, E.A. (2013). "Economic Growth in Developing Countries: The Role of Human Capital". *Economics of Education Review* 37: 204–212.

Kandiko-Howson, C. and Lall, M. (2019). "International Support Boosts Research Development". *University World News* (8 June). Available at: https://www.universityworldnews.com/post.php?story=20190604151019822 (accessed 28 May 2020).

Islam, N. (2017). "Rohingya and Nationality Status in Myanmar". In *Citizenship in Myanmar: Ways of Being in and from Burma,* edited by A. South and M. Lall. Singapore: ISEAS, and Thailand: Chiang Mai University Press.

Jollife, K. and Speers, E. (2016). *Strength in Diversity: Towards Universal Education in Myanmar's Ethnic Areas.* Yangon, Myanmar: The Asia Foundation. Aavailable at: http://asiafoundation.org/wp-content/uploads/2016/10/Strength-in-Diversity-Toward-Universal-Education-Myanmar-Ethnic-Area.pdf (accessed 28 May 2020).

Kapur, D. and Crowley, M. (2008). "Beyond the ABCs: Higher Education and Developing Countries" (February 4). *Center for Global Development Working Paper No. 139.* Available at SSRN: https://ssrn.com/abstract=1099934 (accessed 28 May 2020).

Lall, M. (2010). *Child Centred Learning and Teaching Approaches in Myanmar. Yangon:* British Council.

_____ (2016). *Understanding Reform in Myanmar, People and Society in the Wake of Military Rule.* London: Hurst Publishers.

_____ (2021). *Myanmar's Education Reforms – A Pathway to Social Justice?* London: UCL Press.

Lall, M. and South, A. (2013). "Comparing Models of Non-state Ethnic Education in Myanmar: The Mon and Karen National Education Regimes". *Journal of Contemporary Asia* 44 (2): 298–321.

_____ (2018). "Power Dynamics of Language and Education Policy in Myanmar's Contested Transition". *Comparative Education Review* 62 (4): 482–502.

Lall, M. et al. (2020). MEPP Policy Brief. Yangon: World Bank.

Marginson, S. (2019). "Limitations of Human Capital Theory". *Studies in Higher Education* 44 (2): 287–301.

Mitter, W. (2002). "Transformation Research and Comparative Educational Studies". In *After Communism and Apartheid, Transformation of Education in Germany and South Africa,* edited by L.R. Reuter and H. Döbert. Frankfurt: Peter Lang Gmbh, 197–205.

Naidoo, R. (2004). "Fields and Institutional Strategy: Bourdieu on the Relationship Between Higher Education, Inequality and Society". *British Journal of Sociology of Education* 25 (4): 457–471.

_____ (2007). "Higher Education as a Global Commodity: The Perils and Promises for Developing Countries". *The Observatory on Borderless Higher Education* 14 (2): 1–19.

Ndaruhutse, S. & Plantak, J. (2011). "La Lengua y el Desarrollo Social y Economico - La Educación Multilingüe: Retos y Recomendaciones." Available at: https://www.teachingenglish.org.uk/sites/teacheng/files/381617_COMPLETO.pdf (p.365-372) (accessed 28 May 2020).

Psacharopoulos, G. and Patrinos, H.A. (2018). *Returns to Investment in Education: A Decennial Review of the Global Literature.* The World Bank.

Salem-Gervais, N. and Metro, R. (2012). "A Textbook Case of Nation-Building: The Evolution of History Curricula in Myanmar". *Journal of Burma Studies* 16 (1): 27–78.

Salem Gervais, N. (2018). "Teaching Ethnic Languages, Cultures and Histories in Government Schools Today: Great Opportunities, Giant Pitfalls? (Part I)". *Tea Circle,* 1 October. Available at: https://teacircleoxford.com/2018/10/01/teaching-ethnic-languages-cultures-and-histories-in-government-schools-today-great-opportunities-giant-pitfalls-part-i/ (accessed 28 May 2020).

Schober, J. (2017). "Belonging in a New Myanmar: Identity, Law and Gender in the Anthropology of Contemporary Buddhism". *Religion and Society: Advances in Research* 8: 158–172.

Schonthal, B. and Walton, M.J. (2016). "The (New) Buddhist Nationalisms? Symmetries and Specificities in Sri Lanka and Myanmar". *Contemporary Buddhism: An Interdisciplinary Journal*: 1–35.

Shalom (2011). *Research on Language and Education in Myanmar – Unpublished Summary of Findings in English.* Yangon, Myanmar: Shalom.

Smits, J., Huisman, J., Kruijff, K. (2008). *Home Language and Education in the Developing World,* UNESCO. Available at https://unesdoc.unesco.org/ark:/48223/pf0000178702 (accessed 28 May 2020).

South, A. and Lall, M. (eds) (2017). *Citizenship in Myanmar: Ways of Being in and From Burma.* Singapore: ISEAS and Thailand: Chiang Mai University Press.

Turk, Z. (2014). "Central and Eastern Europe in Transition: An Unfinished Process?" *European View* 13 (2): 199–208.

Walton, M.J., and Hayward, S. (2014). "Democratization, Communal Violence, and Contesting Buddhist Narratives in Contemporary Myanmar". *East-West Center Policy Studies Series* 71: 4.

Wolf, A. (2002). *Does Education Matter? Myths About Education and Economic Growth.* London: Penguin Business.

10

BUILDING A KNOWLEDGE SOCIETY THROUGH LIBRARY EDUCATION IN MYANMAR

Roxanne Missingham and Mary Carroll

In recent years Myanmar has seen great changes in society, politics and economics. The opportunities presented to the people of Myanmar as it emerges to engage with the rest of the world have been extraordinary. Like a chrysalis Myanmar is transitioning from what has been a constrained and tightly controlled society and is now emerging into a new, more expansive world. Such transitions always present challenges and extend opportunities. Education is often a critical element in the success of these transitions.

Education is fundamental and integral to many of the changes which are occurring in Myanmar – both in its capacity to increase knowledge that is relevant to all aspects of life and also to allow Myanmar to engage with the wider world. The individuals experiencing this transformation within the higher education sector need to have access to the principles and research insights from scholarship outside Myanmar to successfully develop policy, science, law, agriculture, library science, health, medicine, economics and other disciplines. Providing open and professionally constructed access to such knowledge underpins the principles which guide the library and information professions around the world.

Library and information studies is a fundamental part of this education revolution and the education and training of qualified library and information professionals has been viewed internationally as a critical element in information access. Education for this discipline was established in Myanmar at the University of Yangon in the 1971 at the height of the development of schools of librarianship worldwide. As with much tertiary education in former British colonies and Commonwealth countries the model adopted was that of British education (see Carroll 2013) with both undergraduate and postgraduate professional entry. This remains the prevailing model. First led by U Thaw Kaung, Chief Librarian of the Universities' Central Library, until 1997 the courses evolved primarily on a print-based culture (University of Yangon 2018). The University is a leader in library studies in Myanmar, consistent with its role as the premier research university in the country. The Department of Library and Information Studies has expanded in 2019 to include eighteen academics, supporting students studying undergraduate and postgraduate, including Masters and PhD, programs. The Department is the largest library education department in Myanmar.

A great challenge for the Department of Library and Information Studies in the twenty-first century is to evolve the courses within the department to address the growing area of digital library and digital literacy capabilities required in the modern age. As Myanmar becomes increasingly part of the digital scholarly world so must the library education program extend its internal capacity and prepare emerging professionals to meet current and future needs. A fundamental component of this new approach is a partnership between the Department of Information and Library Studies, led by Professor Ni Win Zaw and the Australian National University Library, assisted by Dr Mary Carroll from Charles Sturt University's School of Information Studies. Through this activity knowledge of digital libraries is being used to revise the education program which offers hands-on training by providing a digital centre to academics within the Department who have been overlooked by other organisations associated with building library capacity in this area.

In this chapter, we explore the philosophy underpinning the approach taken using both normative and praxis theories, particular challenges, library pedagogy and the outcomes achieved so far. Finally, the lens of the United Nations Sustainable Development Goals is applied to understand the work within a national and international context.

TRANSFORMING LIBRARY EDUCATION IN MYANMAR

Imagine you are sitting in the library of a leading university in your country. You are a postgraduate student wishing to review material on the early twentieth century. You sit with your pen and paper. There is no wi-fi, the library collection is primarily print and your search for resources is through a print card catalogue. There is little space and a dearth of material from other countries. Collection-building has been interrupted over time by budgetry limitations and decades of strict censorship under a military regime. The library has no air conditioning and the collection is adversely affected by the physical environmental conditions, with many parts of the building brittle and crumbling.

Perhaps you are thinking that this is a description of sixteenth-century Europe, or university libraries at a time when books and periodicals had to travel by ship. This situation described above is, instead, the reality faced in many parts of Myanmar. As librarian Myat Sann Nyein (2016, 1) poignantly describes:

> The years before 2011 were very dark, with all information cut off. Librarians in Myanmar worked in what felt like an enclosed society, and libraries in Myanmar were lacking new and updated materials and facilities in those days.

Critical to understanding this feeling of "darkness" is an understanding of the conflict such a situation creates for librarians. Included in the underpinning values librarianship "professes" as part of its credos are freedom of access, freedom to read and impartiality in what is collected and to whom information is provided. Retired New South Wales, Australian State Librarian Alex Byrne describes a basic syllogism at the heart of understanding the importance of libraries in developing open societies which can provide insight into how librarians view their role. The syllogism as described by Byrne is that:

> Firstly—good libraries provide uninhibited access to information. Secondly—a healthy democracy depends on an informed and participative community. (Byrne, 2013)

Thus healthy, well-resourced and open libraries, staffed by professionals cognisant of their professional role and equipped with requisite skills and knowledge needed for organising and providing information are a critical element in open and fully informed societies. Education for the library and information profession in this context is essential in the development of these underpinning values for the profession, and also in equipping emerging professionals with the knowledge, skills and capabilities for their future lives.

The power of knowledge is fundamental to a modern civil society. Accordingly, library education is vital to equip future professionals for their position in transforming the role of knowledge and scholarship in universities, public institutions such as libraries and archives and parliament and non-government organisations. Library practice through curation, digital literacy programs and making collections fosters the development of knowledge capacity within Myanmar. As one of the few services that can be available to the entire community, libraries' vital role in a modern nation contributes to harnessing the power of global research. While there have been some changes since Myanmar's opening, for example the introduction of digital resources and some databases, infrastructure is still limited, as are resources. Perhaps most significantly, the development of the library and information studies education program to equip future librarians to support a more digitally capable nation is in the extremely early stages of development, as yet but a dream in the eyes of the Head of the Department at the University of Yangon. As Dr Hlaing Hlaing Gyi, Librarian, Central Universities Library and one of the passionate advocates for the development of library services noted to us in an interview in 2018:

> Connecting to the world is vital for universities to thrive. While small in number, university library staff must welcome the opportunities and meet the challenges without being afraid of current technological limitations.

EDUCATION: THE POWER OF UNIVERSITIES

University education has been fundamental to the transformation of countries across the world. The dimensions of development explored by theorists include economic, socio-cultural and political spheres (Saha 1991). The relationship between these aspects of development and universities is complex and involves many actors. In a modern, digital society the opportunities created through educational development provide an additional aspect of enabling global participation. This provides a reach beyond the regional and national lenses that have been traditionally applied to development studies. In many ways these are epitomised in the United Nations Sustainable Development Goals.

Transformation through education provides new forms of outcomes including literacy and societal participation. Sen argues that literacy and societal participation are "functionings", "the various things a person may value doing or being" (Sen 1992, 14). The approach provides a stronger intellectual basis to assess social benefit and equity than simple economic figures. These "doings and beings" beyond functionings enable participation in national activities as well as better health and economics outcomes. Education is a means to enhance these functionings that foster capabilities in national social, individual and economic development. Policies and leadership are vital components of these changes, enhanced through an informed citizenry.

If we apply these concepts to university education in Myanmar, in particularly to library and information studies, the relationship between education and development is clear. The nature of individual rewards from better social and economic outcomes are part of an individual's achievement of freedom through capabilities. In order to attain societal freedom of informed choice, enhanced industry and economic capabilities must intersect with policy. These policies need connection with Myanmar history and world knowledge. Libraries and archives are the repositories of the documentary heritage of Myanmar and provide access to ongoing research within the country.

Education can be seen as a precondition for the choice and opportunity to make policy decisions that will result in the better national development explored by Sen. Literacy and capabilities to manage and interpret knowledge fit within a normative framework. In Myanmar, the gap that education can fill has the capability to improve individual and national actions leading to social, political and economic outcomes.

A further theoretical framework that can provide insight into this work is normative theory. Nussbaum's (2011) theory of social justice focuses on developing capabilities to enable individuals through enhanced wellbeing and opportunities to choose to exercise those capabilities for social justice, leading ultimately to the development of nations through individuals. This concept of translation from self-governing agencies to self-governing individuals requires preconditions of will. "Autonomy of the will is the property the will has of being a law unto itself (independently of every property belonging to the objects of volition)" (Kant 1785, 108) therefore there is a requirement for capabilities to exist for autonomy. To translate this to the Myanmar experience, developing individuals and equipping library students with capabilities that provide opportunities for them to make choices increases their ability to express their will.

Interpreting the application of these theories in contemporary national government policy in Myanmar enables a reflection of the importance of educational change. The Myanmar Sustainable Development Plan (MSDP) embodies the creation of a vision that aligns with normative and praxis models. In this document the Myanmar government notes that Myanmar's most invaluable asset is "our people" (Ministry of Planning and Finance 2018). The plan designates the critical role played by the education system as being indispensable to a healthy nation. However, the question is whether there is funding and power to deliver on the promises.

Table 10.1. Myanmar literacy rate, 2019

Literacy rate (2016)	Total	Male	Female
15-24 years	84.75	85.12	84.41
15 years and older	75.55	80.01	71.85
65 years and older	58.2	70.58	49.2

Source: Unesco 2019

MYANMAR: CHALLENGES FOR LIBRARY EDUCATION

Myanmar's library education has been delivered in an environment with many challenges. While literacy overall in Myanmar is relatively high, education and digital capabilities are much lower. The UNESCO statistics indicate literacy is higher for younger citizens, not unexpected given the low participation rate beyond primary school:

School enrolment and completion is essential to ensure literacy as well as a population ready for university education. In Myanmar, the participation rate for education is high for primary education at 91 per cent, whereas upper secondary school participation is low at 28 per cent for females and 26 per cent for males (Education Policy and Data Center 2018). There are complex gender issues that need to be unpacked.

For library educators the potential applicants for places is low because of the low numbers in high school, although the government has committed to increasing education. There is additional complexity from the perspective of the impact of library education. Unlike many parts of the world, schools, in the large part, function without libraries and librarians and thus the contribution that graduates can make to society and the economy is limited because of the limited opportunities for employment of professional librarians – in all sectors. For those graduating into practice challenges include collections that have been limited through lack of funding, the small number of professional librarian positions overall, limited budgets for the delivery and development of library activities, opportunities for professional development, and support for digital information which is still immmature. The capabilities needed for education, industry, research, non-government organisations and development require funding and a recognition of the value of such a national approach to library practice.

To achieve such an outcome, the partnership between the University of Yangon and the Australian National University is based on understanding and capabilities to collaborate over a multiyear period. Drawing together an understanding of the challenges has included research based on knowledge provided through other institutions including the National Library of Myanmar, National Archives of Myanmar, universities (including University of Yangon Library, the Universities' Central Library, University of East Yangon Library and Department of Library Education, University of Dagon Library and Yangon University of Education Library) and the largest library and information science teaching university in Australia, Charles Sturt University (Missingham 2017). This partnership will be described in the following section.

LIBRARY EDUCATION: PILLARS FOR REFORM

The University of Yangon/Australian National University library education project has three pillars. The first is the connection through library studies theory and theorists that stretches back across the centuries. The foundations of our discipline sit in common across Australia and Myanmar, embodied in education and practice. The concepts of modern librarianship are traced to Indian mathematician and librarian, Siyali Ramamrita Ranganathan. His five laws (Ranganathan 1931) are basic to our common understanding of the discipline. The laws are:

Books are for use. Every person his or her book.

Every book its reader.

Save the time of the reader.

The library is a growing organism

For many theorists on resource descriptions, reconceptualising collections in a networked era (Dempsey 2016) and collection access also provide a common framework for library education that crosses national barriers. This pillar provides a common language from which to explore concepts and practice in library education. It enables our collaboration to commence from a set of agreed theory from which to weave in the digital story.

The second pillar is new library pedagogy. Emerging in the past few years the theory embraces the opportunities of information and digital literacy within a praxis of librarianship in action. The most recent handbook (Pagowsky and McElroy 2016) explores the topic through an active framework focusing on social justice and creating new learning tools and environments focused on engaging in developing an independent critical approach to enquiry and reading. It embodies much of the philosophy explored by the development theorists noted above in developing capabilities and functionings.

The background for the emergence of these concepts can be seen in the work on incorporating social responsibility as a goal within library science (Lankes 2016) and the proposition that information literacy must be seen through the lens of a socially constructed "landscape" which an individual inhabits, and not just as a generic set of skills (Lloyd 2010).

Recognition of the need for the development of information and digital literacy capabilities has not been limited to the library profession. Vint Cerf, the "father of the internet", is a passionate advocate for development of these capabilities. He has commented that it is critical to be serious about digital literacy:

> A digitally literate person would understand, for example, the fragility of digital information. Even though bits seem ethereal, as if they will never wear out, the fact is the medium is not guaranteed to last for very long. (Australian National University 2018)

By seeking to incorporate information and digital literacy within the education framework, the University of Yangon is addressing a very real and pressing issue. Funders have seen an opportunity to contribute to development through investing in selected online research resources for university libraries, with information literacy training for librarians in these libraries (Kupryte 2015; Byein 2016). By creating these new opportunities, it was evident that there was a gap within the university education program. To develop the capabilities in future librarians, the pillar of new library pedagogy was vital to enable the profession to develop and provide capabilities required for the emerging nation, as well as provide human collaboration for sustainable outcomes from the funding of the Electronic Information for Libraries (EIFL) program and other projects.

The third pillar is the digital economy into which the capabilities achieved through the transformation of the program by the Department of Library and Information Studies at the University of Yangon can reach. The potential of education to make a long-term change that benefits society and the economy outlined in the National Education Strategic Plan 2016–21 is embodied in the project.

These three pillars – library and information science theory, new library pedagogy, and the digital economy provide a strong basis for the collaboration that has occurred over the past three years.

PROJECT ESTABLISHMENT AND DELIVERY

The project was initially established through a request from the ANU to the University of Yangon that was sent to all departments. The Department of Library and Information Studies had already identified the need to incorporate digital library content into their teaching program. The libraries employing graduates were increasingly advocating for these skills as they incorporated digital library practices into their collection and services. The Head of the Department's goals were to have Australian experts provide workshops and sample course material to enable the lecturers in University of Yangon to develop their courses, incorporating digital library theory and practice into the curriculum.

The first step was a visit to establish the gap in the current program and also the degree of need in employers – both universities and the National Library of Myanmar. Information was collected on the subject areas into which the digital library approach could be added. The analysis included current pedagogical approaches and rubrics used by the Department. Next, experts were identified in Australia and the second stage was delivering workshops and sampled teaching curriculum to the Department of Library and Information Studies lecturers at the University of Yangon. The programs covered digital library theories and courses in collection management and services. During this stage the team from Australia also visited libraries and the National Archives of Myanmar to speak to staff and directors about the changes in the industry and their needs from current and future graduates. The next step was to provide equipment which could be useful as part of the curriculum and also to develop the knowledge of lecturers. The installation of a small laboratory included a laptop, scanner and software for digitisation and digital library collection management.

Discussion with the Head of Department identified that there is a significant gap in archive and preservation education, with no courses being delivered in the country. Further work will be required to develop programs to meet this need. Identification of relevant Australian expertise and sample course content will be the next steps to support a future set of workshops in the University of Yangon.

REFLECTIONS ON THE PROJECT

The scope of the project has included developing a greater understanding of the potential of library education as a transformative tool in development, developing awareness of the challenges and programs to jointly create a strong understanding of digital library theory and practice.

Topics explored in the workshops and seminars topics included:

digital library theory

recreation of concepts of collection description, management and access in the digital environment

innovations in rubrics and subject design

addressing digital content

possible means of digital delivery

the role of libraries in schools

Engagement of University of Yangon academic staff has been extensive. Their participation has been active with exercises designed to relate their current programs and knowledge to new and emerging areas of the discipline. The strong engagement with institutions such as the National Library and other university libraries has supported a collaborative approach to library education within the country. Professor Ni Win Zaw, the Head of the Department at YU, is an active member of the executive of the Myanmar Library Association and her engagement professionally has assisted in understanding opportunities for growth as well as identifying the gap created through funder investment in practice, but not in education.

In reflecting on the work undertaken in the program, it is important to acknowledge the commitment and passion of educators. Their passion and dedication to reform, however, sits within an environment that faces huge challenges. With regular interruptions to power, limited internet speeds and access and extremely limited IT support, the program must remain within the confines of national and university infrastructure at present. Throughout the project there was awareness of the fundamental problems in achieving digital libraries. Power outages, lack of wi-fi and limited collections, in large part due to previous controls on publishing by former governments, meant that the project was focused on the future, acknowledging that digital librarianship is at present available to the academic community in universities primarily from a limited number of computers within each university library. It is, however, building capabilities that will fit within the nation's sustainable development goals and desire to grow economically and socially.

SUSTAINABLE DEVELOPMENT GOALS

The United Nations Sustainable Development Goals are a valuable lens with which to visit this project. Myanmar has committed to a program linking national government-led actions to the goals, building on existing programs. Myanmar's baseline report acknowledges that the nation is in a time of transition – "from war to peace, from military rule to democracy, and from a closed to an open market economy" (Myanmar Central Statistical Organization and UNDP 2017, 2). The framework indicates areas where libraries and library education can provide key elements, such as education, gender equity and jobs, with specific reference to literacy. The government's formal plan places a stronger commitment to activities, noting that education "also contributes to students' overall development in ways that allow them to realise their full potential" (Myanmar Ministry of Planning and Finance 2018, 41). There are, however, limitations because of the lack of funding, and lack of infrastructure issues related to autonomy.

Looking at the SDG goals in a broader framework, the empowerment of individuals explored by Sen and Nussabaum echo in the individual goals, particularly justice and peace. Perhaps the strongest resonance in the library education project is with the goal of partnerships (Goal 17). In this project there has been a genuine partnership both between the two universities, the library sector in Myanmar and Charles Sturt University.

The result has been a stronger, well-formed understanding and long-term commitment for action and serves as a guide for future partnerships which seek to promote sustainable development in Myanmar.

FUTURE DIRECTIONS

Myanmar faces continuing challenges in library education and library practice. The legal framework for libraries is poor, impeding progress and failing to deliver support for national capabilities required for the twenty-first century (Mratt Kyaw Thu 2018). A 2014 study by The Asia Foundation and the Myanmar Book Aid and Preservation Foundation found that library infrastructure has failed to deliver to regional and city communities through a combination of poor funding, poor infrastructure, low salaries, very limited collections and, in essence, a lack of leadership (Ninh 2014). Little has changed since then.

Overall, the need for funding from the Minister of Education for library education, lack of independence of universities and very limited digital infrastructure are significant barriers to the national benefit of reformation of library education. Much more is required. Some of the key challenges for library education are:

- infrastructure – technology and resources
- resources for educators to reform courses within a very tight program
- exploring opportunities to develop school library education, currently lacking
- opportunities to learn and engage in digital libraries and information literacy internationally
- capacity for embedded development in partnership with institutions across the nation

For libraries the challenges include:

- need for infrastructure for delivery of services
- funding for collections, staff and buildings
- support to further develop the workforce to create capabilities for national transformation
- building social justice and strengthening democracy.

The University of Yangon – Australian National University project is one step towards increasing capability (Missingham 2018), with more to come. A new form of praxis combining educators and practitioners from university libraries will provide a platform for the development of the library and information studies program across the nation.

In ending this chapter it is useful to look at some examples of how investment in education is needed. When the authors visited the National Archives in Yangon, an employer of graduates from the University of Yangon Department of Library and Information Studies described their commitment to develop their knowledge of archival practice and theory. A reading group was active, meeting regularly. The source for the reading group was a single photocopied version of the first edition of a publication of the Australian Society of Archivists – *Keeping Archives*. The text is now in its third edition (2008); however, budget and restrictions on ordering books from overseas have prevented the staff from having access to current knowledge.

Perhaps as potently, one of the librarians shared a story with me of a student in a rural community who had been using the public library. Unfortunately the student had been unable to finish primary school as his family needed him to work to support the economic needs of the household. However, he was unable to use the library as the hours of the library were very limited. The library was not staffed by a professional librarian, and without a collection of a reasonable size the whole community was unable to successfully complete their learning. While initiatives for rural libraries are being advocated for by Khin Kyi, mother of Aung San Suu Kyi, amongst others, there remains much ground to be covered.

The creation of a strong library education program is vital for Myanmar's next stage of development. It lays a foundation to support economic, social and political growth through capabilities around digital knowledge and connects those undertaking education activities to a world of information previously inaccessible. It builds bridges for education and social change. If there is one major step needed it is to provide these new capabilities for library educators which, combined with the evolving infrastructure to access digital knowledge, will enable access to Myanmar's history and stories within the concept of world knowledge to create a robust civil society. This requires significant funding and developments in library education.

Notes

1. Library education is also offered at the University of East Yangon and Yadarpone University, but only the University of Yangon offers a PhD program.
2. Thanks to Dr Mary Carroll, Professor Ni Win Zaw for their contribution to the project and inspiration.
3. Praxis is a concept applied to education that describes a process of learning based on cyclical development. In Pedagogy of the Oppressed Paulo Freire outlines praxis as "reflection and action directed at the structures to be transformed" (Freire 1970, 127). In this context, it is used to outline the relationship between education and practice, and the iterative approach to development of digital concepts within the curriculum of library and information science education. The cycle has applied the theory through undertaking the education of educators, reviewing the impacts of the material provided on the program, reflectively analysing the impact of the workshops and activities, altering and revising the education program through a planned approach and implementing these plans in further actions including a new laboratory.
4. The Ministry of Education plan emphasised the importance of education in their report, in particular schooling. "Quality, equitable and relevant education is essential if we are to provide our children with new knowledge and competencies, creativity and critical thinking skills and cultural and ethical values that will enable them to excel in their chosen careers and contribute to Myanmar's socioeconomic development in the 21st century" (Myanmar Department of Education 2016, 4). There is concern that the education standards have been low, and that teaching has been of a poor standard. There are many issues around education that the plan aims to address. For an assessment of some of the issues see Sithu Aung Myint (2018).

References

Australian National University. *J.G. Crawford Oration: The future of the Internet.* Canberra: The Australian National University, 27 June 2018. Available at https://www.anu.edu.au/news/all-news/jg-crawford-oration-the-future-of-the-internet (accessed 12 May 2019).

Byrne, Alex (2003). "Necromancy or Life Support? Libraries, Democracy and the Concerned Intellectual". *Library Management* 24 (3): 116–125.

Carroll, M. et al. (2013). "Commonwealth of Uncertainty: How British and American Professional Models of Library Practice have Shaped LIS Education in Selected Former British Colonies and Dominions". *IFLA Journal* 39 (2): 121–133.

Dempsey, L. (2016). "Library Collections in the Life of the User: Two Directions". *LIBER Quarterly* 26 (4). Available at https://www.liberquarterly.eu/articles/10.18352/lq.10170/ (accessed 12 May 2019).

Education Policy and Data Center (2018). *Myanmar: Education Overview*. Washington, D.C.: EPDC. https://www.epdc.org/country/myanmar (accessed 12 May 2019).

Freire, P. (1970). *Pedagogy of the Oppressed*. New York: Continuum International Publishing Group. Available at https://commons.princeton.edu/inclusivepedagogy/wp-content/uploads/sites/17/2016/07/freire_pedagogy_of_the_oppresed_ch2-3.pd.f (accessed 12 May 2019).

Hmwe Kyu Zin (2018). "National Archives: Where National and Historical Records are Kept, Global New Light of Myanmar". *Global Light of Myanmar* (3 June). Available at http://www.globalnewlightofmyanmar.com/national-archives-national-historical-records-kept/ (accessed 8 May 2019).

Kupryte, R. (2015). "E-libraries Transform Scholarship in Myanmar". *Sci dev net*. Available at https://www.scidev.net/asia-pacific/education/multimedia/e-libraries-transform-scholarship-in-myanmar.html (accessed 12 May 2019).

Kant, I. (1785). *Groundwork for the Metaphysics of Morals 1785*. Translated and edited by M. Gregor and J. Timmermann. Cambridge: Cambridge University Press, 2012.

Lankes, R.D. et al. (2016). *The New Librarianship Field Guide*. Cambridge, Ma.: MIT Press.

Lloyd, A. (2010). *Information Literacy Landscapes: Information Literacy in Education, Workplace and Everyday Contexts*. Cambridge: Chandos Publishing, 2010.

Mratt Kyaw Thu (2018). "Libraries in Limbo". *Frontier Myanmar* (23 May). Available at https://frontiermyanmar.net/en/libraries-in-limbo (accessed 12 May 2019).

Missingham, R. (2017). "Connecting Myanmar Libraries to Global Academia". *New Mandala*. Available at https://www.newmandala.org/new-initatives-help-libraries-myanmar-connect-academics-world/ (accessed 12 May 2019).

Myanmar Central Statistical Organization and UNDP (2017). *Measuring Myanmar's Starting Point for the Sustainable Development Goals SDG Indicator Baseline Report*. New York: UNDP.

Myanmar Ministry of Education (2016). *National Education Strategic Plan 2016–21 Summary*. Naypyitaw: Ministry of Education. Available at http://www.moe-st.gov.mm/wp-content/uploads/2018/01/NESP_20Summary_20-_20English_20-_20Final_20-_20Feb_2023.pdf (accessed 12 May 2019).

Myanmar Ministry of Planning and Finance (2018). *Myanmar Sustainable Development Plan (2018 – 2030)*. Naypyitaw: Ministry of Planning and Finance. Available at http://themimu.info/sites/themimu.info/files/documents/Core_Doc_Myanmar_Sustainable_Development_Plan_2018_-_2030_Aug2018.pdf (accessed 12 May 2019).

Myat Sannyein Nyein (2016). "Transforming Libraries in Myanmar: The e-Library Myanmar Project". Oxford University Press Blog. Available at https://blog.oup.com/2016/07/libraries-in-myanmar/ (accessed 8 May 2019).

Ninh, Kim N.B. (2014). "Myanmar's Libraries: A Potential Catalyst for Community Development". *Asia Foundation*. Available at https://asiafoundation.org/2014/02/05/myanmars-libraries-a-potential-catalyst-for-community-development/ (accessed 8 May 2019).

Nussbaum, M. (2011). *Creating Capabilities*. Cambridge, MA: Harvard University Press.

Pagowsky, N. and McElroy, K. (eds) (2016). *Critical Library Pedagogy Handbook*. Chicago: Association of College and Research Libraries, a division of the American Library Association.

Ranganathan, Siyali Ramamrita (1931). *The Five Laws of Library Science*. Madras: The Madras Library Association.

Russell, B. (1954). *Human Society in Ethics and Politics*. London: G. Allen & Unwin.

Saha, L.J. (1991). "Universities and National Development: Issues and Problems in Developing Countries". *Prospects* 21 (2): 248–257.

Sen, Amartya (1992). *Inequality Re-examined*. Oxford: Clarendon Press.

Sithu Aung Myint (2018). "An Education Policy Disaster, 30 Years on. Yangon". *Myanmar Frontier*, 25 July. Available at https://frontiermyanmar.net/en/an-education-policy-disaster-30-years-on (accessed 12 May 2019)

UNESCO (2019). *Myanmar Country Profile*. Paris: UNESCO. Available at http://uis.unesco.org/country/MM (accessed 12 May 2019).

University of Yangon, Department of Library and Information Studies (2018). *Libraries and Information Studies*. Yangon: The University. Available at https://www.uy.edu.mm/libraries-and-information-studies/ (accessed 8 May 2019).

11

THE WINDING PATH TO GENDER EQUALITY IN MYANMAR

Khin Khin Mra and Deborah Livingstone

Myanmar's transition to democracy has created a critical juncture with both threats to gender equality and opportunities to enhance it. In many ways the enduring legacies of military rule have impacted the scope of what changes are possible, and what can be imagined as possible, in advancing gender equality in the contemporary era. There is a common misperception that gender equality exists in Myanmar (Ikeya 2005; Ma et al. 2018). However, the reality for women and girls shows that gender inequalities persist in many forms. This includes in women's access to jobs, land, and credit (Ministry of Labour, Immigration and Population 2017), political representation (Zin Mar Aung 2015; Maber 2016), participation in the peace process (Alliance for Gender Inclusion in the Peace Process 2016; Williams 2018) and in popular perceptions and beliefs about women's roles and their abilities (The Asia Foundation 2014; Thein 2015). Women and girls also experience high levels of violence (Faxon et al. 2015; MoHS and ICF 2017). Gender inequalities intersect with other factors (Khin Mar Mar Kyi 2012) such as age (Faxon 2017; Agatha Ma 2018), ethnicity (Agatha Ma and Kusakabe 2015), religion (Thein 2015), class (Frydenlund 2019) and disability (Maber and Aung 2019; Khum 2019) to create a complex and varied picture of inequalities in different states and regions.

The National Strategic Plan for the Advancement of Women 2013–2022 (NSPAW) is the first-ever gender strategy of the Government of Myanmar. The NSPAW drafting process was initiated by the former military government after being advanced by women's networks and CSOs following Cyclone Nargis in 2008. The Women's Protection Technical Working Group, which was set up as a response to Cyclone Nargis, played a key role through its advocacy to the Ministry of Social Welfare, Relief and Resettlement (MSWRR). While the initial planning concentrated on women's empowerment in emergency situations, this evolved into a strategy structured around the twelve priority areas[1] outlined in the United Nations Convention on the Elimination of All Forms of Discrimination against Women (CEDAW)[2] and the Beijing Platform for Action (BPfA).[3] In the post-Nargis period, women's networks and organisations took advantage of the space created at a time of great institutional change to leverage a national plan that went beyond addressing women's needs in an emergency to more comprehensively addressing women's rights "so that women and men can play equal and meaningful roles, and women can reach their full potential" (Ministry of Social Welfare, Relief and Resettlement 2013, 1).

However, in 2016 the plan was widely perceived by women's organisations, donors and government actors as having stalled (Khin Khin Mra and Livingstone 2016). As a cross-government strategic plan, NSPAW had not been aligned with other national plans and strategies and other ministries did not see the plan as relevant to them. There was no operational plan or budget to help the Women's Development Division deliver the plan and technical capacity in the Division was insufficient. Development partners were keen to support implementation but offers of support were not coordinated and stretched the capacity of the Department of Social Welfare further. Civil society organisations who had advocated for NSPAW were critical of the government's failed attempts to implement the plan. In this context the Department of Social Welfare sought technical assistance to support the Women's Development Division to implement NSPAW and we were contracted by the UK Department for International Development.

Using the NSPAW as a case study, this paper examines how formal and informal institutions both bolstered and impeded efforts to implement a national policy to support gender equality in Myanmar. The implementation of NSPAW between September 2016 and February 2018 helps to illustrate how gendered institutions and practices continue to affect policy processes in Myanmar. We chose NSPAW as a case study given our experiences working within the Myanmar government. Data comes from our observations and analysis over seventeen months embedded as technical assistants in the Women's Development Division where we supported the creation of four cross-government technical working groups, engaged with international development architecture and developed policy briefs on key areas related to NSPAW. As feminist researchers we had a unique opportunity to see how institutions are gendered, how they interact, and how key actors engaged with them. This allowed us to explore how the legacies of military rule informed how formal and informal institutions evolved during the democratisation period and the impact of this on the implementation of a national gender policy. This paper also draws on both authors' extensive experience working to promote the rights of women and girls in Myanmar.

Using a feminist institutionalist lens this paper makes a key contribution to both practice and theory by generating a more nuanced understanding of policy-making processes and feminist scholarship in Myanmar. New institutionalism theorises that institutions – such as parliaments, the military, governments, constitutions and laws – are governed by formal and informal rules and norms and at the same time they are shaped by informal networks, ways of working and relationships (Ní Aoláin 2018). Feminist institutionalism expands on this to include power dynamics and the gender dimensions of formal and informal rules and practices (Acker 1992; Stivers 2002; Kenny 2007; Krook and Mackay 2011; Mackay 2014). We use this lens to explore how institutions, and the formal and informal norms and rules that governed how NSPAW was developed and implemented during the transition, were influenced by the gendered legacies of military rule, including how patriarchal power structures were normalised and space for civil society or feminist action were limited at a time of transition and institutional reform. We examine the power dynamics between key actors and how formal institutions, like Union-level development architecture, national policy and international frameworks, and informal institutions such as social and cultural norms have evolved and interacted in different ways in the "rounds of restructuring" in Myanmar's transition to democracy. We argue that, while the early stages of democratisation in Myanmar have offered up new spaces and opportunities for gender equality and women's empowerment, it has also strengthened the actors and institutions opposed to change .

GENDER EQUALITY AND THE LEGACY OF MILITARY RULE

Since the reintroduction of democratic processes in Myanmar in 2010, the legacy of military rule has significantly influenced the formal and informal rules that have emerged during the reform process. This has had a major impact on the opportunities for supporting greater gender equality. There are many and multi-layered drivers of inequality in Myanmar. Women, along with non-Bamar ethnic groups and religious and sexual minorities, have been conspicuously absent from discussions related to the political transition (Agatha Ma and Kusakabe 2015; Chua and Gilbert 2015; Faxon et al. 2015; Zin Mar Aung 2015; Mayber 2016; Agatha Ma et al. 2018). While a democratic system of government was institutionalised under the country's 2008 Constitution, the military continued to dominate the transitional system of governance under President Thein Sein (2011–2016), reinforcing patriarchal power structures and obstructing women's political leadership. Where decades of armed conflict in ethnic states led to a "masculinisation" of decision-making, women were also sidelined from the peace process (Ferguson 2013; Hedström 2016; MSWRR et al. 2016; Cardenas 2019). Traditionally, women have held a high social status in Myanmar, for example, as bearers of culture. However, this declined under military rule (Harriden 2012). Few women held senior government positions, they were not recruited for active duty in the Army, Navy or Air Force, and until 2013 they were only recruited for feminised roles in the military such as secretaries, nurses, and support staff (Open Society Foundation 2014). While the State Counsellor Aung San Suu Kyi appears to offer a powerful alternative example of female leadership, her prominent status in Myanmar has largely been attributed to her connection to her father General Aung San, the famous independence hero, rather than for any inherent ability or leadership qualities (Harriden 2012). Ethnic armed forces have also been led almost exclusively by male leaders and women are not usually trained as combatants or encouraged to be involved in political affairs (Hedström 2013).

During military rule (1962–2010), women's organisations such as the Myanmar Women's Affairs Federation, led by the wives of senior government leaders/military officials, were set up as a response to international criticism of the state's human rights record and failure to meet CEDAW obligations (Harriden 2012). Government policies and programs were, however, ultimately directed by men, reinforcing male power and control (Harriden 2012). In effect, many of these organisations were mobilised to encourage women to support the military government and its policies, perpetuating an apolitical notion of women as wives and mothers in need of protection. The expectation that men are leaders, combined with social expectations that women are meant to play a supportive role, is fully engrained in daily life (ActionAid, Care and Oxfam 2011). Women face a double jeopardy: they lack power and resources but are expected to fulfil feminine responsibilities according to customary ideologies (Khin Mar Mar Kyi 2012).

Under military rule, while military wives' organisations flourished, civil society was unable to operate independently as the government outlawed all political activities (Steinberg 2001). After Cyclone Nargis in 2008, however, some opportunities for civil society organisations to operate materialised. The social and political reforms that began in 2011 saw a significant, though ultimately brief,[4] change in the relationship between states and citizens. During this time there was a great sense of hope for Myanmar as political prisoners were released, Aung San Suu Kyi was elected to parliament, media freedoms increased, and the government became increasingly open to grassroots development and collaboration with civil society. Civil society organisations were able to advocate for diverse issues and participate in many policy domains which were previously dominated by the military. During this time, many women used the growing political space to mobilise groups and networks to advocate for gender equality.

Despite the growing sense of optimism afforded by these changes, the space for feminist action remained limited and the relationship between women's rights activists and the state continued to be maligned by a deep sense of mistrust. While Burmese women in exile were able to come together under the umbrella of non-state armed groups and overtly challenge gender inequalities (Hedström 2016; Olivius 2018), women's groups within Myanmar were more constrained by conservative social norms, restrictions on freedom of speech and association and potential negative repercussions including exile and imprisonment (Maber 2016). While there was a growing body of Myanmar-situated feminist theory to ground and support progressive policy and action, women within Myanmar and women in exile continued to use different approaches and language and have different alliances (Hedström 2015; Olivius 2018). This meant that, while political space opened up to support the advancement of women, there was no common basis to work from to unite these groups and to support their engagement in male-dominated policy processes.

Women's efforts to promote gender equality at this time were also impeded by the 2008 Constitution. The constitution guarantees all persons equal rights before the law and equal legal protection (Section 347), the right to vote and run for public office (Section 9), and no discrimination on the basis of sex (Section 348). However, it also guarantees 25 per cent of members of parliament to be appointed by the Commander-in-Chief of the Defence Services (Sections 109 & 141), retaining significant power for the military. As the military is dominated by men this provision plays a major role in restricting women's opportunities for participation in parliament and key ministerial positions. The constitution also requires the president to have experience with military affairs (Section 59-d) and contains references that reinforce gender stereotypes, for example stating that "nothing in this section shall prevent the appointment of men to positions that are naturally suitable for men only" (Section 352). References to women are principally as "mothers", which reinforces gendered stereotypes that women are suited to motherhood above other opportunities and contends that their reproductive roles are in need of protection (Section 32) (Khin Khin Mra 2015b). This constitutionally enshrined narrative structures how policy is framed and embeds gendered social norms and stereotypes in policy discussions and in their implementation.

While the transition brought new institutional arrangements and political space to advance gender equality, the primacy of the old order remained safeguarded by the fact that reforms were initiated by the military. Key institutions, including the constitution and parliament, were highly masculinised with the rules set and created through the leadership of men (Khin Khin Mra 2015a). In 2015, only two of the 110 military appointees in the 440 member *Pyithu Hluttaw*[5] were women. The appointed speakers of both houses of parliament were also men, and both ex-military officials. More "masculine" ministries like Home Affairs and Defence, which were controlled by the military, received by far the majority share of the government budget, whereas the whole Ministry of Social Welfare, Relief and Resettlement (MSWRR) budget accounted for less than one per cent of the national budget in 2015 (Khin Khin Mra and Livingstone 2016). Under the NLD government women's representation also remained limited, impacting women's voices and efforts in demanding legislation to protect their rights or leading initiatives for gender reform. In 2016, there were only two women Union ministers out of thirty-six ministerial positions and they were appointed to "soft" or "feminised" portfolios such as education and social welfare. Women's formal participation in peace talks, political settlement frameworks and development mechanisms also continued to be undermined, restricting their ability to advocate for gender equality within reforming institutions.

Indeed, the normalisation of patriarchal power structures instituted under military rule and the limited space for civil society and feminist action deeply affected the scope of what was possible to achieve during the transition. Male-dominant institutions and ideas remained powerful during the restructuring of institutions rather than evolving to become more gender-inclusive. As shown in the next section, these legacies also played a role in influencing the development of the National Strategic Plan for the Advancement of Women 2013–2022 (NSPAW) and its implementation.

THE ACTORS AND INSTITUTIONS OF NSPAW

Initiated under the former military government, NSPAW is the first gender strategy of the Government of Myanmar to advance women's empowerment. NSPAW is the responsibility of the Women's Development Division in the Department of Social Welfare, Ministry of Social Welfare, Relief and Resettlement (MSWRR), and responsibility for policy decisions and coordination with NGOs sits with the Myanmar National Committee for Women's Affairs (MNCWA). Founded in 1996, MNCWA was designated as the cross-governmental body responsible for NSPAW; however, it had not functioned effectively for years. A proposal for a revised MNCWA, with membership from two women's networks, the Gender Equality Network and Women's Organisation Network, was approved by the Office of the State Counselor in 2016, opening up space for women's voices to be heard at a policy level. A Parliamentary Committee for Women's and Child Rights was also formed, and further opportunities existed to engage MPs in the implementation of legislation related to NSPAW priority areas, potentially with the support of former gender activists who became MPs in the 2015 elections.

Neither committee had fully embraced NSPAW or fought for it to be at the centre of the reforms at the time technical assistance was being provided. Ministry representatives on MNCWA were at Director General rather than

Ministerial level, which meant that no key policy decisions or links to other policy or peace processes were made. While a more open political process offered opportunities for reforming structures and institutions, existing policy institutions were sustained along with the practice of top-down policymaking. Gender focal points had been established in eighteen ministries but they were relatively junior, at Director and Deputy Director level, and had little influence and no terms of reference to support integrating NSPAW into their sector plan and programs. At State and Region levels there were no Women's Development Division staff or budget. To implement any activities staff from the division travelled or made use of other, equally stretched, Department of Social Welfare staff (Khin Khin Mra and Livingstone 2016).

Gender civil society organisations and networks in Myanmar and women's organisations in exile were critical of the development of NSPAW and its implementation. While women working in Myanmar-based CSOs and networks were constrained by conservative social norms and the threat of imprisonment, they had developed a good relationship with MSWRR and had the technical skills to develop and implement gender policy. This raised concerns at the time that they were being co-opted by a government they did not fully trust following years of military rule. Women's organisations in exile, however, were able to challenge the development and implementation of NPSAW more directly and able to use the language and support networks available through their strong links with the international gender community. Much common ground existed in terms of what these organisations wanted to achieve for women in Myanmar. However, as noted in the previous section, different alliances, levels of relationship with the government and international networks, and priorities for action meant there was no single voice from civil society on how to implement NSPAW.

Development partners engaged with NSPAW directly through the Women's Development Division. NSPAW implementation required a clear and shared strategy, with development partners focused on how to ensure NSPAW was integrated across all Sector Coordinating Groups, ensuring development aid effectiveness principles were upheld, and that capacity issues in the Women's Development Division were recognised. Instead, development partner meetings were characterised by reporting back on activities, and relationships with government were fostered individually and separately to further their own agendas. The lack of common aims between gender actors, fragmentation of support to the Women's Development Division, and lack of coordination on policy issues effectively diluted women's voices and their impact on institutional and policy reform.

Development partners also engaged with NSPAW through the Gender Equality and Women's Empowerment cross-cutting Coordination Group, the main institution for gender in the development assistance architecture. At the time the authors were providing technical assistance on NSPAW, the then recently elected NLD Government restructured the development assistance architecture. Ten Sector Coordinating Groups replaced the previous seventeen Sector Working Groups. Gender Equality and Women's Empowerment had previously been a Sector Working Group and, in the restructuring and only after much lobbying from donors and the Department of Social Welfare, it was retained as one of three Cross-cutting Coordinating Groups. This was seen as a demotion in terms of how seriously the government took gender equality; in effect, gender equality was sidelined and separated from what were seen as the key development issues in Myanmar. Responsibility for leading the Cross-cutting Coordinating Group and implementing NSPAW was located within a small and poorly resourced division that had no dedicated staff below Union level. As an institution, or set of rules, this meant that NSPAW effectively sat outside of the overall development architecture and was not aligned with or integrated into national policies and plans (Khin Khin Mra and Livingstone 2017).

At the same time as gender equality was being sidelined in key policy terrain and development architecture, a range of related gender commitments and agendas such as CEDAW, the Women, Peace and Security agenda, ASEAN commitments and various donors began to compete for the time and resources of the new government. [6] The links between the different agendas of each of these institutions were not made either conceptually or practically by the Women's Development Division. Instead, this led to a kind of paralysis, with the division using all its time to respond to the most recent meeting request, donor demand, or instruction from various ministries rather than prioritising, planning or reporting existing related activities relevant to the implementation of NSPAW (Khin Khin Mra and Livingstone 2017).

Informal institutions were also gendered and influenced the implementation of NSPAW. For example, the relationship between the government and civil society organisations and networks continued to be hampered by ongoing historical tensions. In the early stages of the NLD government, there was a great sense of hope amongst civil society for change. However, despite the removal of the previous military-backed government from power, under the NLD the civil society sector continued to face challenges to their participation in the policymaking process. Under the new government, NSPAW was still seen as the sole responsibility of MSWRR by many women's organisations and they continued their advocacy and pressure only to MSWRR with whom they had developed a good relationship. However, opportunities to place NSPAW at the heart of the reform agenda were missed, as they concentrated their efforts on the implementation of other technical frameworks such as CEDAW. Given the positive relationship with MSWRR and CSO's technical strengths, links could have been made between all gender agendas and NSPAW, and advocacy broadened to ministries leading on the relevant agenda and to parliamentary committees such as the Committee on the Rights of Women and Children. Furthermore, distrust between civil society organisations and government also affected CSOs' advocacy to military-dominated ministries such as the Ministry of Defence and the Ministry of Home Affairs. This distrust led to a somewhat combative relationship between the government and women's organisations and made joint action to implement NSPAW challenging.

Social and cultural norms also influenced these processes, where women continued to be viewed as subjects or as "victims", rather than as critical actors in policymaking and institutional reform.[7] In the Burmese language, "culture" is defined as *yin kyae hmu* meaning "politeness or gentleness". The influence of Buddhism on *yin kyae hmu* is perceived by Buddhists as a protective force that counters the negative influences of globalisation (GEN 2015). There is a growing fear in Myanmar that *yin kyae hmu* and its associated traditional cultural values are under threat from both internal and external forces – cultural, religious economic, and political (Steinberg 2014 in GEN 2015). Women are perceived as being the bearers of *yin kyae hmuI,* which places them and their behaviour on a pedestal. At the same time, *hpon* is a concept that gives higher authority and status to men, which suggests that men have innate leadership and decision-making qualities and influences how women can make decisions about issues that affect them, and how they engage in community or policy discussions (GEN 2015). This idea is deeply held and is borne out in research that shows both men and women prefer male leaders (The Asia Foundation 2014). The notion of "*arh nah deh*" also relates to how people behave, reinforced amongst women in particular, whereby they "refrain from asserting themselves, because they feel obliged to maintain the other person's dignity or 'face', or to show respect or politeness" (GEN 2015, 43). Buddhist belief in karma means that it is also widely perceived that acts in a previous life affect what happens to an individual, family or community. This creates social barriers and discrimination against marginalised groups such as women, persons with disabilities and LGBT individuals. Individuals internalise these norms and tend to accept or blame themselves for marginalisation rather than holding actors or institutions responsible for discrimination against them.

The social and cultural norms described above continue to play a significant role in hampering efforts to improve gender equality in Myanmar. For many policymakers, gender equality is perceived as a "Western" concept that conflicts with Buddhist values (GEN 2015) and, in turn, NSPAW is considered by many, including senior government officials,[8] as a "Western" agenda. Perceived threats to *yin kyae hmu*, and the combination of *arh nah deh*, *hpon* and karma, mean that women are significantly constrained in voicing their concerns and engaging with government on institutional reform. This is especially true for women interacting with male-dominated institutions such as the General Administration Department, the Police and Land departments, where policy remains dominated by ex-military male leadership. The combined effects of these social norms leave women disempowered and effectively excluded from policy engagement. As a result, Myanmar's democratisation priorities continue to be defined by male-dominated institutions and women's voices remain unheard in institutional reform and policymaking processes.

ENGAGING WITH GENDERED POWER DYNAMICS AND INSTITUTIONAL COMPLEXITY

This section describes how the authors sought to respond to the above challenges and engage with the actors and institutions in support of the implementation of NSPAW. At the beginning of the technical assistance, it was widely perceived that there had been no action in implementing NSPAW, with several government and civil society interviewees saying it was "a paper exercise", that "the government had done nothing", and it effectively "remained on the shelf". In effect, NSPAW was experiencing "drift", where old institutional arrangements are actively neglected (Krook and Mackay 2011, 186). As such, its influence on policy and legislation was minimal. For example, NSPAW objectives on women's economic empowerment did not feature in the national policy and plans on economic development. NSPAW and the Women's Development Division similarly had little influence over four discriminatory laws on the Protection of Race and Religion, which were advocated for by the group *Ma Ba Tha*, led by nationalist Buddhists and which were passed swiftly (Marte 2015). The Protection and Prevention of Violence Against Women Bill, drafted by MSWRR with support from gender CSOs, remained in draft form for years.

To understand the constraints leading to this, the technical assistance was designed to adapt and respond to the findings of ongoing political analysis. This analysis aimed to understand the institutions, incentives, relationships, and distribution and contestation of power between different groups and individuals. The authors found that the multiple gender agendas created confusion within the Women's Development Division and competition between donors as to whose agenda should be prioritised by the division. This confusion and competition meant that the division and development partners working on gender focused on power dynamics within this "community" rather than engaging in broader development issues and national priorities through the national development assistance architecture (the Sector Coordinating Groups) and existing national policies and plans (Khin Khin Mra and Livingstone 2016). Understanding this meant that we could support the Women's Development Division to coordinate the various gender frameworks under one NSPAW "umbrella" operational plan and work with other ministries to integrate NSPAW into national-level development processes and institutions.

Key actors, their incentives and the power dynamics between them were analysed. We found that the Women's Development Division had little influence in its own department, let alone across other ministries. The analysis did identify allies within the government however, for example in the Myanmar Police Force in the Ministry of Home Affairs, the Ministry of Health, the Hluttaw Committee on the Rights of Women and Children, and the Union Election Committee. These individuals were allies either as a result of personal relationships with the Director of the Women's Development Division and Director General of the Department of Social Welfare or they were already active in promoting gender equality in their sector or committee. A mapping of existing government activities that related to NSPAW (Khin Khin Mra and Livingstone 2016) showed that many actions were being undertaken across different government departments that could fall under the umbrella of NSPAW. These activities were not driven by NSPAW or reported upon by ministries or other stakeholders under an NSPAW planning or monitoring framework, and they were often perceived as being completely unconnected to NSPAW. While there had been little alignment of NSPAW to line ministries' existing strategies and plans, the mapping demonstrated where there was common ground.

An analysis of values and ideas showed how gender norms and gendered practices are reflected in the voice and influence of the Women's Development Division and how this is reflected in the limited resources provided to the division and the attitudes of some government departments to the value and importance of NSPAW. NSPAW was considered by officials in other government departments as dealing with "women's issues" and the business of the Women's Development Division, rather than as a strategic plan that should guide the whole government to achieve gender equality. Deep-rooted social and cultural norms such as *hpon*, politeness and respect, and women as bearers of culture supported the existing patriarchal institutions and their central position, with NSPAW marginalised on the edges.

With this understanding of how the key institutions were gendered, where NSPAW sat in the formal divisions of power and policy terrains, and the actors and power dynamics between them, we used four main approaches to support the implementation of NSPAW: *strategic framing* – changing the narrative; *nudge* – aligning different interests across government and with development partners; *listening and dialogue* – consulting key actors and building consensus; and *adaptive programming* – being able to adapt and respond as the context changed.

While NSPAW was perceived to have stalled, there was significant will from MSWRR, civil society and donors to make it work. The evidence from the analysis and the mapping of existing activities helped identify a set of key messages aimed at changing the narrative of perceived failure. Based on the feminist institutional theory that "ideas and discourses are a potential source of institutional change" (Krook and Mackay 2011, 191), we supported the Women's Development Division to create a new narrative, or "strategic framing", around NSPAW, one that created a broader sense of ownership and located NSPAW within government as a high-level priority.

Three key messages were developed: firstly, that NSPAW supports national priorities such as peace and economic development; secondly, that one coordinated plan to further gender equality and women's empowerment can help Myanmar deliver international gender commitments; and thirdly that while NSPAW sits with the MSWRR, it is the responsibility of all government ministries and all development partners to integrate NSPAW objectives and indicators into their national plans, budgets and reporting. These messages were delivered consistently by the Minister and Director General of MSWRR to government and development partners which helped begin to develop consensus around how to implement NSPAW more effectively.

Given the lack of power and influence the Women's Development Division had within national policy terrains, we applied nudge theory to get consensus on a set of actions that would support coordinated and accelerated implementation of NSPAW. With capacity constraints and coordination issues, a pragmatic approach was agreed, focusing on: building on existing frameworks where objectives have already been agreed such as CEDAW concluding observations and Universal Periodic Review recommendations; engaging with development partners that were already mobilised around a specific issue such as Women, Peace and Security; and using existing objectives and indicators, such as the Sustainable Development Goals, as indicators to align NSPAW more effectively with other national plans and processes such as health, education, economic development and the peace process. Had a more technical approach been taken, developing plans with perfect logframes and narratives, it is unlikely that consensus would have been achieved. The downside of this approach was that alignment with government priorities and plans did not always support a human rights approach, particularly in the context of events in Rakhine State and conflicts in Kachin and northern Shan States.

A year of consultations and dialogue led to consensus and actions supporting the accelerated implementation of NSPAW. The MNCWA had a revised terms of reference though efforts to get the MNCWA to meet and make policy decisions were less successful, leaving a gap in high-level leadership and coordination. At a technical level, government, CSO and development partner stakeholders agreed to develop four initial Technical Working Groups (TWGs). In this way, NSPAW could be seen to drive action forward in a coordinated way that maximised resources and supported reporting. Four TWGs – Violence Against Women and Girls;

Women, Peace and Security; Participation; and Mainstreaming – were agreed based on links to national plans and priorities where there was already momentum, partnership and activity, and links to other gender institutions and agendas. Several ministries were involved in developing the action plans which could be aligned with existing national plans and strategies, for example in relation to health, justice, peace, the economy, elections, and public financial management. They were also intended to be used to guide gender mainstreaming in the new Sector Coordinating Groups.

Being able to adapt to rapid changes in the context was critical and the process leading to consensus on key messages and actions was not a linear one. Without any significant power, influence or budget, progress was highly dependent on our ability to build trust and respond to changing relationships and priorities within government, by development partners, and in the relationship between government and development partners. Engaging with the "ongoing political contestation and the daily 'enactment'" (Krook and Mackay 2011, 186) of the government was critical. For example, getting to agreement on four technical working groups involved much behind-the-scenes consensus building across several sectors in government departments and with development partners, including bilateral donors, the UN, civil society and the private sector. Understanding the power dynamics between actors, and how they engaged with gendered institutions, helped us work with them to try to seize the opportunity afforded by the transition to transform institutions in support of gender equality.

WHAT WORKED AND WHAT DID NOT WORK?

Some fragile gains were made in the implementation of NSPAW with formal and informal institutions both supporting and obstructing progress. Multiple gender instruments created confusion, compounded by limited capacity and no budget in the Women's Development Division, and a lack of cohesion and coordination from donors. While NSPAW, and its grounding in international institutions such as CEDAW, provided a nationally owned cross-government plan for advancing gender equality, it was also imperfect, sidelined and siloed in a division with little capacity, resources or political influence. Critical to getting support from key stakeholders in this context was capitalising on personal relationships and aligning the plan with other existing national plans and priorities. Ongoing analysis revealed where there was common ground and helped identify priorities and build consensus on areas for initial accelerated action. This was time-consuming, but it was essential to understand the scope of what was possible, and how this changed over time. A pragmatic approach, politically rather than technically driven, made consensus on priorities possible. After seventeen months of technical assistance, a roadmap for the accelerated implementation of NSPAW was agreed upon, four technical working groups were established, policy briefs and action plans developed and the narrative around NSPAW shifted from one of failure to joint ownership and action.

Adaptive programming, being able to respond to the changing context and power dynamics, supported these gains. During the period of the technical assistance, the new government established a new development assistance framework, the SDGs became a focus of government planning, and the situation in Rakhine State erupted. The core outcome remained fixed, but the route changed several times. Our ability to respond to the changing context was supported by our understanding of the institutional context and relationships with government and development partners. In fact, we often acted as a bridge between government, the UN, donors and civil society, negotiating complex and sometimes tense issues and discussions.

Gains were made within predominantly patriarchal institutions and in news ways of working with them, rather than taking advantage of the reform process to actually transform or create new institutions. A body of Myanmar research and feminist theory was at the early stages of emerging. The use of "Western" concepts and theories challenges Myanmar social norms, which made it easy for NSPAW to be dismissed as a "Western" agenda rather than a national priority. This led, for example, to the technical working groups predominantly involving gender activists and junior staff from other departments and ministries, rather than senior government decision-makers who could integrate NSPAW objectives within national priorities and plans.

Just at the moment of consensus, with policy briefs and annual plans agreed for the four technical working groups, the technical assistance ended. The gains were fragile and observations of progress since have shown that it has slowed, if not stalled. Long-term, coordinated and properly resourced support, with a coherent, strategic approach from development partners is essential. The department was pulled in different directions and attempts to unite efforts under one plan were challenged by development partners continuing to push their own agendas, claim space without delivering, and fail to take advantage of high-level political opportunities to centre NSPAW at the heart of development coordination efforts. Without strategic and politically aware inputs from development partners, we had serious difficulties in challenging aspects of NSPAW implementation, such as the Human Rights and Humanitarian priority area, especially relating to conflicts in Rakhine, Kachin and northern Shan States.

CONCLUSIONS

The ongoing legacies of military rule, including the normalisation of patriarchal power structures, and the limited space for civil society and feminist action affected Myanmar's political settlement at a time of transition and institutional reform. While the early stages of democratisation in Myanmar offered up new spaces and opportunities for gender equality and women's empowerment, it also unleashed complex processes that strengthened the actors and institutions opposed to change. The case of NSPAW demonstrates how this shaped what was, and was not, possible in terms of institutional reform that supported gender equality in the rounds of restructuring under the new NLD government. Formal and informal institutions continue to be gendered, with the national gender "machinery" sidelined and unfinanced. Multiple gender agendas have also created confusion and development partners stretched government in different directions, failing to put aside organisational agendas to take advantage of a critical juncture to place gender equality at the heart of the reforms. Fragile gains and changes to ways of working were made *within* patriarchal institutions, but these were dependent on personal relationships, lengthy consensus building, and constantly adapting to changes in the context. Change was not linear and depended on understanding gendered power relations and incentives, as well as the social and cultural norms that prevailed.

To generate transformational change and put gender equality front and centre of a reform process it is critical to understand and engage directly with the institutions at the heart of the reforms, rather than shouting from a distance on the edges of the institutions that make all the big decisions. Understanding how formal and informal institutions are gendered, and how power dynamics play out within and around these institutions, is essential in effectively attempting to reshape institutional arrangements and develop strategies to promote gender equality through democratisation. Feminist theory and a body of research generated in Myanmar could help create culturally specific feminist principles and objectives that tackle perceptions of gender equality as a challenge to Myanmar culture, and guide potential new political institutions and cultures that include and benefit women. This would help Myanmar feminists and gender activists, and guide development partners, in jointly engaging with and restructuring gendered institutions and power dynamics, and in developing new institutions and ways of working at a time of transition to democracy.

Notes

1 Livelihoods, Education and Training, Health, Violence against Women, Emergencies, Economy, Decision-making, Institutional Mechanisms for the Advancement of Women, Human Rights, Media, Environment, and the Girl Child.

2 CEDAW (2008) defines what constitutes discrimination against women and sets up an agenda for national action to end such discrimination.

3 The Beijing Platform for Action aims to "remove all the obstacles to women's active participation in all spheres of public and private life through a full and equal share in economic, social, cultural and political decision-making."

4 At the time of writing press freedoms and the space for civil society is shrinking.

5 The *Pyithu Hluttaw* is the lower house of parliament.

6 he agendas and commitments included implementing CEDAW concluding observations, implementing Universal Periodic Review (UPR) recommendations, United Nations Security Council Resolution 1325 on Women, Peace and Security, Sustainable Development Goal 5 on Gender Equality, ASEAN Committee on Women and ASEAN Commission on the Promotion and Protection of the Rights of Women and Children plans, and a UNFPA Violence Against Women National Action Plan for the Women and Girls First Programme.

7 Spelling of Myanmar words has been taken from GEN (2015).

8 Conversations with government officials Oct-Dec 2016.

References

Acker, J. (1992). "From Sex Roles to Gendered Institutions". *Contemporary Sociology* 21: 565–569.

ActionAid, CARE and Oxfam (2011). *If Given the Chance: Women's Participation in Public Life in Myanmar*. Yangon.

Agatha Ma and Kusakabe, K. (2015). "Gender Analysis of Fear and Mobility in the Context of Ethnic Conflict in Kayah State, Myanmar". *Singapore Journal of Tropical Geography* 36 (3): 1–15.

Agatha Ma, Poe Ei Phyu and Knapman, C. (2018) "In the Land of Wise Old Men: Experiences of Young Women Activists in Myanmar". *Gender and Development* 26 (3): 459–476.

Alliance for Gender Inclusion in the Peace Process (2016). Women, Peace and Security Policymaking in Myanmar: Context Analysis and Recommendations, Edition 1/2016, December. Yangon: Alliance for Gender Inclusion in the Peace Process.

Cardenas, M.L. (2019). "Women-to-Women Diplomacy and the Women's League of Burma". In *Peace and Security in Myanmar: Between Feminism and* Ethnopolitics, edited by A. Kolas. London: Routledge.

CEDAW (2008). Concluding observations of the Committee on the Elimination of Discrimination against Women: Myanmar. Available at http://www.refworld.org/pdfid/494ba8d00.pdf (accessed 27 May 2020)

Chua, L.J., and Gilbert, D. (2015). "Sexual Orientation and Gender Identity Minorities in Transition: LGBT Rights and Activism in Myanmar". *Human Rights Quarterly* 37 (1): 1–28.

Connell, R. (2014). "Rethinking Gender from the South". *Feminist Studies* 40 (3): 518–539.

Faxon, H.O. (2017). "In the Law and on the Land: Finding the Female Farmer in Myanmar's National Land Use Policy". *The Journal of Peasant Studies* 44 (6): 1197–1214.

Faxon, H.O., Furlong, R., & Sabe Phyu, M. (2015). "Reinvigorating Resilience: Violence Against Women, Land rights, and the Women's Peace Movement in Myanmar". *Gender & Development* 23 (3): 463–479.

Frydenlund, S. (2019). "Motherhood, Home, and the Political Economy of Rohingya Women's Labor". In *Unraveling Myanmar's Transition: Progress, Retrenchment and Ambiguity Amidst Liberalization*, edited by P. Chachavalpongpun, E. Prasse-Freeman and P. Strefford. Singapore: National University of Singapore Press.

Ferguson, J. (2013). "Is the Pen Mightier than the AK-47? Tracking Shan Women's Militancy Within and Beyond". *Intersections: Gender and Sexuality in Asia and the Pacific* (33): 1–12.

Gender Equality Network (GEN) (2015). *Raising the Curtain: Cultural Norms, Social Practices and Gender Equality in Myanmar*. Yangon: Gender Equality Network.

Harriden, J. (2012). *The Authority of Influence: Women and Power in Burmese History.* Copenhagen: Nordic Institute of Asian Studies Press.

Hedström, J. (2013). *Where are the Women? Negotiation for Peace in Burma.* Stockholm: The Swedish Burma Committee.

_____ (2015). "We Did Not Realize about the Gender Issues. So, We Thought It Was a Good Idea: Gender Roles in Burmese Oppositional Struggles". *International Feminist Journal of Politics,* 18 (1): 6179.

_____ (2016). "The Political Economy of the Kachin Revolutionary Household". *The Pacific Review,* 30 (4): 581–595.

Ikeya, C. (2005). "The "Traditional" High Status of Women in Burma: A Historical Reconsideration". *Journal of Burma Studies* 10 (1): 51–81.

Kenny, Meryl (2007). "Gender, Institutions and Power: A Critical Review". *Politics* 27 (2).

Khin Khin Mra (2015a). Women's Political Rights in Myanmar's Democratic Transition. Masters thesis, Crawford School of Public Policy, Australian National University (unpublished research paper).

_____ (2015b). "A Masculine Myanmar and the Vote". *New Mandala* . Available at: <https://www.nemandala.org/a-masculine-myanmar-and-the-vote> (accessed 20 May 2020).

Khin Khin Mra and Livingstone, D. (2016). *Technical Assistance on the Implementation of the Myanmar National Strategic Plan for the Advancement of Women: Inception Report.* Reading: Coffey International.

_____ (2017). *Technical Assistance on the Implementation of the Myanmar National Strategic Plan for the Advancement of Women: Final Report.* Reading: Coffey International.

Khin Mar Mar Kyi (2012). *In Pursuit of Power: Politics, Patriarchy, Poverty and Gender Relations in New Order Myanmar/Burma* (PhD Thesis). Canberra: The Australian National University.

Khum T.N. (2019). "Women and Girls with Disabilities Face Double Discrimination in Myanmar". Yangon: ActionAid Myanmar. Available at: https://myanmar.actionaid.org/stories/2019/women-and-girls-disabilities-face-double-discrimination-myanmar (accessed 27 May 2020).

Krook, M.L. and Mackay, F. (eds) (2011). *Gender, Politics and Institutions: Towards a Feminist Institutionalism.* Basingstoke: Palgrave Macmillan.

Maber, E.J., and Khin Mar Aung (2019). "Gender, Ethnicity and Disability: Approaching Inclusivity in Myanmar's Education Reforms?" In *The SAGE Handbook of Inclusion and Diversity in Education,* edited by M. Schuelka, C. Johnstone, G. Thomas and A. Artiles. London: Sage.

Maber, E.J.T. (2016). "Finding Feminism, Finding Voice? Mobilising Community Education to Build Women's Participation in Myanmar's Political Transition". *Gender and Education* 28 (3): 416–430.

Mackay, F. (2014). "Nested Newness, Institutional Innovation, and the Gendered Limits of Change". *Politics and Gender* 10 (4): 549–571.

Marte, N.P. (2015). "Buddhist Nationalism Threatens Myanmar's Democratic Transition". *East Asia Forum*. Available at: http://www.eastasiaforum.org/2015/03/12/buddhist-nationalism-threatens-myanmars-democratic-transition/ (accessed 27 May 2020).

Ministry of Health and Sports (MoHS) and ICF (2017). *Myanmar Demographic and Health Survey 2015–16*. Nay Pyi Taw, Myanmar, and Rockville, Maryland USA: Ministry of Health and Sports and ICF.

Ministry of Labour, Immigration and Population (2017). *The 2014 Myanmar Population and Housing Census: Thematic Report on Gender Dimensions*. Census Report Volume 4-J. Nay Pyi Taw: Ministry of Labour, Immigration and Population. Ministry of Social Welfare, Relief and Resettlement (2013). *National Strategic Plan for the Advancement of Women 2013–2022*. Nay Pyi Taw: Republic of the Union of Myanmar.

Ministry of Social Welfare, Relief and Resettlement, Asia Development Bank, UNFPA, UNDP and UN Women (2016). *Gender Equality and Women's Rights in Myanmar: A Situation Analysis*. Manila: ADB.

Ní Aoláin, F. (2018). "The Feminist Institutional Dimensions of Power-Sharing and Political Settlements". *Nationalism and Ethnic Politics* 24 (1): 116–132.

Olivius, E. (2018). "Time to go Home? The Conflictual Politics of Diaspora Return in the Burmese Women's Movement". *Asian Ethnicity* 20 (2): 147–167.

Open Society Foundation (2014). *Rights-based Women's Organisations, Burma: An Assessment and Mapping of the Work of Women's Organizations in Burma*. OSF: New York.

Steinberg, D.I. (2001). *Burma: the state of Myanmar*. Washington DC: Georgetown University Press.

Stivers, C. (2002). *Gender Images in Public Administration: Legitimacy and the Administrative State*. Thousand Oaks: Sage Publications.

Tharaphi Than, Pyo Let Han, and Shunn Lei (2018). *Lost in Translation: Feminism in Myanmar*. Working Paper.

The Asia Foundation (2014). *Myanmar 2014: Civic Knowledge and Values in a Changing Society*. Yangon, Myanmar: The Asia Foundation.

Thein, P.T. (2015). Gender Equality and Cultural Norms in Myanmar. In International Conference on Burma/Myanmar Studies: Burma/Myanmar in Transition: Connectivity, Changes and Challenges: University Academic Service Centre (UNISERV), Chiang Mai University, Thailand, 24–26 July 2015.

Transnational Institute (2017). *Beyond Panglong: Myanmar's National Peace and Reform Dilemma*. Yangon, Myanmar: Transnational Institute.

United Nations (1979). Convention on the Elimination of All Forms of Discrimination against Women. New York: United Nations.

Williams, Susan H. (2018). "Federalism and Gender Equality". *Federal Law Review* 46 (4): 491–519.

Zin Mar Aung (2015). "From Military Patriarchy to Gender Equity: Including Women in the Democratic Transition in Burma". *Social Research* 82 (2): 531–554.

12

WOMEN'S MOVEMENTS IN MYANMAR AND THE ERA OF #ME TOO

Aye Thiri Kyaw and Stephanie Miedema

In recent years Myanmar has seen dramatic social and economic changes. Following nearly sixty years of military rule (1962–2010), the election of the National League for Democracy in November 2015 heralded a new era for democracy and human rights. For those who had led a long campaign for women's rights in Myanmar, seeing Daw Aung San Su Kyi take the helm as State Counselor was a symbolic step forward. In the context of these political changes, a nascent women's movement is making strides toward greater gender equality in the country and to improve the representation and rights of women. Local manifestations of the global #Me Too movement are similarly building new spaces and opportunities for dialogue around women's rights, including the right to be free from violence and exposure to sexual harassment and assault.

In this paper we examine women's activism in Myanmar and how the #Me Too movement has galvanised a discussion around the prevalence of sexual harassment and violence. There is limited data available on women's rights and violence against women in Myanmar, particularly with respect to the #Me Too movement. We do not purport to provide a comprehensive, data-driven evaluation of changes in gender norms around women's rights and discussions of sexual violence in Myanmar. Rather, we draw on discussions in the media and non-for-profit organisations, alongside our collective experiences conducting research and advocacy on women's rights in Myanmar.

Both authors of this chapter are involved in Myanmar's women's rights movement. Aye Thiri Kyaw is a Myanmar national who has been active in the women rights' field in Myanmar since 2013. She has served as a gender analyst to the United Nations and other international organisations and has been at the forefront of public debate and discussion on sexual violence and women's rights in Myanmar. For example, in 2018, the author delivered a TEDxYangon speech, "#Me Too Myanmar: Men of Quality for Women's Equality," in which she openly talked about incidents of sexual harassment that women face in their everyday lives. The content of the talk was informed by the author's personal experiences of sexual harassment in her native town, Sittwe (Rakhine State, Myanmar), where she worked as an aid worker. The talk was meant to provide an example of how women can openly discuss their experiences of sexual harassment, and encourage fellow women citizens to do the same. The talk also served to encourage men to speak out against peers who engage in sexual harassment, and to provide a forum to discuss the silencing of women by society pressure and gender norms. The paper will refer back to this talk in a later section, as an indication of how the #Me Too movement has initiated greater discussion of sexual violence in Myanmar.

Stephanie Miedema is a doctoral candidate who conducts research on gender norms, sexuality and women's experiences of violence in South and Southeast Asia. She has collaborated with the United Nations and international agencies on violence against women research in Myanmar since 2012. She currently is analysing Demographic and Health Survey data on community-level norms around women's resources in Myanmar and their risk of experiencing intimate partner violence. Her work is cited in global development forums and journals, to inform policy and programmatic efforts to respond to and prevent violence against women (e.g. Miedema 2018).

Part of this paper is informed by research jointly conducted between 2013–2015 commissioned by Myanmar's Gender Equality Network on the state of violence against women (see Gender Equality Network 2015a;

Miedema et al. 2016; Miedema and Tharaphi Than 2018; May Sabe Phyu et al. 2018). It is important to note here that this chapter is not meant to capture the experiences of women across Myanmar. For example, our discussions may not apply to the experiences of women who live in internally displaced persons camps, or conflict-affected areas. Rather, our arguments are based on the analysis of incidents inspired by social media conversations and debates, primarily from the perspective of women's rights activists based in Yangon. Thus, this paper reflects primarily the lives and experiences of young, urban women and men. Further research on women's rights and how the #MeToo movement has manifested in other parts of the country is needed.

We begin this chapter with an analysis of key debates around women's rights in Myanmar. We then examine the available data on violence against women, focusing on sexual harassment and assault. Drawing from our collective experience conducting gender research and advocating for women's rights in Myanmar, we discuss evidence of progress made toward greater equality between women and men, and propose that the grassroots activism of a nascent women's rights movement has enabled the global #Me Too movement to gain traction among Myanmar women and open discussions of sexual violence and harassment. The paper will then analyse how these conversations may in part contribute to emerging shifts in gender and sexual norms in Myanmar.

DEBATES ON THE STATUS OF WOMEN IN MYANMAR

There are divergent views regarding the status of women in Myanmar. One narrative, often promoted by elite women using historical accounts of gender stratification, argues that women historically have enjoyed a high status in Myanmar. Pointing to the historically unique position of women in Myanmar, some scholars suggest that women have enjoyed greater legal rights than those in neighbouring China and India (eg. Than Than Nwe 2003). Historian Chie Ikeya (2011) argues that this perception was a popular narrative in the twentieth century, with women widely perceived as keepers of the "family purse" (Mi Mi Khaing 1984, 61). Today, a popular saying, "the man shoulders, the woman carries" is often used to demonstrate women and men's equal and complimentary roles in society (Ma Thanegi 2013). It is widely perceived that Myanmar women take on different roles, but earn the same respect and dignity as their male counterparts. These perceptions have also been compounded by the many years in which feminist social movements were suppressed under military rule (Than 2015).

A second narrative taken up by contemporary women's rights advocates and academics challenges this view and argues that the notion of equal status between Myanmar women and men is inaccurate. This argument often draws on the widespread Buddhist belief that women are spiritually inferior to men. In her work, Mi Mi Khaing (1984) argues that the belief that women are inferior to men is not just an abstract idea, but rather a religious philosophy that infiltrates all aspects of women's lives. For example, an ethnographic study of women in Yangon describes how they often act within a hierarchical gender system according to the prevailing notion of *hpon* (Fennessy 2016). The notion of *hpon* is an underlying driver of gender discriminatory practices in Myanmar society (see also Khin Khin Mra and Livingstone this volume). The concept derives from Buddhist beliefs that position men as superior to women (Gender Equality Network 2015b). These beliefs permeate Myanmar society and are instantiated in many discriminatory beliefs and practices against women (Pansy Tun Thein 2015).

These two conflicting views of women's status in Myanmar came to a head in 2017, with public debates on *Tea Circle Oxford,* an academic platform for social and political academic commentary on Myanmar. An article titled "The Myth Myanmar Can Afford to Ditch", written by Brandon Aung Moe, an engineering graduate from the National University of Singapore, challenged the view that Myanmar women are disempowered. Drawing on the notable examples of Daw Aung San Su Kyi, and elite businesswomen who thrive amid the widespread belief about sexism in Myanmar, he argued that women enjoy the same privileges and rights as men (Brandon Aung Moe 2017). He suggested that women in Myanmar shoulder additional social and economic responsibilities out of love for their husbands and family responsibility, and imply that Westerners misinterpret this as a lack of Myanmar women's rights (see also Ma Thanegi 2013).

In contrast, gender activists and academics counter that, while some elite women may enjoy certain rights and freedoms, this is often not the case for the majority of women in Myanmar. In response to Brandon Aung Moe's piece, May Thu Khine argued that existing data demonstrates the prevalence of widespread gender inequality, gender-based violence, insufficient legal protections, inadequate reproductive health and rights and the persistence of widespread sexist attitudes around women and men's relative status in society. She comments that the article was a disappointing reminder of progress still to be made with respect to women's rights and freedoms in Myanmar society (May Thu Khine 2017). We concur with this position. Myanmar currently ranks 106 out of 189 countries in the world on global gender inequality indices (UNDP 2017). Although, as noted by Brandon Aung Moe, Daw Aung San Su Kyi serves as the de facto leader of Myanmar, participation of women in politics and leadership is extremely low (Shwe Shwe Sein Latt et al. 2017). For example, no women serve as Township Administrators in the General Administration Department, the main government department that operates the country's decentralised governance system (Kyi Pyar Chit Saw & Arnold 2014). Many rationalise this lack of participation as a result of women's innate disinterest in politics, arguing that women are not interested in taking up powerful, decision-making positions (see Shwe Shwe Sein Latt et al. 2017). Rather, as May Thu Khine (2017) argues, the widespread belief that men possess *hpon* enables them to pursue higher political positions and stops women from pursuing those (see also Harriden 2012). Further, women from diverse backgrounds suffer discriminatory social norms and practices, and experts suggest that high levels of violence against women signal the unequal status of women (Miedema & Tharaphi Than 2018; Khin Khin Mra and Livingstone this volume).

These conversations on *Tea Circle* converged with the growth of women's activism globally and the birth of the #Me Too movement. We now turn to a discussion of how the #Me Too movement manifested in Myanmar, shifting the discourse around sexual violence and women's rights.

#ME TOO: A NASCENT WOMEN'S RIGHTS MOVEMENT

In contemporary Myanmar, two emerging phenomena are beginning to expose the silence around women's exposure to violence and the harmful gender norms that underpin abuse and harassment: a nascent women's rights movement that has been growing since its inception in 2010, and the global #Me Too movement. Despite the challenges and limited official government support for women's rights activism, we propose that the traction of the #Me Too movement signals progress towards social norm change with respect to greater rights and freedom from violence for women. In this section, we first summarise the major strides of women's rights activism in Myanmar to situate our discussion. We then turn to the #Me Too movement, and explore the social processes unfolding with respect to women's voice, agency and activism around sexual assault and harassment.

The rise of women's movements in Myanmar

The beginning of contemporary women's rights activism in Myanmar started as part of the political struggle for democracy in the 1990s. A number of women's rights groups emerged as a result of growing frustration with male domination and violence, particularly in ethnic minority areas exposed to civil war. Twelve organisations from different ethnic backgrounds, collectively known as the Women's League of Burma (WLB), came together to champion women's rights and bring attention to women's experiences of sexual violence committed by the Myanmar military, *Tatmadaw*. Led by exiles located outside Myanmar, the group provided a space for women to share their stories, a space that was not possible within the country under the military regime (O'Kane 2007; Olivius 2018). The WLB championed a campaign for peace and reconciliation in Myanmar, preventing violence against women, and building the capacity of women to become politically empowered (Women League of Burma 1999). The WLB also aimed to build solidarity among women from different ethnic groups, who were being targeted under the military government. They built networks and helped to lead regular forums on issues facing women in Myanmar, which in turn morphed into a collective activist space for feminist mobilisation (Hedström 2016). In particular, the backdrop of armed group struggles at the borderlands provided a transnational platform for a feminist movement to thrive. Their international advocacy enabled the group to pursue justice and accountability around issues of sexual violence, as well as address issues around domestic violence in their own communities (Olivius & Hedström 2019)

This collective groundswell advocating for women's rights gained momentum after the 2008 Cyclone Nargis. Devastation from Cyclone Nargis, which destroyed and killed thousands of people in the Ayeyarwady Delta, prompted the founding of the Gender Equality Network (GEN) Myanmar, a technical working group formed to address women's protection and wellbeing in the aftermath of the natural disaster. The strength of GEN from its inception was its broad membership base and strong partnerships with the various women rights groups within and beyond Myanmar (Faxon,

Furlong, & Sabe Phyu 2015). Today, GEN is comprised of more than 130 civil society organisations, national and international organisations, and technical resource persons, all geared toward building and strengthening gender equality initiatives through campaigning, advocacy and research (Gender Equality Network 2018). GEN has spearheaded two major areas of research on women's lives in Myanmar: (1) Myanmar's cultural norms and social practices in the context of gender equality (Gender Equality Network 2015b), and (2) women's experiences of intimate partner violence and sexual harassment (Gender Equality Network 2015a). An early major achievement of GEN included the drafting of legislation on the prevention of violence against women and the official launch of the National Strategic Plan for the Advancement of Women (Gender Equality Network 2018; MNCWA 2018). Overall, the continued work of women's groups to advocate for greater representation, freedoms and rights for women across Myanmar – as well as for rights of women within diverse ethnic groups – signals that these issues continue to gain traction within government and civil society, and that women's voices are increasingly being heard in the halls of power and on the streets.

Still, the women's rights movement – and its activism to change norms and increase accountability – faces many challenges. Challenging gender inequality and promoting gender equality means confronting those who benefit from the status quo, including two powerful male-dominated institutions, the military and the Sangha, that can inhibit progress forward toward gender justice (Miedema & Tharaphi Than 2018) Many feminists in Myanmar argue that feminism is yet to rise in the country. Instead, they argue that "donor-led safe feminism" is booming, and that women's rights groups focus on superficial events such as White Ribbon Campaigns, and the global 16 Days of Activism against Gender-based Violence campaign, rather than fighting the patriarchal norms that are embedded at all levels of society (Than, Han, & Lei 2018). Nevertheless, one would find it hard to downplay the fact that women's rights efforts, both inside and outside the country, have contributed a great deal to raising awareness around women's rights and violence against women in Myanmar since the 1990s. It is within this backdrop of growing women's rights activism and sexual harassment awareness that the global #Me Too era came to Myanmar.

The global #Me Too movement

Before it became a Twitter hashtag, the #Me Too movement, originally founded in the United States in 2006 by activist Tarana Burke, held the vision of creating a survivor-oriented movement to provide resources to survivors of sexual violence (particularly women of colour) and generate a community of survivor-led advocates who would speak up about sexual violence in their communities.[1] The #Me Too Movement went viral in October 2017 with a tweet from a Hollywood actress Alyssa Milano saying: "If you've been sexually harassed or assaulted, write #Me Too." In the wake of articles detailing accusations of sexual harassment and assault by Hollywood producer Harvey Weinstein (Kantor and Twohey 2017), the hashtag quickly gained prominence and it morphed into a global #Me Too movement (Fox & Diehm 2017). In general, most social media users of the #Me Too movement are from the US, the UK, France, Canada and India (Fox & Diehm 2017), although its use has been documented in other Asian countries such as China (Haynes 2018). The #Me Too movement has been credited with bringing to prominence the widespread and pervasive nature of sexual violence against women worldwide (Zarkov & Davis 2018). However, some scholars and activists caution against interpreting #Me Too as a panacea for sexual violence. The #Me Too movement creates an onus on survivors to speak out, keeping the focus of the conversation on women's experiences, rather than men's perpetration (Fulu 2017). Further, the movement is limited to only some women: those with access to social media, those for whom the sanctions of speaking out are bearable, and in turn, those who have the social power to speak out in the first place (Davis and Zarkov 2018). Yet the "viral roar" of narratives, stories and histories of sexual violence captured by the #Me Too movement has also captured and made visible the experiences of marginalised groups and communities (Gieseler 2019).

HOW #ME TOO SPARKED A CONVERSATION IN MYANMAR

When the #Me Too movement started to gain momentum globally, we – and others (e.g. Hogan 2018a; Hogan 2018b) – began to notice a rise in the use of this hashtag within social media and online discussions among Myanmar women. Building on the foundation built by Myanmar women's rights activists, the growth of online use of the #Me Too hashtag widened the space for conversation and more opportunities for women to speak out about their experiences of sexual harassment and abuse. Myanmar women's involvement in the #Me Too movement appears to have contributed to greater collective mobilisation of women, who feel empowered to speak out against their experiences of sexual violence, despite longstanding taboos. In doing so, the #Me Too movement has reinforced the message that sexual assault, regardless of where it takes place, is unacceptable and must be denounced.

It is important to recall here how conversations around sexual assault are generally considered taboo in Myanmar. As we found in our study on violence against women, women often feel silenced by social norms that prevent them from speaking out about their experiences of sexual harassment (Gender Equality Network 2015a). Yet despite these taboos, we have seen a rise of conversations sparked by #Me Too (e.g. Hogan 2018a). While there are still significant hurdles to overcome, we see these as indications of progression toward greater openness and less stigma around confronting sexual violence in Myanmar society.

More specifically, the #Me Too movement, arguably for the first time in history, has given Myanmar women a platform to come forward and speak up about their experiences of sexual harassment. Social media use is exploding in popularity in Myanmar, and greater access to communication technology affords Myanmar women an opportunity to know what goes on elsewhere in the world. The bulk of #Me Too activism occurs online in Myanmar, although it appears to also be exerting influence on in-person activism as well. In the following section, we discuss four major events throughout 2018 linked to the #Me Too inspired incidents in Myanmar, which indicate the influence of the #Me Too movement to inspire women to speak out in person and via online platforms.

Fortune-teller charged with sexual assault

One of the first incidents inspired by #Me Too statements on social media in Myanmar was a situation in which a young woman felt empowered to take action against her abuser, a popular fortune-teller[2] (Han 2018). In January 2018, a university student in Yangon made a complaint with the police against a well-known fortune-teller after she publicly denounced him on Facebook for sexual abuse in 2013. The woman, joined by some friends, described originally seeking out the fortune-teller for advice about their love lives, and in turn experienced sexual harassment and abuse. The fortune-teller denied these claims, arguing that if they had experienced abuse, they should have reported the incident to the trustees of the pagoda in which he was based. A conversation ensued on Facebook and other social media outlets (Naw Betty Han 2018) in which the young women described feelings of powerlessness in speaking out, given both the social standing of the fortune-teller and prevailing gender norms in which women were expected to keep silent about sexual activities – including harassment. Indeed, their public declaration came as a surprise to many, given the gender and age of the girls, and the social prominence of the fortune-teller. The first young woman used social media, and related how she had felt empowered through ongoing use of the #Me Too hashtag to come forward with her experience. She, in turn, inspired four other young women to join her, and together they collectively spoke out against the violence they had experienced at the hands of the powerful man, in part empowered by an increasing number of stories shared in public online and social media forums with respect to women's experiences of sexual harassment in Myanmar.

#Mystorymatters

In July 2018, Myanmar saw another major public incident of sexual violence survivors speaking out publically against their abuser, in this case against a renowned civil society leader whose organisation partners with several UN entities. Initiated by a young woman's social media post, and quickly taken up by other women, the narratives posted on Facebook describe experiences of harassment and sexual assault by their former boss, a CEO of a prominent women's rights organisation (Naw Betty Han 2018), who was allegedly harassing and assaulting his employees during their tenure at his organisation (Goldberg, 2019). The women explained that they were not believed, even by their family members, so they shared their experiences via social media, joining the global #Me Too movement in July 2018. Frustrated by a lack of recourse via formal channels, and disbelief from their families, the women reported being inspired by other Myanmar women and women globally who were using social media as a platform to discuss their experiences of sexual assault. The women reported that they were threatened with dismissal and efforts to blacklist them from applying for other jobs (Goldberg & Myat 2018). The survivors reported having stayed silent for many years as their complaints were dismissed by the organisation. They also shared incidents in which the perpetrator threated to block career opportunities and blackmail their affairs. Before the advent of the #Me Too, the women said, nobody would have believed them, as their former boss was well-connected and perceived to be a respected women's rights champion (Goldberg 2019).

#Me Too Myanmar: Men of quality for women's equality

In mid-2018, Yangon hosted its third TED Talk, titled "Today's future". The event included a #Me Too-inspired talk by this chapter's first author, which was aired live to the public. The talk started with an ice-breaking question about the experiences of sexual harassment on the buses in Yangon. Sexual harassment on the public buses is a well-known phenomenon among Myanmar women who rely on the public transportation to get to and from work. The talk then went from women's general experiences of sexual harassment on public transport to the presenter's own personal experiences of sexual harassment in public places. On one single day, she said, she experienced twenty-nine instances of sexual harassment, even calling out men who were trying to expose their private parts to women. In her talk, she encouraged support of women who disclose experiencing abuse, and advised the community to call out perpetrators and hold them accountable for their actions. The talk emphasised the need for men to be allies with women, to stop perpetrators of sexual harassment and prevent violence in their communities. The TEDxYangon talk shifted the discussion of accountability from women to men: instead of mothers teaching daughters to be demure, the speaker argued, it is time for fathers to teach their sons how to be real men and support gender equality (Aye Thiri Kyaw 2018) .

The Vagina Monologues – in Myanmar

There is no word for "vagina" in the Myanmar language. Talking about sex, let alone sex education, is taboo, especially for women. Yet 2018 saw the first Vagina Monologues presented in Yangon, which featured twenty stories about women's issues, including sexual and reproductive health issues, rights and violence against women (Hogan 2018b). Although the organisers hesitated to convene the Monologues due to the controversial nature of the topic in the social and cultural environment, the first event was successful and sparked further conversation around women's sexuality (Hogan 2018c). In 2019, the second Vagina Monologue was performed in the Myanmar language and was considered to be a revolutionary moment in the trajectory of women's reproductive and sexual health and rights in the country. In particular, the performers kept urging the audience to continue the conversation as an effort to respect women and their bodies/voices (Voice of America 2019). The performance of the Vagina Monologues, a play originally written by Eve Ensler and performed in the United States, in the socio-cultural context of Myanmar provided a compelling case of transnational women's rights activism, as well as an indication of a growing ability of Myanmar women to break silences and taboos around sexual issues.

Although there is continued pushback against women who share their stories, we are seeing more stories shared by women since #MeToo sparked conversations in Myanmar. It would be wrong to conclude that #Me Too alone brought on these conversations. Instead, as we have already shown, these conversations built off years of campaigning and advocacy by women's groups around sexual violence and harassment. In the following section, we discuss the potential role of the women's rights movement and the #Me Too movement in shifting extant social and cultural norms around gender, sexuality and violence in contemporary Myanmar and what we see possible for women in the years ahead as the country continues to transform.

CHANGING SOCIAL NORMS: THE WOMEN'S RIGHTS MOVEMENT AND #ME TOO CONVERSATIONS

In Myanmar, many people use the common expression, "a woman's dignity and grace cannot be exchanged for gold," to describe womanhood. This saying is often accompanied by the phrase "Ah Pyo Sin", which means the purity of a woman is measured by her virginity. When a woman loses her virginity before marriage, the woman and her family members may be subjected to social stigma (Gender Equality Network 2015b). Compared to sons, daughters' movement and freedom is controlled by their partners to conform to expectations of appropriate women (Fennessy 2016). These gendered norms around what it means to be "a good woman" often restrict the mobility of women and their ability to engage in public activities because they are fearful of being in situations where they may be coerced into sex and thus, lose their virginity (Miedema et al. 2016; Gender Equality Network 2015a). Inequitable social forces similarly shape women's life conditions prior to and during the marital transition, with implications for women's power in marriage. In Myanmar, gender relations between women and men historically have been touted as equitable and advantageous to women. Rare qualitative data find that structural gender inequalities permeate Myanmar society, and intersect with other social forces, to constrain women's marital power. In particular, we argue that women's transition into marriage is a critical period to assess how gendered social inequalities determine the future distribution of power within marital relationships. These premarital social processes result in a "preconditioning" of relationship dynamics from the onset of marriage, with long-term effects on women's power within the relationship, and subsequent exposure to intimate partner violence (IPV). Gender norms in Myanmar also include beliefs that women are unable to prevent or stop sexual harassment and abuse from occurring, which further enables these acts to be carried out with impunity by perpetrators. Men's sexuality is understood as something uncontrollable, and as a result, the responsibility and the blame for experiencing sexual violence rest on the shoulders of women (Aye Thiri Kyaw 2018; Pansy Tun Thein 2015). Until recent years, there has been little discussion with respect to the responsibility of the perpetrators (Aye Thiri Kyaw 2018). Myanmar women have largely come of age in an environment where violence and sexual harassment is silenced, and a major expectation of Myanmar women is to be "tolerant"(Gender Equality Network 2015b; Pansy Tun Thein 2015). Women are taught to be tolerant of their brothers, husbands and parents-in-law, and accept their status in the patriarchal family structure (Gender Equality Network 2015b; Pansy Tun Thein 2015) Although these attitudes continue to be widespread, Myanmar has started seeing young people, especially young women, question their current status. We propose that much of the credit for changes in the status quo belongs to the Myanmar women's rights movement, which has been bolstered by the #Me Too movement.

The terms "women's rights" and "violence against women" were not in Myanmar's general lexicon, even ten years ago. Yet, as we demonstrate above with our four case studies, the growing discussion around women's rights as a result of decades-long activism – alongside recent online platforms to speak openly about abuse – has created an environment where these topics are more widely discussed and acknowledged. Notably, since the majority of conversations take place online, we expect that women find social media platforms to be useful to talk about violence in a safe way. Although we acknowledge, as others have done (see also Davis and Zarkov 2018), that these online platforms are limited to a subsection of the Myanmar population, we believe that the case studies described above signal the beginning of a shift in gender norms related to women's status in Myanmar. We are observing a moment of change within Myanmar society whereby the intersection of decades-long women's rights activism and the global #Me Too movement has started to shift the conservation on this issue. A decade ago, it would have been impossible to even talk about violence against women. Today, this topic is publicly debated in Myanmar, reflecting shifting attitudes and beliefs around women's status and freedom from violence – as an indicator of gender equality – in the country.

Here, however, we caution in giving social media platforms and the #Me Too movement more credit than deserved. Activists and researchers rightly argue that progress toward greater gender equality is not just about #Me Too, but also a result of decades-long struggle by women's rights activists, who have worked to raise awareness of violence against women across the country (May Sabe Phyu et al. 2018). We acknowledge both that the conversations around #Me Too are building momentum to end violence against women in Myanmar, even while #Me Too cannot single-handedly end the epidemic of sexual violence against women. Still, #Me Too appears to be part of a global information movement that creates space for conversations on sexual violence and women's equality (May Sabe Phyu et al. 2018). The intersection of these two phenomena are beginning to change norms around women's and girls' place in society. More women are speaking out about sexuality, sexual harassment and their rights in Myanmar. Slowly, but increasingly, domestic violence is not seen as a woman's fault, but rather as a form of widespread gender-based violence. Still, much work needs to be done to increase awareness and public advocacy messages to reach to all areas of the population. A notable gap is the lack of legislation and formal legal channels available to women who seek justice and the continued impunity of members of the military, in particular, for sexual violence committed in conflict areas.

SOCIAL CHANGE AND THE LEGAL SYSTEM

In 2016, Mi Mi, an activist and survivor of an acid attack, was one of the first women to openly call for justice for herself and women who experienced gender-based violence. Her story was shared widely, even before #Me Too made its advent in Myanmar. Yet the perpetrator was sentenced to only seven years imprisonment. Her story continues to highlight the need for stronger laws to address violence against women, and the overall culture of impunity in Myanmar (Rigby 2018, 206).

Myanmar society remains conservative when it comes to addressing sexual harassment, particularly with respect to calling out perpetrators (The Gender Equality Network 2015a). As noted by a prominent lawmaker, a social movement that includes both men and women to call out sexual harassment will send a loud and clear message to perpetrators, and have more strength to shift norms around impunity and acceptance of violence against women (Naing 2017). A law is needed, but it is not enough. The law needs to be enforced and respected. Women need to be aware of the law and know their rights to report incidents of violence. When women report, they must be taken seriously. There are many, multifaceted and multilayered steps that are needed before Myanmar is free of violence against women. Yet the joint intersection of exiled women, a ten-year women's movement and the catalyst of the #Me Too movement has begun to set change in motion.

Although attitudes and beliefs may be changing, so far this has not translated into legal change. Some legislation does exist to criminalise non-partner sexual violence and harassment. Penal code 509 states:

> Whoever, intending to insult the modesty of any woman, utters any word, makes any sound or gesture, or exhibits any object, intending that such word or sound shall be heard or that such gesture or object shall be seen, by such woman, or intrudes upon the privacy of such woman, shall be punished with simple imprisonment for a term which may extend to one year, or with fine, or with both.[3]

However, there remains multiple challenges to its implementation. Penal Code 509 is not widely known to the general public. Women's rights activists argue that the lack of specificity and clarity of the definition of sexual harassment also dilutes the utility of the law (UN WOMEN 2016). Further, law enforcement is weak, and perpetrators often end up paying just a small fine (Naing 2017). The passage of legislation to comprehensively criminalise all forms of violence against women lags behind (Miedema and Tharaphi Than 2018). There is growing concern among women's rights activists and the general public around how perpetrators are held accountable, and how to challenge the culture of impunity, particularly through legislation (see Khin Khin Mra & Livingstone this volume). Although the "Prevention and Protection of Violence Against Women Law" was first proposed in 2013 (Gender Equality Network, 2013), it only has been made available for public consultation in the national newspaper. Increasingly publicised cases of violence against women, combined with the delay of passing the law, has led to public criticism that current laws do not address women's experiences of violence and protect their rights (Walton et al. 2014; Khin Khin Mra & Livingstone this volume). The continued impunity of the military for crimes of sexual violence against women and girls also continues to hamper this process and the ability to implement meaningful reforms. Indeed, like many parts of the world, there is a long way to go before we see a society that is free from sexual violence and in which perpetrators are held to account.

CONCLUSION

Although Myanmar women were once portrayed as equal to men, with high status, women's rights groups challenge this belief and highlight the many barriers to Myanmar women in terms of attaining equal rights. Violence against women, and particularly domestic violence and sexual harassment, have largely been overlooked as social problems that violate the rights of women as human beings. Women's rights have long been hampered by gender and sexual norms that impede their ability and agency to speak out when they experience discrimination, harassment or sexual violence. Strict gender and sexual norms dictate that Myanmar women should be modest and submissive. Parents are expected to control their daughter's virginity in order to maintain the family honour, leading to restrictions and constraints on women's lives. These expectations silence the voices of women who experience sexual violence or harassment.

Awareness around gender inequality and women's rights has been growing through the rise of women's rights movements inside and along the border of Myanmar. The establishment of women's rights groups at the Thai-Myanmar border and the more recent growth of a coalition of women's rights organisations in Myanmar have been vital to changing the dialogue around women's rights and building a platform for women to speak out about gender-based violence in Myanmar. Within this context, the #Me Too movement has catalysed further open discussion and conversation around women's experiences of sexual violence. Conversations around taboo topics such as "sex education," women's sexuality and domestic violence have received attention as important discussions to be continued both at national and local levels. Incidents of abuse and harassment are now more openly discussed, both via social media and at in-person events. The work of the women's rights movement has set up an enabling environment in which women can use the #Me Too platform to speak up and speak out.

Given these changing gender and sexuality norms and increasingly open spaces for dialogue, this is an important time for women's rights activism in Myanmar. Challenges still remain to shift systemic gender inequalities, alongside other intersecting forms of oppression. Yet, particularly in urban spaces, we see how women are beginning to feel empowered to share their stories, creating collective momentum around activism against sexual violence and harassment, and other forms of violence against women. Much work remains to be done, particularly by way of legislative reform. But we believe these conversations and advocacy set the stage for meaningful reform to protect the lives of women and girls across the country.

Notes

1 See https://metoomvmt.org/about/#history (accessed 6 June 2020).

2 In Myanmar, people regularly consult fortune-tellers about their prospects, especially around the New Year and during exam periods. Fortune-tellers are revered in Myanmar society and hold a special cultural status. Many Myanmar women and girls consult fortune-tellers with respect to their love lives and marital prospects.

3 See http://www.*burmalibrary*.org/docs17/1861-Penal_Code-ocr-en+bu.pdf (accessed 6 June 2020).

References

Aye Thiri Kyaw (2018). "#MeToo Myanmar: Men of Quality for Women's Equality". TEDxYangon - YouTube. Available at https://www.youtube.com/watch?v=N9yttv-YgVc (accessed 17 June 2020).

Brandon Aung Moe (2017). "The Myth Myanmar can Afford to Ditch". *Tea Circle Oxford,* 9 August. Available at https://teacircleoxford.com/2017/08/09/the-myth-myanmar-can-afford-to-ditch/ (accessed 17 June 2020).

Faxon, H., Furlong, R., & Sabe Phyu, M. (2015). "Reinvigorating Resilience: Violence Against Women, Land Rights, and the Women's Peace Movement in Myanmar". *Gender & Development* 23 (3): 463–479.

Fennessy, M. (2016). "Marriage, Modernity and 'Manner': A Burmese Buddhist Woman's Agency in Contemporary Yangon, Myanmar. An Ethnographic Portrait". *GISCA Occasional Papers Series,* No. 8. Göttingen, Germany: Georg-August-Universit*ät Göttingen.*

Fox, K. and Diehm, J. (2017). "#MeToo's Global Moment: The Anatomy of a Viral Campaign". *CNN News,* 9 November. Available at https://edition.cnn.com/2017/11/09/world/metoo-hashtag-global-movement/ (accessed 17 June 2020).Gender Equality Network (2013). *Developing Anti-violence Against Women Laws.* Yangon: Gender Equality Network. Available at https://themimu.info/sites/themimu.info/files/documents/Ref-Doc_Developing-Anti-Voilence-Against-Women-Part-1_GEN_Jan2013.pdf (accessed 17 Juen 2020).

Gender Equality Network (2015a). *Behind the Silence: Violence Against Women and their Resilience in Myanmar.* Yangon: Gender Equality Network. Available at https://themimu.info/sites/themimu.info/files/assessment_file_attachments/Behind_the_Silence_Violence_Against_Women_Their_Resilience_-_Gender_Equality_Network_October_2014.pdf (accessed 17 June 2020).

_____ (2015b). *Raising the Curtain: Social Cultural Norms and Gender Equality in Myanmar.* Yangon: Gender Equality Network. Available at https://www.burmalibrary.org/docs22/GEN-2015-11-Raising%20the%20curtain-en.pdf (accessed 17 June 2020).

_____(2018). *10 Years Milestone and Journey.* Yangon: Gender Equality Network. Available at https://www.genmyanmar.org/research_and_publications?year=2018 (accessed 17 June 2020).

Gieseler, C. (2019). *The Voices of #MeToo: From Grassroots Activism to a Viral Roar.* London: Rowman and Littlefield Publishing Group.

Goldberg, J. (2019). "In Myanmar, a Nonprofit Icon Enjoyed Foreign Funding Despite Allegations of Sexual Abuse – VICE". *Vice,* 14 October. Available at https://www.vice.com/en_asia/article/qvgwbd/myanmar-chan-nyein-aung-sexual-harassment-abuse-non-profit?fbclid=IwAR0wIRCrffDcgzN_WDr49IExfC9ZunQTQhgSTctQ2zabPrHAL1AtXG_dERc

Goldberg, J. and Aung Kaung Myat (2018). 'Women Accuse CEO of Myanmar Human Rights NGO of Relentless Sexual Assault". *Coconuts Yangon,* 18 July. Available at https://coconuts.co/yangon/news/women-accuse-ceo-human-rights-ngo-sexual-assault/ (accessed 17 June 2020).

Harriden, J. (2012). *The Authority of Influence: Women and Power in Burmese History.* Copenhagen: NIAS Press.

Haynes, S. (2018). "How #MeToo Is Taking on a Life of Its Own in Asia". *Time,* 9 October. Available at https://time.com/longform/me-too-asia-china-south-korea/ (accessed 17 June 2020).

Hedström, J. (2016). "We Did Not Realize about the Gender Issues. So, We Thought It Was a Good Idea: Gender Roles in Burmese Oppositional Struggles'. *International Feminist Journal of Politics* 18 (1): 61–79.

Hogan, L. (2018a). "In Myanmar, #MeToo Opens Up Conversation on Sexual Harassment". *VOA News,* 21 November. Available at https://www.voanews.com/east-asia-pacific/myanmar-metoo-opens-conversation-sexual-harassment (accessed 17 June 2020).

Hogan, L. (2018b). "Sex, Taboos and #Metoo – In the Country with no Word for 'Vagina'". *The Guardian,* 18 July. Available at https://www.theguardian.com/world/2018/jul/12/why-are-we-afraid-to-say-vagina-myanmar-learns-to-talk-about-sex (accessed 17 June 2020).

_____(2018c). "With Cupcakes and Courage, Myanmar Stages 'Vagina Monologues'". *NPR News,* 29 March. Available at https://www.npr.org/sections/goatsandsoda/2018/03/29/597679722/with-cupcakes-and-courage-myanmar-stages-vagina-monologues (accessed 17 June 2020).

Ikeya, C. (2011). "The 'Traditional' High Status of Women in Burma". *Journal of Burma Studies* 10 (1): 51–82.

Kantor, J. and Twohey, M. (2007). "Harvey Weinstein Paid off Sexual Harrassment Accusers for Decades". *The New York Times,* 5 October. Available at https://www.nytimes.com/2017/10/05/us/harvey-weinstein-harassment-allegations.html (accessed 17 June 2020).

Kyi Pyar Chit Saw and Arnold, M. (2014). *Administering the State in Myanmar: An Overview of the General Administration Department.* Yangon: MDRI and The Asia Foundation. Available at https://asiafoundation.org/wp-content/uploads/2014/10/Administering-the-State-in-Myanmar.pdf (accessed 17 June 2020).

Ma Thanegi (2013). "Our Brand of Feminism". *Myanmar Times,* 10 June. Available at https://www.mmtimes.com/special-features/167-the-modern-woman/7113-our-brand-of-feminism.html (accessed 17 June 2020).May Sabe Phyu, Aye Thiri Kyaw and Miedema, S. S. (2018). "#MeToo in Myanmar: How a Twitter Hashtag Amplifies Women's Agency in a Formerly Isolated Country where Gender Inequality Reigns Supreme". *Tea Circle Oxford,* 29 August. Available at https://teacircleoxford.com/2018/08/29/metoo-in-myanmar-how-a-twitter-hashtag-amplifies-womens-agency-in-a-formerly-isolated-country-where-gender-inequality-reigns-supreme/ (accessed 17 June 2020).

May Thu Khine (2017). "Disappointing Progress on an Dmportant debate: Response to 'The Myth Myanmar can Afford to Ditch'". *Tea Circle Oxford,* 11 August. Available at https://teacircleoxford.com/2017/08/11/disappointing-progress-on-an-important-debate-response-to-the-myth-myanmar-can-afford-to-ditch/ (accessed 17 June 2020).

Mi Mi Khaing (1984). *The World of Burmese Women.* London: Zed Books Ltd.

Miedema, S.S., San Shwe and Aye Thiri Kyaw (2016). "Social Inequalities, Empowerment, and Women's Transitions into Abusive Marriages: A Case Study from Myanmar". *Gender and Society,* 30 (4): 670–694.

Miedema, S.S., and Tharaphi Than (2018). "Myanmar Debates Women's Rights Amid Evidence of Pervasive Sexual and Domestic Violence". *The Conversation,* 10 December. Available at https://theconversation.com/myanmar-debates-womens-rights-amid-evidence-of-pervasive-sexual-and-domestic-violence-104536 (accessed 17 June 2020).

Myanmar National Committee for Women's Affairs (MNCWA) (2013). *National Strategic Action Plan for the Advancement of Women (2013-2022).* Naypyidaw, Myanmar: Ministry of Social Welfare, Relief and Resettlement. Available at https://myanmar.unfpa.org/sites/default/files/pub-pdf/NSPAW2013-2022_0.pdf (accessed 17 June 2020).

Naw Betty Han (2018). "Fortune Teller in Sex Harassment Case Held'". *The Irrawaddy,* 9 February. Available at https://www.mmtimes.com/news/fortune-teller-sex-harassment-case-held.html (accessed 17 June 2020).

O'Kane, M. (2007). "Blood, Sweat and Tears: The Political Agency of Women Activist-Refugees of Burma". *Intersections: Gender, History & Culture in the Asian Context* 15: 1–10.

Olivius, E. (2018). "Asian Ethnicity Time to Go Home? The Conflictual Politics of Diaspora Return in the Burmese Women's Movemen". *Asian Ethnicit,* 20 (2): 148–167.

Olivius, E., & Hedström, J. (2019). "Militarized Nationalism as a Platform for Feminist Mobilization? The Case of the Exiled Burmese Women's Movement". *Women's Studies International Forum* 76: 1–10.

Pansy Tun Thein (2015). "Gender Equality and Cultural Norms in Myanmar". Paper presented at the International Conference on Burma/Myanmar Studies, Chiang Mai University, Thailand, 24–25 July. Rigby, J. (2018). *The Other Ladies of Myanmar.* Singapore: ISEAS.

Shoon Naing (2017). "Sexual Harassment, the Hidden Scourge of Myanmar Women". *The Myanmar Times,* 30 May. Available at https://www.mmtimes.com/national-news/yangon/26185-sexual-harassment-the-hidden-scourge-of-myanmar-women.html (accessed 17 June 2020).

Shwe Shwe Sein Latt, Kim N. B. Ninh, Mi Ki Kyaw Myint, & Lee, S. (2017). *Women's Political Participation in Myanmar: Experiences of Women Parliamentarians.* Yangon: The Asia Foundation and Phan Tee Eain.

Than Than Nwe (2003). "Gendered Spaces : Women in Burmese Society". *Transformations* (6): 1–12.

Tharaphi Than (2015). *Women in Modern Burma.* London: Routledge.

Tharaphi Than, Pyo Let Han and Shunn Lei (2018). "Lost in Translation: Feminism in Myanmar". *Independent Journal of Burmese Scholarship.* Available at https://journalofburmesescholarship.org/pprs/Feminism_in_Myanmar_edited1.pdf (accessed 17 June 2020).

UN WOMEN (2016). *Women' s Access to Justice in the Plural Legal System of Myanmar.* Yangon, Myanmar: UN Women. Available at https://www2.unwomen.org/-/media/field%20office%20eseasia/docs/publications/2016/04/myanmar%20research%20report.pdf?la=en&vs=3114 (accessed 17 June 2020).

UNDP (2017). *Human Development Reports.* Yangon, Myanmar: United Nations Development Programme. Available at http://hdr.undp.org/en/countries/profiles/MMR (accessed 17 June 2020).

UNFPA (2016). "A Silent Emergency: Violence Against Women and Girls". *United Nations Population Fund, Myanmar,* 25 November. Available at https://myanmar.unfpa.org/en/news/silent-emergency-violence-against-women-and-girls (accessed 17 June 2020).

Voice of America (2019). "Myanmar Opens Up for 'The Vagina Monologues'". *Voice of America News,* 7 March. Available at https://www.voanews.com/east-asia-pacific/myanmar-opens-vagina-monologues (accessed 17 June 2020).

Walton, M.J., McKay, M., & Daw Khin Mar Mar Kyi (2014). "Women and Myanmar's 'Religious Protection Laws". *The Review of Faith and International Affairs* 13 (4): 1–20.

Women's League of Burma (1999). *The Founding and Development of Women's League of Burma.* Mae Sot, Thailand: Women's League of Burma.

V

Living with Plural Identities

13

DO PEOPLE REALLY WANT ETHNOFEDERALISM ANYMORE? FINDINGS FROM DELIBERATIVE SURVEYS ON THE ROLE OF ETHNIC IDENTITY IN FEDERALISM IN MYANMAR

Michael G. Breen and Baogang He

Since independence in 1948, Myanmar (then Burma) has grappled with the idea and implementation of federalism. It remains the major demand of the non-dominant ethnic nationalities but has been resisted by many of the majority Bamar community (especially the military and other political elites) despite promises to the contrary. The 1947 Panglong Agreement, which was a precursor to independence, enshrined the idea of "ethnofederalism". That is, provinces (states, regions, divisions) that recognise and institutionalise the rights of ethnic nationalities to their traditional homelands and resources, to use their own languages in official business and education, and to self-determination.

But much has changed since 1947. For one, various governments have pursued a Bamar-based nation-building agenda, which included official status for the Burmese (and not minority) language and special status for the Buddhist religion. There has been significant migration and intermingling of different ethnic communities in many parts of the country. Democracy is (arguably) in its third incarnation, with the National League for Democracy (NLD) winning the 2015 election and establishing a constitutional reform process, under the guise of the 21st Century Panglong Conference, with the objective of establishing a "genuine federal union". However, its progress has stalled, in large part because of (the military's) concerns relating to secession.

The secession risk associated with federalism is a longstanding issue. Paradoxically, federalism indeed can help to prevent secession, while at the same time making it more likely. This is particularly the case with ethnofederalism, the approach favoured by Myanmar's ethnic leaders. The paradox plays into a more general debate about the relative merits of ethnofederalism, where state/provinces are based on ethnicity and language, and territorial federalism (also known as regional federalism), where states/provinces are based on economy, resources, infrastructure, geography, etc.

We implemented a series of experimental deliberative surveys to engage with these debates on the ground, to contribute to feeding a deliberative perspective into the current constitutional reform process, and to refine deliberative democratic methodologies for use in deeply divided societies and constitutional reform processes in Asia. This paper is based on the results of those deliberative surveys.

The deliberative surveys focused on federalism and were held in Shan State and Monywa Region in Myanmar in 2018. We engaged participants (mostly laypersons) from a mix of different ethnic groups in information-sharing and deliberation to reach common understandings of terms, like ethnofederalism, to deliberate amongst themselves, and to respond to a before and after survey that asked their opinions on the issues that were discussed. We asked general questions, like whether Myanmar should have federalism, and more specific questions like whether the existing (Bamar) regions should be merged to form one Bamar state.

This paper focuses on those questions that related to ethnofederalism and the practical implications of the results. It shows that, in contrast to statements of key ethnic leaders, many participants no longer aspire to ethnofederalism. Participants in our forums wanted to retain their ethnic identity and to have it recognised, but ethnofederalism was no longer the main objective. Surprisingly, a form of territorial or regional federalism was preferred by most participants, and increasingly so following deliberations about what kind of arrangements they might imply. Many concluded that ethnic identity should be recognised but not institutionalised as a basis for federal arrangements. Just as much as participants did not want to engage with Bamar-centric institutions, merely replacing them with another ethno-centric set of institutions was also seen as problematic. This perspective was particularly strong among those that did not identify with one of the seven major non-Bamar ethnic nationalities.[1] Participants recognised that an ethnofederal structure left many small ethnic groups even more marginalised. Providing autonomy to all on a group basis was considered impractical and risky. In conclusion, the paper argues that to take Myanmar's federalism further, a territorially focused restructuring of the states and regions would take better account of contemporary laypersons' views and help to mitigate the secession risk, thereby enabling states and regions to be more empowered through constitutional change. In doing so, the paper contributes to the political science literature on how to design federalism for divided societies and to manage a secession risk, and offers a methodology and perspective that can be applied to constitutional settlement and conflict resolution processes in Myanmar and elsewhere.

CONTEXT

Federal institutions in Myanmar have historically been ethnically focused. However, this has not always been with the objective of allowing ethnic autonomy, rather of neutralising it and furthering an assimilationist or integrationist agenda. The 1947 constitution incorporated five asymmetrical constituent units – three ethnic states, two of which had a secession right, and two ethnic divisions with mostly administrative power (see Breen 2019). Most of these had half or all of the parliamentary seats in their state assured for their ethnic group, and important powers allocated to them in the constitution. But implementation and the structure itself were inadequate. Some groups received no special structures, while other groups were dissatisfied with those that they did receive. Conflict started at independence and continued to grow, until the military seized power and suspended the constitution, declaring that "federalism is impossible, it will destroy the union" (cited in Smith 1991, 196). After twelve years of running the country without a constitution, a quasi-federal state structure was re-established in 1974. This time, there were no special rights for ethnic groups in states and divisions (Breen 2019). And, there were now seven ethnic states and seven divisions, the latter of which were understood by some to be representative of the Bamar (see for example Weng 2016; Sakhong 2010; Myanmar News Agency 2016b).

Ethnic identity was recognised, by state boundaries and names, but there was no accompanying institutionalisation of those rights. Over the coming years, the central state implemented an assimilationist nation-building agenda and controlled the ethnic states. For example, the official education system operated in Burmese, the ethnic states were led by appointees of the central state party, Buddhism was intertwined with the governance of the state and civil servants were staff of the military-controlled central department (Breen 2018c, 92–102; South and Lall 2016; Smith 1991; Sakhong 2005). Conflict continued in the ethnic states and many ethnic armed organisations (EAOs) held considerable power in the areas that they controlled. They established institutions, like schools and political wings, and in some cases ran quasi-parallel governments (Callahan 2007; Breen 2018c, 99). Some expect these institutions to be legitimised through the development of an ethnofederal structure.

The 2008 Constitution re-established the fourteen states and divisions (now regions) and introduced new institutions like an upper house of parliament and a multiparty system. The states and divisions remained symmetrical, but six ethnically based self-administered areas were added, along with national race affairs ministries,[2] which operated on a non-territorial basis. The special place of Buddhism and the Burmese language-focused education system remained. Conflict abated in many areas as the military and the then government sought to negotiate a national ceasefire agreement and took steps towards institutionalising democratic practices. But in other areas (notably Shan and Kachin states), conflict restarted, while the Rohingya Muslim-focused atrocities of 2017 forced a mass exodus of that group into neighbouring Bangladesh and elsewhere. These conflicts have significantly eroded trust between the military and EAOs and contributed to the current stalemate. Further, the new National League for Democracy (NLD) government has been accused of simply continuing the Bamar nation-building agenda, and ignoring the priorities of ethnic nationality communities (Aung Aung 2018).

Figure 13.1 shows an approximation of the distribution of major ethnic nationalities, and the state and region boundaries, according to the 2008 Constitution. An overlap between the boundaries and the different ethnic

Figure 13.1: Map of states and regions in Myanmar, overlaid on an approximation of the ethnic distribution of major ethnic nationalities. Source: Ethnic distribution based on data from Smith 1991

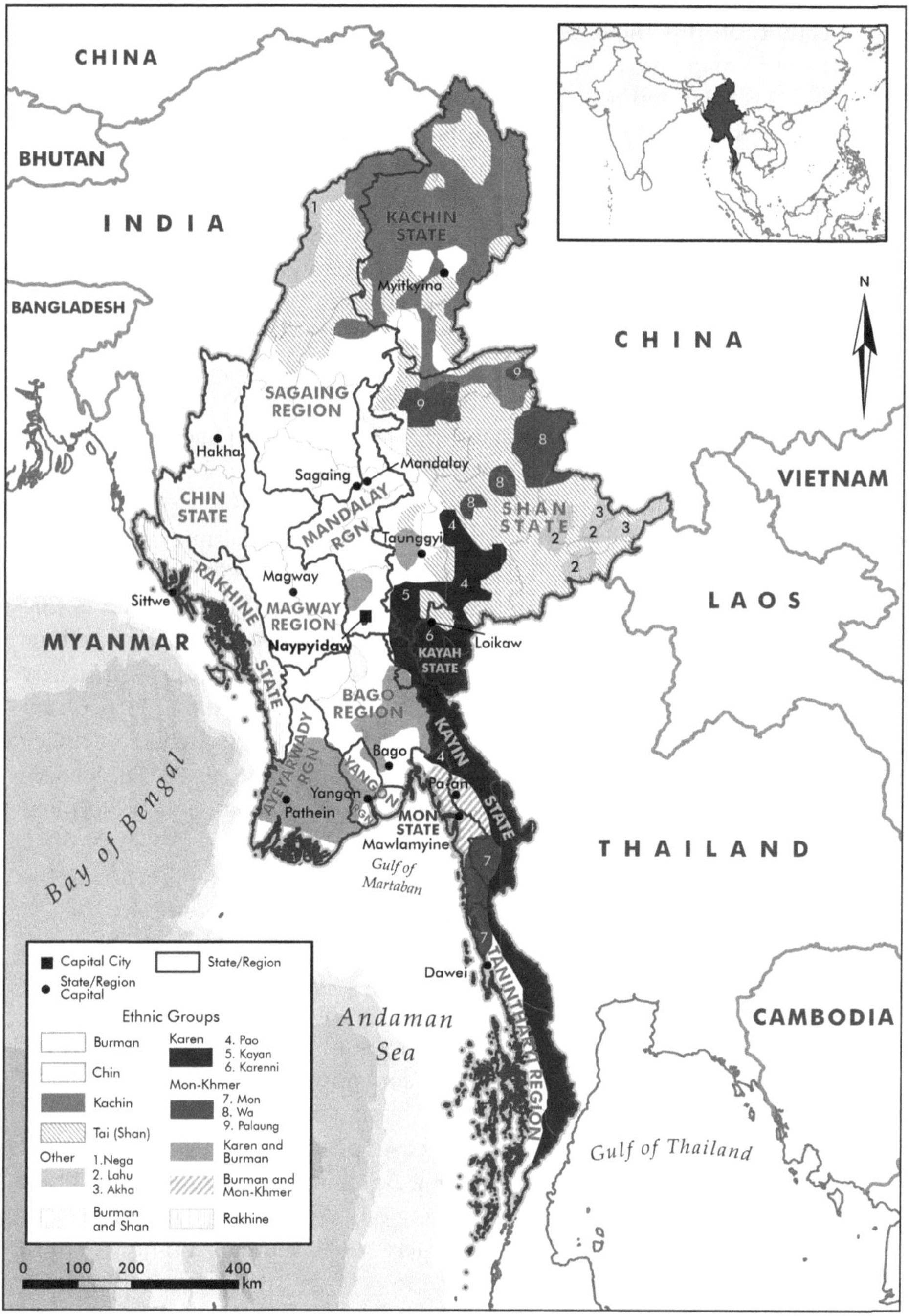

nationalities is apparent, as is the near impossibility of the federal structure neatly capturing the breadth and complexity of this diversity. But in any case, the map shows estimates only, each area is not homogenous and there has been significant population growth and internal migration since 1947 when the initial ethnically focused federal arrangements were agreed.

The 2014 census collected data on the distribution of different ethnic nationalities, but that data has not been released (see Ye Mon and Pyae Thet Phyo 2016). Estimates of ethnic populations remain just that and there is very little reliable data on distribution and how it has changed since 1947. Notwithstanding, the 1983 census did collect data on the ethnic distribution of groups within the states and divisions (as existent under the 1974 constitution). It showed that five of the seven ethnic states had a majority of the named ethnic nationality (two of which were well under 60 per cent of the population) and the remaining two had a plurality of the named ethnic group (Ministry of Home and Regional Affairs 1987, Tables 6 for each state and division).

Since that time, there has been substantial internal migration. Based on the most recent census (2014), around 20 per cent of the population are internal migrants (Department of Population 2016). The UN reports that four states or regions have a net in-migration, three of which are ethnic states (Shan, Kachin and Chin), and that internal migration is primarily motivated by economic opportunity (World Bank Myanmar 2016, 6). In-migration to ethnic states is often perceived to be part of a deliberate policy of "Burmanisation". Further, as at the end of 2018, over 400,000 people remained internally displaced as a result of conflict (Internal Displacement Monitoring Centre 2019).

Yet ethnic leaders still agitate for federalism based on ethnicity, to the extent that the current constitutional reform process, specifically the 21st Century Panglong Conference, has seen debates punctuated by demands for new ethnic states, new self-administered areas and the merging of the seven (nominally Bamar) regions to form one Bamar state (Myanmar News Agency 2016a, b). Many of these demands are still based on promises of the Panglong Agreement, rather than contemporary reality. Khun Marko Ban, from the Karenni National Progressive Party, for example, argued that "the eight states principle is a basic principle, because it stemmed from the essence of the 1947 Panglong Agreement" (cited in Nyein 2016). These demands hark back to the Panglong Agreement, Aung San's oft-repeated promise of ethnic equality such that "if Burma gets one *Kyat* [unit of currency], then you [the ethnic nationalities] will get one *Kyat*" (cited in Walton 2008, 897). But there is no shared vision of what a Panglong-based ethnofederal structure would actually look like. How many groups should get states? Should there be one Bamar state or more? Should states, or ethnic nationalities, have the right to secede?

Demands for federalism are also based on the self-determination principle. Prominent Chin leader and peace negotiator Lian Sakhong highlights the Bamar-centric nation-building, writing that self-determination is necessary because the central state has, *inter alia*, "abused rights of religious and cultural minority groups" (Sakhong 2005, 10). The Wa demand the establishment of a Wa state, covering their self-administered division and ceasefire area, which are both currently part of the Shan State. Practically, they have complete control in these areas and their "leaders want no part of being ruled by any state-level government emanating from what now constitutes Shan State" (Callahan 2007, 30). South and Lall (2016, 2) put the demands for the right to mother-tongue education "at the heart" of the conflict.

Overarching all this is a fear of secession. The fear is present mostly among the military who continue to associate federalism with secession despite its renunciation by EAOs. They fear that empowering ethnic groups will enable them to mount a secessionist movement. Hence, the 21st Century Panglong Conference's progress has stalled on this issue (see for example Shan Herald Agency for News 2017). But what if federalism was not so intertwined with the notion of ethnic identity? It could still deliver many of the benefits attributed to it, which could include an extent of ethnic autonomy according to naturally clustered communities, without raising the risks of secession.

DEBATES ON ETHNO AND TERRITORIAL FEDERALISM

Unlike many Western federations, such as the United States and Australia, Asian countries have needed to take ethnic diversity seriously as they discuss or implement federal governance structures. The major issue that runs through academic examination, and the practical consideration of federalism in Asia, is whether federal institutions should be based on territorial or ethnic factors. Critics of ethnic approaches (ethnofederalism) cite "a substantial body of evidence warning against this" (Roeder 2009,

295). However, practitioners continue to recommend ethnofederalism as a response to ethnic conflict, because in many cases there are no plausible alternatives (Anderson 2014).

The chief criticism of ethnofederalism is that it might lead to the break-up of a country – secession or disintegration. If an ethnic group has its own institutions, it is more likely to be able to secure and develop the resources and basis from which mount a successful secessionist movement (Brown 2007, Roeder 2009). And, they may be more likely to. "Institutionalizing and promoting the separate identity of a titular group increases that group's cohesion and willingness to act" (Cornell 2002, 225). Others argue that ethnofederalism leads to more discrimination, more isolation and distrust, and less intercultural understanding (Bunce and Watts 2005).

But of course, it is never so simple. If ethnic groups are fighting for self-determination, then states and regions that are based on geography only and which incorporate only parts of each ethnic group, are not likely to contribute to a settlement agreement. If ethnic groups gain autonomy, they are less likely to want to secede. Ethnofederalism is regularly promoted as a way to resolve conflict and to facilitate respect for human rights and stable democratic governance in ethnically divided countries (Anderson 2013; Ghai 2000; Lawoti 2010; Stepan 1999; Kymlicka 2007). Today, "virtually all constitutional settlements to self-determination conflicts" incorporate some type of ethnic autonomy (Weller and Wolff 2005, 232).

According to Anderson (2014), ethnofederalism is the least-worst institutional arrangement irrespective of its problems, because no other state structure has been as successful in resolving or reducing conflict in ethnically divided countries. Anderson (2013) shows that its failure rate has actually been less than that of the alternatives. Further, as Hale (2004) demonstrated, ethnofederalism is not more likely to collapse (lead to secession or breakdown) unless there is a "core ethnic region" – one state or region that has a majority or large proportion of the population. This was the case in Pakistan (before Bangladesh split off), Yugoslavia, Czechoslovakia and others, including Burma under the 1947 constitution. So according to this hypothesis, creating one Bamar state by merging existing regions is likely to lead to the failure of federalism in Myanmar.

The use of mixed criteria, like in the case of Nepal, seems obvious. Nepal used identity and viability as the two main criteria to create a kind of hybrid federalism (Breen 2018a). Using mixed criteria for the establishment of provinces also means that the provinces are more likely to be substantively heterogeneous. The presence of a mixture of different ethnic groups in a unit will tend to have a more moderating effect on intergroup politics, especially if new unit-based majorities that are different to those at the centre are created, or if they break up a core region (Horowitz 2000 [1985], 613–619; Breen 2018c, 153–158). Heterogeneous units also contribute to the creation of conditions conducive to democratic deliberation, which have also been shown to have moderating effects and decrease the risk of secession or secessionist conflict (Breen 2018c, 153–172; 2018a).

On the other hand, a more "territorial federalism" will not meet the demands of the minority ethnic groups who are agitating for autonomy, and even less so, when there are ethnically based institutions already in existence. We know this much from the statements and actions of the leaders of ethnic parties and EAOs, as well as the academic debates. However, the citizens' perspective is missing. The federal enterprise is essentially a democratic project. It requires state-builders to listen to the voice of people.

DELIBERATIVE SURVEYS ON FEDERALISM IN MYANMAR

Many constitutional reform processes are elite-driven, based on the power of political parties or militaries, and drafted by legal technocrats with little attachment to the realities on the ground (Fishkin 2018; Elster 1998; Wallis 2014). In Myanmar, these problems are compounded by extreme majoritarianism,[3] an effective military veto (Harding 2017), and the restrictive nature of the constitutional debates (in terms of inclusivity, formality and agenda-control) (International Crisis Group 2016; Breen 2018c, 127–134).

One way to help address these problems is through the development of a more deliberative democracy (see also Walton 2017). Deliberative democracy emphasises the force of reason over military, economic or political power, and aims to ensure that everyone has an equal opportunity to participate in democratic procedures and, in doing so, influence decision-making and the exercise of state power (Habermas 1984; Dryzek 2000; Fishkin 2009). This is especially pertinent when considering constitutional change (Elster 1998; Fishkin 2018). We experimented with deliberative surveys as one way to engage the public and determine how to feed a deliberative perspective into the decision-making process.

Context and methodology

One topic of our research design related to the bases of the states and regions, including whether they should be based on ethnicity or territory. The results were surprising and telling. This is the focus of this chapter. The deliberative surveys covered other topics, namely national identity and religion, federalism and the division of powers, most of which are not addressed here. A separate paper (Breen and He 2020) focuses on national identity and religion and implications for theories of deliberative democracy, while a full report is also available (Breen, He, and Win 2018).

Our deliberative surveys were based on the Deliberative Polling® (DP) methodology created by James Fishkin (2006, 2009). DP uses a before and after survey in order to ascertain a more genuine public opinion on matters of policy and public administration. The survey questions are identical, which enables opinion change to be measured and compared. DP relies on random selection. Our variation used a more targeted approach to selection to achieve "discursive representation" (Dryzek 2005), in this case, that of ethnic identity. We used local civil society organisations to recruit and ensure a mixture of participants. Participants were to be reflective of the region, rather than the country as a whole. We held three forums in Shan State (Lashio and Taunggyi) and two in Sagaing Region (Sagaing and Monywa). Therefore, Shan and Bamar are comparatively well represented. The language of deliberation was Bamar. We also paid

Table 13.1: Statistical breakdown of participants

Ethnic identity*	Bamar	Chin	Kachin	Unspecified
	45	15	10	0
	Various	Shan	Other	
	12	36	48	
Religion	Buddhist	Christian	Muslim	Unspecified
	123	39	4	0
Age range	18-29	30-49	50+	Unspecified
	64	47	46	16
Gender	Male	Female	Other	Unspecified
	116	49	1	0
Education level	Primary	High school	University	Unspecified
	17	56	90	3

*Various refers to Karen, Karenni, Mon & Rakhine. Other refers to small ethnic groups, like Pa-O, Wa etc.

a modest honorarium to participants as an incentive to participate and in recognition of their time and effort. Overall 193 people attended, and 166 people returned both before and after surveys. All statistics provided relate to the 166 people only. All quotes are verbal translations. Attendance breakdowns are provided in Table 13.1. Relevant questions and results are in Appendix 13.1.

Before engaging in a deliberation, the participants first completed the survey, selecting whether they agreed or disagreed with a series of statements using a scale of 1 to 5 where 3 is neutral and 5 is strongly agree. Secondly, participants were provided with an independently reviewed and balanced briefing package on the issues that would be discussed and asked to review the package before attending a deliberative forum. At the forum, the information package was reinforced by a keynote lecture, with opportunity for questions. Then participants broke into mixed small-group sessions ("tables"), facilitated by a trained moderator who asked a series of questions and enforced a set of rules for deliberation. The small groups provided "report-backs" on the outcomes of their deliberations at the end of each session, which provided a further opportunity to ask questions and debate issues. Finally, the participants would complete the same survey.

The average mean of the combined results of each question on the first and second survey are compared. Opinion change was measured in terms of change in mean, and moderation (or convergence of opinion) in terms of change in standard deviation. An opinion change of 10 per cent indicates that around half the participants changed their opinions (in kind or degree). This analysis was also repeated per ethnic group, location, gender, religion and others. This paper discusses the differences between ethnic nationalities ("groups") and between locations, which are most relevant in this instance. Regarding the former, the analysis does not discuss changes in the Karen, Karenni, Mon and Rakhine groups individually as the number of participants was too low to achieve statistical significance. Also, there is an "other" category. Respondents selecting this category identified with a small ethnic nationality, whether or not it was officially categorised as a constituent part of what is defined by the government as a "national race". For example, Pa-O, Lahu, Kadu, Sha-ni, Wa and Jingpo. Three of the five locations comprised mostly laypersons, while two comprised a mixture of local elites and laypersons. Local elites were members of ethnic armed organisations (EAOs), political parties and civil society organisations.

The morning session of each forum focused on identity and religion, and the afternoon session focused on the questions concerning federal institutional design. Each morning, participants extolled their individual ethnic identities and the need for their recognition. We expected, as is the case with the overarching discourse and the thrust of elite negotiations like the 21st Century Panglong Conference, that participants would then argue for the institutionalisation of those ethnic identities in the structures of the states. In other words, we expected (at a minimum non-Bamar) ethnic nationalities to advocate for ethnic states, more self-administered areas and the upgrading of existing self-administered areas into states. Simply put, ethnofederalism. However, this did not occur.

A preference for territorial federalism

When each table reported back on the outcomes of their deliberations about the bases and boundaries of states and regions, we were surprised. With few exceptions, tables reported a general consensus that territorial federalism should be preferred over ethnofederalism. That is, states and regions should be ethnically mixed (heterogeneous), with the boundaries being based on criteria like geographical continuity, economic resources and infrastructure, moreso than ethnicity, language and historical continuity.

The most commonly cited reasons were that: 1) if there are more states or self-administered areas, then the chances of conflict and secession will increase – the participants' overarching priority was peace; 2) the creation of ethnic states and self-administered areas marginalises small minorities and Bamar minorities living in those states and areas; 3) all states and regions are ethnically mixed, and so one ethnic nationality should not be privileged over another; and 4) ethnofederalism is impractical because there are too many ethnic nationalities to give each a state or self-administered area.

But is it dangerous to contemplate a reorganisation or renaming of the states and regions? One table concluded that territorially based criteria are better than ethnic criteria "but the status quo is best". However, the status quo is problematic for many ethnic nationalities, because "some ethnic nationalities are split across states and they are worried for their identity." Further, the states are subordinate to the central government.

The arguments for ethnofederalism were almost entirely based around the promises of Panglong. Yet the survey results showed that less than half of the participants could answer a basic multiple choice question about the Panglong Agreement before the forum, with most of those believing that the agreement was signed between all the major ethnic nationalities (Breen, He, and Win 2018, 18). As Walton (2008) points out, the Panglong Agreement has become much like the country's founding myth, yet with conflicting versions. One is the myth of ethnic unity.[4]

Ultimately, the conclusions reached by the tables and the content of the deliberations themselves reflected a prevailing shift of opinion away from ethnofederalism. The survey results told a similar story. After the participants had become more informed and discussed their reasons and perspectives with each other, they shifted towards preferring territorial federalism.

Specifically, support for states and regions that are based on ethnicity dropped by 8 per cent to become neutral (Question 2), while support for the "opposite" approach, states being based on economic and geographical criteria, increased by 6 per cent (Question 32) – see Figure 13.2. These changes were highly statistically significant. Before the poll, over 60 per cent of participants supported ethnic states, yet after it dropped to 43 per cent, with at least twenty-four persons changing from support to not.

Figure 13.2: Should states be based on ethnic or territorial criteria (before and after survey results)

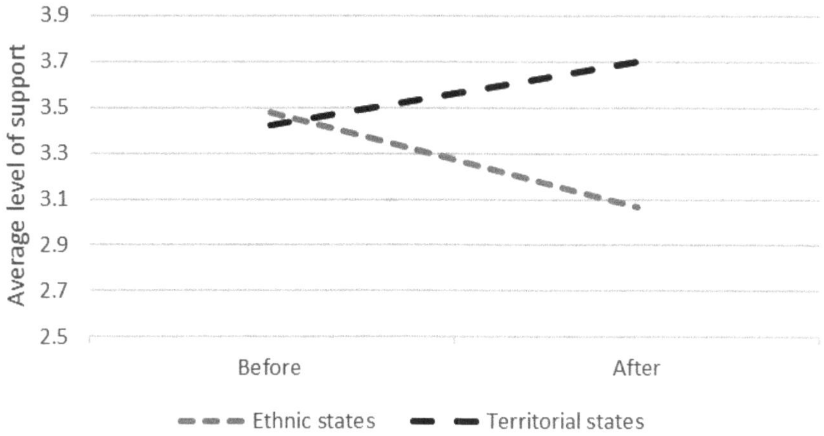

The different ethnic groups changed in a consistent way on these questions, with few exceptions. Support for ethnically based federalism dropped for every group, except for the Chin. However, Chin participants' support for territorial-based federalism was also up, so it follows that many were seeking mixed criteria, which was a point of discussion. Support for ethnic states was also lower among the Bamar as compared to other ethnic nationalities. A comparison of each location (forum) showed the trends to be consistent, with two exceptions. The second forum (Lashio, comprising mostly laypersons) slightly increased their support for ethnic states, while the fifth (Sagaing, comprising mostly laypersons and Bamar) was down slightly on support for territorial federalism (it was also down on support for ethnofederalism).

More ethnic states or self-administered areas

Survey results on the issue of more ethnic states and more self-administered areas also demonstrate the shift away from ethnofederalism. Support for statements that all large ethnic nationalities should have an ethnic state, and that all small ethnic nationalities should have a self-administered area dropped substantially (14 and 7 per cent respectively) – see Figure 13.3.

Figure 13.3: Should all major ethnic nationalities have a state, and should all small ethnic groups have a self-administered zone (before and after survey results)

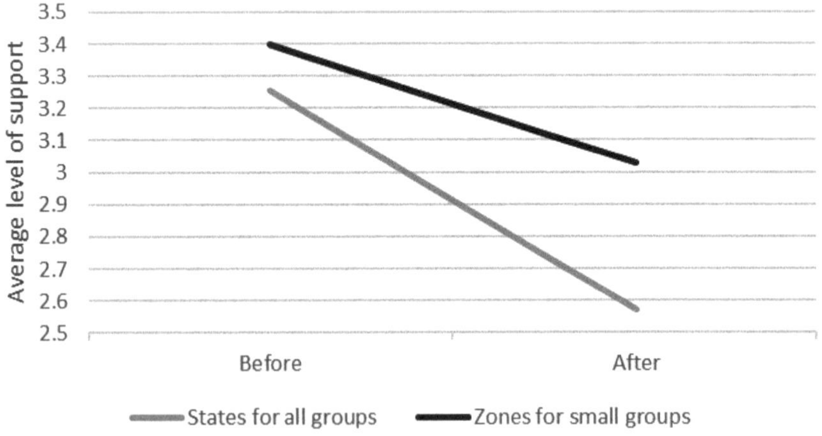

These changes were highly statistically significant at 0.05 confidence level. The number of people who did not agree that there should be more ethnic states more than doubled from forty-six persons to ninety-six (out of 166). Twenty-four remained neutral (see Appendix 13.1, Question 4). Slightly more people ended up agreeing with the idea of more self-administered areas (as discussed below, it is seen as a trade-off for more territorially based states), but the average was neutral, and the shift was substantively towards less support (see Appendix 13.1, Question 7).

There were no substantive differences between groups and between locations on the issue of more ethnic states or self-administered areas with one exception. The second forum, comprising mostly laypersons in Lashio, northern Shan State, increased its support for more self-administered areas. As mentioned, this forum's participants also went in the opposite direction on the question of ethnofederalism, but only just. Lashio is quite close to many active conflict zones and if nothing else, these differences demonstrate that different locations may have different priorities and perspectives. Most particularly, in areas where there has been sustained conflict, the intermingling of different ethnic nationalities has been lower, and the EAOs have maintained and propagated a stronger sense of ethnic nationalism (South and Lall 2016). However, we did have some participants from EAOs in other forums and their positions changed in a way that was consistent with changes in the other participants' positions.

So, while such deliberations can mask a more substantive disagreement and variance of opinion, in these cases, the trends remained consistent. The deliberative survey approach minimises the element of peer pressure and power relations when recording opinions such that opinion change can be attributed to the power of reason. The survey results can thus be considered a more genuine opinion than one communicated verbally or on their behalf.

Overall, the trends were backed by a greater understanding of the potential benefits of federalism. For example, some participants argued that democratisation and regional development can be achieved without a focus on ethnicity. Indeed, some felt that these potentialities would be more likely to be achieved if federalism were more territorially based. Federalism can be designed to maximise resource and infrastructure development opportunities, access to markets and economies of scale. Merely replacing one set of ethnocentric institutions (at the central level) with another (at the state level) has the potential to invite further conflict.

The eight-state approach

Deliberative approaches have also proven their ability to generate innovative and compromise solutions. This was put to the test with the vexed question of whether the existing regions should be merged to form one Bamar state. At almost all tables, the discussion on this question was lively and occasionally animated.

It was difficult to reach agreement in such a short space of time, as can be expected, but the deliberations did lead to the development of innovative potential solutions (even if politically unpalatable at present). During the report-back session, one participant stood up and said that "if we can't agree to merge the regions, then why don't we split the Shan State – already it has four military commanders" (meaning that it is already administratively divided into four areas). This suggestion received a round of applause from the audience and it is not a suggestion we have heard in any other venue. It would achieve at least one key objective sought by proponents of the merger, namely a rebalancing of the upper house of parliament in favour of ethnic states, while avoiding the creation of a Bamar state, which was opposed by most. Besides, if nothing else, the deliberative forum did help people make up their minds. Forty participants were neutral in the before survey, but after deliberation twenty-one of those formed an opinion, which was invariably to not support the prospective merger (see Appendix 13.1, Question 8).

Secession

Just like the elite level debates, secession was an overarching theme. We had some specific questions on this matter, but the quality of debate was low. People were somewhat reluctant to discuss the issue directly but raised it repeatedly. Every other issue, from the boundaries of states and regions and new self-administered areas, to revenue-sharing and natural resources, were discussed in terms of how they may make secession more or less likely.

Most participants did not think federalism would lead to secession and this position was strengthened by deliberation. We asked whether participants agreed with the statement that "federalism will lead to secession". The level of agreement decreased 6 per cent (around one-third changed their view) and participants significantly moderated (see Appendix

13.1, Question 9 and Figure 13.4). The change was highly statistically significant. In addition to those shifting their support to elsewhere, twenty out of forty-three people who were neutral in the first survey later disagreed with the statement (Appendix 13.1, Question 9).

Figure 13.4: Federalism will lead to secession? (before and after survey results)

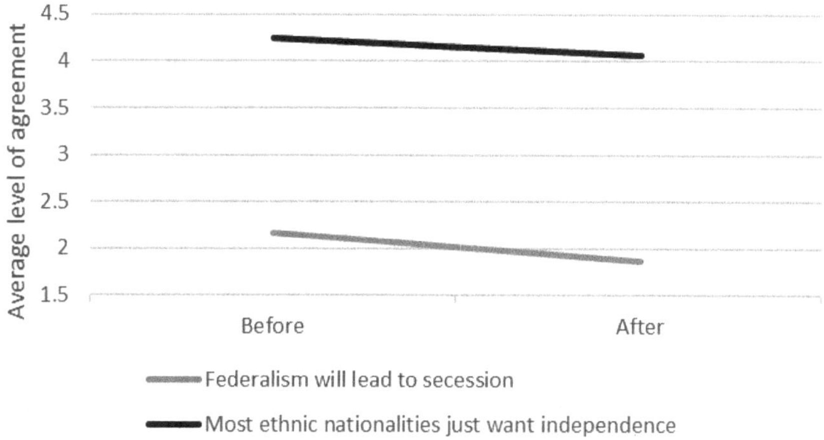

Further, participants' agreement that with the statement that "most ethnic nationalities want an independent state" also decreased. This change was also statistically significant. There were little differences across groups or locations on these matters. However, the Chin group did slightly increase its agreement with the idea that federalism would lead to secession, but on average still disagreed, while the Bamar group was well down in their belief that ethnic nationalities just want independence. Again, this is a positive outcome of the deliberations, given that Bamar are traditionally thought to be most opposed to federalism and more fearful of secession.

The prevailing view was well captured by one participant reporting back on small-group discussion: "In the past federalism was about secession – but today it will unite us". One Bamar participant summed up both the perspective and effect of such public deliberation:

> Before [today] I had thought that federalism meant secession, but now I know what it is and so we should have it. But it should be territorial because people are mixed. If we grant more self-administered areas then others will demand them too. This is problematic. If the people are educated about federalism, then they will not demand pure ethnic states.

SECESSION RISK AND ITS MANAGEMENT

In Myanmar, like in other ethnically divided countries, the secession risk is not just the main reason against federalisation, it is also the main reason for the establishment of modern federal systems (see Breen 2018b). There is a well-established paradox of federalism that on the one hand it can accommodate ethnic diversity, but on the other hand, it can exacerbate ethnic tension and division (Erk and Anderson 2009). It was in the minds of the military negotiators, and it was also in the minds of our participants, as they sought a solution that would not invite more secessionist conflict.

Many constitutions prohibit secession or secessionist activities, usually by declaring a country to be "indivisible" or similar (Novic and Urs 2016). Only Ethiopia's includes an explicit right for secession, while a few others include a process by which a particular province can seek independence. But a secession risk can be managed in a variety of other often interrelated ways.

A secession risk can be understood as a product of four factors (see Breen 2018b). For starters, there needs to be some credible demand or action towards an independent state. Then the risk becomes a matter of degree. One factor is how homogenous a given area is – that is, does it house mostly only one ethnic group, and are most of its members within this area. Secondly, do the groups or institutions have the power of arms, or can the central government simply send in the troops. And thirdly, is there any international support or sympathy, especially by neighbours, to the claims for an independent state. If all these factors exist at once, the risk is too high and federalism is likely to be strongly resisted by central authorities. In Myanmar, there are now few credible calls for independence, and the international support for independence or armed insurgencies has mostly lapsed. Theoretically, the secession risk is now not too high to prevent federalisation. But still the fear persists.

If homogeneity in a federal state or region is a secession risk factor, then one way to reduce secession risk is to create more heterogeneous states and regions (Breen 2018b). It is an unfortunate truth that in some countries, mass migration programs have been implemented by the central state to reduce homogeneity and thereby pressure for secession. But a more benign approach is viable. It is also true that when an ethnic group is fighting for self-determination, an ethnically mixed state or region is hardly going to provide the type of autonomy that is being sought. However, there is a trade-off.

When states and regions are homogenous, central authorities may tend to limit the extent of powers available to them, so that they cannot accumulate the resources to underpin secession. This applies especially to fiscal powers and coercive powers. For example, even though the 1987 amendments to the constitution in Sri Lanka afforded its provinces law and order powers, they were never devolved as it was deemed too risky. Conversely, in Nepal, ethnic autonomy was given effect by drawing provincial boundaries such that each included at least two major ethnic groups. Although some remained unsatisfied, it meant that in practice, the provinces could have strong powers without raising the risk of secession. Arguably, there is far greater ethnic autonomy in the mixed provinces of Nepal, than in the homogenous provinces of Sri Lanka (see Breen 2018c, 153–158).

A further strategy to reduce secession risk is to empower a third (local) tier of government, which is increasingly referred to as the hourglass model (Shah 2012). In this way autonomy can be both more targeted and more relevant to small groups, while the presence of a third tier acts as an additional guard against any independence plans by a state or region.

Traditionally, federal theory would have it that interdependence – or shared rule – will act to prevent secession. A strong upper house of parliament that represents states and regions is one such institution for this. But such houses tend to represent the interests of political parties more so than states and regions. In practice, political parties have a much more integral role in creating interdependence (see Riker 1964; Breen 2018c, 149–182).

Political party engineering has been used in several "deeply divided societies" in Asia and Africa to ensure the development of strong integrative multiethnic parties (Reilly 2001). Indonesia banned regional and ethnic parties (with a couple of exceptions). Nepal recognised the value of small regional and ethnic parties, while at the same time forcing the major parties to put up inclusive candidate lists resulting in more multiethnic parties and policies (see Breen 2018a). In Myanmar, the place of ethnic parties is not likely to be diminished, and nor should it be. However, the major parties should not be explicit or proxy Bamar parties – they should be multiethnic. This would mean both including and representing the interests of different ethnic nationalities.

CONCLUSION

The question of federalism has been the major issue preventing the establishment and consolidation of democracy in Myanmar since independence. It has always been envisaged that federalism would be ethnic in nature (ethnofederalism), incorporating states and regions that would provide autonomy and self-determination for ethnic nationalities on the basis of historical entitlement. However, the central state and the military in particular, have been resistant to the idea, and have instead promulgated a Bamar-centric nation-building agenda. This has served to accentuate the non-Bamar ethnic nationalities' discontent, to increase conflict and imperil democratisation.

Since the election of the NLD in 2015, a constitutional reform process, under the guise of the 21st Century Panglong Conference, has been in place, with a goal of reaching a genuine federal system. This conference has been punctuated by demands for more ethnofederalism but has reached a deadlock over the issue of secession. The concerns about the potential for secession arising from ethnofederalism is a common debate in political science. We sought to find out what everyday people in Myanmar think.

We discussed and surveyed these issues with a selection of laypersons, and some local elites, in order to ascertain a more genuine public opinion on federalism. We were surprised to find that despite the prominence given to the recognition of ethnic identity in deliberations, most participants did not want further ethnicisation of the federal system, and in fact, preferred states and regions that are based on territorial (geographic, economic etc.) criteria, rather than ethnic criteria. Overarching this was their concern about the potential for more conflict – and secession.

So, while the perspectives of elites (as per the 21st Century Panglong Conference) and laypersons seem to differ on the issue of ethnofederalism, there is a shared concern about conflict and secession. The results of the deliberative survey (notwithstanding its shortcomings) suggest that the people (and perhaps the military) would be less concerned about, and more supportive of, federalism if it were designed in a way that decreased the potential or risk of secession (and at the same time increased the potential for economic development and democratisation).

Regardless of whether or not the constitution bans secession, the risk will remain. So, it should be managed. If the names and boundaries of states and regions were refocused to emphasise territorial rather than ethnic factors, and the states and regions became more ethnically mixed, then it may become more politically palatable for the powers of those states and regions to be enhanced. It is counter-intuitive, but such an approach may increase the extent of ethnic autonomy, as although an ethnic group may not form a majority in a distinct state or region, it will (ideally) reach a critical mass where it can have a strong voice and wield important democratic powers. This can be supplemented by autonomy at the local level (a third tier of constitutional government) and non-territorial rights (such as those encapsulated by the national race affairs ministries currently in place), while political parties should continue to play a role in both representing minority interests and bridging differences between groups. It is not so much a question of whether an ethnic minority is empowered as it is a question of whether the hegemony of the dominant group is broken.

Acknowledgements

The authors are grateful for the collaboration of Dr Khin Zaw Win and the Tampadipa Institute in designing and implementing the deliberative forums, along with the Heartland Foundation, Kanbawza Youth Library, Tukhamein Education Institute and Yone Kyi Yar. We also thank the University of Mandalay and the student volunteers who worked with us in various critical roles. We acknowledge the funding from the University of Melbourne, Norwegian People's Aid and Deakin University, and advice from International IDEA and the Forum of Federations.

Notes

1 For example, those identifying as Jingpho, Lahu, Sha-ni, Kadu and Palaung.
2 Also known as ethnic affairs ministries.
3 In 2010, the USDP won 80 per cent of the contested seats in the lower house, and in 2015, the NLD won 77 per cent.
4 Representatives from three ethnic nationalities (Chin, Kachin and Shan), plus Aung San, signed the agreement.

References

Anderson, L.D. (2013). *Federal Solutions to Ethnic Problems: Accommodating Diversity*. Exeter Studies in Ethno Politics. Abingdon, Oxon: Routledge.

_____ (2014). "Ethnofederalism: The Worst Form of Institutional Arrangement...?" *International Security* 39 (1):165.

Aung Aung (2018). "Myanmar's Current Politics: Implications for the 2020 General Elections". In *Perspective*. Singapore: Institute of South East Asian Studies - Yusof Ishak Institute.

Breen, M.G. (2018a). "Nepal, Federalism and Participatory Constitution-making: Deliberative Democracy and Divided Societies". *Asian Journal of Political Science* 26 (3):410–430.

_____ (2018b). "The Origins of Holding-Together Federalism: Nepal, Myanmar and Sri Lanka". *Publius: The Journal of Federalism* 48 (1):26–50.

_____ (2018c). *The Road to Federalism in Nepal, Myanmar and Sri Lanka: Finding the Middle Ground*. Politics in Asia series. Abingdon, Oxon and New York: Routledge.

_____ (2019). "Asymmetry or Equality? Ethnic Nationalities in a Bamar-Dominated State. A Country Study of Constitutional Asymmetry in Myanmar". In *Constitutional Asymmetry in Multinational Federalism,* edited by P. Popelier and M. Sahadzic. Palgrave Macmillan.

Breen, M.G., and Baogang He (2020). "Moderating Polarised Positions on Questions of National Identity and Sovereignty: Deliberative Surveys on Federalism in Myanmar". Inter*national Area Studies Review* 23 (1):93–113.

Breen, M.G., Baogang He, and Khin Zaw Win (2018). *Deliberative Polling on Federalism in Myanmar: Report*. Yangon: The University of Melbourne and Tampadipa Institute.

Brown, D. (2007). "Regionalist Federalism: A Critique of Ethno-national Federalism". In *Federalism in Asia,* edited by Baogang He, B. Galligan and T. Inoguchi, 57–81. Cheltenham, UK: Edward Elgar.

Bunce, V., and Watts, S. (2005). "Managing Diversity and Sustaining Democracy: Ethnofederal versus Unitary States in the Postcommunist World". In *Sustainable Peace: Power and Democracy after Civil Wars,* edited by P.G. Roeder and D.S. Rothchild, 133–158. Ithaca, NY: Cornell University Press.

Callahan, M.P. (2007). *Political Authority in Burma's Ethnic Minority States: Devolution, Occupation and Coexistence*. Policy Studies 31 (Southeast Asia). Washington DC: East-West Center.

Cornell, S. (2002). "Nation-Building and the Treaty Process". *Indigenous Law Bulletin* 5 (17):7–10.

Department of Population (2016). *The 2014 Myanmar Population and Housing Census: Thematic Report on Migration and Urbanization*. Nay Pyi Taw.

Dryzek, J.S. (2000). *Deliberative Democracy and Beyond*. Oxford: Oxford University Press.

_____ (2005). "Deliberative Democracy in Divided Societies: Alternatives to Agonism and Analgesia". *Political Theory* 33 (2): 218–242.

Elster, J. (1998). "Deliberation and Constitution Making". In *Deliberative Democracy*, edited by J. Elster, 97–122. Cambridge: Cambridge University Press.

Erk, J., and Anderson, L. (2009). "The Paradox of Federalism: Does Self-Rule Accommodate or Exacerbate Ethnic Divisions?" *Regional & Federal Studies* 19 (2): 191.

Fishkin, J.S. (2006). "Beyond Polling Alone: The Quest for an Informed Public." *Critical Review* 18 (1–3): 157–165.

_____ (2009). *When the People Speak: Deliberative Democracy and Public Consultation*. Oxford: Oxford University Press.

_____ (2018). *Democracy When the People Are Thinking: Revitalising Our Politics through Public Deliberation*. Oxford: Oxford University Press.

Ghai, Y. (2000). *Autonomy and Ethnicity: Negotiating Competing Claims in Multi-ethnic States*. Cambridge: Cambridge University Press.

Habermas, J. (1984). *The Theory of Communicative Action: Reason and the Rationalization of Society* Vol. 1. Boston: Beacon Press.

Hale, H.E. (2004). "Divided We Stand: Institutional Sources of Ethnofederal State Survival and Collapse". *World Politics* 156 (2): 165–193.

Harding, A. (2017). "Irresistible Forces and Immovable Objects: Constitutional Change in Myanmar". In *Constitutionalism and Legal Change in Myanmar*, edited by A. Harding and Khin Khin Oo, 71–82. Oxford & London: Hart Publishing.

Horowitz, D.L. (2000 [1985]). *Ethnic Groups in Conflict*. 2nd ed. Berkeley, California: University of California Press.

Internal Displacement Monitoring Centre (2019). *Myanmar: Figure Analysis - Displacement Related to Conflict and Violence*. Geneva: Internal Displacement Monitoring Centre.

International Crisis Group (2016). *Myanmar's Peace Process: Getting to a Dialogue*. In Crisis Group Asia Briefing. Yangon/Brussels: International Crisis Group.

Kymlicka, W. (2007). "Multi-nation Federalism". In *Federalism in Asia*, edited by Baogang He, B. Galligan and T. Inoguchi, 33–56. Cheltenham, UK: Edward Elgar.

Lawoti, M. (2010). *Federal State Building: Challenges in Framing the New Nepali Constitution*. Kathmandu: Bhrikuti Academic Publications.

Ministry of Home and Regional Affairs (1987). 1983 Population Census edited by Immigration and Manpower Department. Rangoon: The Socialist Republic of the Union of Burma.

Myanmar News Agency (2016a). "Cries for Federalism Dominate Second-day Session of 21st Century Panglong Conference". *Global New Light of Myanmar,* 3 September 2016. Accessed 18 September 2016. http://www.globalnewlightofmyanmar.com/cries-for-federalism-dominate-second-day-session-of-21st-century-panglong-conference/.

_____ (2016b). "Visions for Federal Union — UPC Continues its Third Day Session". *Global New Light of Myanmar,* 3 September 2016. Accessed 18 September 2016. http://www.globalnewlightofmyanmar.com/visions-for-federal-union-upc-continues-its-third-day-session/.

Novic, E., and Urs, P. (2016). "Secession". In *Max Planck Encyclopedia of Comparative Constitutional Law,* edited by R. Grote, F. Lachenmann and H.D. Rudiger Wolfrum. Online: Oxford University Press.

Nyein, Nyein (2016). "Stakeholder Presentations at Peace Conference Reveal Contrasting Positions on Statehood and Security". *The Irrawaddy,* 2 September 2016. Accessed 4 September 2016. http://www.irrawaddy.com/burma/stakeholder-presentations-at-peace-conference-reveal-contrasting-positions-on-statehood-and-security.html.

Reilly, B. (2001). *Democracy in Divided Societies: Electoral Engineering for Conflict Management.* Cambridge: Cambridge University Press.

Riker, W.H. (1964). *Federalism: Origin, Operation, Significance.* Boston: Little, Brown.

Roeder, P.G. (2009). "Ethnofederalism and the Mismanagement of Conflicting Nationalisms". *Regional & Federal Studies* 19 (2):203.

Sakhong, L.H. (2005). "Federalism, Constitution Making and State Building in Burma". In *Designing Federalism in Burma,* edited by D.C. Williams and L.H. Sakhong, 11–34. Chiang Mai: UNLD Press.

_____ (2010). *In Defence of Identity: The Ethnic Nationalities' Struggle for Democracy, Human Rights, and Federalism in Burma.* Bangkok: Orchid Press.

Shah, A. (2012). *Whither Provinces and States? The Case for an Hourglass Model of Federalism.* Ottawa: Forum of Federations.

Shan Herald Agency for News (2017). "'No-secession from Union' Wording Dominates 21CPC". Shan Herald Agency for News, 30 May 2017. Accessed 5 June 2017. http://english.panglong.org/2017/05/30/no-secession-from-union-wording-dominates-21cpc.

Smith, M.J. (1991). *Burma: Insurgency and the Politics of Ethnicity.* London and New Jersey: Zed Books.

South, A., and Lall, M. (2016). *Schooling and Conflict: Ethnic Education and Mother Tongue-based Teaching in Myanmar.* Yangon: The Asia Foundation.

Stepan, A.C. (1999). "Federalism and Democracy: Beyond the US Model". *Journal of Democracy* 10 (4): 19–34.

Wallis, J. (2014). *Constitution Making during State Building.* Cambridge and New York: Cambridge University Press.

Walton, M.J. (2008). "Ethnicity, Conflict, and History in Burma: The Myths of Panglong". *Asian Survey* 48 (6): 889–910.

_____ (2017). "National Political Dialogue and Practices of Citizenship in Myanmar". In *Citizenship in Myanmar: Ways of Being in and from Burma,* edited by A. South and M. Lall, 95–112. Singapore: ISEAS - Yusof Ishak Institute.

Weller, M., and Wolff, S. eds. (2005). *Autonomy, Self-governance and Conflict Resolution: Innovative Approaches to Institutional Design in Divided Societies.* Routledge Advances in International Relations and Global Politics: 33. London; New York: Routledge.

Weng, L. (2016). "Ethnic Armed Group Leaders Discuss Formation of a Burman State". *The Irrawaddy,* 27 July 2016. Accessed 28 July 2016. http://www.irrawaddy.com/burma/ethnic-armed-group-leaders-discuss-formation-of-a-burman-state.html.

World Bank Myanmar (2016). *A Country on the Move: Domestic Migration to the Regions of Myanmar.* Yangon: World Bank Myanmar.

Ye Mon, and Pyae Thet Phyo (2016). "Long-delayed Religion Census Reveals Only Modest Muslim Increase". *Myanmar Times,* 21 July 2016. Accessed 4 May 2017. http://www.mmtimes.com/index.php/national-news/21510-census-religion-data-reveals-decrease-in-percentage-of-buddhist-population.html.

Appendix 13.1: Survey questions and results regarding ethnic versus territorial federalism and equality

No.	Question	Before (average mean)	After (average mean)	%change ^	Modera-tion^^	%change ^^^	1		2		3		4		5	
							B	A	B	A	B	A	B	A	B	A
2	States should be based on ethnicity**	3.4789	3.0663	-8.3	-0.08	-7	13	18	26	50	28	28	67	43	32	27
4	All ethnic nationalities should have their own state**	3.2560	2.5723	-13.7	-0.05	-4	16	34	30	62	39	24	58	33	23	13
7	Small ethnic groups should have a self-administered area**	3.3976	3.0301	-7.4	-0.07	-6	9	20	28	42	51	35	44	51	34	18
8	All the existing regions should be merged to form one Bamar state	2.5181	2.2892	-4.6	-0.05	-4	48	64	39	44	40	19	23	24	16	15
9	Federalism will lead to secession**	2.1627	1.8614	-6.0	0.17	14	66	77	37	53	43	23	10	8	10	5
17	Most ethnic nationalities want independence*	4.2410	4.0663	-3.5	-0.14	-14	5	7	7	13	12	16	61	56	81	74
32	States should be based on geography and the economy**	3.4217	3.7000	5.6	0.10	9	13	6	18	15	44	34	68	78	23	33

*Statistically significant at $p=0.15$. **Statistically significant at $p=0.05$.
^As a proportion of the scale of possible answers (1 to 5).
^^Difference in standard deviation from the mean between first and second surveys.
^^^Change in standard deviation from the mean.
B=Before (first survey), A=After (second): Frequency of specified response on each survey.
1=Strongly disagree, 2=Disagree, 3=Neutral, 4=Agree, 5=Strongly agree.

14

THE EMERGENCE OF *DAWKALU* IN THE KAREN ETHNIC CLAIM IN THE 1880S AND THE BEGINNING OF CONTESTATIONS FOR "NATIVE RACES"

Hitomi Fujimura

It is widely accepted that language plays a vital role in the formation of nation as well as the sense of unity among its people (Anderson 2006; Gellner 1983). In a multilinguistic society such as Myanmar's,[1] language use has significant political implications at all levels of society. With over 135 officially designated ethnic groups, language is often seen as a marker to identify and differentiate one's individual identity.[2] In Myanmar, Burmese has been the dominant language of power and instruction since the country's independence in 1948 in ways which have marginalised other ethnic nationality groups. Successive governments sought unification through the Burmanisation of ethnic nationality areas, including through the standardisation of the Burmese language in schools and bans on publications in non-Burmese languages (Callahan 2003).

Much scholarly attention has been paid to the relationship between national identity, ethnicity and language. Language is not only a cultural resource which crafts a shared sense of unity amongst a group of people, but also has an instrumental function embedded in the process of nation-building. Benedict Anderson famously demonstrates the principal role that print capitalism has played in the formation of nations (Anderson 2006, 36). He argues that the mass distribution of information *vis a vis* the popular press helped to lay the foundation for a national consciousness in many parts of the world: "an imagined community among a specific assemble of fellow-readers" (ibid., 62).

In recent years, increasing attention has been paid to the development of the idea of nation in Burmese or the conceptual role of religion and nation in the formation of identity in Myanmar (eg. Candier 2019; Turner 2014). While there has been significant work written on Myanmar's multiple ethnic nationality movements, less attention has been paid to the semantics of how a sense of national consciousness emerged among non-Burmese or non-Buddhists. This chapter adds to this literature by providing a historical perspective on how the concept of nation came to be expressed in colonial Burma amongst the ethnic Sgaw Karen.[3]

The Karen are one of the largest ethnic nationality groups in Myanmar and have long been defined through their armed struggle for ethnic autonomy (eg Smith 1991; Thawnghmung 2012; South 2007).[4] Much of the scholarship on Karen nationalism tends to begin with the establishment of the Karen National Association (KNA) in 1881, whose members later appealed to the British authorities for an independent state of their own (Cady 1958, 138; Smith 1991, 45). The KNA was also a forerunner to the Karen National Union (KNU), which was formed in 1947 with the aim of advancing the Karen national cause, across linguistic, geographic and religious lines. In another paper I show the historical significance of the KNA and the importance of understanding their conceptual reference to "nation" in Sgaw Karen (Fujimura 2020). Based on this argument, this paper extends its focus to trace shifts in the usage of the Sgaw term *dawkalu,* nation, in the late nineteenth century and to clarify the political implications of the term.

It is important to acknowledge here the immense variation of the Karennic languages. Officially, there are eleven sub-groups in the Karennic language family, but linguists recognise over forty sub-groups within Karennic (Shintani 2003). Among those sub-groups, Sgaw and Pwo are the two largest groups. While Sgaw has relatively fewer dialects, there are many local differences within Pwo, especially in pronunciations and tones.[5] Because of this diversity within the Karennic languages, different scripts and orthographies have appeared.

The Karennic languages were originally oral languages without their own scripts or writing systems. Several Karen scripts, such as Baptist Sgaw, Baptist Pwo, Buddhist Pwo and Telakhon, were devised throughout the nineteenth century by religious leaders of each community (Womack 2005). It should be noted that those scripts developed alongside each religious aggregation, in conjunction with a growth in national consciousness in each religious community vis a vis British colonialism. The congruence of the Karen writing systems with their respective religious communities is key to understanding the difficulty in promoting a unified sense of nation among diverse Karen-speakers. Religious difference has been identified as one of the main factors driving internal disputes and secession movements from the main ethno-nationalist organisation, the Karen National Union (KNU) (Gravers 2007, 248).

This chapter provides a historical lens to the Karen national movement and how Sgaw Karen elites attempted to overcome these religious and linguistic divides. The argument is based on an in-depth analysis of historical documents written in Sgaw Karen. While acknowledging that there are many Karennic languages, special attention will be given to Sgaw Karen and the Baptist-oriented orthography because it is the very language that the KNA and its successors used in their official names and documents. The Sgaw Karen name of the KNA is *pwakanyaw dawkalu taohhpwoh* (ပှၤကညီဒီကလှာ်တၢ်အိၣ်ဖှိၣ်), and the KNU's official name is also in Sgaw Karen.[6] The political significance of the language allows us to trace the shifts of historical reference to concepts like nation and ethnicity.[7]

The chapter begins with a review of previous literature to clarify the analytical scope of the paper, followed by a brief summary of the importance of the American Baptist mission to Karen speakers. Following on from Anderson, in the third and fourth sections it examines the writings of early Sgaw Karen elites in print media, through which a specific expression of Karen national consciousness began to emerge and the notion of *dawkalu*. The background and intent of such self-expression will also be explained. Finally, the author discusses how political contestations for the status of "native races" begun as early as the late nineteenth century.

IDENTITY POLITICS IN MYANMAR

Since the political transition in 2011 and the inauguration of the National League for Democracy (NLD) in 2016, the landscape of ethnic politics in Myanmar has entered a new phase. As political tensions against Muslims harden, there is an urgent need to seriously engage with the dynamics of ethnic identity politics among the various peoples of Myanmar (Smith 2018, 27).

Myanmar's complex politics of nationhood is not a recent phenomenon. It is embedded in sixty years of ethno-nationalist conflict, which has its roots in the British colonial period. Under colonial rule the concept of nationhood amongst Myanmar's myriad ethnic groups transformed in significant ways. Yoshinari Watanabe examines the palm leaf manuscripts of the Burmese Court to highlight the difference between pre-colonial understandings of ethnic categories and their modern usage. He shows how the Burmese term *lumyo,* for example, commonly translated as "race" or "nation", was merely used to designate those who were subjects of other governing authorities than the Burmese kings, such as Chinese and Indians (Watanabe 2009, 32–35). The differences between various ethnic groups within the kingdom was not an important distinction for Burmese rulers. Rather, what mattered most was whether they were subject to the Burmese king's rule, and therefore taxable (see also Ito 2007). However, under colonial rule conceptual transformations and semantic shifts began to take place, in ways which highlighted the differences between different ethnic nationality groups.

Under British colonial rule, "race" became central to social organisation and the categorisation of colonial subjects, and British officers came up with intricate racial taxonomies of various groups according to scales of evolution and linguistic differences (Ferguson 2015). The British initially sought to categorise the indigenous people in Burma in the same manner as in India; alongside caste. But soon they realized that there was no such social system in Burma, and thus the difference in language and religion became useful indicators for classification. Jane Ferguson shows how British typologies of race were applied in the national census conducted by the British, fixing one's *amyo* with one's language (Ferguson 2015, 6). Aurore Candier (2019) demonstrates how British conceptualisations of race also came to resonate in local Burmese people's terms as a result of diplomatic interactions and negotiations between the Burmese Court and British colonial officers, with *amyo,* meaning "kind," and the idea of nation, *lumyo* (Candier 2019).

Studies of the contemporary period have turned their attention to the popular usage and understanding of the Burmese term *taing yin thar*. This term, usually translated in English as "native races" or "natives of the country" (Department of the Myanmar Language Commission 2011, 180), is deeply embedded in both popular and institutional understandings of citizenship, to the exclusion of groups like the Rohingya (Cheesman 2017; South and Lall 2018). While previous work has highlighted the political functionality of *taing yin thar* and *lumyo,* less attention has been paid to the fact that these terms tend to implicitly reflect the majority perception, since they are Burmese words. When used by the majority Burmese, *taing yin thar* usually designates only minority groups other than the Burmese. An article written by a Shan writer illustrates this well, stating: "it is felt that what is called *taing yin thar lumyo* means other non-Burmese people in everyone's mind" (Hsain Nyun Lwin 2019). For many ethnic nationality peoples, this term conceptually differentiates the Burmese from other various non-Burmese groups, assuming a politically central position of the former.[8]

An examination of these contested political concepts is essential to understanding contemporary Myanmar. However, while it is important to examine how different actors refer to *taing yin thar* and *lumyo* in the Burmese political domain, it is equally worth analysing how other actors comprehend such concepts in different languages and how their understandings and claims became a part of politics of "native races". To give an insight into how different languages used in Myanmar change the meaning of a concept like *taing yin thar,* the Karen case is telling.

In a monthly Karen newspaper called *Kayin Dhadinzin* (ကရင်သတင်းစဉ်, *KD*) in Burmese and *Kanyaw Takahsaw* (ကညီ တၢ်ကစီဉ်, *KT*) in Sgaw Karen,[9] some articles use the Sgaw Karen term *kaludoo* (ကလှာ်ဒူဉ်) as the equivalent term of *taing yin thar* (*KD* 2015, 7, 9; *KT* 2015, 2–3). However, the Sgaw Karen word, *kaludoo,* does not carry the same meaning as *taing yin thar,* "native people of the land." *Kaludoo* literally translates as "a family member of the kind." *Kalu* simply means "a kind," yet it is not an exclusive term designating human ethnic origin. It can be used in expressions to refer to kinds of trees or flowers. When this term is used with another word *pwa* (ပှၤ), meaning people, the literal translation would be "kind of people." *Doo* (ဒူဉ်) means "family" or "kinship."[10] The most recent English-Sgaw Karen dictionary defines *kaludoo* as "ethnic" or "ethnicity." Thus, *kaludoo* designates a sub-category of one group.[11]

This case cautions us not to take for granted a concept like *taing yin thar* as a universal term that can be widely applied for analyses across Myanmar and its ethnic groups. Instead, we should shift the focus to the concept itself and ask how the concept of "native people of the land" (which would become expressed by the concept of *taing yin thar* in Burmese in the twentieth century), came into play in the first place. The following sections examine how this occurred for Karen Baptists in the late nineteenth century, engaged in the politics of "native races" as they began asserting their claims for a Karen nation. Given the ethnic diversity of the country, a multilingual approach should also be applied to understanding the past.

THE AMERICAN BAPTIST MISSION: EARLY KAREN ENCOUNTERS WITH RACE AND NATION

Karen interactions with the American Baptist mission in Myanmar are important when tracing the emergence of the concept of nation among Karen speakers. As Ikeda (2012) shows in his examination of historical sources, the existing Karen ethnic discourse was heavily influenced by the mission in the nineteenth century. The American Baptist mission reached Burma in 1813 and concentrated their efforts amongst ethnic animist groups like the Karen, where Buddhism had not proliferated. The first baptism among the Karen population took place fifteen years later in 1828 (*American Baptist Magazine* 1829, 244). In the 1830s and 1840s, there were many Karen conversions in Tenasserim and the Irrawaddy delta region. Local community-based mission denominations were set up in Tavoy, Moulmein, Bassein and Rangoon, where numerous mission schools were established.

One characteristic of the early Karen Baptist mission was the development of the Sgaw Karen characters and orthography. Rev. Jonathan Wade was prompted to devise a Sgaw Karen script around 1830 to assist with Christian missionisation. Wade describes how he encountered a group of Karen speakers during a missionisation trip in the vicinity of Tavoy, when an elder stepped forward and asked him whether he was the one to bring "the lost Karen script and book" (Wade n.d.). Wade began his work creating a Karen script, aided by his Mon assistant, Myat Kyaw, who was also fluent in Sgaw, Pwo and Burmese. They combined the Burmese and Mon scripts to transcribe the sound of the language properly. Karen evangelists associated this Baptist-oriented Sgaw Karen scrip with their oral tradition in their preaching (*Hsa Too Gaw,* HTG 1846, 174), which is later known as the "Karen's lost Golden Book."[12]

With the newly devised Sgaw Karen script, the American missionaries started to publish schoolbooks and other publications in Sgaw Karen around 1832 (*Baptist Missionary Magazine* 1833, 201). During this period missionaries began to systematically collect and record Karen vocabulary. The vast vocabulary collections found in Karen dictionaries and vocabulary books that were published in the 1840s show no reference to either *kaludoo* or *dawkalu* (Mason 1843; Wade 1849; Kau Too and Wade 1847, 1848). The comprehensive *Sgaw Karen Vocabulary,* edited by Wade and published in 1849, has an entry for "every nation", but is translated as *myo myo kalukalu* (မျိုမျို ကလုာ်ကလုာ်) (Wade 1849, 862). "*Myo*" is a Burmese term carrying the same meaning as *kalu* (kind). When repeated, those terms function as an adjective, in the same way as Burmese. Therefore, the given translation simply means "various kinds of." The absence of the terms *kaludoo* or *dawkalu* in these early Karen dictionaries shows that they were not popular or common among Sgaw Karen speakers in the 1840s.

Educational work was central to the American Baptist mission and the Karen orthography was the first subject to be taught to Karen children. The number of literate Karen Baptists gradually increased as the mission expanded. The Karen Theological Seminary,[13] Pegu High School and Rangoon Baptist College were the main Baptist institutions for higher education and these schools became seminal for Karen encounters with Western ways of thinking, including ideas related to race and nationalism.

These ideas were translated and transmitted to the Karen Baptist community through school textbooks and in class. An initial example is a geography textbook written by Ellen Mason, wife of Rev. Francis Mason: *Lee Hawkhoh, Geography: Ancient and Modern.* Most of its contents were identical to the geography textbooks widely used in America and Britain in those days, but Mason herself wrote the section describing British Burma and its people. A section was entitled "Race" in English and "*pwakanyaw a kalu*" in Sgaw Karen (Mason 1861, 7). The first Sgaw Karen term *pwakanyaw* means "human" as well as "Karen-speakers", depending on the context. The second word *a* is the possessive case, and *kaḷu* means "kind," as explained above.

Mason also inserted her own description of the variety of Karen-speaking people in Burma. This section was entitled "Karen tribes, *Pwakanyaw hpoh adoo tapha*" (ibid., 18).[14] The term *pwakanyaw* here should be translated as "Karen speakers," since it is comparable to "Karen" in English. Translated directly, the Sgaw Karen title means "Karen (*pwakanyaw hpoh*[15]) families (*adoo tahpa*[16])". To the best of the author's knowledge, this is one of the earliest references to the term *doo* to express a human ethnic trait. Although *doo* simply designates one's family relationship or kinship, it is obvious that it here designates the term "tribe," as shown in the English title. It should be noted that this was an American missionary's writing and not a work by Karen converts themselves. Yet this exemplifies how the Baptist education began to transmit Western concepts of thought around human classification and race into the Sgaw Karen Baptist community.

Karen converts' experiences outside of class also laid the foundation for their understanding of race, nation and human classification. Sponsored by the American mission, a selection of Karen Baptist youth studied at universities in America for periods of up to six to nine years. These experiences were formidable in influencing a growing Karen elite in Western understandings of race and nation. One of the first generation of Karen students studying abroad, Theodore Thanbyah, wrote of his experiences with racist attitudes in America (Thanbyah 1920). He retrospectively narrated his own experience in his autobiography in 1920, explaining that some Americans yelled at him on the railway, calling him a "negro," to move away from the seat he was sitting in so they could occupy it (ibid., 70–71). His experience studying in America, wrote Thanbyah, suggested to him "that American people did not wish to be with non-White people" (ibid.). The concept of race and nation gradually appears to have taken hold amongst Sgaw Karen intellectuals close to the Baptist mission as a dominant category of reference. As shown in Thanbyah's story, both inside and outside of class, some young Karen Baptists felt a strong racial consciousness and a growing understanding of its socio-political significance.

THE BEGINNING OF SGAW KAREN EXPRESSIONS OF "NATION": THE FORMATION OF THE KNA

As far as existing documents suggest, the term *dawkalu* was first used by Karen Baptists to refer to themselves in 1881 with the establishment of the Karen National Association (KNA). A group of Karen Baptist intellectuals, including Thanbyah and others who had studied in the United States, became interested in developing a Karen ethnic organisation after their audience with the Governor General of India at the end of 1880, Viceroy Lord Ripon (Fujimura 2020). When Lord Ripon privately visited Rangoon at the end of December of 1880, Thanbyah and Rev. Saw Tay,[17] after their discussion with another Karen teacher Shwe Maung Oung,[18] succeeded in meeting the Viceroy himself. Through their conversation, they learned that the Viceroy would meet with residents of Rangoon, including members of Burmese, Chinese, and Indian populations. This experience triggered the idea to form an association representing the interests of the Karen-speaking community and initial claims to a nation of their own (ibid.).

The founders of the KNA considered it important to negotiate with colonial officers on behalf of other Karen people to secure their rights within Burma on their own terms. One of the founders, Salu, wrote in retrospect about the moment they decided to form the KNA, formed primarily as an entity which would give the Karen a voice to negotiate directly with the British colonial government: [19]

> [a]fter the audience with the Viceroy Lord Ripon, Shwe Maung Oung said that "it should not be as it is. If we do not request the same as others asked for, their influence would be so large that we can do nothing about it. So, we ought to demand for ourselves and we will stand up" (HTG 1906, 190–191).

They named the organisation *pwakanyaw dawkalu taohhpwoh,* literally translated as Karen National Meeting (or Association), using the Sgaw Karen word *dawkalu*. Given that there was no recorded use of the term prior to the 1870s, it is possible to assume that the term *dawkalu* must have been created by Karen Baptist intellectuals during the period in the lead-up to the establishment of the KNA. It remains unknown whether the KNA founders took other nationalist movements in other parts of the world as their model, but it appears that they saw it as important to express the notion of "nation" in their own language. The establishment of the KNA also saw the beginnings of Karen claims to the British government that they were a nation of their own, separate to the Burmese.

THE UNSUCCESSFUL PROMOTION OF THE IDEA OF *DAWKALU* TO KAREN PEOPLE

The establishment of the KNA was indeed a landmark moment for ethnic politics in colonial Burma. However, the KNA membership was very limited, relying on the inner-circle friendship and kinship networks of Karen Baptist educated elites in Rangoon. The usage of the term *dawkalu* as a reference to the Karen "nation" was also limited among other ordinary Karen-speakers, especially from other linguistic and religious groups. Given these circumstances, the KNA sought to actively promote the idea of *dawkalu* to its future followers.

In 1885, the KNA established a newsletter under the name *Pwakanyaw dawkalu atapayuh* (ပှၤကညီ ဒီကလုာ် အတၢ်ပရၢ, *Karen National News*),[20] often referred to in short form as "*dawkalu*" or "*dawkalu atapayuh*." Founded by Thanbyah and three others, it was written in Sgaw Karen and printed in Bassein, with a subscription fee of four rupees. Thanbyah later recalled that the actual subscribers were very few, limiting the circulation of the *Karen National News* (Thanbyah 1913, 94). Their readership was also limited by the fact that it was written in the Sgaw Karen writing system, which was only accessible the Karen Baptist community. Indeed, the work of these early Karen nationalists was not available to non-Sgaw speakers or non-Baptist Karens who had not learned how to read such characters.

Additionally, the *Karen National News* was not widely known even within the Karen Baptist community, because much of the geographically dispersed Karen church was not familiar with the activities of the KNA. Thanbyah recalled in retrospect that their association decided to hold a general meeting once every three years, and that there were few attendees (Thanbyah 1913, 88).[21] This was also reflected in their low subscription numbers. Thus, even though the intention of the newsletter was to develop a concept of nation among Karen people, even amongst Sgaw speakers their promotion of the expression of *dawkalu* was highly limited to a select few.

Despite these limitations, the KNA continued to promote a sense of Karen unity and nationalism in their interactions with the colonial government. For example, in February 1887 KNA members encouraged the Karen Baptist community to travel to Rangoon and attend the ceremony celebrating the Queen's Golden Jubilee as a symbol of Karen unity and support for the British government (HTG 1887, 18–19). The Chief Commissioner of Burma invited British generals, officials, and other personnel to attend the ceremony. The names of the Burmese delegates from Mandalay can be found in the article which reported the program of the ceremony in the *Rangoon Gazette Weekly Budget* (1887, 16–17). Delegates from the KNA also got the chance to attend the ceremony and deliver a message to the Queen, as the representative of the local subjects of British Burma (HTG 1887, 40).[22]

Even though the letter was read out in English at the commemoration, Thanbyah later recalled that it was prepared in two languages, English and Sgaw Karen (Thanbyah 1913, 110).[23] After praising the Queen's fifty years of peaceful reign, the letter said that blessings had arrived for the Karen people since British rule began in Burma in 1826 when they were "liberated from the bad government" (HTG 1887, 42). They obtained blessings in two ways, physically and mentally. Their physical development concerned the increase in their social status, property, and level of education. It was also noted that British officers helped to provide education for the Karen. In the letter they suggested their mental development was mainly a result of Karen people's conversion to Christianity and the rejection of animism (ibid.).

A closer examination of the wording in the Sgaw Karen letter helps to comprehend how the KNA's claim of nation or *dawkalu* was understood in their own terms. There is only one sentence in which the term *dawkalu* was used in the Sgaw Karen version. To interpret the implication of this reference precisely, the phrasing of the letter is very clear, as shown below (punctuation added by the author in italics):

> ...The days under British rule were the time of blessing for *us as one race*....
>
> ...When it was started, *we, one race,* lived under the governance of the English and were liberated from the evil rule and murders....
>
> ...*We Karen* acquired the gospel, believed in Jesus Christ, and became free of all obstacles....
>
> ...*We, the Karen as a nation,* are grateful for the majesty's golden jubilee altogether.... (ibid., 42–43).

As shown in the above extract, the sentences often indicate that "we", the sender of the letter, are "the Karen"(*pwakanyaw*), which is also paraphrased as "one race" (*pwa takalu*). One line reads that "we, the Karen as a nation," implying that the Karen race (*pwakanyaw takalu*) is equivalent to a nation (*dawkalu*). It is noteworthy that the term *dawkalu* is embedded within the narrative, suggesting a greater sense of unity amongst the Karen people than was the case. The wording in this letter, as a whole, gave the impression to its readers that the Karen-speaking population was one united race that could be called a nation.

The contents of the address to the Queen was made public through the KNA's newsletter *The Karen National News* and reprinted in *The Morning Star.* Both periodicals were written in Sgaw Karen and circulated among the Karen Baptist community, and thus the message it carried was only revealed to the subscribers of these two newspapers, mostly Sgaw Karen Baptists. This implies that, even though the letter suggested that the KNA represented all Karen-speakers as one united group, their work was only accessible to the Karen Baptist community. While the KNA hoped that publishing their commemoration letter for the Golden Jubilee of 1887 would help to stir a sense of nation among the Sgaw Karen-speaking population, they made little attempts to reach Karen people outside of the Baptist community. And yet, even within the Baptist community itself, these efforts were far from successful. In October of the same year, the KNA held its general meeting in Rangoon. A short entry in *The Morning Star* reported that there were only eleven Baptist Karen pastors assembled for the meeting (HTG 1887, 162). Indeed, despite their efforts, the KNA was still struggling to get attention from Sgaw Karen Baptist members, and the notion of *dawkalu* or "nation" was still limited to a small number of intellectuals.

LOCALISATION OF THE CONCEPT OF NATION AND THE POLITICS OF "NATIVE RACES" IN COLONIAL BURMA

The observations made above demonstrate the limited reach of the KNA and their attempts to create a sense of nation amongst the Karen. As described, the localisation of the concept of nation, *dawkalu,* was initiated by a small minority of Karen Baptist intellectuals in the early 1880s in the founding of the KNA. The KNA was established to negotiate and communicate with British officers and the colonial administration in a collective form on behalf of a so-called unified Karen nation, which its leading members claimed to represent. The term *dawkalu* was formulated by Sgaw Karen Baptist intellectuals in order to assert (in Sgaw Karen) the notion of a nation amongst the Karen people to British administrators.

While the term *dawkalu* was used in Karen publications to introduce the idea of nation to the Karen-speaking community, their reach was limited. As per Anderson's (2006) notion of nationalism, the development of these newsletters was significant at the time, as it signalled a clear attempt from Karen intellectuals to communicate with ordinary people and to invoke a mutual sense of a Karen nation by referring to *dawkalu*. It was clear from these publications that Karen intellectuals also saw the political benefits of advocating for a shared conceptual understanding of nationhood amongst those they claimed to represent.

Although it was a small movement concentrated in an inner-circle of Sgaw Karen Baptists and rather unsuccessful, the KNA promotion of the concept of *dawkalu* as well as the creation of the term itself was quite modern in two ways. First, it was modern because of the very idea of making a claim to nation. Second, the promotion of the concept through printed newspapers was also very modern at the time. In this sense, it can be said that the print language made it possible for the Karen nation to be "imagined", as Anderson insightfully argues.

While acknowledging the historical significance of these claims and the power of print language to articulate them, this case study also illuminates the limited power of nationalist projects amongst communities as diverse as the Karen. The intellectual claims of KNA members to represent a collective understanding of Karen nationhood was in many ways invalid. Even though Karen Baptist intellectuals started to make use of the idea of *dawkalu* for their own political purposes, they only publicised their assertions in Sgaw Karen, despite the linguistic diversity of Karen speakers whom they aimed to embrace. Its linguistic novelty must have made it difficult to immediately comprehend the meaning of the term *dawkalu* even within the Sgaw Karen-speaking communities. The concept itself was new, and the term to designate nation had an inherent linguistic limitation, since it was also built off Western ideas and thought.

Furthermore, the newspapers, the modern means to make a nation imagined, also hindered the collective imagination of the broader Karen community. The KNA's organisational newsletter and commemorational letter were written in the Baptist-made Sgaw Karen script and did not attempt to engage other writing scripts or religious communities. Thus, the message could only be conveyed to the limited number of Karen Baptists who were literate in the Baptist-oriented orthography. In this sense, their writings did not reach non-Baptist Karens who made up the majority of the

Karen-speaking population and they were unable to promote a common sense of nation amongst those they claimed to represent.

It is interesting to recall here the process in which *amyo* and *lumyo* in Burmese developed in conjunction with the Western concept of race and nation in the nineteenth century and how the ideas of *pwakalu* and *dawalu* in Sgaw Karen synchronously emerged as well. In both Burmese and Sgaw Karen communities, political elites responded to the British colonial state's development of racial categories and sharpened their articulations of such categories and meanings in their own languages. This fact lends itself to a re-examination of the conceptual roots of nation and nationhood in Burma. Indeed, a conception of nation did not emerge first among Burmans as *lumyo*, and then was subsequently imposed upon other language speakers or ethnic groups. Rather, the development and politics of nation were contemporaneous in the two languages (and likely others) and correlative with various vernacular groups. The political projects of other ethnic groups are just as significant in their adoption of racial concepts as their Burmese counterparts.

The other element this case study illuminates is the KNA's eagerness for self-representation as native peoples of the country. The KNA claimed their nation because they sensed the need to differentiate themselves from the majority Burmese-speakers. As the majority, the British government regarded the Burmese as the primary, most important local population.[24] The colonial perception tacitly generated a sense that people who fell into the British colonial category of *Bama lumyo* were de facto entitled to political privilege as *the* local natives. Yet the vernacular term *Bama lumyo* which gradually resonated with colonial political arrangements was originally a category of human traits merely designating Burmese-speakers.

The influence of Western concepts of nationalism pushed Karen Baptist elites to come up with a neologism *dawkalu*, aiming to claim their own distinctiveness as a separate nation of British Burma. The commemorational letter was a highlight of this political attempt. As already shown, one sentence in the letter reads "*We, the Karen as a nation*, are grateful for the majesty's golden jubilee altogether", indicating the Karen nation rejoicing in the Queen's Jubilee as a member of British Burma. This commemoration speech also underscored the Karen peoples' support for the British, in contrast to the Burmese Buddhist community who aimed to resist the colonial government (see Aung-Thwin 2011; Turner 2014). What matters here is not that Karen people showed their support for the colonial government, but that their claim was explicitly political: to be recognised by the official authority as a distinctive nation of Burma.

The KNA's attempt to highlight their status as a legitimate nation of Burma also speaks to today's politics of *taing yin thar* and the way ethnic groups appropriate this Burmese term as a way of maintaining their legitimacy as a national race, within the nation of Myanmar. An examination of historical records shows how the political assertion of native-ness by non-Burmese was already at work in the late nineteenth century, initially among the elite Karen Baptists. Although the political significance of the term *taing yin thar* only became apparent around the time of independence, it is possible to render another historical landscape that the vernacular politics with "*taing yin thar*" type of thinking preceded and was at play many years prior.

CONCLUDING REMARKS: REFLECTIONS ON THE CONTEMPORARY SITUATION

This chapter has provided an analysis of historical documents to examine the linguistic development of the Sgaw Karen term nation (*dawkalu)* and how it was used to promote a sense of unity, ushering in the politics of "native races" in the late nineteenth century. Although the Sgaw Karen term *dawkalu* was initially used among a select few of Karen Baptist intellectuals in Rangoon, this political project preceded what was later to become one of Myanmar's strongest ethno-nationalist insurgencies. While the creation of the Karen National Union in 1947 saw these aims realised in an armed struggle for an independent Karen nation, political attempts to build a distinct sense of ethnic identity and nationhood *vis a vis* the Burmese has a much longer history.

Focusing on the language and writing systems through which the concept of nation was first expressed by Sgaw Karen elites, this paper also points to the intrinsic issues which the nationalist movement has faced since its very inception. With diversity in languages and religious communities spread over a vast geographical area, the notion of a unified Karen conception of nation has been difficult to achieve through oral communications, speech and especially print media over time. The inability of the KNA to convey the new concept of nation through the novel term *dawkalu* to a wider audience clearly demonstrates this.

This challenge of diversity within the Karen ethno-nationalist movement has persisted throughout the twentieth century, into the contemporary era (see Gravers 1996; Rajah 2002; South 2007; Thawnghmung 2012). While Karen political leaders have attempted to cultivate a sense of unity amongst different Karen communities, the concept of nation or *dawkalu* still tends to represent the interests of a minority from the Baptist-oriented Sgaw Karen. The KNU's own history testifies to such internal hardship, as it experienced a series of scissions among themselves, primarily along the axis of linguistic, religious, and socioeconomic divides (see Gravers 1999, 91–95; South 2007, 61–62).

By unravelling how the politics of native races came to play out in the Sgaw Karen nationalist project of the late nineteenth century, this chapter also stresses the importance of turning academic attention towards a multilinguistic analysis of the diverse histories of the development of terms such as *lumyo* (nation) and indeed, *taing yin thar*. Alongside the Burmese, the development of understandings of nationalism and nationhood have been deeply contested political projects across ethnic groups in Myanmar for many years.

Notes

1. In this chapter, "Myanmar" is used to designate the country after its independence. "Burma" is used to discuss the country when it was subject to colonial rule.
2. This list of 135 ethnic groups is based on arbitrary classification systems which stem back to the colonial era (see Ferguson 2015).
3. Sgaw Karen is one of the two major sub-groups of the Karennic languages.
4. Thawnghmung (2012) argues that the image of Karen as being aggressively anti-Burmese is superficial and depicts how the "other" Karen live differently as well as quietly in Burma.
5. Other Karennic speakers, such as Bwe, Paku, Monei, and Mobwa, are concentrated on the eastern side of Toungoo.
6. *Pwakanyaw Dawkalu Suhhpwohkayuh* (ပှၤကညီ ဒီကလုာ် စၢဖိုၣ်ကရၢ).
7. This claim requires more study about the art of reference in other Karennic languages. In this sense, this chapter is limited by its particular focus on the Sgaw Karen, thus excluding the political paradigms possibly taking place in other languages than Sgaw. The author does not intend to suggest the Sgaw Karen is only the Karennic language that should be considered. However, it is still very difficult to conduct a historical analysis of other Karennic languages due to the limited number of archival documents.

8. See Walton (2013) to understand how "Burman privilege" has been institutionalised throughout Myanmar's modern history and how this is likely to impede possible inter-ethnic coalitions in the future.
9. This newspaper had been printed in Burmese and Sgaw Karen for a long period of time. It appears that the editorial board became more conscious of the linguistic variety of Karen languages, as it started to include articles written in Pwo Karen in 2017.
10. Derivatively, it also means "house", where family members live together.
11. In newspaper articles or other writings in Sgaw Karen, usually *pwa htee hpoh kaw hpoh* (ပှၤထံဖိကိၢ်ဖိ) is used for national citizens, literally meaning "people of the land."
12. Stern analyses how Karen speakers understood the socio-political changes along with their oral tradition differently in the nineteenth century (Stern 1968).
13. Initially established in Moulmein in 1845, removed to British Burma's new capital in 1859.
14. The subsequent description concerns different Karen-speaking populations, including Sgaw, Pwo, Bwe, Paku, Monei, Mopwa, Kaya, and more (Mason 1861, 18–22).
15. *Hpoh* in Sgaw Karen means "a child", but it has been commonly used to designate "human" or "people."
16. *Tahpa* is an affix indicating plural forms of the preceding word.
17. Saw Tay was Thanbyah's cousin, and they studied together in bible schools in Bassein. After his baptism in 1851, he attended the Karen theological seminary from 1855 to 1858. After his graduation, he started to work in the same school as a Karen teacher (HTG 1891, 186). He was ordained in 1862. He was dedicated to education in the seminary, while serving on the Burma Baptist Convention and as the editor of *The Morning Star*, in Sgaw, *Hsa Too Gaw* (Shwe Nu 1895, 75–76). He died in Rangoon in 1911 (ibid., 185–186).
18. Shwe Maung Oung was a Sgaw Karen schoolmaster born in Rangoon in 1835 or 1836. Shwe Maung Oung acted as the first Accountant of the KNA in 1881 (Thanbyah 1913, 89).
19. For a more detailed examination and discussion, see Fujimura 2020.
20. *Tapayuh* means "news" in Sgaw Karen. Since *a* (အ) is an affix expressing the possessive case, *atapayuh* means "news of".
21. For example, only eleven pastors and evangelists appeared at the 1887 meeting (HTG 1887, 163).
22. These delegates were Shwe Maung Oung, Thanbyah, Maung Lu Ni, Saw Tay, Tha Lu, Ti Thu Maung, and Shwe Nyaw (HTG 1887, 41). When their turn came, the Acting Chief Commissioner, Sir Crosthwaite, approached and stopped in front of the Karen delegates' seats. After a British officer read out a

brief statement to initiate delivery of an address to the Queen a Karen delegate stood up and read aloud a letter to Queen Victoria in English (*Rangoon Gazette Weekly Budget* 1887, 40). Then, Sir Crosthwaite replied, saying that the KNA's letter would surely be delivered to the Queen (HTG 1887, 40).

23. The original manuscripts may not exist today, as the author has not yet been able to find them, but the complete texts are accessible in both languages. The Sgaw Karen version was published and circulated in *The Morning Star* in 1887, and the whole English text was published in the *Rangoon Gazette Weekly Budget*.
24. This understanding is well exemplified in the speech made by Charles Bernard, the Chief Commissioner in most of the 1880s, stating that "[T]he Burmese are by far the most numerous and most important" among the local peoples (Bernard 1887, 72).

References

Anderson, B. (2006). *Imagined Communities: Reflections on the Origin and Spread of Nationalism* (Revised Edition). London and New York: Verso.

Aung-Thwin, M. (2011). *The Return of the Galon King: History, Law and Rebellion in Colonial Burma*. Singapore: NUS Press.

Bernard, C. (1887). "Burma: The New British Province". *The Scottish Geographical Magazine* 4: 66–83.

Cady, J.F. (1958). *A History of Modern Burma*. Ithaca and London: Cornell University Press.

Callahan, M. (2003). "Language Policy in Modern Burma". In *Fighting Words, Language Policy and Ethnic Relations in Asia,* edited by M. Brown and G. Sumit. Cambridge, MA: MIT Press, 143–175.

Candier, A. (2019). "Mapping Ethnicity in Nineteenth Century Burma: When 'Categories of People' (*lumyo*) Became 'Nations'". *Journal of Southeast Asian Studies* 50 (3): 347–364.

Cheesman, N. (2017). "How in Myanmar National Races Came to Surpass Citizenship and Exclude Rohingya". *Journal of Contemporary Asia* 47 (3): 461–483.

Department of the Myanmar Language Commission (2011). *Myanmar-English Dictionary.* Naypyidaw: Ministry of Education, Union of Myanmar.

Drum Publication Group (2008). *Drum Karen-English Student Dictionary.* Thailand: Drum Publication Group.

Ferguson, J. (2015.) "Who's Counting? Ethnicity, Belonging, and the National Census in Burma/Myanmar". *Bijdragen tot de Taal-, Land-, en Volkenkunde* 171 (1): 1–28.

Fujimura, H. (2020). "Disentangling the Colonial Narrative of the Karen National Association of 1881: The Motive Behind Karen Baptist Intellectuals' Claim for a Nation". *Journal of Burma Studies* 24 (2).

Gellner, E. (1983). *Nations and Nationalism.* Oxford: Blackwell.

Gravers, M. (1996). "The Karen Making of a Nation". In *Asian Forms of the Nation,* edited by S. Tønnesson and H. Antlöv. Richmond: Curzon Press, 237–269.

____ (1999). *Nationalism as Political Paranoia in Burma: An Essay on the Historical Practice of Power*. Richmond: Curzon.

____ (2007). "Conversion and Identity: Religion and the Formation of Karen Ethnic Identity in Burma". In *Exploring Ethnic Diversity in Burma,* edited by M. Gravers. Copenhagen: NIAS Press, 227–258.

Hsain Nyun Lwin (2019). "Thain Yin Thar Hsoda Barle (What is so-called Thaing yin dar?)". *Mizzima Daily,* November 25.

Ikeda, K. (2012). "An Outline of Knowledge Formation on the Karen People of Burma and Saw Aung Hla's 'A History of the Pgakanyaw' (1939)". *The Bulletin of Institute for Advanced Studies on Asia* 162: 154–266 (in Japanese).

Ito, T. (2007). "Karens and the Konbaung Polity in Myanmar". *ACTA ASIATICA* 92: 89–108.

Kau Too, Sau and Wade, J. (eds.) (2001[1847]). *Thesaurus of Karen Knowledge, Comprising Traditions, Legends or Fables, Poetry, Customs, Superstitions, Demonology, Therapeutics, etc.* Cephas Bennett revised in 1915, Vol.1. Tavoy: Karen Mission Press (in Sgaw Karen).

—— (2001 [1848]). *Thesaurus of Karen Knowledge, Comprising Traditions, Legends or Fables, Poetry, Customs, Superstitions, Demonology, Therapeutics, etc.* Cephas Bennett revised in 1915, Vol.2. Tavoy: Karen Mission Press (in Sgaw Karen).

Lieberman, V.B. (1978). "Ethnic Politics in Eighteenth Century Burma". *Modern Asian Studies* 12 (3): 455–482.

Mason, E.M. (1861). *Lee Hawkhoh: Geography: Ancient and Modern.* Moulmein: American Baptist Press (in Sgaw Karen).

Mason, F. (1846). *Synopsis of a Grammar of the Karen Language, Embracing Both Dialects, Sgau and Pgho, or Sho.* Tavoy: Karen Mission Press (English, Sgaw Karen, and Pwo Karen).

Rajah, A. (2002). "A 'Nation of Intent' in Burma: Karen Ethno-nationalism, Nationalism, and Narration of Nation". *The Pacific Review* 15 (4): 517–537.

Shintani, T. (2003). "Classification of Brakaloungic (Karenic) Languages in Relation to their Tonal Evolution". In *Proceedings of the Symposium Cross-linguistic Studies of Tonal Phenomena: Historical Development, Phonetics of Tone, and Descriptive Studies,* edited by S. Kaji. Tokyo: Research Institute for Languages and Cultures of Asia and Africa, 37–54.

Shwe Nu (ed.) (1895). *Saymanayree Ayhoobalee Akhawhtee Tablaw (1845-1895) (The First Jubilee of the Seminary (1845-1895)).* Insein: Seminary Press (in Sgaw Karen).

Smith, M. (1991). *Burma: Insurgency and the Politics of Ethnicity.* London: Zed Books.

—— (2018). "Ethnic Politics and Citizenship in History in Citizenship in Myanmar: Ways of Being in and from Burma". In *Citizenship in Myanmar, Ways of Being in and from Burma,* edited by A. South and M. Lall. Singapore: ISEAS-Yusof Ishak Institute and Chiang Mai University Press, 26–58.

South, A. (2007). "Karen Nationalist Communities: The 'Problem' of Diversity". *Journal of Contemporary Southeast Asia* 29 (1): 55–76.

—— (2008). *Ethnic Politics in Burma: States of Conflict*. London: Routledge.

South, A. and Lall, M. (2018). "Introduction". In *Citizenship in Myanmar, Ways of Being in and from Burma,* edited by A. South and M. Lall. Singapore: ISEAS-Yusof Ishak Institute and Chiang Mai University Press, 1–25.

Stern, T. (1968). "Ariya and the Golden Book: A Millenarian Buddhist Sect among the Karen". *The Journal of Asian Studies* 27 (2): 297–328.

Thanbyah, T. (1913). *Pwakanyaw Daw Atadohhtaw Htawhtaw (1854-1914)* (*Karens and their Development (1854-1914)*). Yangon: Missionary Press (in Sgaw Karen).

——. (1920). *Pwamweeleh tatagha athathamoo* (*A Life of Pilgrim*). Rangoon: Hanthawaddy Press (in Sgaw Karen).

Thawnghmung, A.M. (2012). *The 'Other' Karen in Myanmar: Ethnic Minorities and the Struggle Without Arms*. Plymouth: Lexington Books.

Turner, A. (2014). *Saving Buddhism: The Impermanence of Religion in Colonial Burma.* Honolulu: University of Hawai'i Press.

Wade, J. (1849). *A Vocabulary of the Sgau Karen Language.* Tavoy: Karen Mission Press (in Sgaw Karen).

Wade, J. and Binney, J. (eds.) (1883). *The Anglo-Karen Dictionary*. Rangoon: American Baptist Mission Press (in Sgaw Karen).

____ (n.d.). The First Twenty Years of the Mission to the Karens of Burma: 1828–48. Unpublished.

Walton, M.J. (2013). "The 'Wages of Burman-ness': Ethnicity and Burman Privilege in Contemporary Myanmar". *Journal of Contemporary Asia* 43 (1): 1–27.

Watanabe, Y. (2009). "Ethnic Policy towards Various 'Peoples' in the Early Konbaung Dynasty: Ethnic Awareness in Eighteenth to Nineteenth Century Burma". In *The Changing Self Image of Southeast Asian Society during the 19th and 20th Centuries,* edited by Y. Ishii. Tokyo: Tokyo Bunko.

Womack, W. (2005). "Literate Networks and the Production of Sgaw and Pwo Karen Writing in Burma, c. 1830-1930". Doctoral Dissertation at School of Oriental and African Studies, University of London.

Periodicals

American Baptist Magazine (English)
Baptist Missionary Magazine (English)
Hsa Too Gaw (ဆၣ်တူၢ်ဂီၤ/ The Morning Star : HTG) (Sgaw Karen)
Kayin Dhadinzin (ကရင်သတင်းစဉ်: KD) (Burmese)
Kayaw Takahsaw (ကညီ တၢ်ကစီၣ်: KT*)* (Sgaw Karen)
Rangoon Gazette Weekly Budget (English)

15

THE AMBIGUITIES OF CITIZENSHIP STATUS IN MYANMAR

Peggy Brett*

Section 2 of Myanmar's 1982 Citizenship Law defines four categories – "citizens", "associate" citizens, "naturalised" citizens, and "foreigners".[1] "Foreigner" is a residual category containing all those not falling within one of the other categories; legally, therefore, no ambiguity should exist about an individual's status. Despite this, there are a considerable number of people in Myanmar whose citizenship status could be described as ambiguous. These include: those formally identified through policies and documentation as of undetermined citizenship (notably National Verification Card (NVC) holders); those whose situation is not defined in the law; those who have no formal proof of citizenship and so struggle to access rights associated with citizens; and "associate" and "naturalised" citizens. The scope of the problem is illustrated by the 2014 Population and Housing Census, which found that only 69.8 per cent of those enumerated had one of the three sorts of citizenship card (Union of Myanmar 2015, 2).[2]

There has been little scholarly discussion of these ambiguities. Discussions have instead been dominated by the linked issues of ethnicity, *taing yin tha* status[3] and the Rohingya. Zawacki (2012) sets out briefly the

*The views expressed are solely my own and do not necessarily represent those of the Center for Diversity and National Harmony.

centrality of citizenship and discrimination to "the Rohingya problem". Leider (2014) and Tonkin (2018) provide detailed explorations of the history of Rakhine State, engaging the question of Rohingya claims to be *taing yin tha*, while Ardeth Maung Thawnghmung (2016) examines in detail the narratives put forward by Rohingya and Rakhine actors. Rohingya scholars such as Islam (2018) have also set out their views of the Citizenship Law and the discriminatory practices that continue to exclude the Rohingya. Meanwhile Cheesman (2017) has highlighted the problematic nature of the concept of *taing yin tha* itself. Broadening the discussion, Nyi Nyi Kyaw (2017) emphasises how the failure to implement the Citizenship Law and documentary practices have contributed to the statelessness of the Rohingya and Pugh (2013) stresses the multi-faceted nature of citizenship and inclusion to argue that legal citizenship alone would not resolve the problem of the Rohingya's exclusion. Gibson, James, and Falvey (2016) use a human security approach to explore the relationship between citizenship and insecurity in the context of Rakhine State. Moving away from the situation of the Rohingya, Ho and Chua (2016) explore the situation of the Chinese, while Nyi Nyi Kyaw (2015) has highlighted the situation of non-Rohingya Muslims in Myanmar and explored the concept of "mixed races". The Citizenship Law itself has been scrutinised by the UN Refugee Agency (UNHCR) (2018), José-María Arraiza and Olivier Vonk (2017), the Center for Diversity and National Harmony (2018) and the International Commission of Jurists (2019). Moving away from considerations of citizenship as a legal status, Lall (2018) and Lall et al. (2014) explore how citizenship is understood by citizens and Walton (2018) discusses political participation as a key element of transformative citizenship.

Ambiguity of status is implicitly present in many of these scholarly discussions, but has rarely been their focus. This paper therefore hopes to expand existing scholarship by highlighting ambiguity as a linking feature in many of the problematic situations identified by scholars and civil society. To provide a context for the discussion, it first notes the impact of three linked statuses (statelessness, ambiguous statuses, and lack of documentation) on those affected. It then sketches out some ideas about how ambiguity arises, emphasising that this is a consequence of the multi-faceted nature of citizenship. Turning to the situation in Myanmar, it explores three cases in which ambiguity arises from the Citizenship Law and through procedures, then discusses "associate" and "naturalised" citizenship as ambiguous statuses before turning to the situation of those holding National Registration Cards (NRCs), Temporary Registration Cards (TRCs) and NVCs. The final section suggests three consequences of the ambiguities described in the previous sections: that they act as hidden forms of exclusion; that they contribute to the precariousness of citizenship; and that they empower popular perceptions as a means of determining citizenship.

IMPACT OF AMBIGUOUS CITIZENSHIP STATUSES ON THE INDIVIDUAL

Statelessness – that is, the situation of those persons who are not considered citizens by any state under the operation of its law – has a profound impact on the lives of affected individuals (UNHCR 2010, 2015; Institute on Statelessness and Inclusion 2014; European Network on Statelessness 2014, 2016; Draper 2016). Citizenship status affects the ability of the individual, *inter alia,* to reside in their own country, to work, to marry, to pursue education, to travel, and to access healthcare. Ambiguous statuses can have similar negative impacts (Vlieks 2014; Lori 2017). Moreover, as Lori argues, ambiguous statuses are used by governments to avoid resolving dilemmas about citizenship and inclusion, instead trapping marginalised populations in a perpetual limbo.

A separate but related problem is lack of identity documentation. Without identity documentation, a person will face problems in carrying out any action where proof of identity is needed. For example, opening a bank account or, in Myanmar, checking into a hotel. An identity document may be proof of citizenship status, but not all are. For example, a driving licence is proof of identity, but not of citizenship. This becomes relevant in cases where the individual has to prove their citizenship status (for example, if applying for a passport or documenting that their child is a citizen). Not all citizens have identity documents (or proof of citizenship), nor do all stateless persons lack identity documentation. However lack of documentation is a risk factor for statelessness and one of the consequences of statelessness is often a lack of documentation.

The question of documentation is particularly important in Myanmar. Citizenship cards are the most commonly held identity document, reinforcing the link between citizenship status, documentation, and access to rights. This is further reinforced by the expectation that everyone has documentation and that this will provide evidence of their citizenship. The 1949 Residents of Burma Registration Act established that all residents should be issued with National Registration Cards. This expectation is reflected in the range of actions where identity documentation is required e.g. getting an inter-city bus, renting or buying a house, getting a job, or accessing healthcare. Someone without a citizenship card may be able to complete these actions using alternative proofs of identity or strategies that circumvent the need for an identity document, but they will always face additional difficulties. Such difficulties also increase the chance of these persons ending up in informal and unregulated situations, with all the risks that this entails. However, this expectation of documentation is not met; the 2014 Population and Housing Census found that 27.3 per cent of the population over the age of ten have no identity document. A further 1.7 per cent held NRCs (identity cards which preceded the citizenship card as the main form of documentation) and 0.5 per cent held TRCs (which have since become obsolete) (Union of Myanmar 2015, 2). These figures underestimate the number of those undocumented or holding TRCs, due to the decision not to enumerate the Rohingya population in Rakhine State, many of whom held TRCs.

Lack of documentation of citizenship status is both a cause and a consequence of ambiguity. Without documentation of citizenship status, it becomes hard to prove possession of that status, if it is challenged. On the other hand, when someone's status is ambiguous, they are unlikely to be able to access documentation (Lori 2017). If parents do not have citizenship cards, their children are likely to be undocumented, since a citizenship card is generally needed to register the birth of, and acquire documentation for, a child (Norwegian Refugee Council et al. 2018). This may impact the child's opportunities and development, including the ability to complete their education. Over generations such lack of documentation and any doubt over the parent's status will make it harder for the child to prove their eligibility for citizenship, increasing the risk of statelessness.

SOURCES OF AMBIGUOUS CITIZENSHIP STATUSES

Citizenship is a complex phenomenon. It can be considered: "as legal status and political membership; as rights and obligations; as identity and belonging; as civic virtues and practices of engagement; and as a discourse of political and social equality or responsibility for a common good" (Shachar et al. 2017, 16). This paper is primarily interested in citizenship as a legal status. However, even considered as a legal status, citizenship is always a mixed question of fact and law. As UNHCR's (2014) discussion of how to assess citizenship in the context of statelessness determination procedures stresses, if a person is not recognised and treated as a citizen by the authorities as well as qualifying for citizenship under the law, they are not, in fact, a citizen. The issuing of identity documentation is an important element of such recognition (Lori 2017). Consideration of the factual element of citizenship as a legal status allows it to be linked to broader discussions which ground the idea of citizenship in access to rights or political participation (Bosniak 2000). Although, as Bosniak (2017) notes elsewhere, there are few rights that may, under international law and practice, be limited to citizens. One of these is the right to vote and stand for election.[4] Although non-citizens are sometimes permitted to vote and some citizens may be excluded, this remains in some ways the quintessential marker of citizenship and belonging (Bosniak 2017), since it grants the individual a say in the shaping of the destiny of the state. This is a particularly pertinent consideration in Myanmar. In his speech on the adoption of the Citizenship Law, Ne Win described one of its objectives as ensuring the ability of natives to shape the destiny of the state without external interference (The Working People's Daily 1982). On a more positive note, Walton (2018) highlights that, in order for citizenship in Myanmar to be transformative, it must be participatory. Both from an historical and from a forward-looking perspective it is therefore worth paying particular attention to the ways in which ambiguous statuses in Myanmar engage with the question of political participation.

Consideration of these three dimensions of citizenship – status under the law; treatment by state authorities, including with regard to documentation; and the ability to participate in political processes – provide a framework for thinking about the ways ambiguity arises and manifests in Myanmar.

AMBIGUITIES ARISING FROM THE CITIZENSHIP LAW AND PROCEDURES

Transmission of citizenship to children

The normal means by which citizenship is acquired under the 1982 Citizenship Law in Myanmar is by descent from a citizen parent. The citizenship status of both parents is relevant to determining the child's category of citizenship (i.e. whether each parent is a "citizen", "associate" citizen, "naturalised" citizen, or "foreigner" affects whether the child is a "citizen", "associate" citizen, "naturalised" citizen, or "foreigner"). Sections 7 and 43 of the Citizenship Law set out the rules for the different combinations of parental status, except that there is no mention of the status of a child both of whose parents are "associate" citizens.

The second omission is that the Law does not specify what happens if one or both parents' status is unknown or undocumented. The administrative processes follow the Law in assuming that information and documentation of both parents will be available, with the result that it is virtually impossible to register the birth of a child or acquire citizenship documentation without producing identity documents for both parents (Norwegian Refugee Council et al. 2018). In this case the child is left in an ambiguous situation. They might have a claim to citizenship, but will struggle to prove it.[5] The broad scope of this omission means that it affects both those generally perceived as citizens (or deserving of citizenship), such as the Karen or Kachin, as well as members of marginalised groups like the Rohingya.

The definition of "Nationals"

Section 3 of the Citizenship Law states:

> Nationals such as the Kachin, Kayah, Karen, Chin, Burman, Mon, Rakhine or Shan and ethnic groups as have settled in any of the territories included within the State as their permanent home from a period prior to 1185 B.E., 1823 A.D. are Burma citizens.

This provision has been criticised for making citizenship dependent on ethnicity (UNHCR 2018; International Commission of Jurists 2019), and for essentialising ethnic identity (Arraiza and Vonk 2017). The arbitrary character of the temporal, spatial, and ethnic parameters have also been noted (Nemoto 2014; Center for Diversity and National Harmony 2018). Cheesman (2017) has highlighted the problematic nature of the entire concept and use of the term *taing yin tha.* As he notes, there is no list of *taing yin tha* in the Citizenship Law or Procedures and the oft-cited list of 135 groups has no clear origin or logic to the categories.

Rather less attention has been paid to how this provision operates at the individual (rather than the group) level. It is unclear how the Law and Procedures envisage that the relevant officials should determine whether a person belongs to a group covered by this provision.[6] This is not a theoretical concern, as reports of problems with the listing of individuals' ethnicity on their citizenship cards show (Smile Education and Development Foundation 2016; The Seagull 2016). Some ethnic groups have also started documenting their own members, with a view to facilitating their access to citizenship or ensuring that their ethnic identity is correctly recorded on their citizenship cards (Ann Wang 2017; Myat Moe Thu 2019).

The case of the "fake Kaman" helps to illustrate this problem. These were a group of around 3,000 residents of Ramree Township, Rakhine State, who were issued citizenship cards in 2018. The citizenship cards identified the holders as "Kaman", a group generally recognised as falling within the definition of Section 3 of the Citizenship Law and so qualifying for "citizenship" as *taing yin tha.* The problems arose when locals and politicians began protesting that the individuals were not, in fact, Kaman and had therefore been issued their citizenship cards incorrectly. The authorities eventually yielded to calls for a review of the process, which withdrew the cards of twenty-one persons (Win Ko Ko Latt and Gerin 2018). In effect the identification of these individuals as Kaman was overturned, despite the fact that they had submitted letters from local members of the Kaman community attesting to their status as Kaman as part of the citizenship verification process (Moe Myint 2018).

Lack of direction in the procedures

Sections 44 and 45 of the Citizenship Law set out the requirements for acquisition of "naturalised" citizenship. However, the Procedures provide little guidance on how to assess these requirements. For example, that an applicant is of good character is established through letters of recommendation from the Ward or Village Tract Administrator (*Procedures relating to Myanmar Citizenship Law: Procedures relating to Naturalised Citizenship* 1983, para. 9). However, the Procedures provide no instructions to these officials on the circumstances in which such letters should be issued or denied. The Law and Procedures do not list which languages are included in the requirement that the applicant speak "one of the national languages well". Nor is there any guidance on the degree of fluency required or the manner in which this should be assessed. In some cases this lack of specificity in the Procedures has resulted in flexibility in the process, for instance with regard to proof that an applicant's parents were resident in Myanmar (Advisory Commission on Rakhine State 2017; Nyan Hlaing Lynn 2017). However, this lack of guidance may result in similar cases being decided differently. As discussed below, they also create ongoing ambiguity due to the possibility that citizenship status may be reassessed and a different conclusion reached.

"ASSOCIATE" CITIZENS AND "NATURALISED" CITIZENS

The Citizenship Law treats "associate" and "naturalised" citizens differently from "citizens" in a number of ways, including their ability to transmit citizenship to their children and the grounds on which citizenship can be lost. A child who is eligible for "associate" or "naturalised" citizenship based on their descent from a citizen parent or parents, does not acquire this status automatically, but has to apply and – at least theoretically – be assessed against the standard eligibility criteria (over eighteen, able to speak one of the national languages well, of good character, and of sound mind).[7] In a system where the normal mode of acquisition of citizenship is by descent, as it is in Myanmar, the possibility that a child with two citizen parents may not be a citizen or may have to be assessed as though they were a first-generation applicant for citizenship is a striking demonstration of the limits of their parents' citizenship.

Outside the Citizenship Law there are further restrictions on the rights of "associate" and "naturalised" citizens.[8] These restrictions raise the question of whether "associate" and "naturalised" citizenship in Myanmar should be considered effective citizenship. While "associate" and "naturalised" citizens are able to vote, they cannot form political parties or stand for election. Their political participation is therefore limited. Tellingly, "naturalised" citizenship is also seen as a second-class status by those concerned. There have, for instance, been cases in which individuals who have applied for citizenship have failed to collect their citizenship cards on discovering that these provide only "naturalised" citizenship.[9] This adds weight to the argument that "naturalised" and "associate" citizenship are not seen as effective citizenship.

A further ambiguity arises in relation to "associate" citizenship due to a lack of clarity over who should hold this status. Section 23 of the Citizenship Law states: "Applicants for citizenship under the Union Citizenship Act, 1948, conforming to the stipulations and qualifications may be determined as associate citizens by the Central Body." Authors approaching the question of citizenship from a legal perspective have generally interpreted this as meaning that only those whose citizenship applications were pending in 1982 should be "associate" citizens (Arraiza 2017; UNHCR 2018). Others have described it as covering all those who acquired citizenship under the 1948 Union Citizenship Act (Lall et al. 2014; Kyed and Gravers 2018). The Procedures on Associate Citizenship would seem to support the latter interpretation as they include provisions under which citizenship was acquired automatically and so no application could have been pending in 1982 among those relevant to the determination of "associate" citizenship. For example, section 4(2) of the 1948 Union Citizenship Act, which granted citizenship automatically to individuals born in the state if both parents were also born in the state and all four grandparents were permanent residents, is included as grounds for "associate" citizenship.

These provisions are a source of ambiguity, as they appear to conflict with Section 6 of the 1982 Citizenship Law which provides that those already citizens when the law came into force should retain that citizenship. It seems that the 1982 Citizenship Law anticipated that those who were already citizens would have their citizenship status reassessed following its entry into force, with a chance that some of those who were already citizens might become "associate" citizens rather than "citizens". The second sentence of Section 6 reinforces this view as it states: "Action however, shall, be taken under section 18 for infringement of the provisions of that section". If the intention was not to review of the status of those already citizens it would be unlikely that infringements of Section 18 (acquisition of citizenship by fraud) would be detected.

All of these factors contribute to a lack of clarity about the nature of "associate" citizens and who should hold this status. There is a risk of similar cases being treated differently as a result of this lack of clarity, as well as of individuals' citizenship status being reassessed. Moreover, in the absence of a clear basis for the distinction between "citizens" and "associate" citizens, the main function of this status appears to be to mark these individuals out and provide a basis for treating them differently from "citizens". In doing so, it blurs the definition of citizenship by redefining some citizens as "associate" citizens and treating them differently from those who were previously their peers.

AMBIGUITIES CREATED BY DOCUMENTATION STATUS

National Registration Cards (NRCs), Temporary Registration Cards (TRCs) and National Verification Cards (NVCs) are all seen as indicating something about the citizenship status of holders, although none are citizenship cards and the details of what each proves are contested. NRCs and TRCs were created by the 1949 Residents of Burma Registration Act; the NRCs as identity cards to be held by residents and the TRCs as temporary identity cards to be held by those without NRCs while their status was being resolved. NRCs were the primary form of identity document issued in Myanmar until the introduction of citizenship cards under the 1982 Citizenship Law. These cards were never formally proof of citizenship, although in practice they were only held by citizens. The Residents of Burma Registration Act applied to both citizens and foreigners, but as foreigners were already required to have Foreigner Registration Certificates, they were not issued with NRCs.

Those who retain NRCs, whether deliberately or accidentally, therefore tend to see them as proof that the individual was a citizen at the time the card was issued and should be recognised as retaining this citizenship in line with Section 6 of the 1982 Citizenship Law.[10] On the other hand, there are vocal sections of the population who maintain that these documents do not prove citizenship, which is legally true.[11] Official practice has been similarly ambivalent. NRC holders are permitted to apply directly for citizenship, rather than first being required to accept an NVC (Smile Education and Development Foundation and Justice Base, n.d.), suggesting some sort of recognition of the status of holders. However, they still have to go through the application process; NRCs cannot simply be exchanged for citizenship cards.

In the 1951 Residents of Burma Registration Rules, which put into practice the Residents of Burma Registration Act, it is clear that TRCs were intended as a short-term document issued in place of the NRC, while waiting for the NRC to be issued or replaced or "If there is specific reasons by general or special order" (*Residents of Burma Registration Rules*, 1951, para. 13(c)). From the mid-1990s until 2015, TRCs were issued to otherwise undocumented persons, including some who had previously held NRCs. During this period, TRC holders were able to use these cards to access certain rights, including the right to vote (Sithu Aung Myint 2015). In this way, TRC holders were treated in some respects as citizens. Formally, however, TRCs only provided proof of identity and residence and did not constitute evidence of current or former citizenship status or eligibility for citizenship.

In 2015 all TRCs were cancelled and holders were told to exchange them for NVCs. As an obsolete document, the TRC does not generally enable the holder to access rights, although in practice it may still be accepted as proof of identity. In the perceptions of holders, it retains value and is seen as providing evidence that the holder should be a citizen. In part this is because of the link between the TRC and the NRC, and builds on the claim to citizenship of those holding NRCs. Another aspect is the proof it offers of former official recognition and acceptance of the individual as a person who existed in the ambiguous status created for TRC holders.

NVCs were introduced in 2016, following the cancellation of TRCs. While in some respects they are a replacement for TRCs, there are a number of key differences that have affected how the cards are received and how they are treated in terms of the citizenship status of the holder. Unlike TRCs, which were linked to NRCs, NVCs are a stand-alone document. They identify the holder as a person whose citizenship status is undetermined and who is expected to go through the citizenship verification process to resolve this uncertainty.[12] Like TRC holders before 2015, NVC holders are accorded certain rights not normally available to foreigners or the undocumented (e.g. the ability to get fishing permits), but face greater restrictions than citizens. For example, in Rakhine State, NVC holders are required to get authorisation before travelling outside their township of residence.

The government describes the NVC as a pathway to citizenship (State Counsellor's Office 2016; Union Enterprise for Humanitarian Assistance, Resettlement and Development in Rakhine 2018), and in theory it should be a tool for resolving the ambiguous status of those whose citizenship is undetermined. However, in practice it is not always seen this way.[13] NVCs are said to identify their holders as foreigners and to deny eligibility for citizenship (although those making this claim may more strictly mean that it denies eligibility for "citizenship" as *taing yin tha* (Mohammad Ayub 2017; Mohammad Al-Masum Molla and Palma 2018; Quadir and Shoon Lei Win Naing 2018).

These negative perceptions are partly due to issues of implementation and distrust in the citizenship verification process, not least because of the small number of cases that have so far been processed. However, they are also partly a result of the differences between the TRCs and the NVCs. The connection between TRCs and NRCs makes the TRC seem more valuable as evidence of citizenship status. Moreover, the very ambiguity of the TRC with regards to the citizenship status of the holder allows different interpretations. Because the NVC explicitly states that the holder must go through the citizenship verification process, it makes clear that they are not already a citizen, whatever their eligibility. The NVC thus positions the holder as someone whose citizenship is undetermined, rather than someone whose status is ambiguous because their card may or may not be seen as proving citizenship. The fact that unlike TRC holders, NVC holders are not permitted to vote further sharpens this distinction. With regard to this right TRC holders were treated as citizens, while NVC holders are treated as foreigners.

THE CONSEQUENCES OF AMBIGUITY IN MYANMAR'S CITIZENSHIP LAW

The ambiguities created by gaps and lack of clarity in the Citizenship Law and Procedures and by the existence of statuses which blur the boundaries between citizen and non-citizen have an immediate impact on the individuals affected. It is also possible that they have an impact on how citizenship functions and is understood at the systemic level. Without directly addressing the question of whether such consequences are intentional or not, this paper follows Lori (2017) in considering how ambiguous statuses may be a means for governments to avoid having to resolve questions of belonging for some groups.

Ambiguity as a hidden form of exclusion

Myanmar's Citizenship Law and procedures have created a system in which access to citizenship is narrowly constrained and tightly controlled: only those who were citizens or eligible for citizenship in 1982 and their descendants can be citizens, foreigners cannot become citizens,[14] and loss of citizenship is permanent (*Burma Citizenship Law* 1982: sections 22, 41, and 64). Moreover, while fraudulent acquisition of citizenship and abetting the fraudulent acquisition of citizenship is a criminal offence (*Burma Citizenship Law* 1982, sections 19, 37, and 60), there are no complementary provisions in either Law or Procedures providing penalties for someone who denies an eligible individual citizenship. Nor do the administrative procedures appear to include any penalty for delaying or failing to process a case.

These factors create a system in which granting citizenship without abundant proof of eligibility can have negative consequences for the administrative officials involved; as is demonstrated by attempts to sue administrative officials for their part in granting citizenship to Muslims (Su Myat Mon 2017).[15] On the other hand, delaying a case or refusing to process it if any detail, however minor, is missing has few consequences.

Theoretically, gaps in the Law and Procedures create a space for administrative discretion which could be used either to facilitate or to hinder access to citizenship. However, the narrow definition of citizenship in the Law and the structure of the administrative procedures create a system that favours exclusion rather than inclusion in cases of ambiguity. For example, if one of a child's parents are unknown, absent, or undocumented the child will usually be unable to acquire citizenship because the administrative system treats the lack of information on the second parent as a reason not to process the case.

The second consequence is that cases remain pending for prolonged periods rather than being resolved. It is common to hear of cases where applications for citizenship documentation through the citizenship verification process have been pending for months or years (Smile Education and Development Foundation 2016; The Seagull: Human Rights, Peace and Development 2016; Norwegian Refugee Council et al. 2018). There are far fewer stories of cases being rejected; to date the citizenship verification process in Rakhine State has not issued a single decision where the applicant is not a citizen. This practice of delaying decisions perpetuates the existence of ambiguous statuses. It may even become a way of permanently excluding those in ambiguous statuses (individually and collectively) without formally doing so. If the processes do not produce results there are few incentives for those in ambiguous statuses to apply.[16] Moreover, the intergenerational impact of ambiguity may result in their descendants being formally excluded. This recalls Lori's (2017) argument that ambiguous and temporary statuses are a tool used by states to avoid resolving the situations of those they do not wish to include in the citizenship body.

Precarious citizenship

Lori's description of precarious citizenship as "the structured uncertainty of being unable to secure permanent access to citizenship rights" (Lori 2017, 846) is clearly applicable to those in Myanmar whose citizenship status is uncertain and who have documents that do not provide proof of citizenship. However, it could describe almost all citizenship in Myanmar, due to the existence of documentation procedures that allow for a change in citizenship status.

Under the Procedures on the Citizenship Law, citizens should acquire their first independent citizenship card at age 10, and renew this card at ages 18, 30 and 45. This process requires the submission of information on the individual's identity and, in effect, becomes a reassessment of the individual's citizenship status.[17] There is anecdotal evidence of individuals finding that their status has changed following this process; for example, those who had "citizenship" cards being issued with "naturalised" citizenship cards. Others may not be issued with new cards at all, leaving them undocumented or holding old documents (Smile Education and Development Foundation 2016; The Seagull: Human Rights, Peace and Development 2016). In practice, the re-documentation processes mean that citizenship status is never finally settled, but will always be subject to reassessment.

It is possible that the existence of "associate" and "naturalised" citizenship, and the large number of people whose status is ambiguous, facilitate these reassessments. A person who has their "citizenship" changed to "naturalised" citizenship has clearly lost status and rights, but the provisions on deprivation of citizenship have not been invoked. Becoming undocumented or holding obsolete documents may be a problem for the individual, but this is sufficiently common that it is not unthinkable and so something that could cause popular outrage and demand rectification. In fact, some people choose not to try to renew their cards, preferring the challenge of navigating life with an out-of-date document to the risk of loss of status through the re-documentation process.[18] The presence of a large number of people whose citizenship status is ambiguous makes it easier for others to join their number, whether by their own choice or the act of officials. As a result, their citizenship, and that of all other citizens, and access to the rights associated with citizenship becomes less secure.

The impact of perception

Some of the ambiguities in the Citizenship Law create a situation in which there are multiple possible answers to the question "what is this person's citizenship status?" For example, whether a person should be a "citizen" as a result of prior citizenship (under Section 6) or an "associate" citizen because of the way in which they acquired citizenship. In the absence of clear guidance, the actual outcome for the individual may depend on the views of the person assessing their case and may change when their situation is reassessed through the documentation process.

The number of undocumented persons also has an impact on how citizenship is understood and serves to increase the importance of perceptions (that is, of the belief that the person in question is or should be a citizen). Holding a citizenship card is legally proof of citizenship. However, due to the large number of undocumented persons, not holding a citizenship card does not prove that the person is not eligible for citizenship. In some cases, it may seem obvious to others that the person in question should be a citizen, leading to them being treated as such. Bosniak (2000) calls this dimension of citizenship the "sense of belonging". As she notes, this is often treated as distinct from the other dimensions of citizenship and linked to discussions of group identity and nationalism. However, in the context of Myanmar, such ideas of belonging can be directly relevant to the question of legal citizenship status.

For example, in 2017, an MP from Kayah State asked a parliamentary question about access to citizenship for the children of those working abroad in an irregular situation or who had returned from such work (Htoo Thant 2017; *The Irrawaddy* 2017; "Pyithu Hluttaw Meeting Reports 21 June 2017"). The parents had lost citizenship or were struggling to establish that they were citizens due to documentation issues. The way in which the question was discussed made it clear that not only the MP in question, but also the Ministry of Labour, Immigration, and Population, saw both parents and children as persons who should be citizens. They therefore proposed to facilitate their access to citizenship, including by use of the extraordinary powers of the President or Union Government to grant citizenship under Section 8(a) of the Citizenship Law to by-pass the rule that once lost, citizenship cannot be reacquired.

On the other hand, the reliance on such intuitive understandings of who deserves to be a citizen can result in the devaluing of documentation as proof of citizenship. This is reinforced by the fact that corruption and the use of bribes to short-cut or circumvent problems with access to documentation are common. It is therefore known that in some cases documentation will indeed have been obtained illicitly.

The case of the "fake Kaman" (discussed above) illustrates this problem. These individuals had gone through the process of citizenship determination and their eligibility for citizenship had been established. Despite this, they were not perceived as citizens by local communities. This perception had sufficient traction that it led to a reassessment of the individuals' citizenship status and in some cases the loss of citizenship. It is difficult as an outside observer to be sure how valid the claim that these individuals were not Kaman is. However, what is clear is that popular opinion of who should be a citizen had the power to influence the legal citizenship status of those concerned. At an individual level, such lack of trust in documentation as evidence of citizenship may result in persons holding citizenship cards nonetheless finding their citizenship status questioned.

CONCLUSION

Citizenship in Myanmar is full of ambiguities: people whose status is not defined; people who cannot prove their eligibility for citizenship; people who are perceived as belonging, as citizens, despite a lack of documentation to this effect; people whose documented citizenship cannot protect them from the consequences of not being perceived as citizens; places where a person's documentation does not match their actual identity and legal status; and the odd status of "associate" and "naturalised" citizens. Some of these ambiguities are the result of gaps in the law and issues with administrative procedures. Others result from the complexities of the situation on the ground and the interaction of the legal standards and popular perceptions of belonging.

This paper has suggested that ambiguities may act as covert forms of exclusion and that they reinforce the role that perceptions around who are and are not citizens play in determining whether or not a person is treated as a citizen, as well as contributing to the precariousness of citizenship in Myanmar. Considered in this way, the idea of ambiguity helps to understand the discriminatory functioning of the Citizenship Law and practice and how they are used to exclude individuals or groups who are not perceived as belonging. While this suggests that removing and resolving the ambiguities is desirable, any attempt at reform should be sensitive to the risk of doing so in an exclusionary system. Loss of ambiguity may simply make clear and permanent the exclusion of those whose status was previously ambiguous.

Notes

1 "Burma Citizenship Law", Pyithu Hluttaw Law No 4 of 1982. The text used is the official English translation published as part of a collection of laws on immigration and citizenship. The terms "citizen", "associate" citizen, "naturalised" citizen and "foreigner" are placed within inverted commas to mark that they are used in the particular way defined by the Citizenship Law.

2 The Census Report provides figures for nine categories of identity document (including "none"). The figure given here is the author's calculation based on the figures for "citizenship", "associate" citizenship, and "naturalised" citizenship card holders.

3 Any translation of the Burmese term *taing yin tha* is problematic (see Cheesman 2017). In this paper it is therefore left untranslated.

4 This right is the only one which the International Covenant on Civil and Political Rights limits to citizens.

5 It could be argued that if one parent is a citizen (of any type) the child should be eligible for "naturalised" citizenship (since this would be the case if the other parent was a "foreigner" and so did not provide the child with any additional claim to citizenship).

6 Paragraph 5 of the Procedures Relating to Citizenship indicates some limitations on who qualifies as *taing yin tha,* but does not provide a positive definition.

7 Contrast section 7 "The following persons born in or outside the State are also citizens..." with section 43 "The following persons, born in or outside the State, from the date this Law comes into force, may also *apply* for naturalized citizenship..." (emphasis added). The criteria for "naturalised citizenship" listed here are drawn from section 44.

8 Sections 30(c) and 53(c) of the Citizenship Law explicitly permit the President and Union Government to restrict "associate" and "naturalised" citizens access to rights otherwise enjoyed by citizens.

9 This idea that individuals would not bother collecting "naturalised" citizenship cards was mentioned in several interviews with Muslim and Rakhine community leaders in February–May 2018. It is, however, difficult to draw firm conclusions on how "naturalised" citizenship is perceived based on statements relating to the situation of the Muslim population in Rakhine State as such discussions tend to get caught up on questions relating to the status that this group "should" have. It is therefore not always clear whether a rejection of "naturalised" citizenship is intrinsic to that status or relates back to the belief that the Muslim population of northern Rakhine State should be recognised as *taing yin tha* under their chosen term Rohingya and therefore entitled to "citizenship".

10 This point was made repeatedly in interviews conducted with Muslims (both those who had acquired citizenship and those who had not) between May 2017 and December 2018.

11 An interview with an Arakan National Party member in May 2017 confirmed that this is their official position. This position was frequently expressed in interviews by Rakhine in May 2017.

12 This is reflected in the text included on the NVCs which clearly states that the card is not proof of Myanmar citizenship. The cards also state: "This identity card holder is a person who needs to apply for citizenship in accordance with Myanmar Citizenship Law". This is reflected in official statements, such as the notification issued by the State Counsellor's Office in December 2016.

13 The negative views of NVCs noted here generally reflect the views expressed by Rohingya. Outside Rakhine State the reaction to NVCs has been less negative.

14 Except through an exceptional grant of citizenship under Section 8(a) of the Citizenship Law.

15 This was confirmed in an interview with the Rakhine State Immigration Chief in May 2017.

16 This can be seen in the reluctance of Rohingya to engage with the citizenship verification process in Rakhine State. In interviews between 2017 and 2019 Rohingya community leaders repeatedly noted that one of their major reservations was that the process did not appear to be producing results.

17 In general on the renewal of documents see Procedures relating to Citizenship, para. 12(c); Procedures relating to Associate Citizenship, paras 5 & 9. The provisions, particularly on renewal of documentation at ages 30 and 45 are unclear, but references to this requirement can be found at Procedures relating to Naturalised Citizenship, para. 6.12(c) 5 & 9.

18 This observation is based on comments made in a number of interviews between 2017 and 2019 and discussions with civil society actors involved in citizenship and documentation issues.

References

Advisory Commission on Rakhine State (2017). "Towards a Peaceful, Fair and Prosperous Future for the People of Rakhine: Final Report of the Advisory Commission on Rakhine State". Naypyidaw, Myanmar: Rakhine Commission. Available at http://www.rakhinecommission.org/the-final-report/ (accessed 2 June 2020).

Ann Wang (2017). "How a Kokang Becomes a Citizen". *Frontier Myanmar,* 17 October. Available at https://frontiermyanmar.net/en/how-a-kokang-becomes-a-citizen/ (accessed 2 June 2020).

Ardeth Maung Thawnghmung (2016). "The Politics of Indigeneity in Myanmar: Competing Narratives in Rakhine State". *Asian Ethnicity* 17 (4): 527–547.

Arraiza, J.M. (2017). "Re-Imagining Myanmar Citizenship in Times of Transition". *Statelessness Working Paper Series,* 2017/01.

Arraiza, J.M. and Vonk, O. (2017). "Report on Citizenship Law: Myanmar". Country Report RSCAS/GLOBALCIT-CR 2017/14.

Bosniak, L. (2000). "Citizenship Denationalized (The State of Citizenship Symposium)". *Indiana Journal of Global Legal Studies* 7 (2).

——— (2017). "Status Non-Citizens". In *The Oxford Handbook of Citizenship,* edited by A. Shachar et al. Oxford: Oxford University Press.

Burma Citizenship Law (1982). Pyithu Hluttaw Law No 4 of 1982.

Center for Diversity and National Harmony (2018). "Myanmar's Citizenship Law: An Analysis". Yangon: Center for Diversity and National Harmony. Available at https://www.cdnh.org/publication/myanmars-citizenship-law-an-analysis/ (accessed 2 June 2020).

Cheesman, N. (2017). "How in Myanmar 'National Races' Came to Surpass Citizenship and Exclude Rohingya". *Journal of Contemporary Asia* 47 (3): 461–483.

Draper, J. (2016). "The Enduring Relevance of Arendt's Understanding of the Harm of Statelessness". *Statelessness Working Paper Series* 2016/06.

European Network on Statelessness (2014). "Still Stateless, Still Suffering". Available at https://www.statelessness.eu/sites/www.statelessness.eu/files/ENS_Still_Stateless_Still_Suffering_online%20version_2.pdf (accessed 2 June 2020).

European Network on Statelessness. (2016). "What Does It Mean to Be Stateless?". Available at https://www.statelessness.eu/resources/what-does-it-mean-be-stateless (accessed 2 June 2020).

Gibson, T., James, H. and Falvey, L. (eds.) (2016). *Rohingyas: Insecurity and Citizenship in Myanmar.* Bangkok: Thaksin University Press.

Ho, E. Lynn-Ee, and Chua, L. (2016). "Law and 'Race' in the Citizenship Spaces of Myanmar: Spatial Strategies and the Political Subjectivity of the Burmese Chinese". *Ethnic and Racial Studies* 39 (5): 896–916.

Htoo Thant (2017). "Illegal Migrants' Children to Get Birth Certificates". *The Myanmar Times,* 22 June 2017. Available at http://www.mmtimes.com/index.php/national-news/nay-pyi-taw/26497-illegal-migrants-children-to-get-birth-certificates.html (accessed 2 June 2020).

Institute on Statelessness and Inclusion (2014). *The World's Stateless.* Wolf Legal Publishers.

International Commission of Jurists (2019). "Citizenship and Human Rights in Myanmar: Why Law Reform Is Urgent and Possible – A Legal Briefing". Available at https://www.icj.org/wp-content/uploads/2019/06/Myanmar-Citizenship-law-reform-Advocacy-Analysis-Brief-2019-ENG.pdf (accessed 2 June 2020).

Islam, N. (2018). "Rohingya and Nationality Status in Myanmar". In *Citizenship in Myanmar: Ways of Being in and from Burma,* edited by A. South and M. Lall. Singapore: Chiang Mai University Press, Yusof Ishak Institute.

Kyed, H. and Gravers, M. (2018). "Representation and Citizenship in the Future Integration of Ethnic Armed Actors in Myanmar/Burma". In *Citizenship in Myanmar: Ways of Being in and from Burma,* edited by A. South and M. Lall. Singapore: Chiang Mai University Press, Yusof Ishak Institute.

Lall, M. (2018). "Myanmar's Youth and the Question of Citizenship". In *Citizenship in Myanmar: Ways of Being in and from Burma,* edited by A. South and M. Lall. Singapore: Chiang Mai University Press, Yusof Ishak Institute.

Lall, M., Thei Su San, Nwe Nwe San, Yeh Tut Naing, Thein Thein Myat, Lwin Thet Thet Khaing, Swann Lynn Htet, and Yin Nyein Aye (2014). "Citizenship in Myanmar, Contemporary Debates and Challenges in Light of the Reform Process". Yangon, Myanmar: Myanmar Egress.

Leider, J. (2014). "Rohingya: The Name, The Movement, The Quest for Identity". Available at http://www.networkmyanmar.org/ESW/Files/Leider-Rohingya.pdf (accessed 2 June 2020).

Lori, N.A. (2017). "Statelessness, 'In-Between' Statuses, and Precarious Citizenship". In *The Oxford Handbook of Citizenship,* edited by A. Sachar et al. Oxford: Oxford University Press.

Moe Myint (2018). "Analysis: Party Says Gov't Issuing Fake Kaman Citizenship Cards to Rohingya, Demands Probe". *The Irrawaddy*, 9 December. Available at https://www.irrawaddy.com/factiva/analysis-party-says-govt-issuing-fake-kaman-citizenship-cards-rohingya-demands-probe.html (accessed 2 June 2020).

Mohammad Al-Masum Molla and Palma, P. (2018). "Promises Myanmar Never Kept". *The Daily Star*, 29 April. Available at https://www.thedailystar.net/frontpage/promises-myanmar-never-kept-1569232 (accessed 2 June 2020).

Mohammed Ayub (2017). "National Verification Card (NVC): A Hidden Trap for Myanmar's Rohingya". *Rohingya Blogger* (blog), 22 October. Available at http://www.rohingyablogger.com/2017/10/national-verification-card-nvc-hidden.html (accessed 2 June 2020).

Myat Moe Thu (2019). "Team to Conduct Nationwide Survey of Ethnic Pa-O People". *The Myanmar Times*, 3 January. Available at https://www.mmtimes.com/news/team-conduct-nationwide-survey-ethnic-pa-o-people.html (accessed 2 June 2020).

Nemoto, K. (2014). "Exclusive Nationalism of Burma (Myanmar) Represented by Its Nationality Law". Asia Peacebuilding Initiatives. Available at http://peacebuilding.asia/myanmar-represented-by-its-nationality-law/(accessed 2 June 2020).

Norwegian Refugee Council, The Seagull: Human Rights, Peace and Development, Institute on Statelessness and Inclusion, and Statelessness Network Asia Pacific (2018). "A Gender Analysis of the Right to a Nationality in Myanmar". Available at https://www.nrc.no/globalassets/pdf/reports/myanmar/cedaw-report-web-7-march-2018.pdf (accessed 2 June 2020).

Nyan Hlaing Lynn (2017). "Violence and Fear on Display in Maungdaw Media Trip" *Frontier Myanmar*, 11 May. Available at https://frontiermyanmar.net/en/violence-and-fear-on-display-in-maungdaw-media-trip (accessed 2 June 2020).

Nyi Nyi Kyaw (2015). "Alienation, Discrimination, and Securitization: Legal Personhood and Cultural Personhood of Muslims in Myanmar", *The Review of Faith & International Affairs* 13 (4): 50–59.

——— (2017). "Unpacking the Presumed Statelessness of Rohingyas". *Journal of Immigrant & Refugee Studies* 15 (3): 269–286.

Office of the State Counsellor (2016). "Notification", 26 December. Available at, https://www.statecounsellor.gov.mm/node/769 (accessed 2 June 2020).

Procedures relating to Myanmar Citizenship Law: Procedures relating to Naturalised Citizenship (1983) Notification 15/83.

Pugh, C.L. (2013). "Is Citizenship the Answer? Constructions of Belonging and Exclusion for the Stateless Rohingya of Burma". *IMI Working Papers Series*, No. 76.

Pyithu Hluttaw (2017). "Pyithu Hluttaw Meeting Reports 21 June 2017". Available at http://www.pyithuhluttaw.gov.mm/?q=node/7324 (accessed 2 June 2020).

Quadir, S. and Shoon Lei Win Naing (2018). "Bangladesh, UNHCR Dispute Myanmar's Rohingya Repatriation Claim". *Reuters*, 15 April. Available at https://www.reuters.com/article/us-myanmar-rohingya-refugees/myanmar-repatriates-first-rohingya-refugee-family-government-idUSKBN1HL19C (accessed 2 June 2020).

Shachar, A., Bauboeck, R., Bloemraad, I. and Vink, M. (2017). "Introduction: Citizenship - Quo Vadis?" In *The Oxford Handbook of Citizenship*, edited by A. Shachar et al. Oxford: Oxford University Press.

Sithu Aung Myint (2015). "White Card or Government Political Playing Card?" *The Myanmar Times*, 16 February. Available at https://www.mmtimes.com/opinion/13132-white-card-or-government-political-playing-card.html (accessed 2 June 2020).

Smile Education and Development Foundation (2016). "Assessing the Risks of Statelessness for Religious Minorities in Myanmar".

Smile Education and Development Foundation (n.d.). "A Guide to Identity Documents".

Su Myat Mon (2017). "Fresh Protests in Rakhine over Citizenship Verification". *Frontier Myanmar*, 22 March. Available at https://frontiermyanmar.net/en/fresh-protests-in-rakhine-over-citizenship-verification (accessed 2 June 2020).

The Irrawaddy (2017). "This Week in Parliament (June 19-23)". *The Irrawaddy*, 24 June. Available at https://www.irrawaddy.com/parliament/this-week-in-parliament-june-19-23.html (accessed 2 June 2020).

The Seagull: Human Rights, Peace and Development (2016). "Report for Religious Discrimination and Conflict in Myanmar: National Registration Cards".

The Working People's Daily (1982). "Speech by General Ne Win at the Meeting Held in the Central Meeting Hall, President House, Ahlone Road, 8 October 1982", 9 October. Available at http://www.burmalibrary.org/docs6/Ne_Win's_speech_Oct-1982-Citizenship_Law.pdf (accessed 2 June 2020).

Tonkin, D. (2018). "Exploring the Issue of Citizenship in Rakhine State". In *Citizenship in Myanmar: Ways of Being in and from Burma*, edited by A. South and M. Lall. Singapore: Chiang Mai University Press, Yusof Ishak Institute.

Union Enterprise for Humanitarian Assistance, Resettlement and Development in Rakhine (2018). "The Report to the People on the Progress of Implementation of the Recommendations on Rakhine State", 13 February. Available at https://rakhine.unionenterprise.org/images/pdf/1st-report-eng-01.pdf (accessed 2 June 2020).

Union of Myanmar (2015). *The 2014 Myanmar Population and Housing Census: The Union Report*. Census Report Volume 2. Naypyidaw, Myanmar: Department of Population, Ministry of Immigration and Population. Available at http://www.dop.gov.mm/sites/dop.gov.mm/files/publication_docs/census_main_report_union_-_english_2.pdf (accessed 2 June 2020).

UN Refugee Agency (UNHCR) (2010). "Ending Statelessness within Ten Years".
——— (2014). "Handbook on Protection of Stateless Persons". Geneva: UNHCR.
——— (2015). "I Am Here, I Belong: The Urgent Need to End Childhood Statelessness". Geneva: UNHCR.
——— (2018). "Citizenship & Statelessness in Myanmar: An Analysis of International Standards and the Myanmar Citizenship Legal Framework". Geneva: UNHCR.
Vlieks, C. (2014). "An Obligation for Statelessness Determination under the European Convention on Human Rights?" Discussion Paper 09/14.
Walton, M.J. (2018). "National Political Dialogue and Practices of Citizenship in Myanmar". In *Citizenship in Myanmar: Ways of Being in and from Burma*, edited by A. South and M. Lall. Singapore: Chiang Mai University Press, Yusof Ishak Institute.
Win Ko Ko Latt, and Gerin, R. (2018). "Investigation Finds Few Cases in Which Rohingya Received Improper Myanmar ID Cards". *Radio Free Asia*, 20 December. Available at https://www.rfa.org/english/news/myanmar/investigation-finds-few-cases-12202018114612.html (accessed 2 June 2020).
Zawacki, B. (2012). "Defining Myanmar's Rohingya Problem". *Human Rights Brief* 20: 18.

V

Conclusion

16

EPILOGUE – CONCLUDING THEMES

Jonathan Liljeblad

For the purposes of an epilogue, it is useful to draw some final thoughts from the preceding chapters by reference to the Introduction's observation that the assembly of contributions to this volume reflect "where things are at" in Myanmar at the time leading into the country's 2020 elections. Despite the breadth of topics that are presented in the four categories of parliamentary life, the economy, institutional legacies, and plural identities, the respective chapters serve to present different perspectives on the status of Myanmar's ongoing political and social changes. These perspectives help to delineate the complexities of the country's "transition" – simultaneously addressing historical legacies while progressing towards current aspirations in a context where both frequently exist as opposing forces. In doing so, the disparate chapters identify topics of significance at a national election milestone that will set the larger direction of Myanmar's future.

Among the various prospective concerns of the diverse authors is an underlying theme of significance: cohesion, particularly in terms of its existential nature in sustaining Myanmar as an identifiable entity in the international community. The commentaries of the preceding chapters indicate that Myanmar's cohesion as a nation-state is subject to forces of inclusion and exclusion, with both centrifugal and centripetal dynamics that work to simultaneously pull the country's complexities into a viable whole and fracture its components into irreconcilable division. The dynamics illustrated by all of the authors mark conditions of contestation, and collectively sum to a scale affecting Myanmar's existence. For example, the three chapters regarding parliamentary life demonstrate efforts of parliamentarians to better represent their constituencies (Egreteau, Chapter 2), their deeper engagement with citizens (Nyein Thiri Swe and Zaw Min Oo, Chapter 3), and support for political continuity (Jefferson, Chapter 4). Collectively, they reflect the deep desire of parliamentarians to advance political reform in Myanmar, but also indicate the ongoing issue of elite domination (Egreteau), structural limitations on parliamentary representation (Nyein Thiri Swe and Zaw Min Oo), and the ambivalence of MPs towards the pace and scope of political change (Jefferson). Similarly, the four chapters on Myanmar's economy present comparable complexities. Even as much as the NLD government has pursued broad-based growth and greater equality to extend development to all people across Myanmar (Turnell and Nyein Ei Cho, Chapter 5), the subsequent three chapters note the many issues that plague genuine reform. These factors include increasing inequality in the form of infrastructure development that exacerbates the financial gap between rural and urban populations (Warr, Chapter 6), investments in manufacturing and machine-driven agriculture which has impeded social development in farming communities (Okamoto, Chapter7), and fisheries policies struggling to resolve the inequalities between big-business and small-scale fishing operations (Yin Nyein, Gregory, and Aung Kyaw Thein, Chapter 8).

The challenge of cohesion is not just in terms of parliamentary or economic reform, with the four chapters on institutional legacies highlighting divisions in other spaces too. In education, for example, the Myanmar government seeks to connect reforms with efforts to promote national peace and social cohesion but offers little guidance regarding the concerns of ethnic groups about the treatment of identities and assurance of equal access (Lall, Chapter 9). At the university level, while partnerships between Myanmar and foreign universities work to further information technology, there are continuing inequities in access that marginalise large segments of the country (Missingham and Carroll, Chapter 10). Outside education, despite the NLD's plans to promote women's rights to overcome endemic patriarchal governmental power structures, the inconsistent aims of activist organisations and actors has fragmented their impact on policy

(Khin Khin Mra and Livingstone, Chapter 11). To a degree, the struggles of women's rights groups have been aided by technology which has helped advocates to connect women's rights efforts in Myanmar to other global movements, like #Me Too (Aye Thiri Kyaw and Miedema, Chapter 12). However, it is not clear if technology can play a similar role of connectivity and coalition-building like it has for some women in Yangon, for other, more marginalised groups.

The contest between inclusionary and exclusionary forces is also apparent in the three chapters on plural identities. For example, peace discussions in Myanmar involve complex debates over forming a federal government based on ethnofederal arrangements. However, these debates do not always align with the concerns of the broader population, who instead see a form of territorial federalism as a way of encompassing the country's diversity in a more unified manner (Breen and He, Chapter 13). Continuing on this theme, the notion of "national races" reflects Burmese-language conceptions that overlook the historical linguistic complexities of non-Burmese speakers, and so serve to demarcate people who are included or excluded as citizens of Myanmar as a nation-state (Fujimura, Chapter 14). Ethnically driven exclusion is also apparent in the laws, with ambiguities in text and implementation operating to subordinate groups into limbo over their citizenship status, and hence their legal rights, within Myanmar (Brett, Chapter 15).

The above struggles highlight dynamics of contention across a wide range of areas: parliamentary representation, rural-urban divides, big-business versus small-scale enterprises, gender, technology, ethnicity and citizenship. While not necessarily a comprehensive overview of the challenges facing Myanmar, they are sufficient to demonstrate the scale and complexity of contestation, with dynamics working to further inclusion or exclusion of segments of Myanmar's population along fractures crossing political, economic, and cultural dimensions. Such difficulties draw attention to the prospects for Myanmar in its current state of political change, as they threaten the country's ability to maintain its cohesion in the process of ongoing transformations.

To a degree, internal struggles are inherent to the life of any nation-state, but they take on greater significance if they rise to a level sufficient to threaten its existence. For a case like Myanmar, such risk is more plausible because of the relative fragility of its transition. In particular, the nature of the issues identified by the authors in this volume occur within a context of nascent democratisation, with a state and a society recently departed from an authoritarian past and in the early stages of adaptation to a hybrid regime including both civilian and military presence in government institutions. Compounding the initial phase of democratisation are the challenges of underdevelopment, with extensive lack of capacity in resources and skills that limit the capabilities of actors to address challenges facing them. In combination, the aforementioned conditions leave Myanmar's transition vulnerable to the deep fractures within it.

A DEMOCRATISING STATE?

The concerns over Myanmar's divisions become more clear in light of the larger literature on political transitions, specifically the scholarship on democratisation in developing countries. The notion of democratisation refers to the shift away from an authoritarian system to a democratic one, such that the array of states fall within a continuum between fully authoritarian and wholly democratic regime types (Epstein et al. 2006; Guo and Stradiotto 2016). In countries experiencing regime transformation, the polity is moving its place along the continuum (Guo and Stradiotto 2016). The process of transformation roughly follows three stages, beginning with preconditions that motivate a polity for regime change, continuing with transition wherein diverse political forces work to alter the political system, and proceeding to consolidation of democracy by political actors accepting the new regime as a legitimate and adequate means of solving problems (Guo and Stradiotto 2016). This process, however, is not unidirectional nor assured, as the comprehensive sweep of changes wrought by systemic transformation involves engagement and enfranchisement by a majority, if not all, of the political actors to allow the new regime to be sustainable (Rudra 2005; Diamond 1999). Moreover, the process is not necessarily conclusive, in that the post-Cold War era has manifested a broad array of political transformations resulting in a range of hybrid regimes with varying degrees of authoritarian and democratic qualities (Bogaards 2009; Brownlee 2009; Diamond 2002; Epstein et al. 2006; Levitsky and Way 2010).

Myanmar is no exception to the democratisation literature. Myanmar's 2008 Constitution and subsequent 2010 elections, as much as they represented a formal launch of a new political regime, also marked a relocation of political contestation to the system hosted by the new regime. The commentaries of the chapters in the present volume demonstrate that such contestation is ongoing, and that there continue to be uncertainties about the nature of engagement and extent of enfranchisement for the diverse segments of Myanmar's polity. The resulting implications of such struggles for Myanmar's ongoing political and social change places the country between a transitionary stage – pursuing further alterations to the political system – and a consolidation stage of working to promote the system as the legitimate and adequate means of addressing the country's problems. The tensions highlighted by the chapters follow the democratisation literature, which observes the difficulties facing polities seeking transformation from authoritarian to democratic regimes.

The democratisation literature raises several prospective cautionary notes for Myanmar's current conditions. First, transitional democracies tend to be susceptible to dysfunction in terms of internal dissension between rival actors holding marginal commitment to the new regime (Gurr et al. 2005; Mansfield and Snyder 1995). The dysfunction can result in inactive governance resulting from a perpetual stalemate between incompatible domestic interests and/or a persistent military order (Gurr et al. 2005; Mansfield and Snyder 1995). In extreme cases, political rancour can lead to factionalism, with actors "willing to sacrifice the rights of other citizens and, indeed, the public good to the pursuit of narrow self-interest" (Ulfelder and Lustik 2007, 371). The polarising effects of factionalism are problematic, since democracies are more likely to collapse when political processes serve parochial interests in such "winner-takes-all" conditions or "veto-group" politics (Mansfield and Snyder 2002; Ulfelder and Lustik 2007). The rigidity of factional environments fosters stand-offs, with resolution only occurring when incumbent executives, military forces, or personality-led coups usurp democratic mechanisms to defeat opposition (Ulfelder and Lustik 2007, 371). As a result, regimes with higher levels of factionalism tend to be more unstable (Goldstone et al. 2010). Factionalism is pronounced in contexts like Myanmar with deep ethnic divisions, with ethnic heterogeneity correlated with higher rates of violence and greater risks of internal war (Epstein et al. 2012; Gurr et al. 2005). The implications for Myanmar are disconcerting, with the present collection of chapters describing forces that drive political, economic, and cultural fractures in the country's polity. As much as there are countervailing unitary efforts, the presence of divisive forces raises the risk of fomenting factional behaviour. To the extent that such conditions threaten to become intractable, Myanmar lies within a class of regimes with higher risks of instability. The fragile nature of the country's democratic transformation is compounded by its ethnic tensions, with Myanmar vulnerable to the larger democratisation trends of internal war arising from such divisions.

Second, the risks of instability are heightened for cases involving partial democracies. Hybrid regimes suffer from higher rates of instability resulting in collapse (Goldstone et al. 1999; Goldstone et al. 2010). The danger encompasses various types of hybrid regimes, including exclusive democracies, where segments of the population are denied suffrage; domain democracy, where elements such as the military retain veto powers over democratically elected officials; illiberal democracy, where there is weak rule-of-law and disregard for equality and human rights; and delegative democracy, where there is marginal separation-of-powers and weak checks-and-balances (Goldstone et al. 2010; Merkel 2004). Hybrid regimes tend to struggle because they indicate a lack of will by political elites to commit and comply with more inclusive democratic rules (Dewal et al. 2013). Moreover, they encourage perceptions of favouritism to particular interests, shallow participation, and poor government accountability, inciting frustration with formal political mechanisms and driving use of informal political mechanisms that may not be complementary to state authority (Dewal et al. 2013; Goldstone 2008; Menocal 2008). The problems of hybrid regimes are exposed in situations of polarised politics, where exclusionary ideologies strive to direct political institutions in opposing directions. Myanmar currently constitutes a hybrid regime, with its 2008 Constitution placing the country as a domain democracy in terms of promulgating a political system that maintains a military presence in the Hluttaw, control over several ministries, and effective veto powers over constitutional amendment and civilian government in national emergencies. In addition, for the chapters in the present volume that detail efforts to deny suffrage or suppress the rights of portions of Myanmar's population, Myanmar exhibits qualities of exclusive or illiberal democracy. The consequent implications for the instability of Myanmar's democratisation process are already real, with the respective chapters presenting contests over inclusion and exclusion for groups along political, economic and cultural parameters. Should Myanmar fall to the pattern of other hybrid regimes, the prognosis for its transition becomes perilous.

Third, in cases of developing countries all over the world, economic development is important for improving the sustainability of a hybrid regime (Menocal et al. 2008; Przeworski and Limongi 1997), in that "so long as they fail to make substantial gains in economic development... the political regimes of most developing countries will remain fundamentally unstable" (Ulfelder and Lustik 2007, 365). Democratising regimes are especially affected by inequality, with high economic inequality correlated with factionalism along economic cleavages (Epstein et al. 2012). Ethnic divisions also tend to appear more frequently with higher levels of inequality, further fracturing a polity (Epstein et al. 2012). Such findings are discouraging for Myanmar, with its status as a lesser-developed country matched by its high levels of income inequality. More disturbing are the trends identified by the chapters in this volume, which note patterns of increasing inequality in multiple economic sectors of the country. The resulting consequence is increasing instability for Myanmar's current regime. Furthermore, the extent that the inequalities align with existing patterns of ethnic division, the implication for Myanmar is that any widening of economic inequalities means a corresponding increase in ethnic tensions, threatening the viability of the peace process.

Last, more general studies of state failure beyond hybrid regimes look to the qualities of effectiveness and legitimacy as determinants of stability, with effectiveness referring to how well a regime performs state functions and legitimacy indicating perceptions that regime actions are just or reasonable (Goldstone 2008). Levels of effectiveness and legitimacy are eroded by factors that include state corruption and communal violence, such as ethnic or religious conflict (Goldstone 2008). The dangers are pronounced for new democracies, which tend to suffer from an inability to maintain economic or physical security to mitigate such factors (Goldstone 2008). The contributions to this volume indicate that there are efforts in Myanmar working to reduce corruption and communal tensions and improve state capacity, but the dynamics reflected in the analyses of the disparate chapters point to continuing contention that maintains conditions of uncertainty over these issues. Following from the studies of state failure, these ongoing issues related to identity politics in Myanmar challenge aspirations for regime stability.

In response to the above, the priorities in ensuring the continued stability of Myanmar's regime – and its prospects for continued transformation – are self-apparent: mitigation of factionalism, resolution of its hybrid nature, reduction of inequality, and improving state redress of corruption and communal tensions. These prescriptions are supported by democratisation literature, which argues that the stability of nascent democracies are aided by higher levels of income with low levels of discrimination, a paucity of external conflicts, and most critically a unity of the polity (Goldstone et al. 2010). While Myanmar has no conflicts with its surrounding neighbours, the contributions of the various authors point to continuing struggles to resolve the issues of inequality, discrimination, and unity. Stability is also promoted by policies that discourage factionalism and diminish the causes of social division (Goldstone et al. 2010; Gurr et al. 2005) by fostering political participation based on norms of compromise and collaboration (Gurr et al. 2005). Attendant with such approaches are policies which extend political rights and representation that improves the status of disadvantaged minorities (Gurr et al. 2005). As much as the chapters in this volume indicate diverse efforts to facilitate the aforementioned prescriptions, they also demonstrate the presence of countervailing forces working to destabilise the country. As a result, despite the clarity of priorities arising from the democratisation literature, the current status of Myanmar presented by the previous chapters indicates indeterminate phenomena with uncertain outcomes. Such a cautionary picture may draw sober perspectives for the country, but it also calls for continued engagement by supporters of Myanmar's democratisation to further its transformation via more inclusive mechanisms that sustain the cohesion of its polity.

INCLUSIONARY AND EXCLUSIONARY FORCES

The extent of the above uncertainties – and their existential nature for Myanmar's ongoing process of democratisation – provide impetus for further research on the tensions between inclusionary and exclusionary forces. To begin, Myanmar is progressing in reforms towards market-based economic principles. However, there are divergent conceptualisations of market-based economies in that they seek varying combinations of entrepreneurial or small-to-medium enterprises (SMEs) versus monopolistic or large-scale corporate entities. Even within the Asian region, the historical agglomeration of "Asian Tiger" economies like Japan, South Korea, Hong Kong and Singapore manifested differing orientations between the two aforementioned extremes. For a country like Myanmar, principles of greater participation suggest more encouragement of native Myanmar business enterprises, but it is still unclear what the likely economic system associated with native businesses will be. Moreover, if the desire for more participation extends beyond native businesses to include foreign entities, then how will foreign expectations direct the future of Myanmar's economy in both positive and negative ways?

Further, the struggle between inclusionary and exclusionary politics also leads in potentially divergent political directions. Participatory forms of decision-making appear in different political systems. Even within the scope of a democracy, there are a range of manifestations that extend beyond more commonly understood conceptions of constitutional democracy or parliamentary democracy. We can look to other examples from the region to see how these variations emerge, including in the development of hybrid authoritarian-democratic regimes, democratic institutions subject to elite capture, populist systems exercising illiberal policies, and/or puppet democracies controlled by "strong-man" authority figures. As a result, aspirations for more inclusive decision-making in Myanmar are not necessarily connected to democratic models known to mainstream Western audiences. This raises the question as to what is the significance, if any, of the struggles over participation for Myanmar's transition towards a democracy?

Finally, the notion of inclusion implies a society that is open to diversity and accepting of dissent. For the multiple ethnic nationalities that comprise Myanmar society, such prospects offer the potential to address concerns of cultural preservation and social marginalisation arising from their status as minorities vis-à-vis the dominant Bamar. However, inclusion also implies an expansion in the voices recognised as part of social discourses, with an attendant increase in discord between potentially irreconcilable perspectives. A lack of reconciliation threatens disunity and a continuation of the country's history of internecine conflict. In which case, the question arises as to whether the pursuit of greater participation will result in the easing of tensions between the country's ethnic nationalities or if it will exacerbate them?

The chapters in this volume deal both directly and indirectly with various aspects of the above, but in doing so mark their significance for further studies and future research. Given Myanmar's ongoing transition, the context driving the aforementioned issues continues to be fluid and therefore calls for ongoing monitoring and reassessment are valid. Moreover, given the endemic complexities of the country, the issues also provide opportunities for multiple perspectives to better clarify the disparate scenarios for Myanmar's future – and identify appropriate actions to those deemed more desirable.

CONCLUSION

On a concluding note, it is worthwhile to observe that the present volume achieves a measure of diversity in viewpoints regarding Myanmar, with a mix of established and emerging scholars across a range of disciplines comprised of Myanmar and non-Myanmar authors engaged in both academic and practice settings. Past volumes of works from the Myanmar Update conferences have sought to promote greater representation of non-Western perspectives about Myanmar, particularly in terms of Myanmar voices presenting research on Myanmar issues to allow global audiences a better understanding of the first-hand experiences of native scholars regarding their home country. The present volume hosts seven Myanmar scholars, either as solo authors or co-authors, for five out of the sixteen chapters. In addition, however, it also offers contributions of researchers from China and Japan, marking the growing inter-connections between disparate Myanmar scholarly communities. Such diversity enriches analytical discourse and offers the promise of valuable insights arising from the collaboration of different perspectives. Further collaboration is welcomed by all organisers of the Myanmar Update series, and the expectation is to continue work that fosters Myanmar-related scholarship as a global community – and serves as inspiration for Myanmar society.

References

Aye Thiri Kyaw and Miedema, S. (2020). "Women's Movements and the Era of #MeToo: Changing Norms Around Sexual Harassment Against Women and Girls in Myanmar". In *Living with Myanmar*, edited by J. Chambers, C. Galloway, J. Liljeblad. Singapore: ISEAS-Yusof Ishak Institute.

Bogaards, M. (2009). "How to Classify Hybrid Regimes? Defective Democracy and Electoral Authoritarianism". *Democratization* 16 (2): 399–423.

Breen, M.G. and He, B. (2020). "Do People Really Want Federalism Anymore? Findings from Deliberative Forums on the Role of Ethnic Identity in Federalism in Myanmar". In *Living with Myanmar*, edited by J. Chambers, C. Galloway, J. Liljeblad. Singapore: ISEAS-Yusof Ishak Institute.

Brett, P. (2020). "The Ambiguities of Citizenship Status in Myanmar and Its Implications". In *Living with Myanmar*, edited by J. Chambers, C. Galloway, J. Liljeblad. Singapore: ISEAS-Yusof Ishak Institute.

Brownlee, J. (2009). "Portents of Pluralism: How Hybrid Regimes Affect Democratic Transitions". *American Journal of Political Science* 53 (3): 515–532.

Dewal, S., Goldstone, J. and Volpe, M. (2013). "Forecasting Stability or Retreat in Emerging Democratic Regimes". *Politics & Governance* 1 (1): 32–47.

Diamond, L. (2002). "Thinking about Hybrid Regimes". *Journal of Democracy* 13 (2): 21–35.

-------- (1999). *Developing Democracy: Toward Consolidation*. Johns Hopkins University Press.

Egreteau, R. (2020). "Parliamentary Life Under the NLD". In *Living with Myanmar,* edited by J. Chambers, C. Galloway, J. Liljeblad. Singapore: ISEAS-Yusof Ishak Institute.

Epstein, D., Bates, R., Golstone, J., Kristensen, I. and O'Halloran, S. (2006). "Democratic Transitions". *American Journal of Political Science* 50 (3): 551–569.

Epstein, D., Leventoglu, B. and O'Halloran, S. (2012). "Minorities and Democratization". *Economics and Politics* 24 (3): 259–278.

Fujimura, H. (2020). "The Emergence of Dawkalu in the Karen Ethnic Claim in the 1880s and Its Paradoxical Hindrance to a Sense of Unity". In *Living with Myanmar,* edited by J. Chambers, C. Galloway, J. Liljeblad. Singapore: ISEAS-Yusof Ishak Institute.

Goldstone, J. (2008). "Pathways to State Failure". *Conflict Management and Peace Science* 25 (4): 285–296.

Goldstone, J., Bates, R.H., Epstein, D., Gurr, T.R., Lustik, M.B., Marshall, M.G. Ulfelder, J., Woodward, M. (2010). "A Global Model for Forecasting Political Instability". *American Journal of Political Science* 54 (1): 190–208.

Goldstone, J., Gurr, T.R., Harff, B., Levy, M.A., Marshall M.G., Bates, R.H., Epstein, D.L., Kahl, C.h., Surko, P.T. Ulfelder, J.C. and Unger, A.N. (1999). *State Failure Task Force Report: Phase III Findings*. Available online at < https://www.researchgate.net/publication/247639865_State_Failure_Task_Force_Report_Phase_III_Findings > [Accessed June 10, 2020].

Guo, S. and Stradiotto, G (2016). *Democratic Transitions: Modes and Outcomes*. London: Routledge.

Gurr, T., Marshall, M. and Woodward, M. (2005). "Forecasting Instability: Are Ethnic Wars and Muslim Countries Different?" Available online at https://www.researchgate.net/publication/267220763_Forecasting_Instability_Are_Ethnic_Wars_and_Muslim_Countries_Different [Accessed June 10, 2020].

Jefferson, A.M. (2020). "Carceral Legacies: On Prisons, Punishments and Politics in Myanmar". In *Living with Myanmar,* edited by J. Chambers, C. Galloway, J. Liljeblad. Singapore, ISEAS Publishing.

Khin Khin Mra and Livingstone, D. (2020). "The Winding Path to Gender Equality in Myanmar". In *Living with Myanmar,* edited by J. Chambers, C. Galloway, J. Liljeblad. Singapore: ISEAS-Yusof Ishak Institute.

Lall, M. (2020). "Reviewing Educational Reforms: The NLD in its Fourth Year". In *Living with Myanmar,* edited by J. Chambers, C. Galloway, J. Liljeblad. Singapore: ISEAS-Yusof Ishak Institute.

Levitsky, S. and Way, L. (2010). *Competitive Authoritarianism*. Cambridge: Cambridge University Press.

Mansfield, E. and Snyder, J. (1995). "Democratization and War". *Foreign Affairs* 74 (3): 79–97.

_____ (2002). "Democratic Transitions, Institutional Strength, and War". *International Organization* 56 (2): 297–337.

Menocal, A., Fritz, V. and Rakner, L. (2008). "Hybrid Regimes and the Challenges of Deepening and Sustaining Democracy in Developing Countries". *South African Journal of International Affairs* 15 (1): 29–40.

Merkel, W. (2004). "Embedded and Defective Democracies". *Democratization* 11 (5): 33–58.

Missingham, R. and Carroll, M (2020). "Building a Knowledge Society in Myanmar". In *Living with Myanmar,* edited by J. Chambers, C. Galloway, J. Liljeblad. Singapore: ISEAS-Yusof Ishak Institute.

Nyein Thiri Swe and Zaw Min Oo (2020). "People Power or Political Pressure? Drivers of Representative Performance in Southern Sub-National Parliaments". In *Living with Myanmar,* edited by J. Chambers, C. Galloway, J. Liljeblad. Singapore: ISEAS-Yusof Ishak Institute.

Okamoto, I. (2020). "Myanmar's Rural Economy at a Crossroads". In *Living with Myanmar,* edited by J. Chambers, C. Galloway, J. Liljeblad. Singapore: ISEAS-Yusof Ishak Institute.

Przeworski, A. and Limongi, F. (1997). "Modernization: Theories and Facts". *World Politics* 49 (2): 155–183.

Rudra, N. (2005). "Globalization and the Strengthening of Democracy in the Developing World". *American Journal of Political Science* 49 (4): 704–730.

Turnell, S. and Nyein Ei Cho (2020). "Myanmar's Economy in Changing Times". In *Living with Myanmar,* edited by J. Chambers, C. Galloway, J. Liljeblad. Singapore: ISEAS-Yusof Ishak Institute.

Ulfelder, J. and Lustik, M. (2007). "Modelling Transitions To and From Democracy". *Democratisation* 14 (3): 351–387.

Warr, P. (2020). "Poverty and Inequality in Myanmar: 2005-2015". In *Living with Myanmar,* edited by J. Chambers, C. Galloway, J. Liljeblad. Singapore: ISEAS-Yusof Ishak Institute.

Yin Nyein, Gregory, R. and Aung Kyaw Thein (2020). "Ten Years of Freshwater Fisheries Governance Reform in Myanmar". In *Living with Myanmar,* edited by J. Chambers, C. Galloway, J. Liljeblad. Singapore: ISEAS-Yusof Ishak Institute.

ABBREVIATIONS AND KEY TERMS

AA	Arakan Army
Amyotha Hluttaw	Upper House of Myanmar's Union Parliament
ANP	Arakan National Party
ANU	Australian National University
Arakan	*See* Rakhine
ARFN	Ayeyarwaddy Region Fisher Network
ASEAN	Association of Southeast Asian Nations
Bamar	*See* Burman
Burman	Majority ethnic group (or its language); also known as Bamar
BIA	Burma Independence Army
CAR	Capital-to-Assets Ratio
CBM	Central Bank of Myanmar
CBO	Community-Based Organisation
CDF	Capacity Development Fund
CEDAW	Convention on the Elimination of All Forms of Discrimination against Women
CESR	Comprehensive Education Sector Review
Chin	Ethnic group, language and administrative area in northwestern Myanmar
CSO	Civil Society Organisation
Dawkalu	Sgaw Karen term for 'nation'
DDG	Deputy Director General

DFID	Department for International Development
Dhamma	Buddhist conception of natural law
DG	Director Generals
DP	Development Partners
EAO	Ethnic Armed Organisation
EIFL	Electronic Information for Libraries
FDI	Foreign Direct Investment
FL	Farmland Law
FPNCC	Federal Political Negotiation and Consultative Committee
GAD	General Administration Department
GDP	Gross Domestic Product
GEN	Gender Equality Network
HIES	Household Income and Expenditure Survey
Hluttaw	Parliament
INGO	International Non-Government Organisation
IMF	International Monetary Fund
IRD	Internal Revenue Department
IHLCA	Integrated Household Living Conditions Assessment
JICA	Japan International Cooperation Agency
Kachin	Ethnic group, language or administrative area in northern Myanmar
Karen	Ethnic group, language, or administrative area in eastern Myanmar; also known as Kayin
KED	Karen Education Department
KIOED	Kachin Independence Organisation Education Department
KNA	Karen National Association
KNU	Karen National Union
Kyat	Myanmar currency
LCC	Literature and Culture Committee

Lumyo	Burmese term for race, ethnicity or nationality
MADB	Myanmar Agricultural Development Bank
MDSP	Myanmar Sustainable Development Plan
MEB	Myanmar Economic Bank
MFI	Microfinance organisation
MMP	Military Member of Parliament
MLCS	Myanmar Living Conditions Survey
MoE	Ministry of Education
MoPF	Ministry of Planning and Finance
MNCWA	Myanmar National Committee for Women's Affairs
MNEC	Mon National Education Committee
MOFA	Ministry of Foreign Affairs
MOGE	Myanmar Oil and Gas Enterprise
MP	Member of Parliament
MPLCS	Myanmar Poverty and Living Conditions Survey
MSDP	Myanmar Sustainable Development Plan
MSWRR	Ministry of Social Welfare, Relief and Resettlement
MTB-MLE	Mother tongue-based multilingual education
MUPE	Myanmar-UK Partnership for Education
Nat	General category that refers to a local spirits, Buddhist deities and tutelary spirits
NAQAC	National Accreditation and Quality Assurance Committee
NCA	Nationwide Ceasefire Agreement
NCC	National Curriculum Committee
NECC	National Economic Coordination Committee
NEL	National Education Law
NEPC	National Education Policy Commission
NESP	National Education Strategic Plan
NGO	Non-Government Organisation
NLD	National League for Democracy

NRC	National Registration Card
NSPAW	National Strategic Plan for the Advancement of Women
NVC	National Verification Card
OECD	Organisation for Economic Cooperation and Development
Pa-O	Ethnic group, language, and administrative area in northeast Myanmar
PPP	Purchasing Power Parity
Pyidaungsu Hluttaw	Union Assembly
Pyithu Hluttaw	Lower House, Pyidaungsu Hluttaw
Rakhine	Ethnic group, language, or administrative area in coastal western Myanmar; also known as Arakan
RC	Rectors' Committee
RCSS	Restoration Council of Shan State
RFP	Rakhine Fisheries Partnership
Rohingya	Ethnic group (or language) on coastal border of Bangladesh
Shan	Ethnic group, language, or administrative area in northeast Myanmar
SDG	Sustainable Development Goals
SLORC	State Law and Order Restoration Council
SNLD	Shan Nationalities League for Democracy
SOE	State Owned Enterprise
SPDC	State Peace and Development Council
Taing yin thar	Myanmar's national races or 'sons of the soil'
Tatmadaw	Myanmar national armed forces
TRC	Temporary Registration Card
UN	United Nations
UNDP	United National Development Program
UNESCO	United Nations Educational, Scientific and Cultural Organisation
USDA	Union Solidarity Development Association

USDP	Union Solidarity and Development Party
VAT	Value Added Tax
VFVL	Vacant, Fallow and Virgin Lands Management Law
WLB	Women's League of Burma

INDEX